S0-ARX-183

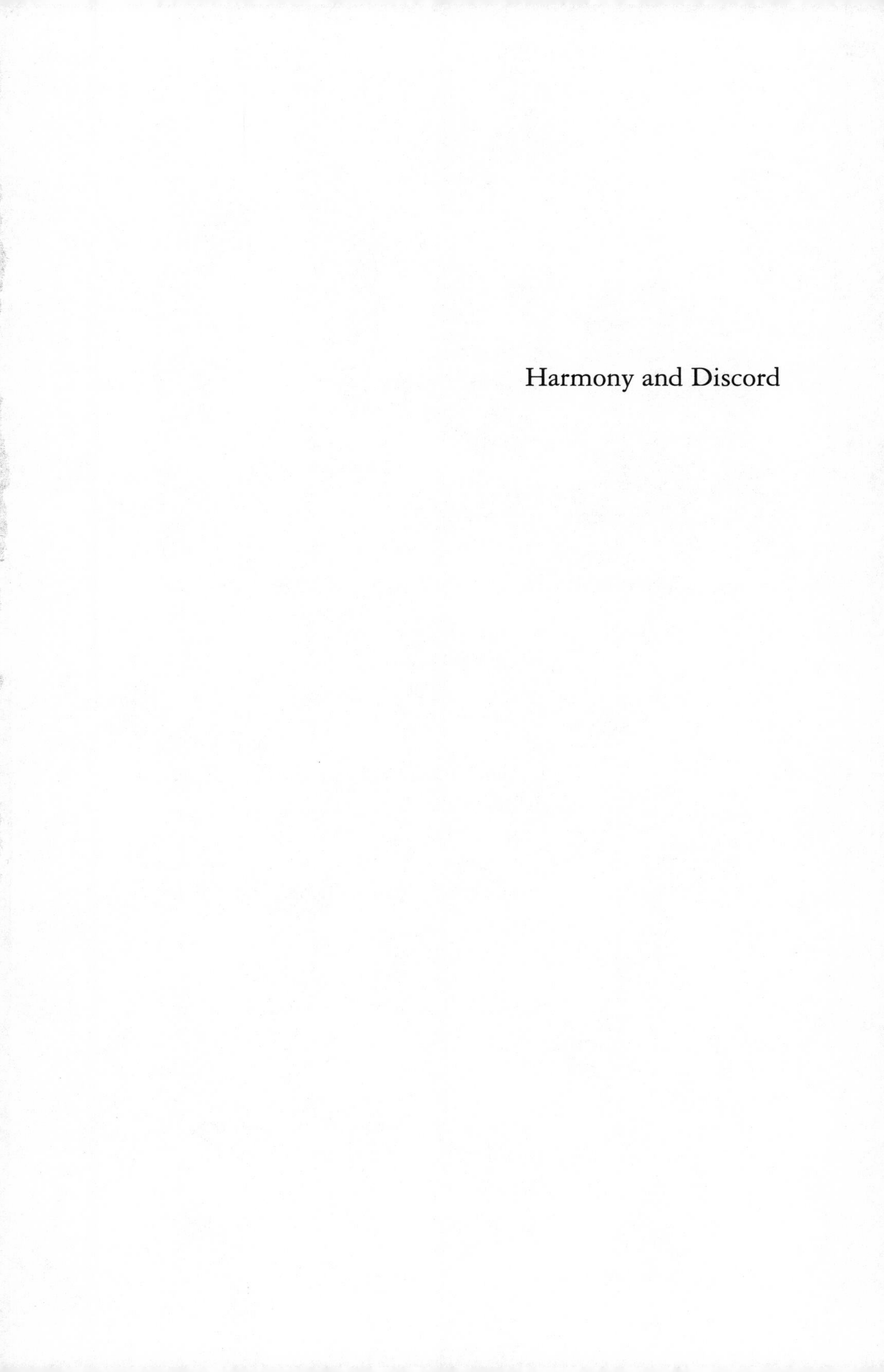

Harmony and Discord

THE NEW CULTURAL HISTORY OF MUSIC

SERIES EDITOR **Jane F. Fulcher**

SERIES BOARD
Celia Applegate
Philip Bohlman
Kate van Orden
Michael P. Steinberg

Enlightenment Orpheus: The Power of Music in Other Worlds
Vanessa Agnew

Voice Lessons: French Mélodie in the Belle Epoque
Katherine Bergeron

Songs, Scribes, and Societies: The History and Reception of the Loire Valley Chansonniers
Jane Alden

Harmony and Discord: Music and the Transformation of Russian Cultural Life
Lynn M. Sargeant

LYNN M. SARGEANT

Harmony and Discord

Music and the Transformation of Russian Cultural Life

OXFORD UNIVERSITY PRESS

Oxford University Press, Inc., publishes works that further
Oxford University's objective of excellence
in research, scholarship, and education.

Oxford New York
Auckland Cape Town Dar es Salaam Hong Kong Karachi
Kuala Lumpur Madrid Melbourne Mexico City Nairobi
New Delhi Shanghai Taipei Toronto

With offices in
Argentina Austria Brazil Chile Czech Republic France Greece
Guatemala Hungary Italy Japan Poland Portugal Singapore
South Korea Switzerland Thailand Turkey Ukraine Vietnam

Copyright © 2011 by Oxford University Press, Inc.

Published by Oxford University Press, Inc.
198 Madison Avenue, New York, New York 10016

www.oup.com

Oxford is a registered trademark of Oxford University Press

All rights reserved. No part of this publication may be reproduced,
stored in a retrieval system, or transmitted, in any form or by any means,
electronic, mechanical, photocopying, recording, or otherwise,
without the prior permission of Oxford University Press.

Publication of this book was supported by the Lloyd Hibberd Publication
Endowment Fund of the American Musicological Society.

Library of Congress Cataloging-in-Publication Data
Sargeant, Lynn M.
Harmony and discord : music and the transformation of Russian cultural life / Lynn M. Sargeant.
p. cm. — (New cultural history of music series)
Includes bibliographical references and index.
ISBN 978-0-19-973526-6
1. Music—Social aspects—Russia. I. Title.
ML3917.R8S27 2011
780.947—dc22 2010010580

9 8 7 6 5 4 3 2 1

Printed in the United States of America
on acid-free paper

R0432000593

For Mom, Dad, and all the folks back home in "God's Country."

ACKNOWLEDGMENTS

Words fail me as I try to express my thanks to all of the friends, family, and colleagues who have helped turn a very rough idea into a finished book. At Indiana University, I had the great good fortune to meet a cohort of fellow students who have become lasting friends and wise colleagues, especially Roark Atkinson, David Fisher, Mara Lazda, Dana Ohren, Matt Pauly, Heather Perry, Sudha Rajagopalan, and Jude Richter. I was equally fortunate in my mentors at IU, first Alexander Rabinowitch, and then Ben Eklof, both of whom began as my advisers and became good friends. To Ben, in particular, I owe a debt of gratitude for his patience, guidance, and support both during graduate school and as I made the difficult transition to faculty member. Malcolm Brown's intellectual generosity and personal kindness also played a key role in bringing this project to fruition. At Cal State Fullerton, I am blessed to enjoy the support of wonderful colleagues in the Department of History, whose fine scholarship and thoughtful pedagogy continue to impress me. I particularly want to thank my mentor, Nancy Fitch, for her friendship, guidance, and, last but not least, fine cooking skills for keeping me happy, healthy, and sane while on the tenure track. Jochen Burgtorf, similarly, has been a good friend, stimulating colleague, and professional guide. Friends and colleagues who are, sadly, more scattered also offered support and constructive criticism. Murray Frame and Benita Blessing read early drafts of the complete manuscript and offered detailed comments and much-needed encouragement at critical points in what has seemed, at times, an endless process of research, writing, and revision. William Weber was not only brave enough to read some of my earliest work on this topic, but still saw enough promise in it to recommend my participation in the European Science

Foundation's project on Musical Life in Europe. The stimulating discussions and critical readings provided during the meetings of our working group on "Musical Education in Europe" profoundly shaped my thinking on the place and importance of the conservatory in society. I would also like to thank my editor, Suzanne Ryan and series editor Jane Fulcher for their support of this project, as well as the anonymous reviewers of the manuscript for their detailed evaluations, which challenged me to think more deeply on key issues and considerably improved this book. Any remaining errors or omissions are, of course, my own.

I owe a debt of gratitude to several institutions and organizations for their generous financial support. It seems particularly fitting to me that a book that focuses on a nineteenth-century voluntary association would be funded in its early stages by a voluntary association. The generous Scholar Award provided by the P.E.O. Foundation supported a critical year of research in St. Petersburg. Funding provided by a Foreign Language Area Studies fellowship and the ACTR/ACCELS Title VIII Combined Research and Language Training program made possible a year of research and Ukrainian-language training in Kiev. A postdoctoral fellowship from the Spencer Foundation and the National Academy of Education provided critical time free from teaching for research and revision. At Cal State Fullerton, I have benefited from consistent support for research and writing from the College of Humanities and Social Sciences, as well as the CSU/CSUF intramural grant program. I particularly want to thank Dean Thomas Klammer for his dedication to facilitating faculty research and publication in the humanities and social sciences.

I truly appreciate the patience and professionalism shown to me by archivists and librarians in Russia and Ukraine. I had the privilege of working in the rich collections of the Russian National Library, the Ukrainian National Library, and the libraries of the St. Petersburg, Saratov, and Kiev conservatories, as well as the Russian State Historical Archive (RGIA), the Central State Historical Archive of St. Petersburg (TsGIA SPb), Russian Institute for the History of Art (RIII), the Russian State Archive of Literature and Art (RGALI), the Central State Archive-Museum of Ukraine (TsDAMLM), and the State Archive of the City of Kiev (DAMK), as well as, briefly, the State Archive of Tambov Oblast' (GATO). I would particularly like to thank Galina Kopytova at RIII for her hospitality and scholarly erudition, as well as her assistance in acquiring key images for this volume.

Finally, I must thank the friends and family who have, with patience and grace, endured my obsession with Russian history and the Russian Musical Society. I would particularly like to thank my parents, who have supported me emotionally as well as occasionally financially through the Bank of Mom and Dad during my long transition from high school band director to tenured university professor. My brother Glen, his wife Felicia, and, of course, my delightful nieces Amanda and Emily have helped me keep it all in perspective, reminding me always that what matters most is family.

A portion of chapter 6 was previously published as "*Kashchei the Immortal*: Liberal Politics, Cultural Memory, and the Rimsky-Korsakov Scandal of 1905" *Russian Review* 64, no. 1 (January 2005): 22–43. Earlier versions of some of the ideas and material in chapters 3 and 4 originally appeared as "A New Class of People: The Conservatory and Musical Professionalization in Russia, 1861–1917" *Music and Letters* 84, no. 1 (February 2004): 41–61, and "Ambivalence and Desire: State, Society, and Music Education in Russia" in *Musical Education in Europe (1770–1914): Compositional, Institutional, and Political Challenges*, volume 1, edited by Michael Fend and Michel Noiray (Berlin: Berliner Wissenschafts-Verlag, 2005), 245–73.

CONTENTS

NOTES ON THE TEXT

Transliterations conform to the Library of Congress system, except that, in the text, soft signs have been omitted in personal and place names and personal names have been Anglicized (i.e., Rimsky-Korsakov, rather than Rimskii-Korsakov, Alexander rather than Aleksandr). References and bibliography entries, however, conform exactly to the Library of Congress system. All events prior to 31 January 1918 are dated according to the "old-style" (i.e., according to the Julian calendar). In the nineteenth century, the Julian calendar was twelve days behind the Gregorian calendar used in Western Europe.

For clarity, I refer throughout to the Russian Musical Society, rather than the Imperial Russian Musical Society, because this work spans the entire life of the organization, including the period preceding the awarding of the imperial title and following its abandonment. In the endnotes, I abbreviate the society as author (as either RMO or IRMO, as appropriate) and in second and subsequent references in titles. Archival identifications have been standardized to fond (collection), op. (opis or section), d. (delo or file), and l. (listok or page).

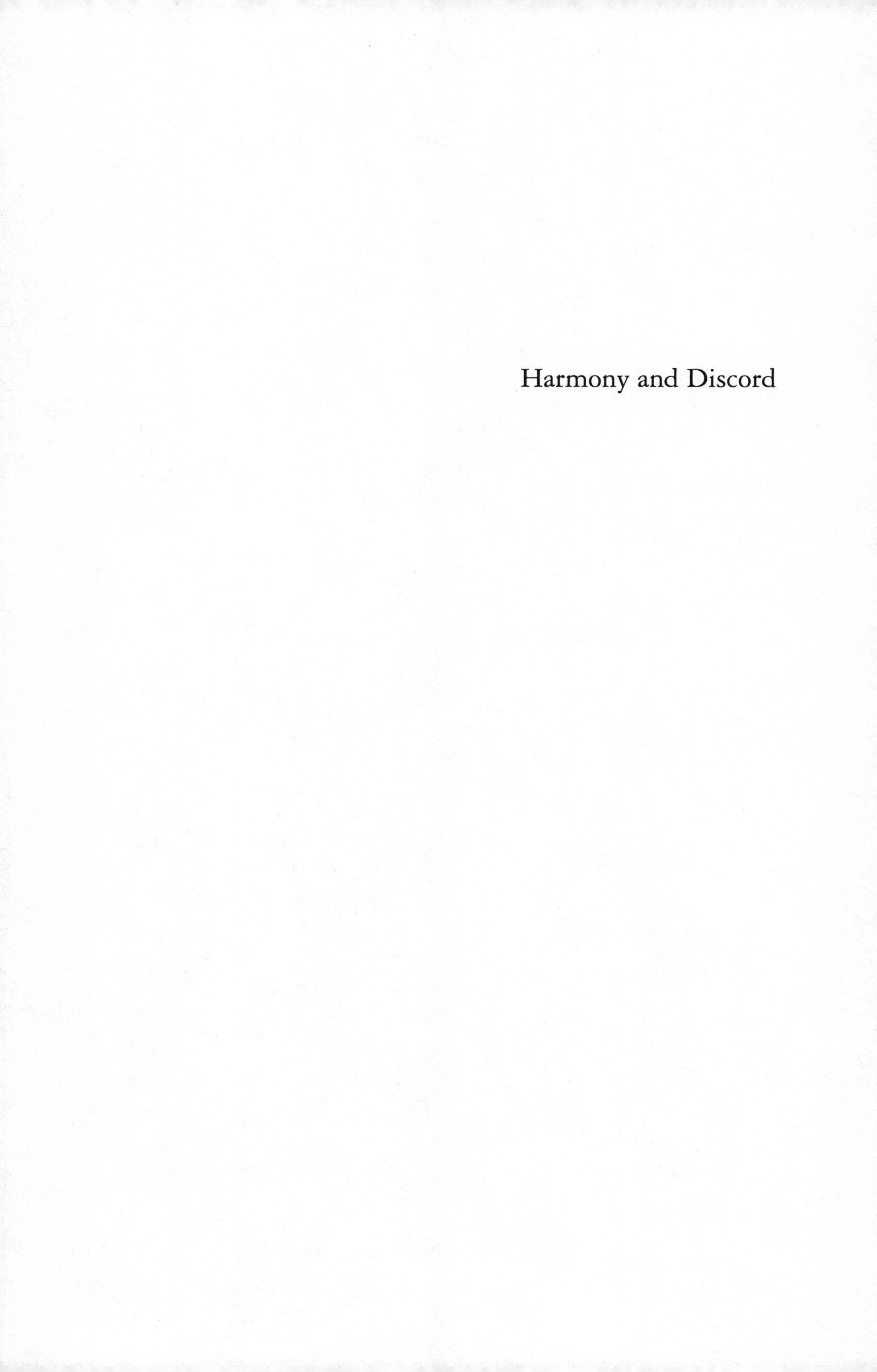

Harmony and Discord

Introduction

In December 1912, the St. Petersburg Conservatory celebrated its fiftieth anniversary. The glamorous jubilee marked the endpoint of a profound transformation of Russian musical life. Over the course of the nineteenth century, Russian musical life was effectively relocated from the private to the public sphere, from the capitals to the provinces, from the intimate confines of the circle and salon to modern institutions such as the conservatory, and from the hands of amateurs to the control of professionals. This transformation owed a great deal to the Russian Musical Society (*Russkoe Muzykal'noe Obshchestvo* or RMO), the voluntary association that had founded and still supported the conservatory. For provincial delegates such as Prince Peter Bebutov, the jubilee celebrations offered a rare opportunity to stand at the epicenter of Russian musical life. Writing for a provincial audience, Bebutov described the celebrations in detail, introducing the readers of *Kavkaz* not only to the formal performances and banquets but also to the commotion and excitement at the heart of Russia's musical world.[1] Interestingly, his tale began not with the formal sessions but with his lengthy journey from Tiflis, a strategy that emphasized both the physical and cultural distance between the provinces and the capital. After seventy-two hours on the train, Bebutov arrived in Moscow, which he found cold, dark, and damp. Glad to move on, Bebutov changed trains for St. Petersburg. Fine weather in the imperial capital set the tone for a glittering celebration.

After checking in to his hotel, Bebutov headed to the conservatory, where complete chaos greeted him as everyone rushed about trying to finalize preparations for the jubilee. Students scurried back and forth, while members of the public begged fruitlessly for tickets to the performances. Unnerved by the commotion, Bebutov was both flattered and relieved when he learned that the conservatory had set tickets aside for provincial delegates. In the midst of all this pandemonium, the unflappable Alexander Glazunov rehearsed his celebratory cantata on a theme by Anton Rubinstein. Although clearly trying to do several things at once, Glazunov nevertheless took the time to greet Bebutov properly.

Bebutov's breathless prose conveyed his almost uncontrollable excitement on this momentous occasion. Describing all of the festivities—from the opening chapel service to the formal program—in loving detail, he emphasized the cultural significance of the celebrations. The conservatory's newly completed theater provided a fitting backdrop for a glamorous audience of beautifully attired women and dashingly uniformed men. The presence of many luminaries of the musical world further enhanced the allure of the evening. On the beautifully decorated stage, busts of Grand Duchess Elena Pavlovna and Anton Rubinstein flanked the student choir and orchestra.

Thunderous applause greeted the performance of Glazunov's cantata, which was followed by a presentation of delegates and congratulatory speeches and telegrams. Bebutov professed amazement at the Russian Musical Society's broad cultural reach as "One after another deputations from the provincial branches" of the Society "filed in." Bebutov's conversations with other audience members, such as the delegates from Sarapul who endured an arduous journey to St. Petersburg by horseback (thirty-one hours) and train (a full day) in order to attend the jubilee, emphasized both the continuing remoteness of the Russian provinces and the Society's success in bridging the cultural chasm between the capitals and the hinterlands. "In a town of only thirty thousand inhabitants," he noted, "they have a branch with two hundred eighty students and are able to produce concerts periodically." Flattering greetings sent by other educational, cultural, and social institutions reinforced both the conservatory's and the Society's claim to leadership in musical life, while telegrams from the emperor and other "exalted" individuals indicated the continuing strength of the traditional social hierarchy and the importance of patronage. Telegrams from Paris, Berlin, Vienna, and other foreign conservatories explicitly placed the St. Petersburg Conservatory and Russian music in the foremost ranks of European musical culture.[2]

Bebutov's tale highlights the depth of the transformation of Russian cultural life between 1801 and 1917. An array of institutions and organizations that were almost wholly absent at the beginning of the nineteenth century structured his cultural world. Foremost among these institutions were the St. Petersburg Conservatory and the Russian Musical Society. Until the Great Reforms, the kind of music individuals made or listened to and the setting in which they engaged in music making depended to a great degree on their identities. In the capitals, the musical life of the nobility revolved around domestic music making, salon performances, the opera, and the occasional public concert. Imported art music was the foundation of this cultural world, a milieu that also encompassed provincial nobles and, to some extent, wealthy and worldly members of other estates. For the vast majority of Russian subjects, serfs and state peasants, their musical world remained a homegrown one of sacred and secular song. These two worlds overlapped, of course. Both nobles and peasants shared the rich vocal heritage of the Orthodox Church. Members of the nobility also increasingly expressed a tender nostalgia for the musical environment that surrounded them, but which they did not really share, as they were tended to by peasant nannies, playmates, and servants. By the second quarter of the century, this nostalgia had crystallized into a reverence for traditional village songs as a source of pure Russian culture. The new composers of the emerging Russian school began to appropriate this peasant musical vocabulary for their own purposes.

The Great Reforms disrupted Russia's traditional cultural structures and ignited profound economic and social change.[3] Culturally, the postemancipation period witnessed determined efforts to create an independent Russian art music, to broaden the scope of musical life, and to use music to temper the consequences of rapid socioeconomic change. Musical life expanded and grew more complex. New groups began to participate actively, showing up in the audiences of concerts and in the classrooms of music schools. A newly confidant cultural intelligentsia and an emerging middle class played the leading roles in the expansion of musical life, but nobles, peasants, and workers also shaped developing cultural structures through the choices they made as consumers of music. Musical life became an arena for intense cultural debate, not only about musical nationalism but also over fluid and shifting conceptions of Russianness, modernity, civilization, and Europeanness.

During the nineteenth century, the conventions and traditions of music making and musical performance helped to define Russian culture and identity. As musicologist Irina Petrovskaia has persuasively argued, a certain scholarly "literocentrism" has blinded us to the daily realities of the production and consumption of culture.[4] For all the importance of literary circles in social and political thought, the number of their participants was limited. For all the brilliance of Russian literature, its consumption was restricted by low literacy levels. Louise McReynolds and Jeffrey Brooks have reminded us that when a broader reading public did begin to emerge, the tastes of these new readers led not to the Russian classics but to *lubok* stories, the yellow press, and boulevard literature.[5] To the dismay of an intelligentsia that hoped to guide the enlightenment of the backward *narod*, peasants and workers displayed a disquieting tendency to manipulate cultural offerings to meet their self-defined goals. Similarly, intelligentsia ideas about music for peasants and workers frequently conflicted with this new public's own sense of its aesthetic, artistic, and entertainment needs.

Music, however, was the art that you could not escape. On the streets, in the home, in parks, gardens, and railway stations, even on the rivers, music was an increasingly insistent component of Russian urban life. For those who actively sought it out, music lessons, public and salon concerts, the opera, and domestic music making completed the rich and increasingly complex fabric of Russian musical life. This study examines Russian musical culture during its most dynamic and creative period, from the death of Mikhail Glinka in 1857 to the Bolshevik Revolution of 1917. However, rather than exploring the creativity of Russia's newly prominent composers and performers, I focus on everyday musical life and the institutional structures that shaped it. I emphasize provincial concerts distinguished largely by the quality of the buffet line or the dances that followed them, the trials and tribulations of struggling piano students, and the small careers of rank-and-file orchestral musicians rather than renowned virtuosi and canonical compositions. By shifting focus from the famous to the prosaic, I hope to demonstrate that the most significant development in Russian music in the nineteenth century was not the birth of its national compositional school, but the creation of the social, institutional, legal, and economic structures that facilitated a dramatic expansion of cultural life.

Similarly, I look for a social and structural explanation for the increasing dynamism of Russian musical life. Late imperial Russia's social structure has attracted significant scholarly interest in the past twenty-five years. Leopold Haimson framed the problem in the 1960s by asking whether, in the absence of World War I, Russia would have developed peacefully into a modern, industrialized, urbanized state with some form of representative and participatory government. Haimson argued that a double social fracture separating educated society (*obshchestvo*) from both the state and the mass of the working population (*narod*) hampered Russia's ability to transform itself.[6] Moreover, although the Emancipation of 1861 eliminated serfdom, it did not eliminate the estate system of social classification as a foundational structure of Russian society. Nevertheless, as Gregory Freeze has noted, the Russian estate system remained fluid in the late imperial period. Indeed, the inadequacy of the system, particularly the limited number of formal estates—nobility, clergy, peasants, and townspeople—virtually assured such fluidity. Under the pressure of profound socioeconomic change, Russia developed new social and occupational categories that awkwardly coexisted with the legal estate structure.[7] Individuals as well as social groups took advantage of the opportunities inherent in this unstable status hierarchy, as Elise Kimmerling Wirtschafter has shown. The estate system proved unable to cope with the social diversification of an industrializing economy and urbanizing society; as a result, individuals frequently occupied multiple social categories simultaneously.[8]

Since the 1960s, historians in the West have increasingly focused on the development of civil society and the middle class in an attempt to understand both Russia's trajectory toward revolution and its broad pattern of social and economic modernization. Yet, "civil society," the "public sphere," and "the middle class," are problematic theoretical terms when discussing Russian society, as their common definitions derive from the West European experience.[9] While wholesale appropriation of these terms and the historical and ideological baggage that accompanies them is not acceptable, they provide a useful theoretical scaffolding on which to examine Russian social developments.[10] Recently, historians such as Adele Lindenmeyr and Joseph Bradley have explored the critical role voluntary associations played in the expansion and intensification of the public sphere in Russia. In the process, they have uncovered a far more complex relationship between state and society than scholars had previously conceived.[11] As Bradley has noted, voluntary associations created alternative, if unstable, sources of power and authority in Russian society that implicitly challenged the autocratic state.[12] They "created the organizational framework" through which an increasingly assertive public could voice its opposition to the tsarist regime. Yet Bradley has also argued that the relationship between the state and voluntary associations was fundamentally a cooperative one, at least until the end of the nineteenth century. Ironically, the autocratic regime emerges as an effective, if somewhat inadvertent, supporter of Russia's emerging civil society.[13] These contradictory roles are visible in the Russian Musical Society, which enjoyed a strong working relationship with the Ministry of Internal Affairs as well as the personal patronage of members of the imperial family, particularly Grand Duchess Elena Pavlovna and her heirs. While the institutional success of the Russian Musical Society was due in large part to its cooperative relationship with the state, this alliance ultimately alienated much of educated society.

This book, it is hoped, will contribute to an ongoing attempt to better integrate musical life into the contemporary narrative of Russian and European history. As William Weber has pointed out, "historians tend to see music as a world apart."[14] Although Weber's comments are now more than a decade old, historians and musicologists still struggle to find common ground. In part, this is due to the specialized, often technical nature of much musicological research. Moreover, where musicologists are apt to focus on the personal characteristics and experiences of prominent composers and performers, historians are more inclined to emphasize the organizational and institutional aspects of musical life. Conversely, as Julia Foulkes has recently noted, social historians have neglected the fine arts, entrusting such research to scholars in other disciplines and departments. Although scholars in these disciplines have been "greatly influenced by the now decades-long attention to the social context of the arts," disciplinary boundaries and, in particular, the opaqueness of formal analysis to nonspecialists has meant that most "historians know little of this work" and "it has made relatively little impact" on their "pedagogical or research agendas."[15] Yet, the potential rewards of crossing such disciplinary boundaries are vigorously demonstrated in the work of scholars such as Murray Frame, whose recent book *School for Citizens: Theatre and Civil Society in Imperial Russia* has considerably enriched our understanding of both theatrical life and Russian social history.[16] This book, similarly, is an attempt to bridge the gap between specialized musicological and historical research on Russian musical life. While aspects of the story, particularly on the founding of the Russian Musical Society and the St. Petersburg Conservatory, will be familiar to musicologists, I hope that this retelling will allow scholars in musical disciplines to see the past of these institutions in a new light.

The activities of the Russian Musical Society take center stage here. Founded in St. Petersburg in 1859, the Society began to expand almost immediately, eventually establishing a network of branch societies and educational institutions that extended over the breadth of the empire. The Russian Musical Society was never alone in attempting to guide musical development. Over the long run, however, the Society became the accepted if not always appreciated leader of musical life. Its very success encouraged the growth of competing voluntary associations, educational institutions, and concert organizations. By the outbreak of World War I, the Russian Musical Society was at the head of a plethora of enterprises that had spun an increasingly intricate web of culture across the empire. One cultural almanac listed thirty-eight musical societies and circles in Moscow alone, ranging from the "Artistic Circle" that organized free concerts on Sundays for workers to the "Pharmacists' Literary-Musical Circle." [17] The Society and its provincial branches were critical components of the cultural infrastructure that supported the extraordinary musical creativity of late imperial Russia, which included not only local music societies, theaters, concert halls, and music schools, but also instrument manufacturers and stores, music publishers, music journals, and concert promoters and agents.

Most cultural organizers directed their attention not at the masses but at the middle. An enormous variety of voluntary associations, including the Russian Musical Society, provided this nascent middle class with an opportunity for public engagement if not political activity. State tolerance of associational activity encouraged involvement, strengthening the group self-identification of an emerging bourgeoisie. In Russia, as elsewhere in Europe, music was an ideal vehicle for the development of cultural identity; for the price of a concert ticket the aspiring bourgeoisie could demonstrate their culture and their ability to participate in educated society.[18] Purchase of a piano or the provision of piano lessons for one's children, similarly, was a manifest symbol of bourgeois status. Differences in the size and quality of the piano allowed further differentiation within the middle classes.[19] By the late nineteenth century, music in Russia was firmly hitched to bourgeois ideas of how life should be lived.

The early years of the Russian Musical Society were a constant struggle as it attempted to carve out a place for itself in the cultural landscape. One consequence of this struggle for existence was a defensive tendency to emphasize its own importance, in part by attempting to create and control its own history. The Russian Musical Society wrote and rewrote its history several times in an effort to sway public and governmental opinion to its favor and to claim credit for Russia's musical development. It created a myth, a heroic tale that emphasized the pioneering role of the Society in creating an effective concert life and establishing music education in both the capitals and provincial cities. In order to justify its existence in the face of sustained, sometimes virulent criticism, the Russian Musical Society created a narrative that presented itself as single-handedly bringing Russian music out of the darkness and into the light.[20]

This narrative, of course, had to accommodate the flowering of Russian composers beginning in the 1830s, especially Mikhail Glinka and Alexander Dargomyzhsky.[21] By emphasizing both the exceptionalism and the dilettantism of Russia's first generation of significant composers, the Society was able to celebrate their genius while still arguing that only the path of institutionalized music and music education could lead Russia to its rightful place within the European musical pantheon. Developing this argument, the Society suggested that pervasive musical ignorance meant that educated society could not properly appreciate a genius like Glinka. Only the Russian Musical Society, they insisted, offered the means to free Russian musical life from decay and stagnation.

In fashioning its narrative, the Russian Musical Society also created its heroes and gave them roles in a novelistic plot: Everyone understood the pervasive problems of Russian musical life, but it was only in Anton Rubinstein that society found an individual with the energy, strength, and independence to forge a path to the musical development of the entire country. Supported by a small but devoted cohort of like-minded musical amateurs and under the patronage and protection of the Grand Duchess Elena Pavlovna, Rubinstein was able to realize his dream of creating a conservatory for Russia. If in the first half of the nineteenth century Glinka brought Russian national music to life, in the second half of the century the Russian Musical Society labored heroically to develop it until it finally earned the justified respect of all of Europe.[22] This triumphal narrative represented an attempt to stake a claim to history. The urgency with which the Society wrote its own history is explained by the unusual hostility it provoked among its contemporaries and competitors.

The opponents of the Society also attempted to control the emerging narrative of Russian musical development. V. V. Stasov—one of the least objective observers of Russian musical life in the nineteenth century, a staunch nationalist, and a wholehearted promoter of Russian culture—strongly shaped Western conceptions of Russian music. In the 1860s and 1870s, Stasov vigorously promoted the creative efforts of both the Balakirev Circle and the *Peredvizhniki* or Wanderers, a group of young painters who broke away from the Academy of Arts in order to pursue their artistic ideal of critical realism. As scholars such as Yuri Olkhovsky and Elizabeth Valkenier have shown, Stasov labored heroically to encourage the art and artists involved, elaborating in the process his own vision of the form and content of a truly Russian artistic culture.[23]

Without negating Stasov's importance in promoting Russian culture, there are many problems with his representation of Russian musical life, not the least of which is his overpromotion of the Balakirev Circle and blithe disregard of the institutional framework developed by the Russian Musical Society. The most vexing problem is a dramatic oversimplification of nineteenth-century debates over music and music education. The strength of Stasov's views has sometimes obscured the multiple visions of Russian music and culture that his contemporaries held. For polemical reasons, Stasov constructed his narrative simply. In it, the forces of good (i.e., the Balakirev Circle) waged an unequal struggle for the development of a truly Russian national art against the forces of evil (i.e., Anton Rubinstein and the St. Petersburg Conservatory), who, tainted by their own Jewish, German, and "foreign" origins and orientations, wanted Russia to become yet another dull cultural outpost of pedantic, stilted, German art. In the long term, Stasov's slanted representation of the development of Russian music proved more influential than the equally biased but highly divergent account promoted by the Russian Musical Society.

Stasov's prominence as a writer and his stature as one of the few surviving participants of the cultural debates of the 1860s made him a natural magnet for early Western scholars seeking to learn more about Russian music. In consequence, as Richard Taruskin has argued, Stasov's sometimes idiosyncratic views shaped the interpretations of Russian musical life offered by the first generations of Western specialists.[24]

In their studies of Russian composers and musical life, later generations of scholars long retained, if only implicitly, Stasov's essentializing polarization of Russia's musical world between the Balakirev Circle and the "Rubinstein party," despite direct challenges by scholars such as Taruskin and Robert C. Ridenour.[25] To be sure, historians and musicologists have produced nuanced and sophisticated interpretations of Russian musical life; the historiography of Russian music is rich and complex.[26] All the same, Stasov's influence can still be seen in both broadly accessible histories of Russian culture, such as W. Bruce Lincoln's *Between Heaven and Hell: The Story of a Thousand Years of Artistic Life in Russia*, and in more specialized studies, such as Boris Gasparov's *Five Operas and a Symphony: Word and Music in Russian Culture*.[27] In Russia, the collapse of the Soviet Union has led to an effort to reexamine musical life and to culturally reintegrate the tsarist and Soviet eras. Denis Lomtev's fascinating case study of the role of ethnic Germans in musical life highlights the possibilities inherent in a more nuanced analysis of the identities of "Russian" musicians. S. V. Belov's recent study of the Iurgenson publishing house, meanwhile, underscores the need for broad research in the proliferating musical institutions of the late nineteenth century.[28] Research on music education, with notable exceptions such as D. L. Lokshin's excellent early study of singing in Russian and Soviet schools, K. I. Shamaeva's rigorously researched study of music education in nineteenth-century Ukraine, V. V. Adishchev's studies of music in the Institutes for Noble Women and the cadet schools, and the work of G. I. Kantor and his colleagues at the Kazan State Conservatory, has centered on pedagogical issues, teacher training, and instructional methodologies.[29] Unfortunately, research in Russian music education has suffered from the tendency, also prevalent in the West, to segregate music education from music per se. In effect, scholars have too often defined music teaching and learning as something other than music. Existing studies of Russian music schools and conservatories, moreover, are largely the product of scholars affiliated with these institutions. These studies often commemorate anniversaries or other important events and are as biased as similar "regimental" histories produced by the Russian Musical Society itself. Although they provide a wealth of information, their primary goal is not scholarly interpretation but the celebration of a particular version of their past.[30] Similarly, studies of provincial musical institutions tend to suffer from a certain scholarly isolationism, as they are frequently treated as an aspect of local history (*kraevedenie*) rather than part of a broader cultural phenomenon.[31]

Yet the conservatory, if approached as a social institution common to modernizing states, offers an opportunity to integrate diverse scholarly threads and create a more synthetic understanding of the role and function of music in society. The European Science Foundation's ambitious multi-year project *Musical Life in Europe* 1600–1900—*Circulation, Institutions, Representation* (1998–2001) included a welcome attempt by a variety of scholars, led by Michael Fend and Michel Noiray, to examine in detail the place and function of the conservatory in European life. As Fend and Noiray note, the conservatory, which rose to prominence in the nineteenth century, had become so dominant by the middle of the twentieth century that they not only trained but also employed "the great majority of performers and composers." Yet, for all their prominence, the "history and sociology of tertiary music education on a European level has virtually remained *terra incognita*."[32]

This study, then, attempts to draw a more complete picture of Russian musical life. It focuses on the provinces as well as on the capitals in an effort to develop a clearer understanding of the development of Russian cultural networks. It seeks to bridge not only musicological and historical approaches to cultural life, but also to link the recent work of historians such as Richard Stites, on the cultural life of the early nineteenth century, and Amy Nelson and Kiril Tomoff, on the development of musical policy and institutions in the Soviet period, by constructing a complex portrait of musical life in the second half of the nineteenth century. Chapter 1 uses the periodical press to introduce the musical world of Russia before the Great Reforms in an attempt to provide readers with a sense of its emotional and intellectual impact. The Russian Musical Society, although innovative, was not intended to be a radical departure from earlier patterns of cultural organization. In order to understand its emergence and significance, we must first understand the milieu that gave birth to it. Richard Stites has recently made a notable contribution toward this project in his magisterial study on the arts and culture in the prereform period.[33] This chapter complements his work, exploring musicians not as a social group but as an amalgam of Russian society whose disparate and distinct parts—amateurs, artists, serfs, foreigners, and students—were all essential to the proper functioning of musical life. The interaction of individuals and events generated a distinct rhythm to musical life, a rhythm that is explored by examining concert-going as a social process rather than a static event. Finally, music criticism is explored in an attempt to understand the intellectual imperatives that both encouraged the establishment of the Russian Musical Society and made its activities so controversial.

Newspaper and journal articles provide a rich window into Russian musical life that complements and complicates the representation of musical culture offered by archival sources and the memoir literature. Throughout this study, a close interpretive reading of periodical sources allows us to move beyond the ideologically shaped debates within musical circles to explore how educated society responded to the cultural transformation occurring around it.[34] Educated society's perception of Russian musical life as a success or as a failure, as riddled by crisis or developing normally, as meeting European standards or inferior and ineffectual, determined the prestige and influenced the development of Russian musical institutions. Newspaper and magazine accounts permit a shift in focus from the development of Russian music per se to the changing role of music in Russian society.

The establishment of the Russian Musical Society and the foundation and development of its flagship institutions, the St. Petersburg and Moscow conservatories, are the focus of the second and third chapters. Everywhere in Europe, the conservatory emerged in the nineteenth century as a real force in musical life, although it did not always serve in practice the professionalizing intentions of its founders, whose goals were subverted by the bourgeois demand for piano instruction. The drive for professionalization and the consequent undermining of the status of amateurs was the common subtext for most of the debates and controversies of musical life in the nineteenth century. Chapter 4 looks at the process of musical professionalization from both a personal and a legal point of view. Struggles to elevate and codify the status of musicians proved successful in the long run, but legal decisions failed to adequately grapple with the practical realities of life as a working musician. The indeterminate professional identity of musicians was further compromised by the presence of prominent subgroups—women, Jews, and poorly educated and socially inferior orchestral musicians—whose demands for inclusion weakened societal acceptance of the music profession.

Chapter 5 examines the expansion of musical life beyond the capitals, using the development of the provincial branches of the Russian Musical Society as a focal point. The transformation of musical life accomplished under the leadership of the Russian Musical Society reached its apogee with the 1905 Revolution. Chapter 6 looks at the traumatic impact of that event on the Society, its branches, and its educational institutions. The firing of Nikolai Rimsky-Korsakov from his post at the St. Petersburg Conservatory weakened public confidence in the Society and created fissures within it that ultimately led to its disintegration under the Bolsheviks. An analysis of the ritual celebration of the 1909 and 1912 jubilees of the Society and the St. Petersburg Conservatory leads to a final discussion of their fate during World War I, the revolutions of 1917, and the early years of Soviet power.

From 1859 to 1918, the Russian Musical Society strove to institutionalize and professionalize music education and concert life in the Russian Empire. From modest beginnings, the Society ultimately developed into a powerful musical institution that provided a degree of coherence and consistency to an increasingly diverse musical life. Its ultimate collapse in 1918 led not to the demise of its educational institutions and cultural networks but to their absorption into the emerging Soviet artistic system. The Society's network of conservatories and music schools became the foundation for a system of musical education and cultural development that, as of this writing, still survives and still serves the needs of the Russian people.

CHAPTER 1

A Far from Silent World

Russian Musical Life before the Great Reforms

WHEN ASSESSING THEIR OWN ACHIEVEMENTS, the patriots of both the Balakirev Circle and the Russian Musical Society sometimes suggested that Russian music scarcely existed at the beginning of the nineteenth century.[1] It bears remembering, however, that a nearly silent early nineteenth century made the subsequent achievements of both parties appear far more heroic. They become the bearers of light into the darkness, of enlightenment to the backward and spiritually impoverished Russian people. For the Russian Musical Society in particular, the supposed absence of music before midcentury reinforced its self-image: it had single-handedly developed musical life and brought culture to the wilderness, or at least to the provinces.

Those familiar with Russian intellectual history will recognize this impulse. Throughout the nineteenth century, the intelligentsia repeatedly assigned themselves the missionary task of uplifting the backward *narod*, a task they pursued with considerable zeal. Musicians and their critics appropriated these intelligentsia values in the drive for musical development that began in earnest in the 1860s. Yet Russia was hardly a silent world in the first half of the nineteenth century. Although prominent composers of European fame were slow to emerge, Russian musical life was dynamic and successful, meeting the needs and expectations of its participants and the public. Music, Irina Petrovskaia has argued, was so prevalent that it was virtually inescapable.[2] It could be found in every corner of Russian life and, unlike literature, it permeated every layer of society. Especially in St. Petersburg, enthusiasts and casual observers could partake of a wide variety of musical evenings, balls, operatic performances, *tableaux vivants*, and concerts both large and small. Music could also be found on street corners and in the courtyards as itinerant musicians and buskers played for an audience that had little choice but to listen. In Moscow and in the provinces, unsurprisingly, musical offerings were less diverse. While the capital reaped the benefits of a relatively rich stock of both local musicians and touring foreign artists, in the provinces musical life depended on the abilities of local amateurs. But even there, music was an important feature of social life.

This cheerful portrait must be qualified and complicated if we are to understand the whole of Russian musical life over the course of the nineteenth century. The fashionable, lively, yet limited musical life of the first part of the century met the needs and expectations of the audiences of that time. As that audience became more sophisticated and diverse, however, it grew increasingly dissatisfied and began to demand change.

Artists, Amateurs, and Serfs: Musicians in Russian Society

Foreigners were the mainstay of Russian musical life in the first half of the nineteenth century. St. Petersburg was a featured stop on the European concert circuit and regularly attracted famous and fashionable performers, while provincial cities such as Moscow, Odessa, and Kiev attracted a more modest but still significant number of touring artists, especially after the first quarter of the century. As glamorous as such touring stars could be, the legions of ordinary musicians and singers who poured into St. Petersburg and Moscow hoping to make a substantial profit, if not a career, were perhaps more important. These humble individuals ensured the orderly conduct of musical life, supplying the orchestras and stages of the two capitals with rank-and-file players, singers, and soloists. These working musicians were craftsmen, well and diversely prepared, willing and able to capitalize on whatever opportunities might be available. At the beginning of the century, one unnamed newcomer from Vienna advertised his services in the newspaper, emphasizing his ability to satisfy the most varied needs of potential employers. He was able to "teach the piano, violin, and all music, as well as to sing in French, Italian, and Russian." Clearly hoping to find a well-placed and well-off patron, our anonymous Viennese suggestively noted his ability "if desired . . . to direct an entire orchestra."[3] Although the fate of this Viennese musical adventurer is not known, for some of the most fortunate arrival in the Russian capital led to stable employment with the Imperial Theaters. The stars of the operatic stage tended to be singers with European reputations and Italian surnames who enjoyed tremendous popularity as well as the financial rewards that accompanied success on the stage and in aristocratic salons. The theaters also attracted rank-and-file musicians and singers from many European countries, enticing them with good salaries, generous pensions, and the lucrative opportunities believed to accrue to those able to sate the musical hunger of the Russian capitals.[4]

Yet, foreigners were only one face of Russia's musical world. Trained in apprenticeships or through formal education, they formed a caste apart from native-born musicians. Less attractive, less visible, but no less important were the serf musicians whose labors enabled the nobility to sustain a fashionable musical life.[5] Skilled serf musicians were bought, sold, traded, and if they escaped, tracked with zeal. In 1806, for example, the violinist and domestic serf, Ivan Dmitriev, son of Sokolov, fled the household of Agrafena Fedorovna Skulskaia. Skulskaia advertised in the pages of *Moskovskie vedomosti* for the return of her property, human and otherwise. Claiming that her runaway violinist had taken "clothing and other items" valued at "eighty-five rubles," she offered a reward of 100 rubles to anyone able to bring him in. The value attached to the fugitive, a mere 15 rubles, underscored the debased position of serfs within Russian society, a humiliation that would have long-lasting repercussions for orchestral musicians.[6]

The important cultural roles played by the Sheremetev and Vielgorsky families, among others, rested on foundations provided by enserfed musicians. Because these noble magnates hired professional, often foreign-born, musicians to train and conduct their private orchestras, choruses, and theaters and sometimes sent their own serf musicians abroad for advanced training, the status of orchestral musicians grew increasingly muddied. Despite the burdens of serfdom, many Russian musicians and singers made careers in the orchestras and choruses, more rarely on the stages, of the Imperial Theaters. If aristocratic music lovers fell into financial difficulty, they might resort to the expedient of selling their highly trained serf musicians to the Imperial Theater. Employment by the theater brought freedom, but the degraded origins of the musical rank-and-file remained an impediment to the professionalization of music until the twentieth century.[7] Russian orchestral musicians, in particular, suffered from low social status and lacked professional recognition. Trained on the job, through apprenticeships, in the Moscow Theater School, the Chapel Choir School, or more rarely sent abroad, they remained artisans, not artists.[8]

Educated society throughout the empire depended on its own members for much of its musical entertainment. In smaller provincial cities, amateur performers were the mainstay of musical life as traveling artists were a rarity before the second half of the century. Everywhere, however, balls were a particularly attractive and enjoyable aspect of musical life. They provided an opportunity to socialize in a glamorous setting, or, at any rate, as glamorous a setting as local resources would allow. In Ufa in 1811, a masquerade ball that was intended to aid an impoverished local family lightened the late winter gloom. "The building was entirely illuminated: characteristic masks and quadrilles in an Asiatic style presented a pleasing variety, but Islamic splendor, for all its magnificence, dimmed next to the beauty of Slavic-Russian attire." Although a ball in the capital would have featured an orchestra of hired professional musicians, this provincial ball relied on the enthusiasm of local society, whose members made up the "orchestra ... of amateurs."[9] What richness and variety provincial cities enjoyed in their cultural life depended on the aesthetic sensibilities and artistic training of local society.

Enthusiasm for music was not always accompanied by skill. *Literaturnaia gazeta* sardonically described midcentury St. Petersburg as so enamored of music that its inhabitants could not "live without music, ... eat or drink without music, ... go for a stroll without music, ... even ... get medical treatment without music." Music was inescapable, the piano an insidious influence on all layers of society: "You will find a piano, or some kind of box with a keyboard, everywhere.... If there are one hundred apartments in a St. Petersburg building, then you can count on ninety-three instruments and a piano tuner," who was guaranteed to "never die from hunger." All of these pianos and the well-employed piano tuner mirrored society's passion for amateur music making. As the commentator for *Literaturnaia gazeta* darkly reminded his readers, the grim realities of the city's musical life hardly stopped at the domestic piano invasion. Taverns provided no relief, as most seemed to view an organ or player piano as an absolute necessity in order to stay in business. Neither would one's home provide a refuge, because an endless army of little orchestras from all corners of the world, "these Tyroleans, Bohemians, Saxons, Piedmontese, and finally, the endless multitude of Italians and Germans, all with barrel organs," would only be waiting to "besiege your courtyard from ten in the morning until late at night."[10] Music was no longer a cultured respite from urban bustle; it had become an unwelcome contributor to the cacophony of the city.

Because of music's pervasiveness, musical training was an issue of considerable public interest. As Richard Stites has emphasized, in Russia as in the rest of Europe, piano, vocal, or instrumental lessons were an accepted part of an aristocratic education, especially for women.[11] At home, the daughters and sons of the nobility learned music from an early age as part of their upbringing. At school, their musical educations often continued. Elite women's institutions, such as the Institutes for Noble Girls, offered their pupils instruction in voice and piano. Male gymnasia pupils also studied music, with supplementary lessons on the piano or orchestral instruments usually available as well. The purpose of musical instruction in these institutions was not to train professional musicians or music teachers. The goal was to provide wellborn and well-off students with the rudiments of an aesthetic education, as well as an agreeable and civilized pastime. Nevertheless, it was in the Institutes for Noble Girls that musical instruction reached its highest development in Russia before the founding of the conservatories in the 1860s.[12]

Especially in the provinces, school music lessons were viewed as important factors in the social and educational success of students.[13] In 1809, the leading citizens of Vladimir turned out in force for the dedication of new music classes in the city's gymnasia. The provincial governor and local notables lent dignity and prestige to a formal ceremony that featured a fully illuminated building, speeches, and "resounding" music. The classes were the creation of a foreign musician, one Freideker, who had generously offered to organize and teach them without payment, although one should perhaps read effective advertising rather than altruism into this act. Freideker directed the musical part of the dedication ceremony and clearly received a healthy dose of positive publicity as well as goodwill from the event. It seems safe to assume that his charitable impulse did not go unrewarded in the long run.[14]

Throughout Russia, annual examinations of *institutki*, gymnasia students, and military cadets included highly ritualized performances by the best piano, violin, and voice students. Choral performances by the graduating class or the entire student body ceremonially displayed their aesthetic development and cultural maturity. Musical excellence was rewarded in the same manner as distinction in other subjects, with students receiving prizes and public recognition. If music did not occupy quite as prestigious a place as more academic subjects, these performances nevertheless reinforced pervasive ideas of the cultural attributes of an educated member of polite society. In the ceremonies, music played a symbolic and celebratory role, with a march accompanying the students' entrance or trumpet fanfares signaling the distribution of awards. The music itself was of little interest; works performed were listed simply as "a symphony," "choral music," or even just "trumpets."[15]

Musical instruction in the schools supplemented but did not replace musical training in the home. The demand for effective and reasonably priced musical instruction encouraged enterprising individuals to establish music schools, but results were uneven at best. Most of these schools offered instruction only on piano or voice, occasionally combined with classes in basic music theory. Such schools sometimes tried to make a virtue out of a necessity, as when one St. Petersburg music school promoted its "modern" program of small group instruction in voice, piano, and music theory. The piano classes, for example, each enrolled up to five students, who were grouped by ability. Although the group lessons were touted as a pedagogical innovation, allowing students to improve their technical proficiency by observing others, it seems more likely that this was an attempt to lower the cost of instruction at the sacrifice of some quality, as well as the instructor's nerves. Even this somewhat compromised form of instruction did not come cheap; the piano and vocal courses each cost 100 rubles (assignats) for twenty-four lessons, over three months for piano students, two months for voice students.[16]

Piano instruction, particularly for girls, served as a metaphor for the broader preparation of the younger generation for a successful life. Consequently, fears of inadequate or ineffective instruction reflected broader anxieties about the proper roles of women. When the popular sheet music magazine *Nuvellist* offered detailed advice on the training of young ladies as pianists, it focused on the supposed tendency to emphasize technique at the expense of understanding. Similar complaints about the superficiality of music lessons persisted throughout the century. In this case, the complaint was an economic as well as an aesthetic one; after ten or more years of training, the neglect of music theory produced girls with superficial technical skills but no real knowledge—or love—of music. Even for a reasonably well-off family, the cost of this failed training could be catastrophic. "For ten years [girls] study the mysteries of the piano, taking two lessons per week, at ten rubles each, which over ten years amounts to nearly nine thousand rubles." Lessons, however, were not the only expense. To arrive at the total cost of a musical education one also had to factor in "expenses of two hundred rubles per year for music, [and] two pianos, each at two thousand rubles." Such substantial expenditures, moreover, yielded little if any real benefit, amounting to "almost fifteen thousand rubles thrown into the fire, because the young lady has learned nothing and rejects music from the day of her wedding." The disdain expressed here toward musical training reflects a broader complaint about the preparation of girls for the practicalities of married life. Rather than expending a small fortune on the frivolous and fruitless musical education of daughters, "Wouldn't it be better to add this fifteen thousand to the dowry?" Her husband, it was assumed, would surely prefer a well-endowed bride to one encumbered by a superficial aestheticism and "a useless piece of furniture, a piano." Despite endless hours of lessons and practicing, such girls only learned to perform prettily a few showpieces. Because these girls had not internalized music, commentators presumed, they would abandon their pianos at the first opportunity following their marriage and "forget music, which they have learned so poorly!"

On the surface, *Nuvellist* absolved young women of responsibility for their failure to learn music, presenting them as victims of inadequate or unscrupulous teachers. Yet, the magazine's specific complaints about piano instruction hid much broader criticisms of Russian musical life. As these girls matured into mothers, they would return to the much-hated piano as their daughters' first teachers, locking both their families and Russia into an endless cultural loop without exit or opportunity for advancement. The magazine's practical advice on the musical instruction of children offered broader lessons for the cultural development of the nation.

In particular, *Nuvellist* chided parents who economized where they should have invested. Rightfully concerned about the cost of a musical education, parents hired the cheapest instructor they could find, rather than looking for a skilled musician and able pedagogue. Lessons, the magazine insisted, should proceed logically and gradually, with a strong foundation in theory and solfège (sight-singing) leading to the study of high-quality repertoire and instruction in accompaniment as well as solo playing.[17] The advice of the *Nuvellist* critic, although practical, ran counter to prevailing attitudes. The critic was concerned with the development of musical skill and ability, first of the individual and ultimately of the nation, whereas most parents emphasized the acquisition of the social skills and graces necessary in Russian society. This tension between what musicians viewed as the purpose of music education and what society understood as the value of musical instruction would persist throughout the nineteenth and well into the twentieth century.

Those who obtained some musical proficiency, and sometimes those who failed to do so, performed with eagerness for audiences composed of their friends, family, and members of their social circle. Amateur recitals and musical evenings offered enthusiasts the opportunity to display their hard-won skills and garner public acclaim with minimal risk to reputation or social standing as the press glossed over less-than-polished performances but lauded more or less successful renditions of the usual operatic arias and salon pieces as evidence of a lady's or gentleman's sophistication, erudition, and aesthetic depth. Grander homes were frequently the sites of semipublic concerts and salon performances distinguished by their uneven, highly variable, even incoherent programming. Aside from a fad for the arias of Gioacchino Rossini, such concerts featured a mixed repertoire of solo vocal and instrumental performances sandwiched between overtures that, in the absence of an orchestra, might be performed in a piano arrangement for four, eight, or more hands. Such concerts were more about social obligation than about aesthetic pleasure, entertainment, or even education. It seemed as if everyone was learning to play music and that all of these new enthusiasts were determined to demonstrate their skills. Whether or not this was advisable, given the quality of the skills acquired, and whether or not anyone had any desire to hear them play, were questions few considered.

The Sites of Musical Life: Salons, Societies, and the Concert

St. Petersburg was the epicenter of Russian musical life. It was only in the capital that the landscape of musical life was completely drawn. In the first half of the nineteenth century, musical life occupied a variety of public and private spaces, each with their own distinct meanings and each attracting their own set of participants and observers. These sites included not only the court, the aristocratic salon, the opera theater, and the public or private concert, but also the home, the intelligentsia *kruzhok* or circle, and the social organization. It is worth remembering that the street, the urban courtyard, and the tavern were also important sites in Russian musical life during this period, as well as later in the century.

The boundaries between these different cultural spaces were not fixed, but highly porous. Musicians, music lovers, and the music itself moved between private and public settings, grand and modest, with surprising ease. This fluidity emphasizes the transitional nature of Russian musical life in the first half of the nineteenth century. The division between music purely for the court and aristocratic elites and music for the peasant and urban masses began, slowly at first, to blur. Noble enthusiasts began to purposefully explore and then exploit native Russian musical traditions, recasting them into idioms and tonal patterns familiar to aristocratic listeners accustomed to fashionable Italian, Viennese, and German musical languages. At the same time, opera arias, romances, and even piano pieces filtered down the social scale to the point where listeners complained, only slightly facetiously, that the most popular operatic themes seemed to be on the lips of every street musician if not every common laborer. As Russian educated society began to diversify and the *raznochintsy*—the people of various ranks—emerged as an economic, social, and political force, both the audience and the structures of musical life broadened. New intelligentsia circles and civic-minded social organizations began to compete with aristocratic salons and the state theaters for cultural leadership.

The Imperial Court played an important but limited role in Russian musical life during this period. Its institutions, such as the Court Chapel Choir, served not only the aesthetic, spiritual, and entertainment needs of the tsar and his immediate family and retainers, but also facilitated the broader development of musical life by training singers and musicians, attracting and supporting foreign and Russian virtuosi, and setting the tone and taste for St. Petersburg's musical life through court balls, concerts, and entertainments. The court or, more precisely, the state also shaped musical life through its support and administration of the opera theaters in St. Petersburg and Moscow.[18]

Opinions differ as to the affective importance of music in the lives of the imperial family. On the one hand, contemporaries have argued that the emperors displayed little interest in music. Alexander II, for example, was described by Anton Rubinstein as "indifferent to music" and inclined to play cards during performances.[19] Such a criticism, of course, could have been laid on any number of the tsar's masculine contemporaries. On the other hand, more sympathetic observers, such as A. F. Lvov, portrayed the family of Nicholas I as much like other families, actively engaged in intimate domestic music making that included the tsar on trumpet, the empress on piano, and the young grand duchesses on the violin.[20] Other members of the imperial family, moreover, were certainly musical enthusiasts, a fact that would have long-term significance for Russian musical life because of their patronage of the Russian Musical Society and other organizations. Grand Duke Konstantin Nikolaevich was a keen amateur cellist, while his wife, Grand Duchess Aleksandra Iosifovna tried her hand at composition. Both the Empress Maria Fedorovna and the Grand Duchess Elena Pavlovna were important hostesses of musical salons.[21] Thus music was a domestic focal point for the Romanovs as for most Russian noble families.

The home was the heart of Russian musical life. In its modest incarnation, the home served as the site for a multitude of music lessons, on voice, piano, or another instrument, for the daughters and sons of the nobility and the merchantry. In theory, if not always in practice, the skills acquired in these lessons created the basis for a domestic musical life of mutual performance and shared music making. As Richard Stites has argued, domestic music making was often another expression of the "sentimental romanticism that infused literature at that time."[22] Domestic music making, with its reliance on sentimental romances, salon pieces, and piano transcriptions of larger orchestral and operatic works, brought into the home the passionate emotions that characterized the sacralized art of the Romantic era.

Aristocratic salons provided a similarly domesticated setting for musical life, but on a far grander scale. These semipublic events brought together skilled artist-professionals, ordinary working musicians, artist-dilettanti, rank-and-file amateurs, and casual listeners. On one end of the scale, the salons approximated the intimacies of music making among one's family. They featured informal performances of solo and chamber works for one's peers, often in the midst of a variety of other entertainments and diversions, conversations, and card playing. At the other end of the scale, salons provided the site for private concerts that featured both noble amateurs and the finest virtuosi in the city. Salon concerts of this type also introduced visiting foreign artists to the city's arbiters of taste prior to their formal, public debut.[23]

The leading musical salons in the two capitals, such as those of Mikhail Vielgorsky, Princess Zinaida Volkonskaia, V. F. Odoevsky, and Grand Duchess Elena Pavlovna, did more than just bring together musically and socially inclined members of Russian society. These salons, which attracted the finest professional and dilettante artists, were the proving ground for new and challenging works by Russian and foreign composers. They were also the center for serious music criticism, discussions of theoretical questions, and heated aesthetic debates that resonated with contemporary intellectual currents. Romanticism, Nationalism, the Masonic movement, the Decembrists, the Slavophile-Westernizer debates, and Pan-Slavism all played a part in shaping the discussions and the music that flourished in these artistic salons. The intimate connections of individuals such as Odoevsky, Volkonskaia, Matvei and Mikhail Vielgorsky, and Mikhail Glinka with their peers who possessed more radical inclinations led to a blurring of the distinction between these artistic salons and the more philosophical intelligentsia circles.[24]

Both the salon and the intelligentsia circle were relatively intimate gatherings, restricted to those whose personal connections or relationships to the host or hostess permitted them entrée. As the century wore on, however, musical life increasingly began to take place on a public stage, although the public remained small and limited by wealth and social status. Public concerts were largely but not entirely restricted to the Lenten season in February and March, when operatic and ballet performances were prohibited. These performances were uneven draws for the public. Their repertoire, and often their performers, had much in common with salon and semipublic concerts in private homes. Amateurs shared the stage with local and touring artists; both the skill of performers and the amount of time devoted to rehearsal varied significantly. Concerts that could not offer some novelty—whether famous virtuosi, unusually large orchestras or choirs, fashionable charitable goals, or less tastefully, soloists who were child prodigies, dwarves, or women on unusual instruments—faced difficulty in filling seats. Even in the provinces, where concerts were much rarer than in St. Petersburg or Moscow, empty seats were common. Although this public indifference to culture was troubling, the reasons behind it were hardly mysterious. High ticket prices, mediocre performances, dull or repetitive repertoire, poor acoustics, uncomfortable listening conditions, and bad weather all contributed to the perceived inadequacies of Russian musical life.

In St. Petersburg, venues for public concerts were relatively few in the first half of the century. One of the most important was the Hall of the Assembly of the Nobility (*zal dvorianskogo sobraniia*) on Mikhailovskaia Square. The building, designed by architect P. Zhako and completed in 1839, was part of an ensemble of buildings originally laid out by Carlo Rossi.[25] Over the years, the concert hall hosted not only the balls and masquerades that delighted St. Petersburg society, but also concerts of visiting artists, the Philharmonic Society, and, eventually, the Russian Musical Society. Although glamorous, the "White-Columned Hall" of the Noble's Assembly had a reputation for poor acoustics, making it a less desirable venue than its primary competitor, the hall of the Engelgardt House.[26]

Originally built by F. B. Rastrelli as a private residence for A. N. Vilboa, the Engelgardt House subsequently passed into the hands of Prince A. M. Golitsyn and then, in 1799, to the wealthy merchant S. Kusovnikov. By 1802, the building was a center for local musical life, its hall the site of the Philharmonic Society's annual concerts. When Kusovnikov's daughter married the grandnephew of G. A. Potemkin, Vasily Vasilevich Engelgardt, the building became part of her dowry. Rebuilt by Zhako in 1829 at Engelgardt's orders, the building housed not only the concert hall but also M. I. Bernard's music shop, a focal point in the lives of St. Petersburg's musicians and music lovers. The beautiful and well-appointed building was devoted entirely to music and other entertainments, the Engelgardt family choosing to live elsewhere. Until 1835, masquerades and balls were the featured entertainment, but when the right to present public balls was restricted to the Imperial Theaters, Engelgardt devoted his hall to concert life.[27] By the middle of the 1840s, however, the hall began to lose its allure as both artists and audiences complained about its discomforts. According to Clara Schumann, the hall was dark, dirty, and frequently cold; she wondered at the continued willingness of polite society to attend concerts there.[28] Unsurprisingly, the hall ceased to make a profit and was rented to the Merchants' Club, which used it for dances and masquerades. In 1846, the building was sold and turned into a store, a turn of events that provoked Nestor Kukolnik to voice his outrage in the press. "When this building was first built, all of Petersburg rushed to look at this new, at that time amazing, at that time incomparable phenomenon. The whole city was full of gossip about its Gothic and Chinese rooms." For Kukolnik, the Philharmonic Hall had been not so much a concert venue as a temple of worship, a wellspring of enlightenment where one could hear "the great works of Handel, Haydn, Mozart, Elsner, [and]

Mendelssohn-Bartholdy." Now, this temple was being turned into a commercial center where Petersburgers could pause "to buy everything that you might need."[29] For Kukolnik, the change of ownership represented not a business transaction but the defilement of a sacred space.

Specialized musical societies, some with charitable goals, played important but unstable roles in the city's musical life. As early as 1802, the Philharmonic Society emerged as a significant force, usually presenting two annual concerts devoted to oratorio or other large vocal and instrumental works. The Philharmonic Society was a mutual aid and philanthropic organization devoted to the welfare of musicians, rather than a voluntary association. By August 1805, membership was limited to musicians employed in the orchestras of the Imperial Theaters; the funds raised by the society's concerts supported the widows and orphans of its members.[30] This organizational strategy proved very effective at first, attracting a substantial number of musicians to the society, but became a weakness by the second half of the nineteenth century because it excluded so many potential members—not only amateurs but also professional musicians employed in other capacities. The membership both aged and stagnated in absolute numbers, prompting concern over the society's ability to meet its financial obligations.[31] Nevertheless, the society's annual concerts featured prominently in St. Petersburg's social calendar, attracting a large audience.

If the Philharmonic Society was the prototype for Russian musical organizations, other societies emerged to fill other unmet cultural needs, with varying degrees of success. The unavoidable first step was the decision by an individual or small group of musical enthusiasts, dissatisfied with some aspect of local musical life, to form a society. The founding members of a society accepted responsibility for it, frequently risking their personal reputations and sometimes their fortunes. The charters of voluntary associations, as Joseph Bradley has argued based on his analysis of the Free Economic Society, established the parameters of a given society's relationship with the state and "functioned as a microconstitution written in the language of representation, which gave associational life autonomous existence and a special meaning."[32] The charters of musical societies, although formulaic and in many ways determined by legal requirements, nevertheless provided a platform through which their leadership could declare their principles and present their ideals in the hope of persuading the public to support them. Ultimately, as we will see with the Russian Musical Society after 1905, a charter could become the battlefield in an ideological war.

For a music society, the success or failure of early membership drives significantly determined the likelihood that it would survive past its birth.

Some societies were more restrictive than others, excluding, for example, women from active membership or simply from leadership roles. Even if a new musical society attracted a substantial number of members, its success was far from guaranteed. Leadership failures and internal divisions often thwarted ambitious goals. As often as not, problems arose within a society over financial issues; costs for concerts and musical evenings always seemed to be higher than anticipated. Problems could also emerge if the society failed to meet the musical and/or social expectations of the membership, or if the interests of members began to diverge.

The 1820s and 1830s witnessed the emergence of a number of musical societies devoted to symphonic music. The Musical Academy, for example, was founded at the end of 1827 at the instigation of F. P. Lvov, the well-known director of the Court Chapel Choir. It provided its members with a pleasant way to pass the time as well as an opportunity to perfect their musical abilities. Its membership included both men and women, subdivided into multiple categories: active (performing), listening, honorary, and contributing members. Active membership, in theory at least, was limited to those able to read music freely. Dues were 60 rubles per year, although the society admitted women and girls willing to perform in its musical evenings as active members at no cost.[33] Commenting on the Academy's first concert, A. V. Nikitenko highlighted the importance of individual leadership, noting that the new organization had been established "mainly through the efforts of the Lvovs, the entire family of whom are excellent musicians." Despite his recognition of the importance of professional leadership, Nikitenko noted with approval that the "active, that is, singing and playing, members of this academy are all amateurs, including young ladies." This first concert boasted the talents of well-known members of both St. Petersburg society and of Russian musical circles: "Three young ladies from distinguished families sang. First-rate voices! The elder Lvov brought everyone to rapture with his violin playing; the younger also played superbly on the cello."[34]

The establishment of the Symphonic Society in 1840 represented an early attempt to reshape Russian musical life through institutional means. In a scathing article published in *Sankt-Peterburgskie vedomosti*, Modest Rezvoi itemized the numerous deficiencies of Russian musical life. Rezvoi was a prominent amateur cellist, composer, and critic as well as a member of several musical societies. His point of comparison was Germany, that bastion of culture where, supposedly, high-quality music was available in even the smallest town. Russia seemed impoverished by comparison. Even in its capital, Rezvoi noted with despair, musical life was limited to "Russian and foreign (*nemetskaia*) opera, and concerts during Lent."[35] Rezvoi's litany of complaints included a limited and too frequently repeated operatic repertoire and a highly compressed concert life. The attempt to cram an entire year's worth of performances into a thirty-five-day period during Lent, with concerts two or even three times a day, doomed even the most dedicated concertgoer to either exhaustion or failure. Moreover, as Rezvoi noted, most ordinary concertgoers were unlikely to restructure their lives and neglect other interests to attend concerts daily during Lent. The compression of musical life consequently limited its significance for educated society. Rezvoi envisioned a more elevated musical life in which concerts provided more than a distraction during long Lenten evenings, an opinion the broader concertgoing public did not necessarily share. His purpose in identifying the weaknesses of Russian musical life was to call attention to the newly formed Symphonic Society, of which he was a devoted member. Rezvoi hoped to help the new society avoid the financial difficulties, artistic failures, and quick decay of its predecessors.

In its first seasons, the Symphonic Society attracted a relatively modest number of members that included many of St. Petersburg's leading amateurs.[36] Its members met weekly, with the orchestra attempting a variety of mostly classical works, including multiple symphonies by Haydn, Mozart, and Beethoven. The new society, like its unsuccessful predecessors, could never muster a complete orchestra from among its own members and was forced to hire outsiders for the wind parts in particular. Nevertheless, the society's members did not simply fill the traditional role of the noble amateur, that of vocal or piano soloist; the society's members were a considerable presence in the orchestra, including some thirty violinists, nine violists, eight cellists, and even two of the four bassists.[37] The choir, similarly, was comprised of male and female members of the society. During its heyday, the Symphonic Society was a significant force in Russian musical life, presenting concerts that featured serious and substantive repertoire. In the winter of 1848–1849, for example, it offered a series of twelve concerts, the last of which included Felix Mendelssohn's Symphony No. 1, Beethoven's Missa Solemnis, and a festive overture on the Russian national hymn. A quartet from the mass attracted particular attention as it "showed to what extent our so-called amateur music lovers (*liubiteli*) love and understand music." Critics such as Platon Smirnovsky invested their hopes in the society, noting with approval that its relatively well-attended concerts featured "the classical creations of the great maestros" rather than light salon music. Expressing his own desire to transform Russian musical life into a more elevated experience, Smirnovsky fervently prayed that the society might eventually establish a

Russian conservatory.[38] Although this was not to be, the remnants of the Symphonic Society survived long enough to serve as the legal precursor to the Russian Musical Society in 1859.

Musical societies varied in their level of cultural sophistication and social exclusivity, depending in part on the personal and artistic prestige of their leadership. The Lvov family, so important in the establishment of the Musical Academy in the 1820s, was similarly crucial to the emergence of the Concert Society, established in 1850 on the initiative of A. F. Lvov. The Concert Society reaped the benefits of Lvov's connections, receiving a modest subsidy from the Ministry of the Imperial Court.[39] In addition, the choristers of the Imperial Chapel Choir and the musicians of the Imperial Theater orchestras, supplemented by leading dilettantes and occasional guest soloists, provided the musical expertise for the society's three annual Lenten concerts in the hall of the Chapel Choir. Grand Duke Konstantin Nikolaevich, for example, played cello in the orchestra. Given the location of the performances and the cost of a membership (10 silver rubles), the Concert Society was intended for and attracted an elite audience. From 1852 to 1853, for example, the more than two hundred members included Tsarevich Alexander Nikolaevich, the Grand Dukes Mikhail Nikolaevich and Nikolai Nikolaevich, as well as prominent music lovers such as the Vielgorsky brothers, V. A. Kologrivov, Odoevsky, and the Stasov family. Although the quality of concerts was very high, by the late 1870s the Concert Society faded into the shadow of the Russian Musical Society.[40]

The Rhythm of Musical Life: Concertgoing as a Social Process

In the first half of the nineteenth century, Russia's musical seasons, like its natural ones, were distinct and regular. The opera season was the highlight of the year. It opened at the end of August and closed in April or May, interrupted only by Lent when operatic performances were forbidden. In an effort to limit competition to the Imperial Theaters, concerts were restricted outside of the Lenten season. Touring artists and charitable concerts were generally exempted from these regulations, so vocal and instrumental concerts were never completely banished even during the opera season. The intensity of the Lenten season, however, left the rest of the year seemingly barren. During Lent, St. Petersburg rang with the sound of music as concerts became the primary form of entertainment. In the spring, the opera theaters closed again as society left the city to summer at their country homes or rented *dachas*. Light concerts and dances appropriate to the pleasant spirit of summer filled this third season, which revolved around pleasure palaces such as the one in Pavlovsk.[41]

The intensity of the Lenten season created a sense of excitement, but it also created problems. Audiences grew tired of repetitive concerts with familiar performers and worn-out repertoire. Although the best concerts featured polished, well-known performers, the Lenten season also provided amateur musicians and enthusiasts with an opportunity to display their skill, taste, and wealth. While a relatively small number of "truly expert amateur musicians," hosted significant concerts, there were "entire streets of the dwellings of self-styled music lovers" whose homes resounded with an unceasing cacophony of "*sextexts, quintets, quartets, trios*, or if necessary, *duets*," which the hosts, "worthy heir[s] of Midas," insisted on calling concerts, but more impartial observers damned as chaos. "How many times (to my sorrow) have I suffered at such barbaric concerts," moaned the critic for *Russkii pustynnik* in 1817. "How many times have I cursed my passion for music, which brings me to these dens of *lovers of discord!*"[42]

Although the quality of performances during the Lenten season was decidedly mixed, charitable concerts often drew together a city's finest musical and vocal talents, amateur and professional. The anticipation of fine performances attracted substantial crowds. For these prestigious events, high ticket prices failed to discourage concertgoers, often prompting especially philanthropic—or publicity seeking—individuals to pay two, three, ten, even twenty times the face value of a ticket. The most important musical charity event, the annual Invalid Concert, commemorated the entrance of Russian troops into Paris at the end of the Napoleonic Wars.[43] This concert was one of the most spectacular events of the season. It generated funds for the support of wounded officers and soldiers by presenting St. Petersburg society with a splendid opportunity to display their patriotism, their wealth, and their appreciation for culture all at the same time. The concerts themselves did little to demonstrate the refined tastes of the Russian nobility, however, featuring as they did pompous cultural displays of Russian imperial might, with orchestras of hundreds and choirs of thousands.

When it was established in November 1813, the Invalid Concert was quite an innovation. *Russkii invalid* promoted the concert energetically, underscoring the event's social importance with increasingly detailed information in the issues leading up to the performance. The newspaper endorsed the concert as a union of leading artists and prominent amateurs famed for their artistic abilities.[44] The patriotic impulse behind the concert was unambiguous; it was intended to "support those Russian Invalids who saved their Fatherland in the present war and who, with their blood, redeemed the freedom of Europe."[45] The militaristic and patriotic program featured a martial symphony by Romberg and a similar chorus with orchestra by Sartii, as well as regimental marches and the patriotic hymn, "God Save the King."[46] Patriotic and philanthropic impulses resulted in a healthy profit. Although tickets were priced at 5 rubles, nearly two-thirds of the total proceeds of the concert came from additional charitable contributions. *Russkii invalid* published a careful accounting of receipts, listing the initials of all those who donated.[47]

Forty years later, in 1853, the Invalid Concert remained a fixture of St. Petersburg social and cultural life. It continued to attract a glamorous and sizeable crowd; one critic argued that had the hall been twice the size there still would not have been an empty seat. Although such claims might have been patriotic hyperbole, they nevertheless evoked the social, if not necessarily artistic, significance of this annual event. The presence of many veterans, seated at the front of the hall, made the concert even more poignant. The repertoire and performances capitalized on the emotionally arousing qualities of musical pageantry; the evening featured a "huge" military orchestra that performed "rather difficult" pieces with "precision." Most important was the singing of the national hymn, "Bozhe, tsaria khrani," which was repeated several times at the demand of the audience.[48]

Charitable concerts were about sociability and display as much or more as they were about music. These concerts had another purpose as well; they provided respectable occasions for public performances by wellborn amateur musicians. One such concert, in 1823, attracted the attention of *Damskii zhurnal*, a frequent chronicler of such events. Music, of course, was not the only topic that interested the journal's readers; comments and essays on musical life shared space with recipes and dressmaking patterns. The concert opened with the overture to Rossini's opera *The Thieving Magpie* and concluded with Franz Joseph Haydn's *Creation of the World*. In between, an assortment of vocal and instrumental solos and ensembles showcased the abilities of these noble amateurs. "What could be more touching than this rare spectacle!" the magazine's reviewer gushed. "Harmony has never had such sway over the sentiments of the heart." Such comments emphasized the concert as a site of romanticized and feminized sociability, where "loud applause served on the one hand as a sincere expression of delight, and on the other as a pleasant reward for a good deed. Talent is even more precious when it is used in aid of those close to us!"[49] The emphasis on charity, sociability, and social purpose shifted attention away from the quality of the repertoire or the performance and refocused it on the personal qualities and good intentions of the performer.

Even at amateur charitable concerts, professional musicians were essential to fill out ensembles and strengthen the overall quality of the performance. Ideally, a concert would feature a "star," usually a popular opera singer, in order to increase its appeal and charitable potential. This structure further reduced the possibility for critical judgments of either the performances or the performers. Instead, the role of the press was to acknowledge and compliment the performers. The *Damskii zhurnal* "review" of a charitable concert held at the Moscow Assembly of the Nobility in 1825 highlights the way such musical criticism served, in effect, as a society page. "After a wonderful Mozart overture from the Magic Flute, there appeared six Ladies who sang a touching cantata by [Johann Gottlieb] Naumann . . . with harp accompaniment. These were: Countess Richchi, who was recognized for her talent in Italy, Princess Trubetskaia, the Mrs. Gedeonova, Barteneva, Rakhmanova, and Princess Zinaida Aleksandrovna Volkonskaia, [who is] adorned with the gifts of Nature [and is] famous across all of Europe as an outstanding singer and erudite writer." Despite the fact that the performers include notable musicians, the performance was described simply as "most charming." Once the performance itself was dealt with, the reviewer resumed his recitation of the list of performers, listing among the members of the choir "Count Richchi, the Counts [Mikhail and Matvei] Vielgorsky, Mr. Aliabiev, Mr. Verstovsky, and Mr. Shotten." Like its many competitors, this concert featured a mix of genres and composers chosen to conform to fashion and to pique the audience's interest. It featured a choir and quartet from Rossini's opera *Semiramide*, another aria from his *Tancredi*, several selections from Carl Maria von Weber's *Der Freischutz*, as well as a virtuoso performance by Count Matvei Vielgorsky on his "magical" instrument, the cello. In this case, fashionable repertoire and interesting performers attracted a large audience drawn from "the best society." In the end, the concert generated more than 22,000 rubles for charity.[50]

Concerts were located at the intersection of the public and private landscape of Russian cultural life. Because fashionable concerts were held in elegant homes, décor and atmosphere frequently rated a mention in the press. When the gracious home of Maria Ivanovna Rimskaia-Korsakova provided the setting for several concerts in the spring of 1827, the quality of the furnishings and the beauty of the rooms captivated the readers of *Damskii zhurnal* as much or more than the music did. In the first concert, "the piano was placed on a platform in an attractive room between two columns, which separated it from the oblong hall, [finished in] white marble with gold and with three mirrored walls."[51] The second concert exceeded the first, being held in the engraving room, where the "golden frames of the engravings, many quite large, glitter[ed] on the green walls and the grand chandelier pour[ed] forth a brilliant light," giving an impression of great elegance.[52]

Musical life might have been glamorous, but it was also sometimes a chore for even dedicated music lovers. Cardplayers and late-arriving guests disrupted performances when they moved about the hall. A substantial portion of the audience considered the performance a mere accompaniment to conversation and card games. Clearly, enthusiastic concertgoers had much to complain about. Even in major cities, weak performances were abundant. Concert organizers often had greater aesthetic ambitions than they had the resources to realize them, as one observer of the 1828 Lenten concert season in Moscow noted with frustration. Mozart's G Minor Symphony (No. 40), portions of his *Requiem*, and the ears of listeners were all "tortured" by performers who unwisely chose to present these complex pieces after only a single rehearsal.[53]

Improvements in concert planning consequently attracted public attention. In 1828, a concert sponsored by the Assembly of the Nobility was most remarkable for an innovative seating plan intended to make the space both more attractive and more convenient for the audience. The chairs immediately in front of the orchestra were arranged to allow concertgoers to be able to get up and move about the hall between numbers without a crush. If the chairs in front of the orchestra were intended to appeal to passionate music lovers, the rest of the audience was not forgotten; the concert organizers placed card tables in another section of the hall. The repertoire for this concert featured the usual array of Rossini arias, as well as two sets of variations for the cello and a tender romance. As usual, the concert ended with a wind band playing as the audience dispersed. Dinner and conversation brought the pleasant evening to a close.[54]

By the late 1830s, concerts, their audiences, and music criticism had all grown more sophisticated, although the structures of Russian musical life had not yet experienced substantial change. The St. Petersburg Lenten season remained the centerpiece of Russian music. Amateur musicians and armchair music lovers looked forward to it with hope and anticipation. For others, such as V. F. Odoevsky, the season also served as a barometer of Russian cultural development. Because concerts lacked visual distractions, they were seen as the best indicator of the aesthetic taste of the public. From Odoevsky's perspective, Russian audiences still needed substantial instruction in music. He pled for the replacement of vocal pieces in the intermissions between major concert works with overtures or symphonic excerpts.[55] Beneath this criticism was a much broader one on the neglect of the orchestral repertoire in favor of the opera, even on the concert stage, which he believed was a symptom of the deep inadequacy of Russian musical life. Audiences remained indifferent to concert music except when they had no other choice, in other words during Lent. Even then, concert organizers were happy to pander to the operatic tastes of the temporarily concertgoing audience, leading to a tragic impoverishment of the repertoire. Moreover, underneath the glitter the musical aspects of concert life often languished. Odoevsky's praise for one modestly sized orchestra, for example, hints at the poor performance skills of too many ensembles. He emphasized the professionalism of this orchestra, noting that these "German artists proved the kind of effect that can be realized by no more than forty men, when each of them knows his business and is zealous, when each begins his part at the proper time, not waiting for his compatriot, and observes rests, *f*[*orte*] and *p*[*iano*] markings, etc."[56] By inverting this simple observation, one can almost hear the less-than-accomplished playing that marred the performances of the overly large, inexpertly led, and inadequately rehearsed ensembles that still populated Russia's musical landscape in the 1830s and 1840s. Indeed, despite the admonitions of critics such as Odoevsky, the organizers of charitable concerts still placed grandiose, sometimes absurdly large, ensembles front and center in an effort to attract the public's curiosity, if nothing else. The Invalid Concert of 1839 attracted the attention of both the public and reviewers for its unusual "musical" attributes: "Six hundred musicians [and] four hundred singers present a difficulty just in their direction." Showy, flamboyant pieces by massed military bands further impressed the audience and perhaps even Odoevsky, who found it "difficult to describe the degree of perfection of our military bands."[57] Although such concerts were often great successes from an entertainment standpoint, their aesthetic and artistic success was highly doubtful.

Despite the reproaches of critics, the Russian public persisted in its pursuit of musical entertainment rather than aesthetic enlightenment. Balls and evenings with "living pictures" were especially appreciated by audiences, both in the capitals and in the provinces. "In the evening, the theater was full.... Living people—as paintings!" The presentation of the tableaux was punctuated by a series of purely musical acts that featured "soloists and singers of the Moscow theater... each performing in turn some musical thing."[58] Such tableaux vivants provided a novel substitute for the opera during Lent, skirting the ban on stage performances but still accommodating listeners accustomed to theatrical musicality and uninterested in "difficult," i.e., purely instrumental, music.

From the mid 1830s, interest in specifically Russian music grew substantially. This reflected both broader changes in society, including the impact of nationalist intellectual currents and official policies, as well as the growing confidence of Russian composers. Nevertheless, events such as the St. Petersburg "Russian Concert" of March 15, 1850 remained novelties. The concert, which featured works by luminaries such as Glinka and Dargomyzhsky, as well as by composers less familiar to us, such as A. F. Lvov, F. M. Tolstoy, and M. P. Shchulepnikov, benefited the Society for Visiting the Poor, a worthy cause. It was a desire to draw a larger audience and generate greater profits for charity that prompted the organizers to plan and promote a *Russian* concert. They counted on the novelty of the event to attract casual listeners as well as dedicated concertgoers, a strategy that Odoevsky recognized immediately. "There is no doubt that the hall of the Noble's Assembly will be full; in the first place because the Petersburg public loves to be philanthropic, especially when it can be charitable while enjoying itself; in the second place because this Russian concert . . . will pique the interest of Russian music lovers."[59] As Richard Stites has argued, the concert "can be seen as an early instance of musical nationalism," but of a nationalism that yet lacked the aggressiveness that would characterize the musical ideologies of the 1860s.[60] More prosaically, for audiences grown weary of an endless diet of Rossini and Meyerbeer, the Russian concert promised relief.

Although the repertoire was unusual, much of the coverage of the event focused more on its charitable intent than on its artistic presentation. Readers of *Sankt-Peterburgskie vedomosti* were reminded that thirty concertgoers, each paying 2 rubles, could provide for the maintenance of one poor soul for the small price of spending an evening listening to good music.[61] Despite the focus on philanthropy, the repertoire for the evening did excite comment. The day before the concert, *Sankt-Peterburgskie vedomosti* advertised the importance of an event that featured both Russian composers and a number of new and unknown works. Odoevsky took upon himself the duty to "direct the attention of our readers to a new composition by M. I. Glinka: 'Ispanskiia vospominaniia,' written especially for this concert, and also his Russian dance tune (*Kamarinskaia*)—a fantasia for orchestra."[62] An eighty-member orchestra and an equally large chorus promised an evening of unusual artistic polish.

In retrospect, one cannot help but be struck by the unusual significance of this concert for the development of Russian music. The program consisted of:

Part I

1) Overture from "Torzhestvo Vakkha" by A. S. Dargomyzhsky (premiere)
2) Prayer, verses by M. Iu. Lermontov, music by F. M. Tolstoy (premiere).

3) Recuerdos de Castilla (*Souvenir d'une nuit d'été à Madrid*) by M. I. Glinka (premiere)
4) The Song of the Orphanages (premiere)

Part II

5) Overture from "Starosta" by A. F. Lvov (premiere)
6) Concerto for piano, by M. P. Shchulepnikov, performed by the composer.
7) Spanish Overture (*Jota Aragonesa*) by M. I. Glinka (premiere)
8) "Tuchki," a romance, with words by M. Iu. Lermontov and music by A. S. Dargomyzhsky.
9) Russian Dance Tune (*Kamarinskaia*), fantasia for orchestra by M. I. Glinka (premiere)
10) Russian military chorus by A. F. Lvov

The concert prompted one critic to reflect on the public's neglect of Russian composers and repertoire: "For several years we have been listening only to Italian and German music, almost forgetting about the existence of the Russian opera, although we have our own music and our own composers."[63] But, as this critic noted, this was an unusual concert. Not only was the repertoire exceptionally strong, but it consisted almost entirely of premieres. Such a concert was a rarity and few others could compare with it. As a result, the concert, and a second one that followed in April, captured the attention of critics. Panegyrics substituted for reviews. By the time the newspapers were through with them, the cultural and national significance of these concerts must have been familiar to the whole of St. Petersburg's newspaper-reading public.[64]

Such remarkable concerts were almost certain to draw a large crowd, but this was not always the case even for well-regarded and talented performers. The failure of Anton Rubinstein's March 1850 concert at the Bolshoi Theater in St. Petersburg provided an excuse for a broader critique of the general state of musical affairs in the city. The critic for *Sankt-Peterburgskie vedomosti* complained in particular about the Symphonic Society's increasing inability to make a significant contribution to local musical life. In this critic's opinion, none of its concerts that year had been noteworthy and the society seemed to lack any plan for the future. This left the Philharmonic Society—with its two annual performances—the only reliable producer of substantial concerts in the capital.[65] Despite the gloomy predictions of this critic, musical life in the capital continued apace. Even the Symphonic Society continued to function, although perhaps not at its previous intensity. Ultimately, this critic's negative assessment reflected not a real decline in the quality of the city's musical life but a significant increase in the expectations of the most skilled and devoted listeners. Complaints ranged from the quality of performances by both amateurs and professionals to the quality and variety of the works being performed, in particular the seemingly endless round of Rossini arias. The behavior of audiences also came under fire. Critics protested the incessant talking and disruptive strolling about the hall of "listeners" who showed much greater interest in their card games than in the performances. By the 1840s, musical writing in the newspapers and journals had developed pretensions as a serious literary genre and critics used their new authority to take both audiences and musicians strongly to task. Audiences, moreover, were beginning to express their own dissatisfaction, showing clear signs of both greater sophistication and boredom. Concertgoers voted with their feet, avoiding events that looked unlikely to be sufficiently diverting.

If dissatisfaction was widespread, neither the diagnosis of the underlying problem nor of the necessary solutions was self-evident. Some observers blamed low performance standards and the frivolous repertoire favored by both artists and amateurs. Yet efforts to raise standards, elevate the repertoire, and thus transform highly social musical evenings into more reverential formal concerts provoked resistance among audience members for whom the musical aspects of a concert were an accompaniment rather than the focal point of an evening. Certainly, Russia was beginning to develop its own compositional school and produce composers with authority. Increasingly self-confident music critics began to demand more serious repertoire from musicians and more respectful behavior from audiences. Much of the public, however, still held to traditional ideas of the structure and significance of musical life. In 1853, a major charitable concert, which offered listeners "free surprises," caught the attention of one feuilletonist, whose coverage of the event simultaneously derided and reinforced the prevailing attitudes toward musical entertainment. Neither the audience nor the feuilletonist appears to have been much interested in the repertoire or the quality of the performance. The concert drew a large audience from all corners of the city and all layers of educated society. "We saw there sparkling uniforms, foppish tailcoats, and modest coats, both white and colored ties, silk and... we assure you, calico dresses." The listeners themselves were as varied as their attire, including elderly faces and very young ones, beautiful faces and others that the author "gallantly" declined to describe. Clearly, the feuilletonist argued, this enormous audience had not been attracted by the music itself; not only were three-quarters of them new to concerts, most showed complete indifference to the music being performed, preferring to wander about the hall, chattering loudly. It was the chance to do good, to contribute to the poor, the author concluded, that drew

St. Petersburg society that evening.[66] Yet, as dismissive as the critic was of the audience, his comments hint at its increasing breadth. If most of the audience was new to concertgoing and unfamiliar with standards of conduct or even dress, then the boundaries of musical life had begun to shift, drawing in new and still awkward members of a slowly expanding educated public.

Yet, traditional expectations for musical life still held. The quantity of concerts, not their quality, remained a point of interest and even pride for some well into the 1850s. The 1853 season in St. Petersburg was noteworthy to *Russkii khudozhestvennyi listok*, a one-page publication with a picture supplement, for the stunning diversity of performers and performances. In rather breathless prose, it described the nearly eighty concerts of the five-week Lenten season. "Concerts in the morning, concerts at noon, concerts in the evening; five, six concerts in one day; charitable concerts, concerts with surprises, concerts with *tableaux vivants*, Russian concerts, concerts on the violin, on piano, cello, guitar, harp, and on wind instruments of all types and sizes," gushed the sheet's reviewer, V. Timmom. The overabundance of concerts was a symptom of the capital's passion for music. Virtually every citizen seemed to be striving to become a virtuoso on some instrument or another; the fad for music spilled over into other areas of social life. "It's now rare to receive a written invitation to an evening party without the inevitable concluding phrase: there will be music." But Timmom also noted the changing landscape of musical life. Music had begun to penetrate to the lower depths of Russian society, thanks to low-priced suburban concerts, organs in taverns, street orchestras and organ-grinders, which, he insisted, was all to the good, given music's "beneficial influence on morality."[67]

The actual behavior of the concertgoing public belied Timmom's simplistic confidence in music's moral influence. Presumably, for music to "soothe the savage breast" audiences actually needed to listen to it. Audiences seemed to be both smaller and increasingly jaded. Only the most fashionable events of the season, the benefit concerts of the artists of the St. Petersburg theaters, whose popularity was on the rise due to a dearth of touring celebrities, attracted large crowds. The audiences who attended these concerts, the critic for *Biblioteka dlia chteniia* charged, often did so for reasons having little or nothing to do with art. "One went to the theater in order to hear a little music, the second was enticed by the *tableaux vivants*," while the third, a woman, had the vague idea of showing off her new dress. A fourth man went to look at the ladies in their new dresses, and a fifth "simply because it was boring at home." The list of reasons for attending a concert, most having little to do with music, was virtually endless.[68] However, if concertgoers were not particularly pure in their behavior, perhaps they were not entirely to blame. Artists and organizers of concerts, especially those with "living pictures," exploited the audience's inattention by presenting the same tableaux, the same musical pieces, and the same artists over and over again. *Biblioteka dlia chteniia* offered an extended review of the 1854 concert season that both condemned the audience for its dismissive attitude toward concerts and displayed that attitude itself. The reviewer provided only simple lists of performances and repertoire with few details and little real criticism, betraying by his prose his lack of enthusiasm. These concerts seem to have left no impression on either the critic or his readers.

The state of Russia's musical life depended largely on the perspective of the commentator, however. While critics increasingly found much to complain about, more tolerant observers found much to celebrate. In 1857, a popular women's magazine, *Severnyi tsvetok*, published a long article on music that purported to be the commentary of a musical dilettante. As with earlier publications such as *Damskii zhurnal*, articles on music shared space with more homely topics, such as the preparation and cooking of varenniki (traditional Ukrainian filled dumplings). The article provided the uninitiated with a guided tour of St. Petersburg's musical venues. Although the Italian Opera set the tone for musical life and determined most listeners' expectations, readers apparently needed more guidance with regard to symphonic music, which was defined for them as "symphonies, overtures, and in general compositions of a similar format." Works of this type, readers were assured, could be heard at the University concerts, where each performance included one symphony, one overture, and one work with soloist. Private musical evenings, the writer confided, were the place to hear quartets, quintets, trios, and so on. The writer had not the slightest doubt that St. Petersburg was a "musical city," offering as proof the existence of "innumerable" musical circles "where amateurs of all possible instruments and voices gather." Most who attended the opera, concerts, and recitals, the author conceded, were not "initiated into the mysteries of art." Instead, they relied on their own tastes to make their judgments. "If they like it—that means it's good, if they don't like it, it's bad." Amateur musicians, unsurprisingly, were described as more exacting in their expectations and more willing to express their opinions. The city could also claim what the magazine described as a small number of "very strict" experts, a hint at the aesthetic divisions between a broad public that approached music as a form of light entertainment and an emerging critical class that viewed music as an elevated and sanctified art.[69]

At midcentury, St. Petersburg remained the center of Russian musical life. Its reputation for great musicality enticed foreign musicians hoping to make a quick profit by servicing the city's alleged hunger for music. The city's reputation began to sour, however, as its musical life became increasingly competitive. The available number of listeners did not grow at the same pace as the number of concerts. Smaller audiences forced many foreign musicians who had confidently traveled to St. Petersburg seeking riches to "go after applause and rubles in the depths of Russia."[70]

Provincial Pastimes: Music Making and Concertgoing in Provincial Towns

St. Petersburg, it must be remembered, is not Russia. Despite the limitations of the capital's cultural life, especially those imposed by the short Lenten season, St. Petersburgers nevertheless enjoyed a much richer and more dynamic musical life than residents of other cities. This does not mean that provincial towns did not have a musical life of their own, but that it was more limited in scope and ambition. Newspaper and magazine commentaries reveal the considerable cultural condescension of the capitals toward the provinces. Certainly public musical life in the provinces remained episodic and unsystematic. The limitations of provincial cultural life, however, reflected a lack of resources—artistic, financial, and structural—rather than a lack of interest. Domestic music making was as popular in the provinces as it was in the capitals, although good teachers, new sheet music, and performance opportunities were all much scarcer. Moreover, because of their rarity, concerts, balls, and operatic performances held additional values for provincial audiences. Sensitive to the low expectations of outsiders who viewed them as uncultured, uncivilized, and unfashionable, provincial elites strenuously attempted to counter such dismissive views and to celebrate their cultural achievements.

Observers from the capitals did not entirely write off provincial musical life, but even their praise carried a strong note of disdain. In 1829, *Moskovskii telegraf* published a "Letter from Tobolsk," devoted to the musical impressions of a traveling Muscovite. The musical highlight of his trip was a charitable concert featuring local notables. The author assured readers that, despite their likely amusement at the image of a concert in Tobolsk, the evening exceeded all expectations and, implicitly, at least approached acceptable standards for musical entertainment. The street in front of the local gymnasia, where the concert was held, was filled with "several coaches [and] a multitude of sleighs," while the building itself was beautifully illuminated. This favorable impression continued inside the hall, which was dazzlingly lit. Although the repertoire was uneven in quality, the concert attracted a large audience with three choirs and a well-organized orchestra of one hundred, with the musicians drawn from local military forces. The distance of the concert from the heart of Russian cultural life undoubtedly strengthened the overall effect. Each of the concert's two parts began with an overture, the first from *Don Juan*, the second composed especially for the occasion, followed by a selection of solo pieces with orchestral accompaniment. An emotional *Elegy* composed in memory of Empress Maria Fedorovna, who had recently died, and the national anthem—performed by the orchestra, all three choirs, and an additional eight-trumpet fanfare—were the twin highlights of the evening. For all his praise, the author's remarks, including the comment that he had "hardly expected" to find such an interesting concert in "far-off Siberia," reinforced rather than contradicted readers' surprise that "talents also flourish here."[71]

More than a decade later, the newspaper *Moskvitianin* explored the musical life of Voronezh, exposing both the possibilities and the practical limitations of culture far from the capital. This was the author's second article on the subject; the first had been a discussion of the "scene" in Revel, suggesting that provincial cultural life was a topic of some interest and anxiety for Moscow's cultural elite, which was conscious of its own uncertain cultural status, simultaneously provincial and metropolitan. The continuing dependence of Russian musical life on foreign musicians and entrepreneurs could not be sidestepped in this article. In 1833, Voronezh welcomed a new arrival from Vienna, a watch repairman by the name of G. Braun. Gradually, Braun became a prominent local figure. He opened a music store that served as a "musical rendezvous" and a local cultural center. Musical life in the city went up another notch in 1837, with the arrival of Colonel Ivan Vasilevich Romanus, commander of the Voronezh Battalion of Military Cantonists. Romanus was regarded locally as both a virtuoso and a composer of note. Together, Braun and Romanus enlivened local artistic life; by 1838, musical evenings had become a regular social event. Concerts gained substance through the leadership of Colonel Romanus as well as the participation of other ranking officers. Infrastructure, manufacturing, and communications all played a role in Voronezh's cultural revitalization. It was the broader availability of keyboard instruments, such as the twin-pedaled reed organs (harmoniums) that Braun had begun ordering from Vienna for sale in his music shop, that made musical life possible. By 1844, the city could boast of several music teachers as well as two instrument makers who made pianos to order and for public sale.

The willingness of citizens to accept leadership roles in their cultural community allowed Voronezh to transform itself from a sleepy provincial town into a "musical city." With effective and energetic leadership, even a small city could develop a successful, if limited, cultural life; should that leadership fail—through loss of interest, internal rivalry, or the death or departure of key figures—musical life could collapse as quickly as it had arisen as there was no other basis to support it. In Voronezh, effective leadership turned the city into one where "music finds a home." Artists from St. Petersburg performed in its concerts, which drew the attention even of the celebrated amateur cellist and confidante of Beethoven, Prince N. B. Golitsyn, whose willing participation inspired the support of other music lovers.[72]

In the provinces, as in St. Petersburg, public musical life was both by and for the nobility and, to a much lesser extent, merchants and other well-off and socially ambitious members of local society. The increased interest of the Voronezh nobility in music noticeably influenced the merchantry, which began teaching their children music. In order for the nobility to participate, however, musical performances could not compromise their social standing. Concerts had to reflect "noble" sentiments and support charitable goals, even if these were sometimes fictions meant to preserve the carefully cultivated amateur status of the best (as well as the worst) noble virtuosi. The recruitment of prominent nobles, such as Prince Golitsyn in Voronezh, could be counted on to generate enthusiasm on the part of ambitious, but not necessarily musically inclined, lesser members of the local nobility, eager to be seen rubbing elbows with the great.

The desire of a provincial city such as Voronezh to be seen as "musical" reflected not only the influence of St. Petersburg but also the common identification of a few provincial cities as unusually rich in culture. Odessa, and to a lesser extent Kiev, were among the cities identified as "musical" owing to the relatively large number of concerts held annually, the presence of a significant amateur community, and in the case of Odessa the existence of a prominent opera theater. Provincial cities such as Kiev and Odessa, Voronezh and Tobolsk, followed their own rhythms in their musical lives, determined by local fairs, seasonal residency of the nobility, and the sporadic appearance of foreign and Russian touring artists. Local musical life was a source of both pride and exasperation for provincial critics and music lovers, often one-and-the-same individuals. They celebrated the ability of their quite small cities to present concerts, but bemoaned a troubling lack of enthusiasm on the part of much of the potential audience, who frequently disdained to attend them.

Kiev could boast an active musical season revolving around an annual contract fair that attracted artists with significant reputations. Even so, the quality and quantity of concerts fluctuated from year to year, which both local critics and correspondents to the St. Petersburg and Moscow-based press noted with disapproval. In 1844, the season included successful concerts by the violinists Karol Lipinski and Teodor Gauman, both much appreciated by local audiences. A third violinist, Tereza Ottavo, gave a concert that was also well received, despite, or perhaps because of, the unusual spectacle of a woman performing publicly on the violin. One critic was certainly unable to escape Ottavo's femininity, offering a highly gendered review of her performance. Her playing was described as reminiscent of Lipinski's, but not an imitation of his style. Where Lipinski plunged the listener into deep, masculine emotions, Ottavo's playing brought forth "more delicate, intimate . . . and soothing feelings. . . . A woman lives more through the heart, her world is . . . inspired by love." For a female artist, then, feeling would, or should, play the most important role.[73]

Kiev's relative musical sophistication was apparent in the rigorous evaluation of its concert life by the press. Real criticism, rather than simple description or flattering imagery, characterized press reports on performances. Thus, concerts by the child prodigies and future leaders of Russian musical life, Anton and Nikolai Rubinstein, were received with reserve. While the critic for *Literaturnaia gazeta* recognized the boys' substantial technical abilities, he identified their extreme youth as their greatest weakness, one that led to a limited command of both technique and musical expression. They surprised their listeners most often not with the quality of their playing so much as with their ability to play so well "at that age."[74] Similarly, a review of the 1847 contract fair season in *Russkii invalid* questioned the city's reputation for musicality but nevertheless reflected its significance as a cultural center. "Last year . . . we told you about our musical novelties. . . . We have kept silent for an entire year since then. Why, you ask? For a very simple reason; there was nothing to talk about." As in St. Petersburg, in Kiev the official musical season was concentrated in a very short period. However, Kiev had a smaller local base for amateur music making and domestic concerts and was less likely to appear on the itinerary of traveling virtuosi. Nevertheless, the complaints of critics also reveal that the level of local expectation was very high; their desire for sophisticated musical entertainment was not being realized. To this critic, it seemed as if Kiev's worthwhile musical life virtually ground to a halt outside of the contract fair season. But musical life did not really come to an abrupt stop; it was simply that the music available was of a poor quality. The local opera troupe was a particular source of pain. It lacked a choir. Its performances were miserable at best. The singers could not stand up to any serious criticism, although the critic acknowledged that in the "sticks" even these wretched singers could be real finds. The performances were so execrable, he concluded morosely, that they merely *reminded* the audience of the operas the company was supposedly presenting.[75]

This critic's own complaints suggest that the dire picture he painted was exaggerated. The array of musical opportunities he found so inadequate would have more than satisfied most provincial cities. Although he lamented that "Besides the highly musical singing in one of the monasteries, besides the very successful occasional musical evenings in one residence, we cannot boast of riches," the complaint itself highlighted venues where musical life was thriving in the city, albeit behind doors closed to the general public. Although he claimed to despair because "[t]hey do not love music here," the examples he listed to prove his argument, such as the existence of a "shameful and impoverished orchestra, . . . several quartets without pretensions, . . . [and] two or three violinists and one pianist with talent," hint at a semipublic musical life that, although not meeting the aesthetic standards of this critic or, perhaps, the capital, met the entertainment and sociability needs of its consumers. Despite the critic's insistence that this list constituted the whole of the city's "musical luminaries," he quickly undermined his own disparaging assessment of local musical life. As he noted, "there are comets and then there are brilliant comets," which, for Kiev, included not only the appearances of "unexpected guests, European artists," but also the biannual performances accompanying the graduation ceremonies of the Institute for Noble Girls. "At these two happy times we sometimes hear outstanding music, both vocal and instrumental, and we hurry to share our pleasant impressions with you."[76]

Equally noteworthy, in the opinion of this critic, was a concert given by Franz Liszt and the graduation performances of young noble ladies. His praise of the Institute was nearly boundless. He professed amazement over how it transformed little girls into young women fit for the highest society. Their musical educations were particularly fine; acquaintance with the Italian and German masters of vocal and instrumental music, as well as practical training in voice and piano, he asserted, gave many of the students a right to real recognition in music. While it is difficult to say to what degree other local music lovers shared this critic's opinion of the city's young *institutki*, Liszt's appearance definitely created quite a stir. His performance in Kiev was a matter of pride for the city, placing it on a more equal cultural footing with the capitals because it, too, was able to attract Europe's leading piano virtuoso. The great artist filled the hall to overflowing despite high ticket prices. But the critic took pains to present Kievans as sophisticated and knowledgeable concertgoers who were not cowed by the fame of their musical guest. Response to the concert, the critic noted sagely, was mixed, with the comments of one, "experienced," concertgoer singled out for attention: in his estimation the performance was not equivalent to earlier ones by Liszt in

Moscow. Liszt himself was honorably acquitted from criticism; all faults were blamed on an overfilled hall, poor acoustics, and an inadequate piano, which conspired to prevent the pianist from demonstrating his art to the fullest.[77] Because this critic described Kiev's musical life on the pages of the widely circulated *Russkii invalid*, he invoked the cultural world of a provincial center for a reading public centered in the capitals. The author implicitly compared musical life in Kiev not just to St. Petersburg and Moscow, but also to European musical centers. He found Kiev lacking culturally not because he compared it to an abstract notion of Europe, but because he compared it to a Europe of capital cities.

Odessa, too, sometimes suffered a sense of musical inadequacy. According to its critics, the city's Lenten season in 1844 was noteworthy mostly for a shortage of concerts, only five or six during the entire period. Although some concerts were of a very high quality, others were simply awful. The contribution of two opera singers, formerly of the local Italian opera troupe, was particularly dubious; the two featured "artists," it was reported, were the kind whose names never appeared in programs except in the aggregate, as soldiers, villagers, townspeople, and so on. Most of the other concerts were more successful, although even those given by the singer Berlendis and the pianist Tedesco, both local favorites, failed to attract a sizable audience. The problem came to a head with the final concert of the season. A local music teacher, Mr. Bush, sadly turned out to be an unsuccessful performer despite his pedagogical talents. Perhaps fortunately in this case, he failed to attract many listeners. Although he had managed to cobble together a full, if amateur, orchestra, the hall was nearly empty.[78] As this critic noted, these two deficiencies in musical life were related. Small audiences meant small or nonexistent profits for performers, which led to fewer and weaker concerts, which led in turn to still smaller audiences.

Despite these complaints, Odessa was still a "musical" city, albeit an unevenly developed one. Exactly a year later, a concert by local amateurs prompted a more hopeful assessment of the state of local musical life. The concert was seen as a sign of the cultural development of the city, a reflection of the idea that "art is the child of civilization." The city's increasing ability to sustain an orderly and well-rounded musical life proved its growing maturity and civility. Particularly important, given the concert's symbolic importance as a marker of civilization, was the opening number, a Beethoven symphony. Equally significantly, the evening presented an opportunity to demonstrate visibly the cultural unification of one of the empire's most diverse cities. "It was gratifying to look at the stage, raised up in the depths of the hall. In the orchestra... officers epaulets and black tailcoats were visible; there were Russians, and Italians, and Frenchmen, and Germans. . . . The symphony of the great Beethoven, who together with Mozart and Haydn forms the [inextinguishable trio of stars] of the German musical world, was performed superbly." The concert was impressive in its scale as well as in its repertoire. The reviewer could not recall another public concert "where such a work was performed by such a large orchestra," further cementing by his comments the event's importance as a civic and cultural achievement.[79]

The inclusion of a Beethoven symphony was of great symbolic importance. The ability of a provincial orchestra to perform such a work was an important marker of musical development. The willingness of an audience to listen to such "advanced" and "difficult" music was also an indicator of the sophistication and taste of local society.[80] In its entirety, however, this concert suggested a more ambiguous level of cultural development. The repertoire that followed the symphony was typically mixed; it included an aria from Rossini's *Stabat Mater*, a cavatina from Federico Ricci's *Prigione di Edimburgho* (*Edinburgskaia temnitsa*), as well as an aria from Vincenzo Bellini's *I Puritani*, before concluding, as always, with the Russian national hymn "Bozhe, tsaria khrani." Noteworthy as well, and again reflecting more traditional concert mores, were the female members of the choir who, as the critic took pains to point out, graced the stage with their beauty and youth as well as with the freshness of their voices. This concert, at least, was well attended.[81]

Practically speaking, it was the weakness of Russia's cultural infrastructure, which was still unable to sustain the circulation of music and musicians throughout the empire, rather than public indifference or a lack of "taste" that restricted provincial musical life. Nevertheless, the repeated complaints of critics in "musical cities," such as Kiev, Odessa, Moscow, and even St. Petersburg, reveal the anxieties latent in Russian cultural life, particularly the constant fear of somehow failing to measure up, whether in comparison to other Russian cities or to some ill-defined European standard. Descriptions of decidedly nonmusical cities, true provincial backwaters, reveal the depth of these fears even more clearly. A summertime trip to Ekaterinoslav prompted a distinctly unflattering portrayal of its musical life in *Russkii invalid*. A concert in the local club by a traveling singer and her husband, a trumpeter, constituted the sum total of the musical offerings of the city. The hall was bad enough, with plain furniture and unattractive chandeliers, but the concert was worse. The audience was not only small, but also ill omened, numbering thirteen, only two of whom were women. The "hideously dressed" singer, accompanied in a "murderous" fashion on a "wretched" piano, warbled several songs. Her husband did somewhat better, adequately performing some undistinguished piece. And that, according to the author, was the whole of a concert that had warranted printed posters.[82] The piece dripped with the condescension of a "cosmopolitan" resident of the capital toward mere provincials, but it also unintentionally suggested that Ekaterinoslav's residents might not have been as culturally backward as the author assumed. The population of the city pointedly avoided this rather pathetic concert.

Provincial audiences asserted both their sophistication and their well-developed sense of the value of music, monetary and otherwise, through their concertgoing habits. There was a litany of complaints about the high cost of concert tickets. Artists had only themselves to blame, the authors of reviews and feuilletons defensively asserted, for pitiful box office receipts. "Arriving in Kazan, (artists) always set the cost of tickets at three silver rubles, just as in St. Petersburg or Moscow." No matter how sophisticated educated society might be in a provincial city, it was inevitably numerically small and, as *Moskvitianin* noted, not all local enthusiasts were "in a position to freely give three silver rubles for every concert."[83] Such cold realities forced provincial concertgoers to make refined choices. Since they literally could not afford to be undiscriminating consumers, they saved their rubles for the most enticing fare.

Enticing fare took several forms, including the grandiose charitable concert also favored by the St. Petersburg elite. In Kazan, for example, one philanthropic concert drew roughly three hundred concertgoers in 1846. The event featured a long list of noble amateurs, whose zealous playing was shielded from real criticism by the charitable intentions of the concert. Some of the performers apparently played with skill as well as enthusiasm, including four young ladies who performed a quartet by Czerny on four pianos with orchestral accompaniment. The orchestra, comprised of both amateurs and military musicians, would have been a draw itself, as substantial orchestras were a rarity in the provinces. Even so, the orchestra's playing was described not in superlatives, but simply as "very satisfactory." Every effort was made to make the venue as attractive as the program; the hall was pleasantly illuminated and greenery graced the stage. The overall effect was one that allowed the audience "to forget the Russian winter" and the melancholy of Lent.[84] As this review suggests, music alone did not attract the audience; the music was not necessarily even the most important lure. Concerts provided a complete sensory experience that included the atmosphere of the performance, the glamour of the artists, the interest of the repertoire, the beauty of the hall itself, and even the qualities of the other members of the audience, determined in part by prevailing expectations of deportment and dress.

Musical Criticism: Art and Social Politics Intertwined

If one were to judge simply by the commentaries in the press, the concert world of early nineteenth-century Russia was one where everyone was wonderful, most were beautiful, all had charitable hearts and noble souls, musicians always played fabulously, and musical compositions were invariably extremely interesting. In short, it was a world where personalities, not art, were the focus; it was a world where the primary purposes of a concert were charitable and sociable, not aesthetic. The music performed, the choice of the performers, and the behavior of the audience all reflected this sensibility. Real musical criticism was largely absent in the first quarter of the nineteenth century. In its place one finds commentary that better suited the needs of the concertgoing public: whenever possible, odes, laurels, and songs of praise to performers, both professionals and amateurs. When such words would clearly have been inappropriate, writers either shyly offered excuses or delicately sidestepped the problems of the performer or the performance. Such "criticism" was not an effort to evaluate the professional abilities of a performer or the aesthetic qualities of a performance. It was an attempt to attract and sustain the interest of the upper reaches of society by flattering its image of itself as charitable, tasteful, cultured, and gracious.

As the first quarter of the century came to a close, broader currents in Russian intellectual life began to have a profound influence on Russian musical criticism. The emergence of the intelligentsia created a social context for the discussion of progressive ideas in literary and political circles, Masonic lodges, and secret societies. The desire to transform Russia into a new, more egalitarian society reached a premature climax in the Decembrist Uprising of 1825. Leading amateur musicians and artist-dilettanti frequented these same progressive circles. Meanwhile, the social and intellectual currents that spurred interest in charitable activity and philanthropy sparked conscious efforts to create social structures for the promotion and development of musical life. V. F. Odoevsky, perhaps the most important critic of the first half of the nineteenth century from an artistic standpoint, was also a founding member of the Society for the Lovers of Wisdom, a progressive intelligentsia circle, and a prominent writer of socially conscious prose. Even in his capacity as a philanthropist—he was a leading figure in the Society for Visiting the Poor—he furthered the cause of Russian music.[85]

Music critics, such as Odoevsky, Rezvoi, and F. Tolstoy (Rostislav), attempted to bring a more serious tone to musical life. Although their commentaries on compositions, performances, and music education rarely explicitly articulated progressive ideologies, their vision of Russian cultural life was structured and sustained by the progressive ideas of the emerging intelligentsia. Their attacks on "illegitimate" critics and self-styled musical experts undermined the authority and public role of the noble amateur and the traditional social ethos of musical life. Their championing of the early Romantic movement supported their calls for a more substantive social role for music, which would require a more contemplative and intense concert experience. Their demands for more challenging, "difficult," and serious repertoire jeopardized the entire structure of Russian musical life. Their ridicule of frivolous concerts, inattentive and overly fashionable concertgoers, and subpar performers, whether amateur or professional, began a drawn-out process of disciplining not only the audience, but also Russian musical life in general. Of course, not all music critics sympathized with progressive ideas. Musical criticism in *Severnaia pchela* catered to more conservative tastes, although the caustic writing of Faddei Bulgarin surely also appealed to readers who simply enjoyed flamboyant polemics.[86] The newspaper was a major source of information about St. Petersburg musical life, attracting readers with feuilletons written not only by the pugnacious Bulgarin, but also by critics such as Odoevsky, who adopted a more moderate tone in the hopes of influencing a broad readership.[87]

The difficulty of reconciling the aesthetic viewpoints held by expert critics with the expectations of the reading and concertgoing public are well illustrated by a series of feuilletons that appeared in *Sankt-Peterburgskie vedomosti* over the course of 1839. Written by Odoevsky under the sigil W. W., these extended essays suggest that older "Classical" ideas of concert life as social event were beginning to give way to newer "Romantic" ones that foregrounded the music and offered composers up as demigods for a worshipful public. Despite his pleas for more serious repertoire, despite his urgent calls for musicians to inject greater "feeling" into their performances, Odoevsky himself failed to make the transition completely; these articles provided long-winded discussions of concerts but lacked substantive critical analysis of either the performance or the repertoire. Russian music (good, bad, or indifferent, absent or lacking, etc.) was barely mentioned, suggesting that it was still not an issue of much importance to mainstream opinion. The very length and prominence of these articles gave new weight to Russian musical life, however.[88]

By the late 1830s, specialized periodicals appeared to service a growing interest in both concert life and domestic music making. The musical journals *Nuvellist* and *Muzykal'nyi svet* quite literally tried to cover the musical world, or at least musical Europe. There was nothing particularly Russian about them; *Muzykal'nyi svet* was printed with parallel texts in French and

Russian, with the Russian text in a smaller typeface and clearly subordinate. Coverage of Russian musical issues, moreover, was always relative to their Europeanness. *Nuvellist*, similarly, was not really *of Russia*. Its European character reinforced the Europeanized identity of its intended audience—educated society in the capitals. Coverage of the Paris, London, and Berlin seasons was at least as complete as that of St. Petersburg.

Russian efforts to chronicle and capture musical life in written form were flavored by the deep interest and involvement of women and girls. *Nuvellist* in particular was clearly marketed to women. In a determined effort to both meet the expectations of its subscribers and distinguish itself from the competition, *Nuvellist* offered not a musical supplement to a ladies-interest periodical, but a magazine of sheet music with a literary-musical supplement. The journal thus satisfied women's hunger for new music by supplying interesting and high-quality pieces accessible to amateurs of varying skill levels. As *Sankt-Peterburgskie vedomosti* noted approvingly, the magazine was an unusually well designed, useful, and, above all, economical publication. On their own, the newspaper cautioned, amateurs were sure to waste money trying to choose appropriate sheet music. A subscription to *Nuvellist* provided an abundant supply of new music to amateur musicians, more than a hundred piano pieces a year, all of which had been vetted for interest and skill level. "Here there are serious pieces and light music, and dances, and romances, and finally a whole section of pieces for children."[89] Musical variety, in a society hungry for new music and increasingly mad for the piano, ensured the magazine's long survival when most other music journals soon perished.

The journal's efforts at musical criticism developed much more slowly. Early attempts, beginning in 1846, were "only tales from musical life, biographies of musical figures, correspondence from various Russian cities, and news from abroad." Tellingly, the determined focus on European musical life that characterized the early years of the magazine was a sensitive issue by the end of the century. In 1889, the fiftieth anniversary of the founding of the magazine, a commemorative pamphlet written by a frequent contributor, the music critic M. M. Ivanov, explained this early neglect as a "natural consequence of the weak development of musical life." He cautioned readers not to forget that the "general press, in the 1840s and 1850s, still lacked sections devoted to theater and music and that in the 1840s even musical feuilletons were still comparatively rare."[90] In the 1850s, however, musical criticism grew more sophisticated. Feuilletons grew longer and their musical coverage became more detailed, although it remained formulaic, depending on extensive descriptions of the playing styles, abilities, and mannerisms of performers. Evaluations of the qualities of musical works were increasingly common, especially if they were new to the St. Petersburg public. These changes signaled the development of a more modern style of musical criticism, one that revealed a greater interest in the musical, rather than the social, aspects of musical life on the part of writers, newspaper publishers, and editors as well as the reading public. Increased attention to the quality of musical performance created a growing sense of the social, cultural, and moral importance of musical life.

Coverage of the St. Petersburg University Concerts highlights this transition. The University Concerts were an important part of the St. Petersburg musical scene from 1842 through the end of 1859. Because of their ambitious and noble goals—presenting serious repertoire performed by young musicians—the concerts were much appreciated by critics if not always by the concertgoing public. In 1850, the critic I. A. Mann took offense when some audience members complained that there was "nothing special" about these performances. The concerts were indeed special, Mann insisted, because they furthered the musical education of their young participants. The purpose of these exercises, as they were accurately described on the tickets, was to develop the aesthetic and moral qualities of the students, not fill the idle hours of frivolous listeners.[91] While they lasted, the concerts retained their special quality as a "school" for young amateurs, both university students and "young ladies from Petersburg society." The audience attended the same school in a sense, because the challenging repertoire, including Mendelssohn, Weber, Bach, and Mozart, demanded that they focus their attention on the music.[92]

By the middle of the 1850s, the growing monotony of the concert season had caught the eye of the critic A. Serov, who evaluated the matter quite candidly. He identified two types of concerts: those for music and those for profit. A recent concert by the Philharmonic Society, he noted rather sadly, was of the second variety, for which reason he refused to offer any artistic criticism of the evening because "commercial goals have nothing in common with art." The program consisted of fashionable numbers from popular operas, including the sextet from Mozart's *Don Giovanni*, which, he noted, had just been performed at a jubilee concert in honor of the composer. Serov sarcastically observed that, given its enthusiasm for this piece, one might conclude that the Philharmonic Society deemed the sextet to be the only part of Mozart's entire operatic repertoire worthy of performance. The instrumental repertoire of the evening was similarly unremarkable: the most prominent piece was the overture from Meyerbeer's *L'Etoile du Nord*. "And that was it. An anti-artistic choice of program, a complete absence of major works for voice and orchestra from the broad repertoire of 'oratorios,' 'cantatas,' and so on . . . in direct contradiction of the appellation *Philharmonic* Society, founded with the goal of propagating a taste for truly good music." The aesthetic aridity of the concert did not trouble the audience, however much it appalled Serov. The critic himself noted that not only was the "enormous hall" full, "the box office receipts were huge, and consequently the *goal* of the concert was achieved."[93]

From tentative beginnings, Russian musical criticism developed over the first half of the nineteenth century into a powerful force that enthusiastically passed judgment on the artistic, aesthetic, and social worth of composers, performers, and musical works, both Russian and European. By the end of the 1850s, conflicting intellectual interests, personal animosities, public ideological persona, and varying aesthetic tastes created significant tension among the leading critics. The prominent place of musical criticism in the newspapers of the two capitals encouraged critics to adopt flamboyant styles that captured the reading public's attention. The high profile of the feuilletons helped to educate the public about new music, aesthetic standards, artistic styles, and the social importance of music, but it also created opportunities for highly visible polemics, thus sustaining a vigorously partisan cultural politics. Moreover, the cultural world described by the music critics of the 1850s was in many ways a world of their own creation. The most legitimate critics, such as Odoevsky, sought to influence Russian society aesthetically, artistically, and morally. They wanted to reshape Russian cultural life, to bring it closer into line with a Europeanized Romantic ideal which nonetheless celebrated and nurtured Russian aspects of this ideal. By highlighting events, musicians, composers, and performances they deemed worthy and ignoring or ridiculing those persistent elements of musical life that they scorned, these critics created in the public imagination a musical world that did not yet exist but which they fervently hoped they could bring into being.

CHAPTER 2

Zealots of Culture

The Russian Musical Society, Voluntary Associations, and Cultural Life

IN THE AFTERMATH OF THE Great Reforms, voluntary associations developed into a potent force. Educated Russians began to use them as the vehicle through which they pursued their cultural, philanthropic, and economic goals. Although cultural voluntary associations, including musical societies, existed prior to the Great Reforms, most were relatively weak. Many were plagued by financial and leadership problems that severely reduced their influence and frequently hastened their decline. Even the most successful, such as the Philharmonic Society, offered little prospect for the broad development of cultural life. By focusing on the needs of its members and their dependents, the Philharmonic Society consciously declined to pursue cultural innovation. Yet, ironically, it was the demise of one voluntary association, the Symphonic Society, that paved the way for the emergence of the most successful and effective musical organization of late imperial Russia—the Russian Musical Society. The founders of the Russian Musical Society seized on Dmitry Stasov's membership in the Symphonic Society as a convenient legal fiction that allowed them to incorporate not as a new organization but as a reinvigoration of an already existing society, thus sidestepping the state's efforts to restrict social organization and public initiative.

Although in its formal structure the Russian Musical Society conformed to the standard model of cultural voluntary associations, in other ways it diverged sharply from previous patterns.[1] Like the musical societies that preceded and followed it, the Russian Musical Society formulated a statement of purpose, established a charter and regulations, and elected members and a governing board. The Ministry of Internal Affairs approved its charter, along with those of all other cultural organizations, and provided nominal oversight. However, the new society's goals were unusually ambitious. Optimistically and somewhat arrogantly, the Society assigned itself the task of not only promoting the performance of good music, but also developing the taste of the Russian people, disseminating music education throughout the empire, and fostering the creativity of native composers and performers.[2] As a consequence, popular expectations for the new society were lofty, perhaps even unattainable.

Conscious of the weaknesses and failures of earlier associations, the Russian Musical Society introduced structural and organizational innovations intended to ensure its survival. Yet, even as it tentatively emerged onto the public stage in 1859, the Russian Musical Society was forced to respond to a well-developed set of popular expectations about musical associations, their cultural roles, appropriate structures, and the practical, legal, and financial limitations on their activities. While most commentators relied on these expectations to frame their welcome to the infant society and its leadership, others adopted a more radical and highly critical response. They demanded that the Russian Musical Society stretch beyond the established limits of musical associations, transform itself into an advocate of national music, and forge a new social role for Russian music and musicians.

Continuity and Change: The Birth of the Russian Musical Society

Although the basic events that led to the establishment of the Russian Musical Society are well known to musicologists, if not necessarily to historians, the Society has rarely been placed in its broader social and historical context as a voluntary association. Scholars have tended to explore the Society in isolation, focusing on leading personalities rather than institutions, on periods of strife rather than on long-term development, and on the capitals rather than the provinces.[3] Such criticism is not meant to detract from the contributions of these scholars, but rather to point out that the Society and its institutions have been too narrowly construed. Robert C. Ridenour's *Nationalism, Modernism, and Personal Rivalry in Nineteenth-Century Russian Music*, perhaps the most important work in English, provided scholars with a thorough and detailed treatment of the Society's early years. Nevertheless, Ridenour's interpretation of the artistic and social role of the Society was limited both by his own scholarly choices and by circumstances beyond his control. He focused on St. Petersburg in the 1860s and 1870s, a decision that allowed him to effectively support his central argument: that the conflict between rival "camps" in Russian musical life in this period was based on personal conflicts rather than a nationalistic artistic ideology. This question, however, kept his focus on key personalities, particularly Anton Rubinstein, Serov, Stasov, and Balakirev, which reinforced, rather than challenged, a traditional tendency to understand musical life through the personalities and careers of the canonical composers and, to a lesser extent, leading performers. Moreover, Ridenour was a victim of Cold War politics (he was denied a research placement in the Soviet Union); his lack of access to archival materials limited the scope of his study and the range of his conclusions. As a result, although the Russian Musical Society has attracted a fair degree of scholarly attention, its broader social resonance and its critical role in the development of the empire's cultural infrastructure has long been underestimated. Its real significance only emerges when we begin to appreciate both its fragile beginnings and its eventual strength as a voluntary association, one among the many that gave shape to Russia's emerging civil society.

The Russian Musical Society emerged out of a desire to give new purpose to musical life. Its founders included Anton Rubinstein, the piano virtuoso and composer and Grand Duchess Elena Pavlovna, the German-born wife of Tsar Alexander II's uncle, Grand Duke Mikhail Pavlovich, as well as Matvei Vielgorsky, patron of the arts and renowned "amateur" cellist, and Dmitry Stasov, brother of Vladimir Stasov, soon to be the new Society's fiercest critic.[4] The familial bond between the Stasov brothers underscores the intimacy of the St. Petersburg cultural milieu. The Society's most partisan critics were not only close colleagues, competitors, and rivals of its equally determined supporters, but sometimes their friends and family. Such polarized attitudes produced a pronounced tendency to rewrite and recast the history of the Society in order to support shifting ideological positions, with the contributions of key individuals, such as Elena Pavlovna and Anton Rubinstein particularly malleable.

Even the most sympathetic observers sometimes had very different views on the same events. For Prince Dmitry Aleksandrovich Obolensky (1822–1881), the successful establishment of the Russian Musical Society was a testament to the leadership of his close friend and confidante, Elena Pavlovna. Although Elena Pavlovna has been unfairly vilified as a "meddler" in musical life, her contributions to Russian society and culture were considerable. A. P. Shestopalov, for example, has recently reminded us not only of her energy and determination, but also of her wide-ranging interests, in which music played an important, but by no means dominant part. The Grand Duchess had long played a formidable cultural and political role in court circles, serving not only as an important patron of the arts but also as a facilitator of political events, such as the movement to emancipate the serfs. At Elena Pavlovna's initiative, Dmitry Aleksandrovich served as the vice-chair of the Russian Musical Society in its early years. Indeed, the Russian Musical Society became a noteworthy project of the Obolensky family; the Prince's son, Alexander Dmitrievich, later became a prominent member of the Society's governing board.[5]

Obolensky's sympathetic treatment ascribes considerable responsibility for the early success and stability of the Russian Musical Society to the Grand Duchess's patronage. As he tells the tale, it was the desire of Elena Pavlovna to develop the musical taste and further the musical education of Russia that provided the necessary stimulus for the Society's creation. The Grand Duchess emerges in Obolensky's memoir as the guarantor of the Society's survival. She opened her home, the Mikhailovsky Palace, to the first classes offered by the Society, which served as the embryo of the St. Petersburg Conservatory.[6] Not only did she lend the new association her personal prestige, serving as the Society's official patron and protector, she also provided significant financial support through both direct subsidies and student scholarships, as well as by covering the St. Petersburg Conservatory's deficit in its early years.[7] Clever strategies, such as the use of the Grand Duchess's residence as the site for public graduation exercises and student performances, burnished the reputation of the Society.[8]

Without question, the staunch support of members of the imperial family and the high nobility contributed enormously to the successful establishment of the Russian Musical Society. Because of their connections and personal prestige, Elena Pavlovna and later imperial patrons could secure a more sympathetic state response to funding petitions and subsidy requests. Initially, the state's formal involvement in the Society was limited to a modest subsidy from the Ministry of the Imperial Court to the St. Petersburg Conservatory. The difficult first years of both the St. Petersburg and Moscow conservatories made state support increasingly urgent as start-up costs and low revenues threatened these institutions and the Society as a whole. It took the personal intervention of Elena Pavlovna to secure modest state subsidies for the conservatories. In 1869, the St. Petersburg Conservatory was awarded an annual grant of 15,000 rubles, while the Moscow Conservatory began to receive a 20,000-ruble annual subsidy in 1872.[9] Yet the granting of these subsidies underscores not only the importance but also the fragility of aristocratic patronage, as Elena Pavlovna secured them by persuading the tsar to take a personal interest in the new conservatories.[10] Elena Pavlovna's intercession set a pattern that would be repeated until the very eve of the revolutions of 1917. State support for the Society was highly dependent on the personal mediation of members of the imperial family or representatives of the high nobility and strongly reflected traditional forms of imperial largesse. As Joseph Bradley has noted, imperial patronage of voluntary associations was far from unusual. Like the Russian Musical Society, the Free Economic Society, the subject of his scrutiny, enjoyed "imperial patronage, accepted members of the royal family as officeholders, received . . . government grants, and petitioned government offices for favors and privileges, such as free postage."[11] In the case of the Russian Musical Society, the initial subsidies for the conservatories were, in effect, generous gifts by the tsar via the state treasury, rather than a decision by the state to assume financial responsibility. Most significant, perhaps, in the end, was the awarding of the imperial title to the Society in the wake of Elena Pavlovna's death, a gesture intended to acknowledge the leadership and contributions of the Grand Duchess by honoring one of her most cherished achievements. The imperial title, however, clouded the status of the Society, giving rise to questions about its independence from the state, particularly during the 1905 Revolution. The imperial title has also misled scholars, most notably Robert Ridenour, who interpreted its awarding as a "takeover" of the Society by the autocratic state.[12] Although the imperial title gave the Society greater prestige and public stature by making transparent its connection to the imperial family, it did not make the Society an official state institution, nor did the government assume financial responsibility for it.

Moreover, notwithstanding the ability of aristocratic patrons to intercede with the state, their own contributions were inherently unstable. From 1872 to 1873, Elena Pavlovna contributed over 11,000 rubles to the St. Petersburg Conservatory, including a small direct subsidy and wage supplements for key faculty members, as well as student scholarships, small grants, and funds for the student cafeteria.[13] After her death in 1873, her heirs refused to continue supporting the conservatory. They only reluctantly agreed to fund existing scholarship students until graduation, as well as to honor the Grand Duchess's contracts with conservatory faculty until their expiration. Direct funding of the conservatory ceased, leaving the Russian Musical Society scrambling to cover this deficit.[14]

The Grand Duchess's efforts to support the Russian Musical Society, according to Obolensky, were simply another example of her concern for the common good. Certainly, her generous financial and moral support legitimized the Society, but it brought risk as well as reward. As Russian social and political attitudes matured, the status of the professional and middle classes increased while the prestige of the aristocracy declined. We can glimpse the limits of noble patronage in a changing society through Obolensky's description of Elena

Pavlovna's struggle to balance her elevated position in society with her desire to participate directly in public life. During a heated dispute with Anton Rubinstein over the direction of the Society, she displayed just how "jealously she guarded her power," by attempting to extend her influence into the smallest affairs of "a society that, by form and structure, belonged to the category of private institutions, which were not subordinate, of course, to the power of one person." The Grand Duchess found justification for her actions in her "boundless desire for the prosperity of the Society and in the significant financial contributions which she had made" to it. As even Obolensky acknowledged, Elena Pavlovna had great difficulty accepting limitations to her authority. Nevertheless, he insisted that she knew that such limitations were necessary both to ensure the Society's success and to guarantee that she did not unduly influence the public through her own personal preferences.[15]

Anton Rubinstein also recalled the establishment and early years of the Russian Musical Society in his memoirs, published in *Russkaia starina* in 1889. Although Rubinstein acknowledged Elena Pavlovna as an important patron, his account focused on the contributions of an emerging civil society rather than on those of a noble elite. Rubinstein ascribed the ultimate stimulus for the Society to conversations held in the Grand Duchess's salon in Nice. Despair over the "sad" state of Russian music fueled a determination "to do something . . . for the musical education of Russian society."[16] The education of society and music education in its more narrow sense were already intertwined. Rubinstein's narrative minimized the importance of patrons and maximized the role of educated society. The heroes of his tale are not traditional aristocratic patrons, such as Elena Pavlovna, but more modern civic leaders, such as V. A. Kologrivov.

Kologrivov, according to Rubinstein, was a landowner from Tula who had spent some time in government service, an unexceptional background for a Russian noble of the era. A moderately skilled amateur cellist and a musical aficionado, Kologrivov was a natural supporter for a new musical society. As described by Rubinstein, he appears the prototypical cultural evangelist, an individual willing to go to great lengths to secure the future of the arts. "Full of indestructible energy, a man of initiative, [Kologrivov] abandoned himself to the establishment and organization of the musical society so passionately and with such fanaticism that it bordered on rudeness. . . . He recruited everyone and everything to the Society; he practically seized [people] on the streets" in an effort to win over converts and locate funds for the cause he had so ardently adopted as his own.[17]

And funds, of course, were desperately needed. Without adequate funding, the Russian Musical Society would have been doomed to follow in the dismal footsteps of so many of its predecessors. There was, after all, a long list of musical organizations that had attempted to raise the aesthetic level of Russian society only to fail within a few years over a lack of funds or internal strife. Worse still, some had lingered, surviving on paper but failing to make a significant impact on cultural life. The search for support, consequently, was intense. As Rubinstein noted, the direct approach was often the most successful one: "We . . . visited a number of wealthy people in Petersburg, asking for their help for our endeavor and in the first year or so collected . . . several thousand rubles." Hat in hand, Rubinstein, Kologrivov, and other leaders of the society made the rounds from house to house: "We went to Prince Iusopov, to Benardaka, to Vasily Feduloich Gromov and several others, who gave—one hundred, three hundred, even five hundred rubles. Several ladies of high society worked particularly enthusiastically for the founding of our conservatory. Sofia Iakovlevna Berigina (wife of A. I. Berigin, a member of the State Council) collected at one point almost three thousand rubles by subscription. . . . and princess Elizaveta Vitgenshtein (née Eiler) collected money ruble by ruble for our work."[18] Although Rubinstein's narrative was one of success, it also hinted at the significant obstacles faced by any new cultural endeavor. The Society won the enthusiasm and support of prominent members of the nobility, but the funds contributed were modest gestures rather than statements of conviction and faith in the Society's cultural project. The survival of the Society from its very inception depended not on the patronage of the wealthy, but on the determination of a handful of zealots of culture.

Kologrivov, as Rubinstein noted, was an exception in terms of his loyalty, enthusiasm, and devotion. But he was not alone. A handful of others, including I. Kh. Pikol, I. A. Veikman, K. B. Shubert, and A. I. Fitstum, labored alongside Kologrivov for the benefit of the Society. Kologrivov's "circle," as Rubinstein described it, was made up of "people who breathed music, for whom it was the alpha and omega of their existence."[19] Social initiative of this kind, purposefully spilling beyond the bounds of a small aristocratic salon, reflected the changes that Russian society began to face as it moved into the era of the Great Reforms. Russian society was reshaping itself. The "public" was becoming a more important force, estate boundaries were both calcifying, as people sought to protect their own identities and privileges in a fluid social situation, and loosening, as people more and more frequently crossed estate boundaries in pursuit of self-defined goals, whether these were economic, political, social, or cultural.[20] In its infancy, the Russian Musical Society gained momentum from this process. Ultimately, the Society's success furthered these fundamental changes to the social structure.

The Russian Musical Society quickly assumed a leading role in the musical life of St. Petersburg, where it benefited from the cultural resources of the capital. The Society's leadership was drawn from among the city's social, intellectual, and cultural elites. But the Russian Musical Society remained a St. Petersburg affair only briefly as its founding principles virtually demanded expansion to the provinces. In the context of the Great Reforms, cultural activism limited just to the capital could no longer claim to be an effort at reshaping Russia. By 1860, the Russian Musical Society expanded to Moscow, where an affiliate society opened under the leadership of Anton Rubinstein's younger brother Nikolai, an accomplished pianist who was both well liked and prominent in local cultural circles. The new Moscow branch of the Society clearly benefited from the experience of its older sibling. While the St. Petersburg Society spent its early years bitterly feuding with its ideological opponents, the Moscow Society experienced little controversy and enjoyed overwhelming public support.[21]

In both cities, the Society's symphonic and chamber music concerts attracted substantial audiences and significant, if not always favorable, critical attention. Innovations intended to provide a stable foundation for the new society sometimes inadvertently provoked a strongly negative popular reaction. In particular, the question of access to the Society's concerts proved difficult to resolve. In an effort to simultaneously build the new organization's membership rolls and create a strong financial basis for further activity, concerts were initially open only to members. Membership was divided into categories, with only active members, who paid dues of 100 rubles, entitled to vote at the Society's annual meeting or be elected a member of the board. Fifteen-ruble "attending" memberships provided admission to ten orchestral concerts, a very fair price as concert tickets in the capital ordinarily ranged from 1 to 3 rubles. As the Society's concerts were generally considered to be of both extraordinary interest and unusually high quality, the average cost per concert was seen as very reasonable. However, an initial decision to restrict the concerts to the Society's members and to sell *no* individual tickets proved controversial. As logical and reasonable as the decision was for the Russian Musical Society, it was perceived as exclusionary. Membership required payment of 15 rubles up front, a far more significant financial burden than the purchase of a single concert ticket for a ruble or two. Under this policy, the Society's critics argued, it was difficult, if not impossible, for those most interested in "good" and "serious" music—students, artists, musicians, and so on, all of whom possessed high aesthetic sensibilities but low incomes—to attend the concerts except at enormous personal sacrifice. The members-only policy also left the Society open to the charge that it had been appropriated by fashionable but aesthetically philistine youth, more interested in making an appearance than listening to the music. Although the democratization of cultural life was an implied goal in the Society's charter, the social context of concertgoing thwarted its realization. Moreover, critics complained that even many who could afford the cost of membership could not afford to compete socially with the lavishly attired and coiffed members of high society. If too large a percentage of the educated public was discouraged from attending, the Society's potential to further Russian cultural development would be dramatically reduced.

The Russian Musical Society did not immediately stake a claim to a more democratic musical life. Appearances, at least for some members of the audience, still were everything, as the reviewer of an early concert of the Moscow branch makes clear. Setting aside the concert itself, the reviewer turned to the audience, in other words, to the members of the Society. Rather than gushing about glamorous individuals and their lavish ensembles as a reviewer might have only a few years previously, the commentator for *Sankt-Peterburgskie vedomosti* noted disapprovingly that the "whole of the *beau monde* had appeared" for the concert. The appearance of the audience threatened to undermine the importance of the event. Here were "men in white tie and tails, the ladies *en grande toilette*," but to the critic this was all "completely unnecessary, because it inhibits the other members, whose material means do not permit them to get so dressed up." For women in particular, the emphasis on appearance was culturally debilitating. The cost of gowns quickly put attendance at such concerts beyond the means of many ladies. The only solution, the critic argued, was to "let everyone attend the concert in whatever they have." Moreover, as the critic acidly noted, the Society would better serve its own goals for "the development of musical education" by not allowing its concerts to be transformed into "a fashion exhibition." The intentions of the Society were clearly in the right place, according to this reviewer. The problem was a practical one. It was unlikely that many would-be concertgoers possessed the self-confidence to weather the disdain and slights of wealthier, more powerful members, whose unrestrained and unnecessary "exhibitions" were distasteful. More important, by failing to encourage simple dress, the Society allowed the wealthy few to claim it as a private club.

On the off chance that readers did not quite understand his point, the critic "reported" several putative conversations. In the first, two members evaluated the success of a recent concert, using fashion as a barometer of class standing. Art and aesthetics were simply ignored:

—Well, how are our concerts going?
—Good, Very good.
Both members, in tailcoats, yawned.

—You weren't there? The second asked.
—No, I couldn't go. I hope that everything was proper?
—It goes without saying: in tailcoats.
—Ah! That means the evenings are good. Well, and the music?
—And the music . . . as well!
—Ah! I will have to get myself to the next concert.
—Yes, you must; all the best people are going.

Later, readers eavesdropped on a conversation between a mother and a daughter in the luxurious boudoir of a fashionable home. The conversation, readers were pointedly reminded, was in French, a marker of the cultural alienation of the aristocracy.

—Well, was the concert good? The mother asks,
—Yes, several of the outfits were magnificent.
—Really?
—I assure you.
—That's too bad; you cannot go to the next concert.
—Why?
—Your new dress will not be ready yet.
—I really cannot go in the same dress?
—I would never allow that; you yourself said that at the concerts everyone is flaunting their attire.
—But, I love music so much, mama.
—A well-educated young lady should love respectability more, and above all else.

This mother was no more inflexible with her daughter than another mother, less wealthy but no less determined to be proper, who also starred in this essay. Two women, mother and daughter, both respectably dressed, sit on a divan and sip tea. The mother speaks:

—No, that is enough. . . . Today was the first and last time that we were at a concert.
—But why, mama?
—What, didn't you notice that we were dressed worse than everyone else?
—And what of it?
—What of it? Whatever gave you the idea that I would voluntarily subject myself to ridicule. Our financial position does not allow us to dress as we should, and thus it is better that we do not go to the concerts.

To drive the point home, one final vignette was set in a tavern where two artists sat drinking tea and debating at length the finer details of the concert. Unlike the previous pairs of members, the primary concern of these "gentlemen" was the music itself. Both loved music so much, that they had deprived themselves in order to scrape together 15 rubles for membership dues. Dressed in tired frock coats, with shirtfronts that had seen better days, their violations of fashion also represented a transgression of class boundaries. Such trivialities, however, did not hold their attention; they were interested in the music and the performances, not the attire of the audience. Clearly, they represented the ideal audience: educated and culturally aware, determined to extract every drop of enlightenment from the Society's concerts even if their financial circumstances meant that they had to attend every performance in the same, somewhat disreputable suits.[22]

Despite the serious criticism directed at the Society's concert policies, early membership drives were highly successful, driven both by the novelty of the endeavor and the promise of high-quality entertainment for a reasonable cost. In 1860–1861, its first year of existence, the Moscow branch of the Society attracted more than six hundred members, although only a handful were active, i.e., voting, members. Within five years, membership had doubled; the branch now boasted over 1,200 attending and more than one hundred performing members, but still only twenty-one active members.[23] Nevertheless, early public enthusiasm and budget surpluses encouraged the Society to quickly develop its music classes into a conservatory, which opened in 1866. Too confidently, the Society's leaders assumed that it would attract an ever-increasing membership.

At first, these hopes seemed justified. In the Moscow Conservatory's first year, membership in the Society increased, as did financial contributions. Predictably, the Society's ability to provide interesting and varied programs and appealing soloists determined public interest. However, concert promotion was a risky venture. Production costs—artists' fees, wages for hired orchestral musicians, and the rental, heating, and lighting of a venue—could add up to a substantial figure not always recouped by sales at the box office. The high cost of supporting both the conservatory and the concert series strained the branch's budget. At the same time, the branch faced renewed competition for the attention—and rubles—of educated society. The Italian Opera, previously a weak competitor, gained new strength. As a result, the concertgoing public, preferring spectacle to more sober concerts, began to transfer its enthusiasm to the Opera. The Moscow Society lost both members and funds.[24]

Individual local support—i.e., ticket sales and concert attendance—was a crucial if still developing form of public or bourgeois patronage in late imperial Russia. The purchase of individual or season tickets to concert series, whether or not they were disguised as membership dues, reflected the emergence of a modern, bourgeois public and a cultural public sphere.[25] However, the Russian Musical Society needed public engagement as well as financial support. Yet, even most active members seem to have viewed membership as a season ticket to the Society's concert series; their complacency threatened the Society's success and even its survival. Many active members were so disengaged that low attendance sometimes forced the cancellation of annual meetings.[26] For those few willing to take a more active role, patronage and civic leadership blurred into each other, particularly as the ideology of the Society emphasized social and cultural modernization and enlightenment as much as it did artistic excellence. Ultimately, a handful of individuals dominated the branches of the Russian Musical Society, serving simultaneously as patrons of the arts and leaders of a voluntary association.[27]

Within a short time, the Moscow branch quickly grew tired of being a mere appendage to the St. Petersburg-based Society, a position that left it clearly subordinate to the capital's agenda. Its demands for greater independence led to a renegotiation of the Society's charter that, predictably, generated significant opposition. Once again, Elena Pavlovna took a leadership role, supporting the demands of the Moscow branch and taking it into her personal patronage, thereby securing the antagonism of leading members of the Society as well as the disdain of later chroniclers for her supposed meddling in artistic affairs.

The Russian Musical Society, like other voluntary associations, was governed by a charter that laid out in some detail the structure of the organization, its goals, and the scope of its work. Although the published charter of the society changed relatively little from 1859 to 1905, both seemingly minor structural changes and the process by which they were negotiated and finalized reflected shifting ideas of the role of voluntary associations and the relationship between state and society. In 1864, much to the chagrin of Anton Rubinstein, who hoped to strengthen his own authority, Elena Pavlovna moved to amend the society's statute and to fundamentally restructure the Russian Musical Society. Traces of the deep power struggle that subsequently developed can be teased out of the placid, bureaucratic phrasing of the revised charter of 1869. The central issue was over the relationship of provincial outposts to the founding association in St. Petersburg, more specifically, over whether the Society would expand to the provinces through independent provincial branches or through dependent extensions of the original St. Petersburg society. After much debate, the revised charter formalized a layered structure that declared local branches of the Society, whether in St. Petersburg, Moscow, or in other provincial cities, nominally independent in terms of their artistic, financial, and educational activities. Each local branch would raise its own funds, program its own concerts, recruit its own teaching staff, and negotiate its own compromises with local authorities and educated society. Above all of these branches now stood the Main Directorate (*Glavnaia direktsiia*), which coordinated policy, interacted with the state and its ministries, and represented the Society as a whole before the public. The Main Directorate also assumed responsibility for approving the establishment or closure of provincial branches. Provincial branches, in turn, were required to inform the Main Directorate of their activities through annual reports and other communications.[28] The Main Directorate consisted of the president of the Society (its imperial patron), the directors of the conservatories, and representatives from each of the local branches. At various times, the Main Directorate also included additional members, most notably the conductor Eduard Napravnik. The St. Petersburg branch of the Society now acquired a board of directors of its own, distinct from the Main Directorate. Through this process, the St. Petersburg branch was effectively demoted and deprived of its leading role, although in practice it remained the most important branch and the line between the Main Directorate and the board of the St. Petersburg branch blurred due to shared personnel.

Over time, the charter was amended to respond to changing legal and social conditions, as well as the expansion of the Russian Musical Society. Drafts and proposals for revisions to the charter became a field for renegotiating not only the status and structure of the Society, but also the role it claimed in Russian cultural life. The discrepancies between one draft version of the 1873 charter and the final version of that charter are telling. In the draft version, the goals of the society were simplified in the first article to the "development of the study of music and the encouragement of native musical talent," but this more modest declaration was belied by the second article, which attempted to stake the Society's claim to authority over *all* musical institutions within the empire, except for those whose charters explicitly indicated their independence. At the same time, the Russian Musical Society made a bid for its own independence from creeping state control, arguing that it was under the exclusive authority of its president and as such did not form a part of any ministry but was an independent institution. Any affairs of the society that required state approval would be handled through the Fourth Department of His Majesty's Imperial Chancellery. This draft also attempted to undo the recent restructuring of the Society; the branches of the Society were to be brought back more firmly under control of a Council, a restructured version of the Main Directorate. In this draft charter, the local branches were envisioned to be "independent" only with regard to purely local affairs, but subordinate to the central administration of the Society in educational affairs, in the development of art, and in their financial matters.[29]

The final version of the 1873 charter did not include any of these bold administrative initiatives. As previously, the first few articles of the charter outlined the goals of the society and the appropriate means of achieving them. The Society proposed to serve its purpose of "disseminating music education in Russia, aiding the development of all areas of musical art, and encouraging talented Russian artists (composers and performers) and teachers of musical subjects," by founding music schools and conservatories, sponsoring concerts and recitals with Russian and foreign repertoire of a high standard, and establishing competitions, prizes, and performance and publishing opportunities for Russian composers. In addition, the Society accepted responsibility to petition before the state on questions relating to musical life.[30] Less insistent on either its own independence or the subordination of its branches or other musical institutions, the Russian Musical Society, in the final version of the 1873 charter, nevertheless staked its claim to leadership in Russian musical life.

Discordant Voices: Controversies, Ideologies, and Russian Music

In choosing the appellation of Russian Musical Society, Rubinstein and his compatriots created the nationalistic framework within which both early supporters and critics of the new organization operated. In the process of naming, the leadership of the new organization made a bold statement about their determination to develop an independent and well-rounded national musical life. This vision included the promotion of a robust concert culture that presented a wide array of high-quality, challenging works that demanded the audience's attention. It also presupposed a willingness on the part of the public for self-education, as well as a more sophisticated and institutionalized approach to music instruction. In short, the self-declared mission of the new organization differed considerably from what many other cultural observers expected from a "Russian" society, that is, an overt emphasis on national identity through the promotion and sponsorship of Russian musical works, composers, and musicians.

Even before the Russian Musical Society was officially constituted, rumors about its establishment had reached the press. The popular magazine, *Severnyi tsvetok*, greeted these rumors with enthusiasm. The "ardent desire" of music lovers was going to be realized. A Russian Musical Society was going to be founded! As the critic T. Vladimirov suggested, the new society promised to further the progress Russian music had already made toward independence. No longer "infected" by the European-wide tendency to slavishly follow the latest Italian fashions, Russian music had begun to choose its own path, following the trail blazed by Glinka. "It's time that we . . . cast off the chains of our slavish imitation of foreign music; it's time to understand that we can compose and create" as well as or better than foreign composers. Such sentiments, while heartfelt expressions of a rising national cultural pride, reveal the persistent anxiety felt by Russian musicians, composers, and critics as they measured themselves against an arbitrary but nonetheless powerful European standard.

As Vladimirov's commentary suggests, the rumored establishment of the Russian Musical Society fostered in many critics a sense of hope for a musical world they believed to be mired in outdated cultural and aesthetic traditions. Vladimirov laid most of the blame for what he saw as the woeful state of Russian musical life at the doorstep of "society." Educated society, he argued, failed to appreciate the importance of music "as a separate and independent field of study," viewing it simply as "a remedy against boredom, as a means to while away free time." Consequently, society denied the practitioners of the art due respect. Because of such prejudices, not only did amateur musicians and music lovers suffer ridicule if they took their music making too seriously, but professional musicians were almost entirely lacking in Russian society. "The bureaucrat, the doctor, the officer, the merchant might be at the same time a musician, but a musician by vocation, one who lives only for music, who plays not just for a crust of bread, but who engages in music as an art to which he has devoted himself—such a class of people does not exist among us." A man of independent means who chose to devote his time to music, moreover, was not a musician in the eyes of society, but merely a man wealthy enough to entertain himself and occupy his time with the arts.[31] Vladimirov, like Anton Rubinstein, identified the uncertain status of the musician as the crucial impediment to the development of a vigorous Russian national musical life. Both of their voices, however, were soon drowned out by the chorus of critics, led by Vladimir Stasov and Alexander Serov, who insisted that in Russianness per se, not in professionalization, lay the salvation of national culture.

The problem of "Russianness," and, especially, the degree to which the Russian Musical Society and its leaders could lay claim to it, became the central issue in the controversies that dogged the early years of the Society.

One of the most persistent critics of the Society on this count was Serov. In his articles and reviews, Serov took the Society and, especially, Anton Rubinstein, to task for their failure to promote Russian music. Clearly, part of the hostility was due to bruised feelings; Serov used his position as music critic to air his grievances and frustrations with what he saw as an "anti-democratic" organization. However, the "anti-democratic" tendencies of the Society seem to have been revealed primarily in its failure to invite him to take a leadership role. Nonetheless, Serov did not completely reject the Society's efforts to improve Russian musical life. He greeted its first concert with some warmth, noting that the program presented was in many ways exemplary, if not particularly Russian. The program that Serov and other critics objected to as insufficiently national included the overture to the opera *Ruslan and Ludmila* by Mikhail Glinka, the finale to the second part of an unspecified Handel oratorio, the G-major piano concerto by Anton Rubinstein, the finale from Mendelssohn's unfinished opera, *Lorelei*, and Beethoven's Eighth Symphony. From Serov's perspective, with the exception of the overture to Glinka's opera, which was tossed in as a sop to patriotism, "the *entire* program of the first concert of the *Russian* musical society in the *Russian* capital could have belonged to any mediocre German *musikverein*." The absence of an overtly Russian national program irked Serov, who followed these complaints with others about the quality of the choir (an amateur choir, he noted, is an amateur choir) and Rubinstein's inadequacies as a conductor, although he willingly accorded Rubinstein laurels in his "appropriate" role as a piano soloist. Despite his displeasure, even Serov was able to recognize the Society's potential contribution to cultural life. "The more societies, the more 'symphonic concerts,' the better it will be for music. Listeners can always be found."[32] Moreover, Serov was not the only observer who noted the slight "Russianness" of the *Russian* Musical Society's concert programs. Even Vladimirov hoped that soon there would be "more in the *Russian* Musical Society that is *Russian*."[33]

As the complaints of Serov and Vladimirov demonstrate, nationalist cultural debates colored early critiques of the Russian Musical Society. Sustained scholarly attention to these nationalist debates, however, has veiled the complex initial reception of the Society in the Russian press. Moreover, although scholars have recently labored to preserve this complexity, it is often lost as diligent research is translated into the popular imagination through textbooks, concert programs, and popular writings.[34] At the time, the relative "Russianness" of the Society, its concerts, and its leadership was hardly the only concern of contemporary observers and critics.

The concerts of the Society, especially in their first season, were major cultural events that piqued the interest not only of the residents of the capital but also of educated society in other cities. Vladimirov, for example, placed the Society's first concert in the context of other musical events of interest to provincial residents, such as the arrival of new sheet music in the shops. The Society attracted attention not only because it was new and fashionable, but also because it directly responded to long-standing complaints about Russian cultural life. Music critics, the self-defined cultural voice of educated society, had spent much of the past ten or fifteen years vociferously complaining about the poor quality of the repertoire and performances at charitable concerts and recitals. Both they and their constituents, educated amateur musicians and musical enthusiasts, welcomed the promise of an annual series of ten substantial orchestral concerts with well-trained orchestras, prominent soloists, and challenging repertoire. For those less concerned about the threat posed by frivolous concert repertoire to Russian culture, the new society offered a fashionable place to see and be seen, and the opportunity to associate with prominent social and cultural figures such as Anton Rubinstein and Grand Duchess Elena Pavlovna.

The new society struggled to keep the focus on the music rather than on sociability, in part by disciplining the audience in new and unexpected ways. Although some critics, as we have seen, complained about the Society's ticketing and membership policies, others praised its innovative approach to concert organization. *Russkii invalid* declared the third concert of the first season an enormous success. It featured a high-quality program that drew a large crowd. The newspaper's critic particularly appreciated the serious tone set by the society's concert practices. This was no casual gathering for the purpose of showing off one's wardrobe, playing cards, or catching up on the latest gossip. By managing both the venue and the audience's behavior, the Russian Musical Society consecrated the hall to the service of art for the duration of the concert. Every audience member received a detailed program that listed the names of the works to be performed, the dates and locations of each composer's birth and death, the texts of the vocal pieces, and, perhaps most significantly, the admonition to "not move about the hall during the performance." Such detailed programs not only focused listeners' attention on the music and the composer, they also emphasized the artistic significance of the Society's concerts and heightened the distinction between them and more ordinary musical offerings. To be sure, such efforts to discipline the audience were neither new nor unique to Russia. As scholars such as James Johnson have shown, the disciplining of the audience was a crucial aspect of the transition to modern, i.e., bourgeois, patterns of cultural and musical life. Silences, Johnson has argued, had social roots. The display and enforcement of proper manners in the concert hall became a way to "confirm one's social identity by noticing those who didn't measure up."[35] Nevertheless, these strategies reflected the seriousness with which the Russian Musical Society approached its civilizing mission. The music was paramount and listeners' were expected to devote their full attention to it. The doors to the hall were closed at the start of each number so that latecomers would not disturb the concentration of either the performers or the audience. Instead, such inconsiderate individuals were forced to wait by the doors until the conclusion of the piece before they would be seated. Such innovations not only satisfied the professional integrity of Rubinstein and his compatriots, but also fulfilled the expectations of an increasingly sophisticated public that had grown tired of concerts devoted more to gossip than to music. The needs of less-sophisticated listeners were also recognized, however, in keeping with the Society's goal to educate the aesthetic taste of the Russian public. Because intermissions and intervals between pieces were kept brief, the concert, consisting of six works, took no more than two hours, making the evening far more bearable for those audience members still unaccustomed to "serious" music. For the anonymous critic from *Russkii invalid*, the Society's innovative and effective concert practices outweighed complaints that it failed to program enough Russian music. The Society, however, was absolved of this charge not because the critic saw it as particularly patriotic but because of the inadequacies of the Russian repertoire. Because so little secular Russian music existed, the critic noted, the Society could not possibly fill its concerts with Russian works without undue repetition. Nevertheless, the critic encouraged the Society to devote a single concert to Russian music, performed in chronological order.[36]

Nationalistic attacks on the Russian Musical Society focused as much or more on personnel as they did on repertoire. As Ridenour has argued, personal rivalries exacerbated by a limited array of professional opportunities strongly shaped the initial reception of the Russian Musical Society in St. Petersburg.[37] Far from being hidden from the public eye, these rivalries and jealousies were directly addressed by the newspapers, which treated the brewing scandals with a degree of ambivalence. Leaving a detailed discussion of the Society's "first-rate" concerts to a later date, *Sankt-Peterburgskie vedomosti*, for example, instead focused on what it saw as "a strange state of affairs." The newspaper described the Russian Musical Society as the natural and appropriate result of the labors of "several gentlemen, . . . one of whom enjoys the most famous and well-deserved reputation within the musical world," who hoped to "lay the basis for the lasting development of music education in Russia," who lacked "any ulterior motives," and whose efforts were "not guided by any material calculations." Despite the purity of their intentions and the nobility of their purpose, the founders of the Russian Musical Society were "now being met by the... petty nagging" of various parties. The critic blamed much of the conflict on the petty jealousies, easily offended sensibilities, and jostling for rank of the musical world, noting that attacks on the Society took several forms. Some complained that the new society unjustly neglected to invite many well-known composers and musicians to serve as founding members. Others complained that the Society was "too bureaucratic." Still others played the "patriotic" card and demanded that the "Russian" society perform "Russian" music; some even flaunted their grammatical knowledge and demanded that the new society label itself not the *Russkoe Muzykal'noe Obshchestvo* but the *Rossisskoe Muzykal'noe Obshchestvo*, to more accurately define the scope and limits of the Society's "Russianness."

In exasperation, this critic opened fire on the detractors of the Russian Musical Society, arguing that their demands were both unreasonable and harmful to an organization whose goals were wholly beneficial. Perhaps most significantly, he defended the right of a private society to organize itself as it saw fit. If several friends established a society for the spread of reading through the publication of useful works and the organization of public lectures, the critic asked rhetorically, would they be obliged to invite all well-known writers to be founding members? As far as the criticism of the Society's "patriotism," this critic dismissed these charges as well, arguing that it could only educate society if it introduced them to "the great works of the great geniuses." Demanding that the musical society restrict itself to the Russian repertoire was the equivalent of expecting his hypothetical literary society to exclude Shakespeare, Byron, and Goethe from their reading list. Russians, the critic concluded, needed to put aside their false pride and understand that "we have been badly outstripped by other nations and that we still need to learn a great deal from them."[38]

Such intense arguments hint at the emerging but still malleable constructions of Russian civil society on the eve of the Great Reforms. As educated Russians faced a profound readjustment of their social structure, they also confronted the need to redefine public life. Voluntary associations and social organizations would play an ever-larger role in this process, but, as this critic divined, it was not yet clear who would have the right to determine how social organizations constructed their field of work. Inherent in the scuffling over the structure and purpose of the Russian Musical Society was a broader debate over whether social or civic organizations were bound to serve the whole of society as "public opinion" defined it. Both this feuilletonist, in the pages of *Sankt-Peterburgskie vedomosti*, and the founders of the Russian Musical Society, in the charter and program of their infant association, insisted that there was room for competing visions of civil society, social engagement, and public life.

Other critics, however, continued to snipe at both the Russian Musical Society and its defenders. Early in 1860, *Severnyi tsvetok* described the Society as "under the dictatorship of an artist of a non-Russian family, Mr. Rubinstein, who has courted fame not in musical Rus' but abroad."[39] Both the nationalistic attacks on the Society and the attempts to defend against them reflect broader Russian debates over national identity, particularly those of the Slavophiles and Westernizers of the 1840s.[40] Much of the dispute over Russian music and music education in the press borrowed the vocabulary and ideological categories of the Slavophile-Westernizer debate and adapted them to suit musicians' cultural agendas. Such rhetorical strategies may have been an attempt to appropriate the cultural legitimacy and intellectual prominence of literary criticism for the far more marginal and newly established field of music criticism. Interestingly, as the debate over the Russian Musical Society grew more heated, the critics themselves took starring roles in the conflict. However, the increasingly virulent and overwrought attacks on the Society by critics such as Serov and Rostislav (F. Tolstoy) attracted a fair share of mockery and ridicule. The satirical journal *Iskra* took aim at the controversy and its major players in a paired set of caricatures early in January 1860. The first of these, "A Musical Evening in the Society of Music Lovers," made gentle fun of music societies in general, and the Russian Musical Society in particular, making clear that the lofty goals encoded in their statutes were not always realized in practice. In this caricature, a young gentleman bearing some resemblance to Anton Rubinstein struggles to capture the wandering attention of a gaggle of amateur singers. Chaos reigns as the director tries, but fails, to establish order. The text of the caricature is significantly more pointed. The director/Rubinstein imperiously demands that members be silent when he speaks and orders them to sing. The "softhearted" members of the society take no offense and dutifully open their mouths to sing. Only one "brave soul" in the back rows whispers to his neighbor of his plan to give the director/Rubinstein a good dressing down after the rehearsal. At the end of the evening, this "hero" decides not to confront the artist but to choose a "cheaper" form of revenge—to nurse a grudge against him.

The meaning of this caricature is clarified by its companion, which depicts a meeting on the street between the director of the musical society and two critics. Contrasts in the physical appearance of the three men make the target of this barbed commentary quite clear. The director is young, tall, and energetic looking. The two critics are older, shorter, and rather comical in their appearance. The text clearly references the controversies surrounding the Russian Musical Society when the first critic complains:

> Well, you did not want to give me a ticket to the opening of the musical society you founded—so don't blame me. You didn't bribe me—so that means [you] have no right to demand favorable reviews.

The second critic, meanwhile, ventures to undercut his competitor and vent his own spleen:

> Why are you listening to this scandalmonger (*spletnik*) from a dark alley? I have more serious business. From all of the cities of Russia I have received letters, where they ask only one question: Why did the Musical Society elect to its board several unknown individuals, but not me—the well-known author of romances that were sung for a while, thirty years ago?[41]

The second critic above would have been unmistakably identifiable to readers as F. Tolstoy, aka Rostislav, the often-vitriolic critic for *Severnaia pchela*. In one of his articles, Tolstoy foolishly drew attention to a letter from a reader in Kursk who complained that the board of the Russian Musical Society was comprised of individuals unknown in the provinces. Although the writer conceded that Rubinstein "had achieved some kind of public notice," he insisted that the pianist's reputation in the provinces was based only on rumor, rather than direct experience with his performances or compositions. The critic for *Russkoe slovo* mocked his competitor's arrogance and vanity by quoting at length the offending letter: "I don't know how you think about these things, but we in the provinces say that at the head of a serious Russian musical society there needs to stand out the name of the well-respected, well-known . . . chair . . . of the Russian musical world, Alexei Fedorovich Lvov." It was not only the absence of Lvov's name that caused provincials to distrust the motives and capabilities of the new society, the letter writer insisted. It was also the absence of other names, including that of Rostislav himself, whose romances, which had been popular in all corners of Russia twenty years before, were still played and sung by "provincial orchestras and sentimental young ladies."[42]

Rostislav's pride presented an irresistible target for other critics. *Russkoe slovo* crowed, "Dear God, I have not read anything like this for a long time! The name of Mr. Rostislav is well known . . . to all of Russia, but the name of Rubinstein only *somehow* has reached the attention of the public. . . . Even in Kursk! . . . Such naïveté would be very sweet if it belonged to someone of the fair sex who had just reached her seventeenth spring."[43] The critic for *Svetoch* also ridiculed Rostislav, expressing complete faith in the authenticity of the letter and its sentiments and advising the critic, on the strength of the endorsement of the letter writer, to abstain from music criticism in the future. *Svetoch* deliberately emphasized the limited cultural horizons of would-be provincial elites, casting the letter writer as "One of your neighbors, an inveterate hunter, who owns thoroughbred borzoi hounds." Such an individual would have little right to comment on cultural affairs except that he enjoyed the talents of "a governess, or perhaps a wife, who plunks out *sad* romances and *sultry* waltzes with *melancholy* introductions." Such music provided the provincial notable the inspiration to write to Rostislav and give vent to his criticism of the Russian Musical Society: "And why did they elect the *German* Rubinstein to the board of the *Russian* Musical Society, and not elect A. F. Lvov? Why did they not elect other *Russian* composers...for example: Verstovsky, Dargomyzhsky, or *even you?*"[44] By highlighting the limited cultural and aesthetic credentials of this would-be musical critic from the provinces, *Svetoch* undermined the legitimacy of not only this episode but also all of Rostislav's complaints against the Russian Musical Society.

Rostislav's hubris and the caricatures and mockery it inspired underscore the fact that educated readers, in addition to being entertained by the vitriolic attacks against the Russian Musical Society, also had every opportunity to read the bemused and sometimes outraged responses of other critics and commentators on the growing conflict. It would have been abundantly clear to anyone at all interested in Russian musical life that the conflict had many levels. On one level, it was indeed about conceptions of Russian identity and Russia's place in European culture and society. On other levels, however, it was about the deficiencies (real or imagined) of Russia's hierarchical society, which bred, among other things, thin-skinned critics prone to taking offense at the slightest excuse in order to defend their position in the social order. Finally, as Ridenour has shown, it was about the narrowness of Russian cultural life in the 1850s and 1860s that fostered intense competition for a limited number of professional opportunities.[45] In the end, Anton Rubinstein, whose public reputation was wounded more than once in these polemical battles, was able to dismiss the hostility of his opponents as simple jealousy provoked by the new society's failure to court them. In his memoirs, Rubinstein painted Serov's frequent public accusations of "German pedanticism" against the Russian Musical Society as the childish reaction of a vain individual whose feelings were hurt because he was not invited to serve as a board member. Rubinstein argued that such rabid hostility was tamed primarily through the mechanism of creating roles for opponents within the Society, thus satisfying the vanity of the organization's most virulent critics.[46] Although Rubinstein's explanation is more than a bit self-congratulatory and self-serving, it nevertheless points to the success of the Russian Musical Society in transforming and broadening the structures and institutions of musical life.

The Changing Shape of Russian Musical Life

Polemical battles over Russian musical life were taken most seriously by musicians themselves. The broad interest of the concertgoing public in the Russian Musical Society reflected the hopes educated society invested in it: for an enhanced public life, for improved entertainment, and, ideally, for the advancement of Russian culture. Consequently, the early concert series presented by the Russian Musical Society in St. Petersburg and Moscow aroused significant interest and excitement. *Sankt-Peterburgskie vedomosti* greeted the Society's newly established concert series with enthusiasm, declaring that they met with "complete sympathy" from ardent local music lovers (*melomany*). In responding to the concerts, the newspaper emphasized both the public's clear support for the new society and its importance in fulfilling a recognized but previously unmet social need. With more than a little satisfaction, the feuilletonist noted that the Society was already beginning to fulfill its stated goals. It had already announced the theme for its first cantata competition, giving young Russian composers a chance to compete for the opportunity to be featured in concert. Continuing in this well-satisfied vein, the feuilletonist insisted that the Society's concerts were extremely good, with well-chosen repertoire, a fine orchestra, and high performance standards that allowed artists to present their talents in the best possible light. For young artists in particular, the opportunity to appear in one of the Society's concerts could secure their local reputation. "Thus," the feuilletonist asserted boldly, "the Society satisfies artists and composers and the public with its concerts."[47] This self-satisfied description, however, is as much a representation of the hopes the Society had for its concerts and the role they might play in shaping Russian cultural life as it is a description of their actual achievements at the time. The concertgoing public was still quite small and, as we have seen, not all of it shared the cultural values of the Russian Musical Society. The Society, as it attempted to improve the public's taste and discipline concertgoers behavior, soon faced the resistance of a significant part of the audience. In response, the Society gave voice to a complaint that would remain familiar throughout the century, loudly bemoaning the indifference of educated society and its incomprehension of "serious" music.[48]

The public's presumed indifference was not simply a matter of a lack of taste or cultivation. A whole host of social and cultural assumptions and categories were wrapped up in this one word, all of which, on the eve of the Emancipation, were under renegotiation. Tension over Russia's cultural relationship to Western Europe underpinned this discourse of "indifference." As Russians struggled to reshape their society with the Great Reforms, they also were forced to choose whether Russian culture would follow the fashions, styles, and modes of entertainment prevailing in the West or strike out on a new path. Many questions remained unanswered and many problems remained unsolved on the eve of Emancipation. Cultural leaders, among them the founders of the Russian Musical Society, seemed unconvinced that Russians were educated enough to participate in a cultured public life. For the Society, this lack of confidence translated into an emphasis on education and acculturation. Not only students, but also the whole of Russian society needed to be "taught" music. In the context of the Great Reforms, the shift from aristocratic concert structures, especially salon performances and benefit concerts, to modern concert forms raised questions of class and social identity. By determining ticket prices, repertoire, concert venues, and performance practices, the Russian Musical Society and other musical organizations redefined the concertgoing public. No one knew what the consequences of this transformation of concert life would be. New venues, performance standards, and audiences were a potential threat not only to aristocratic values but also to traditional Russian ones. On the eve of the Emancipation, as the Russian Musical Society began its endeavors, Russia was poised on the brink of profound change.

Commentaries on concerts hint at the social changes that increasingly left traces in cultural life. Clothing, manners, and social behavior were all in a state of flux. *Russkoe slovo* recreated this fading social world when it commented on a concert promoted by the Philharmonic Society in support of the private schools of the Women's Patriotic Society. Everything about this concert and its coverage reflected an older sensibility about public musical life. The concert was intended to benefit charity, but a charity that focused on meeting the needs of the nobility: the practical needs of its impoverished members and the status needs of those wealthy enough to desire a public presence through social engagement. At this particular concert, the enormous crowd complicated the lives of the ladies, who found it difficult to maneuver in their "unusually broad crinolines and fashionable, endlessly long trains." The male members of the audience included a large number of officers, who, apparently, were now much more interested in music than had previously been the case. The audience rained its applause on the performers, especially on its favorite singers.[49] This type of commentary, which reported on a musical event without any substantive comment on the music or the performances, represented precisely the public's "indifference" to music that became such an ideological issue not only for the Russian Musical Society, but also for the Balakirev Circle and others striving to reshape Russian musical life.

One could certainly argue that the fault lay not with the supposedly indifferent public but with the musicians. Critics still complained about the high cost of concert tickets, which drove away audiences not because they were uninterested, but because they were unwilling or unable to devote such a substantial sum to the pursuit of an evening's entertainment. The public clearly hungered for music, especially for interesting concerts featuring leading performers. In Moscow, as a correspondent for *Russkii invalid* noted, even miserable weather did not necessarily deter audiences. However, even popular virtuosos could not persuade audiences to part with their rubles. Anton Rubinstein's concerts in Moscow were poorly attended and "coldly" received, but the blame was on the pianist's own shoulders for he had been the one who set the ticket prices at such a "legendary" level, thereby excluding all but the "elect."[50] This resistance to high ticket prices can be read as a sign of increasing audience sophistication; it also signaled the start of a process of audience "democratization" that extended from the 1860s into the 1920s, ultimately transforming not only the structures but also the underlying ideals of Russian musical life.

Most of these changes were still on the distant horizon in the early 1860s. Initially, the problem of "indifference" was due largely to the conflict between musicians who demanded the consecration of the concert and an audience that still expected a pleasant social experience accompanied by, rather than focused upon, the performance of music. If the audiences at public concerts were sometimes thin, music was hardly absent. In addition to the concerts of local and visiting virtuosi, nobles still held concerts in their homes, a custom now aped by "lesser people" as well. There was "no salvation from music" during the winter season of 1860, according to *Russkii invalid*. "Even the walls of your apartment will not save you, because even if neither you yourself nor any member of your family succumbs to the musical madness, then you probably have neighbors under you, over you, or around you, who pluck out some symphony or other on the piano (symphonies, as is well known, are currently in fashion), or who mournfully draw out [the tune] 'Tell Her!' (*Skazhite ei!*)." The event of the season was the house concert given by the director of the Imperial Theaters, Andrei Ivanovich Saburov, which merited a loving description in the pages of *Russkii invalid* despite the fact that the critic was not able, or was not invited, to attend. Reportedly, the flower of Russian society attended the concert, which was held in Saburov's "sumptuous palazzo," with its many "rare and expensive works of art," and strolled in his winter garden under palm trees, accompanied by the sounds of a burbling fountain as well as Beethoven and Haydn.[51]

The popularity of music as a domestic as well as public entertainment could be a very mixed blessing, as a caricature from 1864 made perfectly clear. The still popular romance, "*Skazhite ei!*" was depicted in its natural habitat, the parlor of a modest home. The lady of the household sat at the keyboard of an attractive but fairly simple piano; her rather ample hindquarters were somewhat precariously perched on the piano stool. She sang the words, "Tell her, tell her!" while accompanying herself on the piano, but her musical efforts were accompanied as well by the expressions of pain on the faces of her husband and son, both of whom had their hands clapped over their ears. Without question, someone needed to tell this good lady something, ideally that she should cease her efforts at music making.[52]

Complaints about the inescapability of music, the overabundance of concerts, or, alternatively, vapid praise masquerading as criticism were all familiar patterns from earlier decades. And yet, things were clearly changing. Among the many commentaries on the 1860 Lenten season, the first for the Russian Musical Society, some focused not only on the overwhelming number of concerts available, but also on the overwhelming boredom many of them generated in their listeners. Only the most masochistic music lover, one critic suggested, would continue to subject himself to the concerts with *tableaux vivants* that were still a featured part of the Lenten season. The height of fashion only a few years before, now these concerts were distinguished only by "their utter tedium . . . if there are many thorns in the path of a feuilletonist, the most painful . . . is the obligation to attend concerts with 'living pictures.' Gods! What kind of torture is this!" For ten years, the critic complained, he had struggled "to decide whether the music is worse than the *tableaux* or whether the *tableaux* are worse than the music." All of those "*mermaids, bathers* . . . [and] *venetians in gondolas*" had grown unbearably tiresome, as tiresome as articles on "rubber galoshes." Was there no one, the reviewer plaintively asked, who could come up with something new?[53] In its concert offerings, the Russian Musical Society, innovative though it was, did not so much force change as respond to an undercurrent of cultural frustration and offer a potential solution to it.

In their polemics, cultural critics implicitly separated music into categories: good or serious music, Russian music, and the Italian opera. Serious music was an ideological construction that reflected the conservative cultural values of the Russian Musical Society, particularly its orientation toward the West European symphonic and chamber repertoire and the institutional structures that supported this music. Opponents of the Society rejected this formulation, placing a premium instead on innovation and national identity. In St. Petersburg, a city enmeshed in the ideological battles between the Society, the Balakirev Circle, and the critic Serov, not all music composed by Russians qualified as Russian music. The Balakirev Circle and its supporters promoted the innovative works of their own initiates and sought to identify them with the works of advanced Western European composers, such as Berlioz, Liszt, Schumann, and Beethoven. Serov, in addition, promoted Richard Wagner.[54] To the disgust of all parties, the public, and not only in St. Petersburg, overwhelmingly favored the fashionable Italian opera at the expense not only of instrumental music but also of the Russian opera.

Rubinstein and the Russian Musical Society confronted significant obstacles in their crusade to elevate the taste of the Russian concertgoing public. "Serious" music was also "difficult" music; it made far greater demands on the audience than did Italian operatic pieces, light classical works, or salon music. In order to appreciate the new, more complex works, audiences needed to listen more actively, more analytically, and pay more attention to the conductor and musicians and less attention to their fellow listeners. Audiences took some persuading that such a more rigorous musical culture was in their best interests. Commentary in *Illiustratsiia* on a concert from the Russian Musical Society's first season hinted at some of these issues. Rubinstein's conducting, so ridiculed by Serov and others, was here praised for its circumspection. Unlike some other conductors, Rubinstein was restrained and did not distract the audience by flailing his limbs about wildly. Nevertheless, the concert was a mixed success. One of the performers, a Miss Ingeborg-Shtark, was faulted for choosing inappropriate repertoire, in this case a technical, chromatic fantasia by J. S. Bach, which generated muttering among the audience that "such things are fine to play at home, but not in public." Wagner's music also generated bemused commentary by the critic, who complained of the difficulty of comprehending this so-called "music of the future." Beethoven's Ninth Symphony was performed quite capably, despite problems with the balance between the choir and the orchestra in the finale.[55] Perhaps most striking in this review is that there is no mention, not one word, either positive or negative, about Russian music and the "Russian" musical society.

Although, at its birth, the Russian Musical Society differed from previous musical voluntary associations mostly in the scope of its ambition, its growth coincided with a period of dramatic economic and social modernization that spilled over into the concert hall as musicians and audiences responded to new cultural challenges and opportunities. Shifts in social power were reflected in the concert hall, as broader layers of society, in particular the *raznochintsy* and members of the urban estates, began to appear more regularly at concerts. Even if the *beau monde* still sometimes used concerts to flaunt their wealth and power, there was now a greater acceptance of the modest, bourgeois, and serious listener, whose tickets were purchased at great sacrifice because of a hunger for culture and a desire for enlightenment as well as, one must suppose, a desire for social acceptance and advancement. As the century wore on, cultural organizations began to cater to new audiences with inexpensive concerts designed to attract, educate, and civilize the urban masses, a musical reflection of the growing concern of the educated classes with the social consequences of rapid modernization. The availability of music per se also increased as musical publishing grew more profitable. As Russian society changed in the aftermath of the Great Reforms, P. I. Iurgenson, head of the Iurgenson publishing house, wagered that the social changes inherent in the elimination of serfdom would lead to a flowering of cultural life and a much broader demand for music.[56] The Russian Musical Society, like other musical organizations and institutions, both responded to and attempted to control the social and economic changes that were reshaping the structures of Russian cultural life. As the Society grew stronger, however, it became more central to musical life, serving as a center of gravity, at once a producer of music and musicians through its concert series and educational institutions as well as a reliable consumer of musical goods and services.

One consequence of the Russian Musical Society's increasing focus on music education, and especially its focus on the success of the conservatories, was less attention devoted to concert life. In 1886, more than a quarter century after the founding of the Society, the concert life of the St. Petersburg branch still consisted primarily of a ten-evening series of symphonic concerts and an additional series of chamber music. Ten concerts were no longer enough to meet the needs of the public, V. V. Bessel insisted in the pages of his journal, *Muzykal'noe obozrenie*. Ten concerts did not provide sufficient room for a satisfactory exploration of the Russian repertoire *and* new works by foreign composers *and* the standard classical symphonic repertoire. Arguing that the city had boasted twenty-five or more concerts annually in the 1860s, Bessel estimated that the city now should need as many as fifty each year. This would correspond, he argued rather ingenuously, to the greater general musicality of the population that had developed because of the Society's educational efforts. Yet, this greater musicality had not translated into a broader concert life. Bessel complained that concerts frequently failed, filling only half their seats. The "majority of the public" had been "weaned from concerts" and now considered them to be a luxury for the rich, while the Russian Musical Society had grown complacent and had forgotten that its primary mission was the development of Russian musical life as a whole, not simply the management of the conservatories. Bessel advocated a reconceptualization of the Society's mission, one that would reach out to new audiences and emerging sectors of Russian society through the establishment of popular, inexpensive symphonic concerts with exemplary repertoire and high performance standards.[57] Bessel's article was not just another in the seemingly endless string of articles through which critics voiced their dissatisfaction with the Russian Musical Society. Calling as it did for the "democratization" of cultural life, if only on a limited scale, it anticipated deeper shifts in Russian cultural ideology that would structure the debates over the Society and the conservatories from the 1890s and into the Soviet period. The legitimacy of musical democratization was by no means unquestioned. In the early years of the twentieth century, N. D. Kashkin insisted that the Society resist pressures to reach out to broader publics, if that required a lowering of artistic standards. Fearing the cultural threat implicit in a broader audience and holding to the ideals of the Society's founders, Kashkin demanded that the Society continue to reflect the highest artistic standards, not pander to the tastes of the bourgeois public.[58]

CHAPTER 3

The Conservatory in Russian Society

The Institutionalization of Musical Life

WITHOUT QUESTION, THE MOSCOW AND St. Petersburg conservatories are the most lasting legacy of the Russian Musical Society. Although musicologists are familiar with their key role in sustaining Russian musical life, historians have tended to overlook their social and cultural complexity. Moreover, the Russian conservatories were progeny of a much broader nineteenth-century cultural movement that established the conservatory as the most legitimate training ground for skilled musicians. Yet, although musicologists have examined in detail a variety of aspects of conservatory training as well as the institutions themselves, significant misconceptions about the conservatory persist, most specifically the idea that the primary function (as opposed to stated goal) of the conservatory has been to train students for professional musical careers.[1] When scholars have looked more deeply at the broader symbolic and social role of the conservatory, whether in nineteenth-century France or early twentieth-century China, the contested nature of the institution begins to emerge.[2]

In Russia during the Great Reforms, elite musicians and cultural critics struggled to address what they saw as the pressing need to modernize cultural life in order to establish a robust national musical culture. For Anton Rubinstein and the Russian Musical Society, the answer lay in the establishment of a conservatory, which would provide its students with formal training in an institutional setting as well as academic credentials that, they hoped, would persuade the Russian state and educated society to accept musicians as professionals. Russia, they argued, needed not just a handful of dilettante composers, however gifted they might be, but an army of composers, performers, orchestral musicians, and, above all, music teachers.[3] If the conservatory could not create genius, it could nevertheless supply young musicians with a comprehensive understanding of music history, theory, and repertoire, as well as performance skills. Rubinstein envisioned an elite academy, a temple of art intended to initiate only the most able into the mysteries of the musical profession. His vision of an institution by and for art and artists competed with an equally persuasive understanding of the conservatory as a factory producing the multitude of modest practitioners needed to disseminate culture widely through the empire. If the temple would produce artists, the factory would produce artisans; the temple would train composers and virtuosi, the factory orchestral musicians and music teachers. The conservatory as factory, complete with musical proletariat, flatly contradicted the professional and artistic self-image of the musical elite. Yet, if it offended the sensibilities of elite musicians such as Rubinstein, it also had powerful advocates, not least the Grand Duchess Elena Pavlovna, because it responded more concretely to the apparent deficiencies of Russian cultural life. These two visions of the conservatory contested for dominance both within the institutions' walls and on the pages of the press.

Internal debates within the musical world aside, in the establishment and growth of the conservatory we witness the development of Russian civil society. While the Academy of Arts, the conservatory's closest analogue, and other iconic cultural institutions, such as the Academy of Sciences and Moscow University, were established and financially supported by the state, it was a voluntary association, namely the Russian Musical Society, that created and sustained the conservatory.[4] The development of the conservatories highlights the increasingly ambivalent relationship between educated society and the autocratic state. Not only did a voluntary association play the leading role in establishing and administering the conservatories, but the state also repeatedly refused to assume responsibility for them. At the same time, the conservatories distinguished the Russian Musical Society from other voluntary associations, most of which lacked a robust institutional focus. Although private institutions, the conservatories openly aspired to, and ultimately achieved, iconic status, eventually becoming repositories of Russian cultural identity. In retrospect, in the establishment of the conservatories, the state abdicated its role as the builder of national culture, and consequently national identity, to educated society. For the Russian Musical Society, the conservatories, as they grew into substantial and prestigious institutions, gave it authority to assert itself as the arbiter of musical life.

Broader European and Russian cultural and social dynamics shaped the conservatories as well. During the "long" nineteenth century from 1789 to 1914, European musical life experienced an era of tremendous creative energy and productivity. Charismatic virtuosos, innovative composers, and the rise of large symphony orchestras transformed Western musical life. The manners, as well as the canonical music, of modern concerts were developed in this period as the public concert triumphed over older, more intimate, performance practices. Simultaneously, European society changed dramatically in response to rapid industrialization, urbanization, and the concomitant rise of the bourgeoisie. The modern conservatory was born out of the intersection of these forces. A more complex public musical life required highly trained musicians, while musicians themselves, subscribing to bourgeois conceptions of status, struggled to acquire recognition as a profession. Meanwhile, the piano, which physically embodied both the power of industrialization (it acquired its modern shape and power through the incorporation of iron and steel into its frame, while improved manufacturing methods lowered its price and made it broadly accessible to consumers) and the power of the bourgeoisie (which adopted it as a symbol of feminine domesticity, culture, and refinement), grew exponentially in popularity, which both created a demand for and legitimized specialized music education among the middle classes. This would have profound consequences for the Russian conservatories, which, as private schools, were dependent on student tuition fees for their survival. The nascent bourgeoisie subverted the conservatory as a training ground for professional musicians—whether artist or artisan—by the sheer weight of their numbers. Overwhelmed by the demand for the piano, the Russian conservatories struggled to fulfill the tasks of either the temple or of the factory.

The Difficult Birth of a Russian Institution

The Russian Musical Society's early efforts at music education clearly reveal the intersection of old and new models of social and cultural life. The quick introduction of music classes underscored for the public the new society's determination to serve as a missionary of culture. The Society began to offer classes as early as the spring of 1860, but they acquired social prominence only the following fall, when they moved out of instructors' homes and into the spectacular Mikhailovsky Palace, home of Grand Duchess Elena Pavlovna.[5] The controversies surrounding the Society infected its educational efforts as well. Although its classes were relatively inexpensive, some critics complained that even modest fees prevented many potential students from enrolling. Such demands reveal the depth of the social expectations placed on the Russian Musical Society from its infancy; it was being held to the letter as well as the spirit of its charter, particularly the promise to disseminate music education. Faculty, including leading musicians such as N. I. Zaremba, Theodore

Leschetizky, and Henriette Nissen-Saloman, taught classes for one ruble a lesson. At such prices and with such teachers, as well as the glamour lent to the enterprise by the conspicuous patronage of Grand Duchess Elena Pavlovna, students were not hard to locate. Anton Rubinstein recalled those early, enthusiastic days as "simply incredible." The halls of the Mikhailovsky Palace teemed with "Crowds of students of all social positions, means, and ages" who "quickly filled the classes."[6] The problem lay in balancing the expectations of students, faculty, and society with the resources of a newly established organization. Informal classes failed to satisfy either Rubinstein's or the Society's broader artistic and cultural goals. A real conservatory, following West European models, promised both the significant advancement of Russian musical life and a new public role for Rubinstein, similar to that achieved by Felix Mendelssohn with the founding of the Leipzig Conservatory.[7]

In 1862, with Rubinstein at the helm, the Russian Musical Society established the St. Petersburg Conservatory, thereby laying the foundation for the reorganization of musical education and, ultimately, the broad transformation of Russian musical life. From that point, Rubinstein would later claim, the study of music in "all institutes, social institutions, [and even] in families" was restructured. "Until then, music for the young was limited, in most cases, to clanking away (*briatsanie*) on the piano." It was the influence of the conservatories, Rubinstein insisted, that transformed music into a serious subject in the schools, where it came to be viewed as "a very important part of the overall development of students." He praised the Society's alumni (*pitomtsy*) for accomplishing "a complete revolution in music education in Russia."[8] Rubinstein's confident retrospective, however, glossed over not only the financial, legal, and administrative obstacles the conservatories faced, but also his own stormy relationship with them. Moreover, although Rubinstein was clearly the driving force behind the establishment of the St. Petersburg Conservatory, the broader development of the Society and its educational institutions was a product of social and cultural initiative far beyond the scope of one man. Traditional representations of Rubinstein as "the" founder of the St. Petersburg Conservatory (or for that matter of the Russian Musical Society) discount the degree to which these institutions were a part of a broader phenomenon of associational life. The Russian conservatories were the offspring of a collaborative effort by an intimate circle of cultural enthusiasts—with Rubinstein perhaps at the center, at least initially—along with a much larger cast of educational, cultural, and social activists determined to modernize Russian music.[9]

Although the battle lines were already clearly drawn, the creation of the St. Petersburg Conservatory drew a wide range of critical opinion. Some critics still viewed Russian musical life complacently and saw the conservatory as a welcome but not particularly significant new institution. The critic for *Russkii listok*, for example, saw no great need for the conservatory, suggesting that existing institutions already satisfied the needs of the church, the *narod*, and music lovers. Although such placid views must surely have infuriated more partisan critics, they probably accurately reflected the perceptions of the broader public. *Russkii listok* offered a utilitarian view of Russia's cultural needs; with some distaste, it suggested that, in a year when there were only 128 openings for new students in the city's gymnasia, the impassioned rhetoric over the conservatory seemed overblown.[10]

The lack of Russian names among the proposed faculty raised eyebrows in many quarters and broadened debates about the conservatory's responsibilities as a Russian institution. Even some critics who viewed Rubinstein as a foreigner reluctantly acknowledged his right to staff the conservatory with those he found competent and compatible. Others sympathized with the Society, arguing that a foreign-born faculty was unavoidable given Russia's failure to nurture native musicians and composers.[11] For such critics, the scarcity of Russian names reflected broader failures of Russian culture rather than the specific inadequacies of the Society. *Russkii listok* complained that the purportedly *Russian* conservatory boasted "only four Slavic" names; moreover, its critic sighed, "only the name of Mr. Davydov sounds purely Russian" and "he is only a native of the Russian Empire, not of Russian blood."[12] This critic's complaint differed significantly from that of the conservatory's real opponents in that it recognized that the conservatory replicated the weaknesses of other important Russian institutions. Like the Academy of Sciences, the conservatory was a transplant, dependent on the importation of knowledgeable, skilled professionals who were alien to Russian culture, oblivious to Russian values, and ignorant of the Russian language. Lacking a Russian faculty, it would forever be alien, clinging to life in a hostile environment. Yet, this critic did not reject the fundamental principles behind the conservatory or the Russian Musical Society. Like them, he accepted the need to transform Russian cultural life but believed that the new conservatory was too simple a solution. By itself, it could not modernize and invigorate Russian music. Like the establishment of universities without primary schools, the conservatory without elementary music instruction could never satisfy the aesthetic needs of the empire. Moreover, if music became a core subject in the primary and secondary schools, the conservatory would be free to concentrate on its "proper" task of training professional musicians. Children and amateurs would be driven from its walls.[13]

The official opening of the conservatory in September 1862 intensified existing polemical battles as Serov, Stasov, and the proponents of the Balakirev

Circle took advantage of every perceived weakness or inadequacy to attack it. Rubinstein and the Society, however, were hardly in danger of collapsing under the onslaught. In addition to their own strategically placed articles, they enjoyed substantial moral support from prominent members of society as well as from some of the more fair-minded critics. Claiming neutrality, the critic for *Russkii mir* waded into the fray in November, singling out the outrageous behavior of Serov, particularly his coarse anti-Semitic attacks on the conservatory's founders and supporters, for condemnation. Serov, the critic complained, had damned the conservatory before it had even opened as the "future breeding ground for talentless musical bureaucrats." Deriding Rubinstein and the Society's leadership as "Iankels," he had accused them of scheming to seize "despotic" control of musical life and "crush" any expressions of musicality that did not conform to their standards, thus blocking the natural development of Russian music. These complaints, the critic insinuated, simply reflected Serov's fear of competition. In any case, by objective measures the new conservatory was a success, with more than 150 students and a well-qualified faculty that scarcely deserved the derisive sobriquet of "Iankel," although the critic carefully sidestepped the issue of "foreignness."[14]

The initial dependence on foreign specialists reflected the unquestioned acceptance by Rubinstein and the Society of the credibility of the Western European conservatories, themselves rather recently established, and of educational certification as a marker of professional standing. Certainly, those Russians who met the conservatory's requirements were mostly products of Western European conservatories or advanced private training abroad. Ironically, many of the "foreigners" whose presence aroused so much indignation were Russian subjects of non-Russian, primarily German, descent.[15] Others were Jewish; anti-Semitism left a deep mark on Russian musical life. Some truly were foreigners, several of whom, such as the violinist and pedagogue Leopold Auer, devoted their careers to Russia.[16] Not all commentators, of course, objected to the German cultural origins and orientation of the conservatories. Some suggested that Russia might do well to emulate Germany, the recognized leader of European musical life.[17]

With the St. Petersburg Conservatory seemingly besieged by hostile critics, the decision to found a second conservatory in Moscow might seem reckless overconfidence. The cultural politics of Moscow, however, were far less contentious than those of the capital and the Moscow Conservatory never attracted the kind of hostility that afflicted its sister school. Moreover, the conservatory was now a familiar Russian institution rather than a novel foreign transplant; it garnered particular praise when it hired graduates of the *Russian* conservatory, such as the young Petr Ilich Tchaikovsky, for its faculty. The celebratory rhetoric surrounding its opening in 1866 illuminates the still evolving cultural ideology of the Russian Musical Society as it attempted to establish itself as the focus of Russian musical identity. Prince N. P. Trubetskoy delivered a speech littered with celebratory platitudes that nevertheless persuasively promoted twin themes of Russia's cultural barrenness and the consequent significance of the Society's civilizing mission. Emphasizing music's moral influence on society, he stressed the need to bring culture to the provinces as well as the capitals and thereby to transform the Russian people. The establishment of the Moscow Conservatory, he insisted, reflected the Society's conscientious attempt to fulfill its self-imposed mandate to satisfy the cultural needs of the empire.[18]

Although the conservatories remained vulnerable to attacks on their "insufficiently Russian" faculty well into the 1870s and 1880s, strategic decisions in the early 1870s helped cement the Society's claim to a guiding role in Russian musical life. In St. Petersburg, the appointment of Rimsky-Korsakov as a professor of theory and composition in 1871 allowed a rapprochement between the Society and some of its most virulent critics, particularly Cesar Cui.[19] An innovative new course in the history of Russian sacred music at the Moscow Conservatory emphasized its commitment to native musical traditions.[20] The purpose of the conservatory and the social role of musicians, however, remained controversial topics; they both mirrored Russia's confusion over its cultural identity vis-à-vis Western Europe and reflected the difficulty of harmonizing Romantic ideals of the artist with the precarious social position of musicians in Russian society. In this context, the subdued assessment of the theatrical critic for *Syn otechestva*, M. Rappaport, was certainly more convincing than either the hysterical polemics of the determined opponents of the conservatory or of purists who argued that it should be a temple of art dedicated to the glory of Russian culture. Rappaport focused on the conservatory as a useful institution, noting its efficiency in providing students with practical technical skills as well as the theoretical knowledge required of a working musician. He valued it as an institution capable of producing rank-and-file orchestral players and singers, not brilliant composers or virtuosi. Like some of the conservatory's fiercest critics, Rappaport doubted that any educational institution could foster real genius. Yet, unlike these critics, Rappaport viewed such expectations as unrealistic and unfair. The inability to produce genius, he suggested, did not negate the conservatory's value as an engine of cultural development.[21]

Whether conceived of as modest artisans or geniuses in the making, conservatory students came under intense public scrutiny. In this context, the feminization of the student body became a particularly contentious issue. It also, ultimately, became one of the characteristics that distinguished the Russian conservatories from most of their Western European counterparts. By 1868, as table 3.1 shows, women constituted a majority of the student body in the St. Petersburg Conservatory. Moreover, the pattern of female domination of the piano department was already well established.[22]

Women were far more likely to be declared frivolous dilettantes than were their male colleagues, so their presence in significant numbers threatened the conservatory's representation of itself as a serious institution of advanced learning. As early as 1863, the newspaper *Golos* charged that it was not some sinister Jewish conspiracy but too many light-minded students that jeopardized the conservatory's ability to advance Russian music. Students' scornful attitudes were mirrored by the broader public, for whom the "word 'artist' ha[d] become almost a synonym for 'idler.'" Only after the temple of art was cleansed of its unworthy children, this critic implied, would the conservatory claim its place at the pinnacle of musical life. With the amateurs and dilettantes driven away by a rigorous curriculum, the conservatory would finally be able to nurture its true students, Russia's future professionals, worthy devotees of art.[23] The persistence of the conflict over the social purpose of the conservatory, and the intensity some devoted to the idea of the "temple of art," can be seen in the fact that some sixty years later, Soviet educational authorities would employ much the same argument to justify a purge of the conservatory student body, in which the primary casualties were young bourgeois women.

Perhaps because of the criticism the conservatories endured, their first few years were marked by particularly self-congratulatory festivities. At graduation ceremonies in the spring of 1869, the director of the St. Petersburg Conservatory, N. I. Zaremba, attempted to connect the young institution to

TABLE 3.1. St. Petersburg Conservatory, Fall 1868

Students by Specialization	Males	Males as % of Total	Females	Females as % of Total	Total	Specialization as % of Total Student Body
Piano	23	21%	87	79%	110	48%
Voice	7	15%	40	85%	47	21%
Orchestral	60	98%	1	2%	61	27%
Special Theory/ Composition	9	100%	0	0%	9	4%
Harp	0	0%	1	100%	1	>1%
Total	99	43%	129	57%	228	100%

TsGIA SPb, fond 361, op. 11, d. 4

the honor and identity of the Russian people, employing in his speech arguments that would resurface repeatedly until the revolutions of 1917. Contesting the idea of the conservatory as a temple of art, Zaremba insisted that it achieved its real purpose only when it satisfied the empire's needs for musically educated teachers, citizens, wives, and mothers. These modest and anonymous figures, not glittering virtuosi, Zaremba suggested, were the conservatory's most important contribution to the cultural development of Russia.[24]

The Keys to the Temple: Admissions, Tuition, and the Conservatory Student Body

Despite the polemical attacks of hostile critics, the conservatories quickly proved popular with their core constituency—students and their parents. Indeed, the very popularity of the conservatories soon provided another basis for attacks on the Russian Musical Society and its flagship educational institutions. The definition of talent lurked in the background as the Society and the musical community struggled to define the purpose of the conservatory and the role of musicians in public life. Despite the criticisms of the conservatories in the press and among the cultural cognoscenti, for many young musicians the conservatories held out the promise of personal aesthetic fulfillment and a Romantic life of art. Several significant hurdles stood between these young musicians and their goals, however. First and foremost was the need to pass admissions examinations sufficiently brilliantly to warrant placement in the class of their choice.

In the first decade or so of the conservatories' existence, the admissions process, although sometimes quite daunting, could also be strikingly informal. The Moscow Conservatory seemed a natural haven for the ten-year-old V. A., whose mother was a highly accomplished pianist.

> In 1873, I turned ten and they decided to send me to the conservatory.... Fees for the conservatory were half that of today (100 r.). However, the main issue in terms of enrollment was not the fees, but [securing] the consent of director N. G. Rubinstein. In order to get his consent, my grandfather put on his full general's uniform, put me and my mother in the carriage, and we set off [to find] Rubinstein.[25]

They trusted the director's local fame to help them locate him, finally landing on his doorstep after learning his address from a passing coachman.

Rubinstein was more than accommodating to his unexpected visitors, receiving them in his housecoat and allowing the boy to deliver an impromptu audition.

> My successes up to that point were not very significant, which is apparent from the fact that [the music I had brought with was] R[obert] Schuman's *Album for the Young*, a very childish work. However, Rubinstein's exam was of a completely different kind than we expected. Pointing at No. 2 [in the collection], "The Soldier's March," he said to me: "Play this a whole step lower," than it should be, not expecting that the performer of such easy pieces would be able to do it. Fortunately... because of the structure of the piece, this was rather easy, so that I, largely by ear... was able to play the first line without stopping. Any further and I would probably have gotten mixed up, but Nikolai Grigor'ich said: That's enough. He's in (free of charge).[26]

This charming story reveals much about the position of both Nikolai Rubinstein and the Moscow Conservatory in its first decade of existence. On the one hand, Rubinstein was already sufficiently beloved and renowned in Moscow for his address to be common knowledge. On the other hand, the conservatory was still such a fragile and immature institution that would-be students and their determined parents could aggressively seek out the director.

The role of the conservatory as the gatekeeper of the musical profession gave the process of admission an unusual significance, long remembered and recorded in the memoirs of alumni. A conservatory education, moreover, especially when pursued with openly professional goals, required a willingness to take considerable risks. The singer A. Nezhdanova's recollections of her conservatory training bear many of the hallmarks of a "rags to riches" story (see figure 3.1). She highlights the both literal and artistic distance she had to travel in order to secure her dreams, leaving a secure home in Odessa and her profession as a schoolteacher for the uncertain promises of the capitals. Although her risk taking ultimately paid off with a stage career, a professorial appointment, and popular acclaim, her recollections of her student years emphasize her poverty, self-sacrifice, and dependence on the charity of acquaintances and relations as she struggled to achieve her goals. Having been informed by several potential teachers in St. Petersburg that her voice was "too small" or "too weak," and that it "wasn't worth it" for her to invest in advanced training given that she had "no other means of support" beyond her teacher's salary and that she should "continue to work in the school and

FIGURE 3.1. "Singer Antonina Nezhdanova in P. I. Tchaikovsky's opera *Eugene Onegin* staged by the Bolshoi Theater, c. 1906." From the collection of Antonina Nezhdanova's house museum. Credit: RIA Novosti/Lebrecht Music & Arts

sing only for her own pleasure," Nezhdanova set off on the long road back home to Odessa, bitter that judgments about her talent as a singer seemed to have more to do with her ability to pay for lessons than with her musical abilities. Although discouraged, she had not yet given up hope and was easily persuaded by friends to make one last attempt to achieve her dreams by auditioning for the Moscow Conservatory. Despite the fact that she had appeared after the school year had already begun and all vacancies filled, she persuaded the director, V. I. Safonov, and voice professor Mazetti, to permit her to audition. "Exiting [Safonov's] office, I began to wait in the foyer of the conservatory for the results of my audition. After several minutes, professor Mazetti exited and, approaching me, announced that I had been accepted in his class.... At that moment I experienced an overwhelming rush of emotions... joy or fear in the face of an unknown future,... a completely new world for me,—a new life. I was giving up everything, leaving Odessa and the school behind, separating myself from my family."[27] Although Nezhdanova's very success makes her exceptional, the passion she invested in her musical education was widely shared by other prospective conservatory students. No obstacle, whether a lack of means, a lack of preparation, or the discouragement of well-meaning acquaintances, family members, and expert musicians, could deter these young dreamers from the pursuit of a life in music. Nezhdanova's tale, like others published to commemorate the conservatories over the years, not only allows readers a glimpse of the inner workings of the conservatories, it also reminds us of their role in the cultural transformation of both individuals and society.

Although memoirs dwell on the emotional weight of the admissions process, entrance examinations attempted to eliminate the clearly unacceptable and identify the truly talented few. Although the conservatory's initial charter required that applicants demonstrate only basic skills, including literacy, numeracy, and some knowledge of music notation, entrance standards were raised as the conservatories became increasingly popular.[28] As early as 1878, more rigorous entrance requirements were imposed, in part to reinforce the conservatory's stature as a higher educational institution. Theoretically, students were expected to have an education equivalent to that of the progymnasia, although this requirement was readily modified for exceptionally promising students.[29] Despite stringent demands on paper, students willing to study an orchestral instrument other than the violin frequently enrolled with little or no prior preparation in music, a reflection of the persistently low social status of orchestral musicians.[30]

Conservatory enrollment demanded not only talent, persistence, and the ability to pay tuition, but also a series of documents indicative of the invasive bureaucratism of Russian life. Students were required to present the conservatory administration with an internal passport in order to receive a certificate for residency in the city, while those under fifteen also needed written permission from their parents. They also had to furnish their birth certificate, proof of their general education, a certificate of release if they were members of a taxable estate, evidence of their draft registration, if applicable, as well as testimony as to their political reliability, a medical certificate testifying that musical study would not be harmful to their health, and, if requested, proof of inoculation against smallpox.[31] For Jewish students, bureaucratic control was even more intrusive as they needed temporary residency permits just to sit the entrance exams. If successful, they usually received residency permits for the period of their enrollment. When, on occasion, the Moscow or St. Petersburg city government refused to issue such permits, Jewish musicians were effectively barred from enrolling in the conservatory.[32]

Over the years, the piano, voice, violin, and composition departments became highly competitive.[33] By 1908, entrance requirements were precisely articulated. Applicants were tested for inherent musical ability, including pitch sense, musical memory, and rhythm. Would-be students also needed to be able to read music in both the treble and bass clefs and demonstrate comprehension of musical meter, note division, and the fundamentals of rhythmic notation. The examination process also evaluated the applicant's level of preparation relative to his or her age. The faculty now scrutinized the physical health of applicants in detail, appraising the lungs, heart, teeth, and lips of woodwind and brass students.[34] The examination process, however, still struggled to identify and categorize musical talent. Absolute pitch, for example, was specifically identified as a propitious gift, but was not considered a sure sign of talent. An ability to unhesitatingly repeat scales, intervals, and phrases with correct pitch, rhythm, and emphasis after a single hearing strongly implied talent, while hesitation or uncertainty suggested its likely absence.[35]

When necessary, some of the most determined applicants resorted to subterfuge and cunning to secure their admission. Such was certainly the case for the young Latvian Iazep Vitol, who achieved success as a composer, critic, and pedagogue despite disasters early in his conservatory career. He connived with his sister Agnes to secure admission to the St. Petersburg Conservatory as a violist, despite the fact that he hoped to be a pianist. "The conservatory received me sternly. At the examination, they asked me why I had chosen the viola; wasn't it true I was an unsuccessful violinist? Vacant places? Well, this year there are no [vacancies] in the viola class. It was the end of all my hopes!" Vitol burst into tears, earning him the sympathy of one key member of the examining committee. "In spite of the fact that I did not play the viola at the level demanded by the conservatory, the elderly and kindhearted professor Veikman (the violist in the Auer Quartet) took me under his wing and even said: 'Aus Ihnen wird einmal ganz gutter Bratschist warden.'" Despite Veikman's confidence that he could make a violist of him, Vitol never really succeeded on the instrument. Nevertheless, entry into the conservatory brought his real goals within reach when he successfully insinuated himself into the composition class.[36]

Vitol's desperate efforts to enroll might seem overblown, especially when preserved in the celebratory memoirs of a highly successful professional musician, but they echo the determination displayed by much more ordinary students and their parents. When, in 1884, Aron Iakovlevich Kuts, a retired military musician, learned that his son Mordukh had been rejected by the St. Petersburg Conservatory for the third time in as many years, he refused to accept the examination results. Kuts's faith in his son's ability was belied by the examining committee's report. Although young Mordukh possessed a good sense of pitch, a musical memory, and the ability to read music, his knowledge of elementary theory was limited and his violin technique inadequate. Unwilling to accept the judgment of the examining committee, Kuts played on the patriotism of the conservatory leadership, demanding a "just" explanation for his son's rejection. Surely, he insisted, they would not deny a place to the "minor son of an old soldier?" As "humane and modern" men, it was their responsibility to "open the doors of their temple to youth." Neither the "title nor the position of the parents," or "other prejudices," he insisted, should prevent students, such as his son, from achieving their educational goals.[37] As a military musician, Kuts occupied one of the lowest ranks in Russia's musical hierarchy. As a father, he hoped to secure a brighter future for his son, seeing the conservatory as a source of social advancement as well as an educational institution.

Although it is easy to dismiss parents' insistence regarding the ability of their offspring as merely a product of their emotional attachment to their children, talent is, in fact, notoriously difficult to quantify or define. As Henry Kingsbury has shown in his sociological analysis of an American conservatory, evaluations and declarations of talent are highly subjective and reflect the biases of the observer.[38] It is particularly difficult to assess the ability of conservatory students retrospectively, not least because the public debates over musical talent and conservatory admissions tend to reveal more about the cultural, gender, and class biases that permeated public discourse than they do about the skills and abilities of conservatory students as individuals or as a group. The St. Petersburg Conservatory, for example, enrolled more than three hundred students in 1872–1873 but only one unfortunate youth was expelled for lack of ability. Tuition, however, served as an important marker of a student's perceived talent; those viewed as particularly promising were rewarded with scholarships and membership in the subsidized-tuition *complekt*, the conservatory's core student body.

In effect, the high fees charged to those considered less able subsidized their studies. Gender, in particular, influenced perceptions of talent, and therefore the availability of financial support because the ideal professional musician was presumed to be male, whether composer, virtuoso, or orchestral musician. As table 3.2 clearly shows, men were more likely than women to receive subsidized tuition, although this was due in part to efforts to sustain the (virtually all male) orchestral division by offering scholarships and stipends to woodwind, brass, and low string specialists. Interestingly, at least in this case, tuition levels failed to predict student educational persistence; those paying the highest tuition fees had the lowest dropout rate.

Tuition was the lifeblood of all of the Society's educational institutions. Although a conservatory education was quite expensive, the broad curriculum at least partially justified its cost. The curriculum included music theory, history, musicianship, and ensemble playing and, if needed, general secondary education courses, as well as lessons with a skilled and reputable teacher in the chosen specialty. A relatively large percentage of students, however, enrolled as auditors, studying only a performance specialty. They paid the highest rates; a coercive measure intended to encourage students to enroll in the full course of study. Although consistent with the Society's efforts to create an educated class of professional musicians, such coercive measures sparked resistance. Beneficial as theory and aesthetics were to musicians in the abstract, one critic argued, they did little to help the timpanist strike the timpani or the singer stay on pitch.[39] Tuition rates, moreover, fail to provide a complete picture of the costs of a conservatory education. Incidental costs, including instrument purchase or rental, books, and sheet music, as well as room, board, and transportation for non-local students,

TABLE 3.2. St. Petersburg Conservatory, 1872–1873

	Women		Men		Total
Student Body	204	62%	127	38%	331
Subsidized *complekt*	63	31%	100	69%	163
Partial tuition or stipends	26	68%	12	32%	38
Full tuition	115	88%	15	12%	130

TsGIA SPb, fond 361, op. 11, d. 1, ll. 29v–30

FIGURE 3.2. "Group of Conservatory Students with Instructors A. K. Glazunov and A. N. Esipova, St. Petersburg, 1910." Permission of the Central State Archive of Documentary Films, Photographs, and Sound Recordings, St. Petersburg

could significantly exceed annual tuition fees. Room and board in one *pansion* for female conservatory students, for example, cost 300 rubles annually in the 1870s.[40] By the early 1900s, tuition for pupils at the St. Petersburg Conservatory was 200 rubles annually. Auditors and those studying with a few of the most prominent professors, such as the pianist Anna Esipova or the violinist Leopold Auer, paid an additional 50 rubles.[41] The conservatories' multitiered tuition structure reflected an attempt to balance demands for accessibility against financial pressures. Nevertheless, the high cost of a conservatory education reinforced its popular image as an institution for the well-off and well-bred (see figure 3.2).

Because the conservatories were dependent on student fees to pay the bills, critics from the 1870s to the Bolshevik Revolution accused them of accepting everyone able to afford the cost of tuition, regardless of their talent, while neglecting poor but talented students.[42] After 1917, the "new" Soviet conservatories resurrected this complaint as a way of distinguishing themselves from their prerevolutionary counterparts; their success in "proletarianizing" the student body was limited at best, as we shall see in the conclusion. Moreover, despite the popular perception of the conservatory as a playground for the elites, it remained surprisingly accessible to less-privileged students through a complicated and extensive system of scholarships and subsidies. By the turn of the twentieth century, a surprisingly high proportion of students received either completely or partially subsidized education; nearly 14 percent of the student body of the Russian conservatories between 1906 and 1914 were released from paying tuition.[43] In addition, the conservatories fought to preserve their core professional mission by consciously exploiting those who contradicted it; scholarships for poorer students were subsidized by the profits generated by the haven of the middle class, the piano department. In the St. Petersburg Conservatory, wind and string bass students automatically received a scholarship releasing them from tuition for up to five years, while only those piano students pursuing a free artist's diploma—and by extension a professional career—were even eligible for scholarships.[44] Such subsidies allowed poorer students to pursue a musical education, but reinforced the class divisions between applied specialties.

The presence of dilettantes in the "temple of art" offended the sensibilities of leading musicians everywhere, but none more than Anton Rubinstein, who resented the Russian conservatories' dependence on student tuition payments. In both words and deeds, especially his resignation as director of the St. Petersburg Conservatory in 1867, he fought what he saw as efforts to compromise high professional standards. Rubinstein's own need for professional recognition, as well as, perhaps, a lingering hope that he could reposition the conservatory on the path he had intended for it, prompted him to return as director in 1887. He struggled to bring the conservatory back into alignment with his own artistic principles by reducing the size of the student body and raising entrance and graduation standards in an effort to eliminate those students he considered unnecessary "ballast." The purpose of the conservatories, he insisted, was to give a relatively small number of talented and dedicated individuals the musical skills, theoretical knowledge, general education, and credentials necessary for successful and respectable professional careers as orchestral musicians, composers, or virtuoso performers.[45]

Rubinstein's ideals conflicted both with the conservatories' financial needs, which demanded liberal admissions policies, and with societal demands for music education, particularly piano instruction. Frustrated at his inability to impose reforms, in 1891 Rubinstein abandoned his efforts and the conservatory as well. The size of the student body, however, continued to be a source of both pride and anxiety. On the one hand, the large number of conservatory students could be used as "proof" of the success of the Russian Musical Society as it fought to extract financial and administrative support from the state, its ministries, and local governments. On the other hand, the enormous size of the conservatories undermined both their status as "temples of art" and their ability to serve as disciplined training grounds for professional musicians. Limits on enrollment, perhaps to one thousand students, were proposed but never implemented. On several occasions, attempts were made to subdivide the conservatory student body into academic and general-musical divisions, thereby formally acknowledging in the curriculum the fact that only a portion of the student body was preparing for a professional career.[46]

Increasingly sensitive to public criticism, the conservatories tried to improve their image by halfheartedly discouraging auditors and repeatedly emphasizing their rigorous professional standards. Certainly, entrance requirements, publicized with pamphlets and advertisements in musical periodicals, created the impression of an institution dedicated to professional training. The St. Petersburg Conservatory, as described in a 1908 pamphlet directed at potential students, was a "higher musical educational institution with the purpose of educating orchestral performers, instrumental virtuosi, concert and operatic artist-singers, composers, bandmasters, and music teachers." This pamphlet might be read as a statement of belief, an effort by the conservatory's leadership to create, on paper at least, the kind of institution that they could not establish in reality.[47] In this, Russia's conservatories were hardly unique. Across Europe and in North America, the professionalizing rhetoric of the conservatory movement concealed the appropriation of these institutions by the bourgeoisie. The intermingling of preprofessional and dilettante students in the conservatories was not necessarily incompatible. Indeed, the bourgeois "invasion" can be seen not as a fatal compromise of the institution's professional purpose but rather as a reflection of its broad social and cultural significance. The modern conservatory, seen only as an institution for the training of professional musicians, would have limited cultural impact regardless of its graduates' technical skills. Instead, the professionalizing ethos of the conservatory masked its more important but less definable role in disseminating and developing new middle-class patterns of cultural engagement.

Turning Dreams into Reality: The Idea and the Experience of the Conservatory

To young musicians, the conservatory was the Promised Land where their dreams might become reality. For the lucky and talented few whose dreams led to successful careers, memories of their studies follow a familiar pattern. The recollections of former conservatory students, whether published in prerevolutionary newspapers, collected in commemorative volumes, or preserved in the archives, need to be read not as straightforward accounts of an artistic education but as expressions of identity. The authors' memoirs reinforced the institutional identity of the conservatories; simultaneously, the conservatories shaped the authors' sense of self on both a professional and personal level. In part, this was due to the intimate nature of musical instruction, even within institutions as large as the St. Petersburg Conservatory.

Memoirs of conservatory training often emphasize the deep emotional connection that developed between teachers and their successful students. The reminiscences of A. N. Amfiteatrova-Levitskaia, a student during the 1870s, are emphatic on this point. Failure to prepare adequately, for example, was interpreted by her principle voice teacher, A. D. Aleksandrova-Kochetova, as "disrespectful to art and to one's teacher." Amfiteatrova-Levitskaia idealized her teacher as exceptionally devoted to her students; many of her pupils, moreover, addressed her as "mama." In Amfiteatrova-Levitskaia's case, this was almost literally true as she lived for a while with her teacher and her family.[48] Talented and promising students warranted such care. The attention teachers devoted to students not only fulfilled artistic ideologies that demanded the nurturing of talent but also promised more tangible returns as successful students brought recognition to their teachers as well as to themselves.

If teachers nurtured their students, the conservatories provided them with a comprehensive musical education. Each conservatory established its own curricula within the limits imposed by its charter and that of the Russian Musical Society. The length of study varied by applied specialty but tended to increase with time. The course of study was divided into two or three levels, with students progressing through each level in two to four years. Thus, a full course of study could take eight or nine years. Many students, especially pianists, enrolled directly in the advanced courses, having attained a degree of technical proficiency through private study. Many more enrolled for a year or two, withdrawing before completing requirements for a diploma. As a result, the student body was unusually fluid and diverse. Students ranged in age from eight or nine years to the middle to late thirties, with most in their midteens to midtwenties.

In addition to one or more applied specialties, courses in music theory and solfège were mandatory for all students, except auditors; those pursuing a free artist's diploma studied some combination of music history, harmony, instrumentation, form, and counterpoint as well. Classes in ensemble playing, choir, orchestra, and opera studio supplemented the core requirements. In addition, every applied specialty had a defined course of study and examination requirements. For example, pianists were expected to study music theory, choral singing, chamber music, music history, aesthetics, and notation, as well as take piano lessons.[49] To receive a diploma, students had to pass all required musical subjects while those pursuing the less rigorous *attestat* could graduate upon successful completion of their applied subject and the minimum course of study in theoretical musical subjects. The auditors, who refused to study theoretical musical subjects, were not entitled to either an *attestat* or a diploma.

The emphasis on theoretical knowledge and musical understanding, as opposed to simple technical proficiency, reflects the essential conflict between the professional ideals of the specialists guiding the conservatories and the pragmatic goals of most students. It suggests a contradiction between the conception of who would (or should) be a conservatory student and who, in the end, these students turned out to be. The conservatory, under the moral and musical leadership of Anton Rubinstein, was created to train professional musicians and to secure for them both rights and public recognition as members of a legitimate profession. Mechanical skill was not the only attribute of the professional musician; well-educated musicians should also be able to understand and interpret the meaning of a composition and to place it within its historical context. The professional's sophisticated, theoretical understanding of music justified his superiority over the dilettante. Conservatory proponents argued that a low level of musical understanding, the result of an educational tradition that rarely devoted significant attention to theory, harmony, or other technical subjects, had condemned Russia to musical dilettantism and the fringes of European musical culture. Only by training educated musicians could Russia transform its musical life. Theoretical subjects became the conservatories' most effective defense against dilettantes. Here was the means to separate the wheat from the chaff; to restrict the arena of public musical life to those entitled to participate by virtue of their expert knowledge. However, many working musicians lacked the education and cultural polish to function effectively in polite society. In an effort to ensure that professional musicians were prepared to satisfy their social, as well as artistic, responsibilities, the conservatories awarded diplomas only to candidates with a secondary education.[50] To help students meet these educational standards, the conservatories offered six to seven years of general secondary education within their walls. These classes, designed to broadly replicate a gymnasia or real school education, offered students from less-privileged backgrounds opportunities for real social and cultural advancement.

The conservatory curriculum did more than simply provide students with technical skills and theoretical knowledge. In many ways, the curriculum encoded a particular conception of the social role of music. Music theory courses represented an idealization of the professional identity of conservatory students. Similarly, music history courses were a reflection of the faculty's conception of music and, in particular, Russia's place within it. In the 1880s, Professor L. A. Sakketti prepared two syllabi for music history at the St. Petersburg Conservatory. The first, a standard one-year course intended for instrumentalists in their fourth year of study and theorists in their third year, attempted to cover the whole history of music as then conceived, beginning with the study of the "music of savages" (*muzyka dikikh*) and ending with the music of the Slavic peoples, especially the Czechs and Poles. Only the final section focused on music in Russia from ancient times to the present. Several years later, the decision to expand the music history course from one to two years prompted Sakketti to revisit and expand his syllabus. As before, Slavic music lay outside the course of European development and was treated separately at the end of the program, although it had been broadened to include the South Slavs as well as Czechs and Poles. Russian music was now divided into three unequal subsections. An examination of the "primitive" or "primordial" epoch, which focused on folk song and native instruments, preceded a detailed discussion of sacred music including its periodization, notational systems, and its alteration under the influence of foreign operatic composers. Finally, students studied secular Russian music. National identity and pride emerge with force in the selection of topics and their description, from music in Muscovy, to "secular music under the influence of foreigners" in the time of Peter the Great, to "national tendencies in opera" under Elizaveta Petrovna and Catherine the Great to "Kavos and Verstovsky as precursors of the emancipation of Russian music" from West European influence. To underscore the point, Sakketti titled the last two sections of the course "Independent Russian music (Glinka and his successors)" and "The Russian Musical Society, its mission, and the results of its activities in propagandizing music among the Russian people."[51]

Proving Their Worth: Student Performances and the Conservatories' Image

The training of a young musician in the conservatory system, then and now, depends on the mastery of three sets of skills. Formal theoretical coursework, although important, represents only one-third of the equation. Intimate, highly personalized instruction on one's instrument or voice initiates the would-be musician into the craft of musicianship. Conservatory students also need well-developed performance skills, as soloists and as members of ensembles. In Russia, however, student performances also served the conservatory's need to prove itself as a useful and successful institution. Consequently, conservatory performances struggled to balance the educational needs of students and the prestige needs of the institution.

The St. Petersburg and Moscow conservatories presented a variety of recitals, concerts, and showcases that offered students a chance to gain performing experience. Beginning and intermediate students usually performed only in closed recitals, which protected both the conservatories and the students from humiliation and ridicule. Yet, because the conservatories needed to demonstrate their success on the public stage, once or twice a month, they invited the listening public, parents, and members of the Society to open recitals that showcased more advanced students. The "competitive" public recitals introduced by the St. Petersburg Conservatory in 1870–1871 presented the most brilliant students to a broad public. These performances attracted a large audience that reassured the Society's leadership that "the conservatory enjoy[ed] the sympathy and trust of society."[52] Moreover, like any modern educational institution, the Russian conservatories relied on formal assessments to evaluate students. Semester exams served to determine which students should move from preparatory to advanced courses, which were ready to take graduation exams, and which should be dropped from the program. Public graduation examinations, however, had symbolic as well as practical functions. In addition to certifying the competency of newly minted professionals, these performances sought to demonstrate the efficacy of the Society's ideology of the "educated musician." Consequently, these examinations initially included questioning in theoretical and general musical subjects as well as instrumental and vocal performances, which tried the patience of state representatives and other observers.[53]

The critic Rostislav used the first graduation examinations of the St. Petersburg Conservatory as a platform from which to both critique the institution and call attention to its financial needs. He snidely noted that he had actually attended the graduation examinations, unlike many other critics who appeared to base their judgments more on ideology than on observed reality. The public examinations, held in the Mikhailovsky Palace, fully convinced Rostislav of the "rational" education provided by the conservatory. In particular, he praised the conservatory's commitment to the education of broadly trained music teachers skilled in both music theory and instrumental or vocal technique. Yet, this first graduation examination revealed ideological, pedagogical, and aesthetic weaknesses that would continue to trouble the conservatories until well into the twentieth century. Although the graduating composition students—including a very young Tchaikovsky—displayed real promise, the immature student orchestra performed very poorly.[54] Despite Rostislav's conviction that this problem would soon correct itself, the struggle to field adequate orchestra programs remained a persistent issue for all of the Society's educational institutions until 1917.

Rostislav grumbled a bit about the inadequately national character of the conservatory, its faculty, and its curriculum. The reviewer for *Nuvellist*, conversely, was largely oblivious to this issue, focusing instead on the conservatory's gift to society of new *Russian* talents, although, like many other critics, he complained about the inability of the foreign-born faculty to prepare singers to cope with the Russian operatic repertoire because they not only lacked an understanding of the Russian style but also the ability to speak Russian. Unlike Rostislav, moreover, he felt free to name names, identifying students and noting their strengths and weaknesses, presumably on the grounds that, as graduates, they no longer enjoyed any immunity from public scrutiny.[55]

In truth, public examinations and other student performances were something of a double-edged sword for the Russian Musical Society and its conservatories. On the one hand, successful performances attracted the attention of the public, potential students and their parents, and possible patrons. Positive reviews helped the Society construct and sustain its image as an agent of cultural enlightenment. Conversely, weak performances, especially by graduating students, gave the conservatories' critics additional ammunition for their attacks. If graduating students performed poorly, or if they appeared inadequate to or uninterested in their appointed task as cultural missionaries, they undermined the very reason for the conservatories' existence.

Cui exploited this vulnerability repeatedly in his attacks on the St. Petersburg Conservatory. In 1870, Cui described a student performance of scenes from *Rusalka* and *A Life for the Tsar* as so "disgusting... in all respects" that he had never heard the like before and hoped never to experience such a performance again. The soloists were "untalented" and "unable to sing." The soon-to-graduate student conductor appeared ignorant of basic conducting patterns and oblivious to the orchestra's wrong notes. The performance was "distorted" from beginning to end. "*All* the tempos were wrong and, in addition, there were not *two measures* in a row performed in the same tempo!" Such an amateurish performance, Cui asserted, called into question the conservatory's frequent assertions about its usefulness and, especially, its attempts to cast itself as a "treasure house" of Russian culture.[56]

In 1871, Cui, referencing his earlier article, charged that graduating voice students lacked musical knowledge but were well able to "pervert" the classics of Russian opera.[57] This time, however, Cui's attacks called forth a vigorous rebuttal by Alexander Famintsyn. Castigating Cui for his underhanded and slanderous articles, Famintsyn accused him of trying to deceive the reading public with regard to the achievements of the conservatory, the leadership of conservatory director N. I. Zaremba, and the abilities of students. In particular, Famintsyn praised Zaremba for his efforts to acquaint the public with the day-to-day activities of the conservatory by opening the annual examinations to a limited public that included parents and relatives of students as well as interested music lovers.[58] Zaremba, in a sense, enabled Cui's attacks; by opening more student performances to the scrutiny of the public, he provided Cui with ammunition to relentlessly assault the conservatory.

For the students themselves, weekly recitals and public examinations provided an opportunity to prove their artistic mettle before their teachers, parents, and peers. Such performances could profoundly shape the emerging artistic sensibilities of artists-in-training. In her memoirs, Amfiteatrova-Levitskaia recalled the strong impression made on her by fellow students such as Alexander, "Sasha," Ziloti, who later became a leading piano virtuoso and prominent conductor. Such performances also strengthened the bonds between students and faculty and heightened their sense of loyalty to their alma mater. At the Moscow Conservatory, for example, Nikolai Rubinstein played the artistic paterfamilias, presiding over an informal salon at the intermission of student recitals. Students, faculty, and guests enjoyed abundant refreshments and good conversation; the second half of the performance was signaled not by a bell, but by Rubinstein, who rose from the table and returned to the hall, followed by the audience.[59]

Amfiteatrova-Levitskaia focused on the importance of weekly recitals in introducing conservatory students to a broad repertoire. Student recitals, unsurprisingly, showcased the solo repertoire and small chamber ensembles, although orchestral overtures and even symphonies were sometimes performed, usually under the direction of a student conductor. Separate symphonic concerts with an orchestra comprised entirely of students, a significant feat, further advertised the conservatory's successes. The first symphonic concert of the St. Petersburg Conservatory, presented on November 25, 1876, not only set the pattern for later concerts with its mixture of symphonic works and solo vocal and instrumental pieces, it also reminded the audience of the conservatory's ideological mission. The evening began with Beethoven's Fifth Symphony, a challenging and monumental work that explicitly expressed the conservatory's indebtedness and lineal connections to the best traditions of Western European art music. This was followed by four solo performances, with pianists and vocalists alternating. Dargomyzhsky's *Rusalka*, the first movement of Mozart's Piano Concerto in D Minor, an aria from Rossini's *Barber of Seville*, and two short piano pieces, a ballad by Chopin and a rhapsody by Liszt, outlined the borders of the conservatory's musical universe, before returning firmly home to pay homage to the father of Russian music, Mikhail Glinka, with the orchestra's performance of the overture to *Ruslan and Ludmila*.[60]

Reviews acknowledged both the significance of a student orchestra and the difficulty of sustaining one. In 1880, for example, one reviewer declared the establishment of a student orchestra and chorus capable of public performance to be one of Karl Davydov's most important achievements as director of the St. Petersburg Conservatory. For the first time, the orchestra consisted entirely of students; it boasted fifty-five members, including twenty-six violins, five violas, seven cellos, three basses, a full complement of orchestral winds, and even a harp. Its three concerts had featured symphonies and overtures by Mozart, Haydn, Beethoven, Glinka, and Mendelssohn, as well as smaller scale works for vocal and instrumental soloists. The repertoire won the critic's approval; while hardly innovative, it was both pedagogically appropriate and culturally useful, as it reacquainted the public with works, such as the Mozart and Haydn symphonies, no longer frequently programmed.[61]

Repertoire choices, however, were also fraught with danger. Students who performed pedagogical etudes, salon romances, or empty virtuoso pieces presented an easy target for hostile critics, who emphasized such vulgar choices as proof of the conservatories' failure to elevate the taste of their students, much less of Russian society. Conversely, the conservatory risked being labeled conservative, pedantic, and anti-Russian if, in an effort to discipline students' taste and expand their artistic range, performances emphasized classical pieces at the expense of more recent or more Russian repertoire. As the conservatories grew in size and public stature, student recitals grew increasingly diverse. Russian pieces appeared with greater frequency, as did new and innovative works by foreign composers, but they still shared the stage with technical showpieces of little aesthetic value. By the mid-1880s, Cui had tempered his style as a critic; he offered a balanced review of the St. Petersburg Conservatory's first public recital of 1885–1886, taking care to outline both students' professional strengths and their artistic limitations. Cui commended the pedagogical tone of the evening, which encouraged young performers to demonstrate their still-developing skills. He further praised the musicality, well-defined sense of rhythm, and self-possession displayed by many of the students. Only the repertoire provoked exasperation. Too many students chose music that was beyond their ability, while too few chose works by Russian composers.[62] Cui's complaints were at least somewhat justified. Concert programs from the St. Petersburg Conservatory show a clear preference for Baroque and Classical solo repertoire; Russian composers appeared more frequently on the programs of chamber ensembles and the student orchestra. More problematically, the required examination repertoire betrayed few Russian influences, although by 1912 the St. Petersburg Conservatory required graduating piano students to perform a Russian composition of their choice, in addition to a Bach fugue, a Beethoven sonata, and pieces by Mozart, Haydn, Schumann, Chopin, and Liszt. For most musicians, however, the greatest concern was not the lack of Russian repertoire, but the predominance of teaching pieces and technically brilliant but aesthetically arid works.[63] Still, as Cui had sardonically remarked in 1885, the absence of Russian repertoire and the fondness of the vocal soloists for French songs, French performance styles, and the French language sometimes left him wondering if he was at the Paris Conservatory or in St. Petersburg.[64]

Building the Temple of Art: The St. Petersburg and Moscow Conservatories

The physical presence of the conservatories testified in brick, mortar, and plaster to their importance to Russian cultural identity. During the nineteenth century, the St. Petersburg Conservatory moved to new quarters several times, with each move reflecting the changing public role of the institution. Its earliest home was in the apartments of its instructors and in the halls of the Mikhailovsky Palace, but such ad hoc arrangements quickly proved inadequate. The rental of more appropriate facilities provided much needed space but placed a considerable financial burden on the young institution. Consequently, early in the summer of 1865, Grand Duchess Elena Pavlovna asked the Ministry of Finance to allocate one of its buildings for the conservatory's free use. The ministry obliged, offering a building on Zagorodnyi prospekt. Although the conservatory quickly outgrew the building, the exchange established a precedent by which the state, although not accepting financial responsibility for the support of the conservatory, proved willing to ensure its institutional viability. The Society also continued to rely on the personal connections of its patron as it sought to move on to more spacious accommodations. Fortunately, the personal appeals of the Grand Duchess once again proved successful. Unfortunately, the building that was allocated to the Society, although in an ideal location on Theater Square, was in such a poor state of repair that even a 5,000-ruble grant from the tsar did not cover the required renovations.[65]

Renovations, however successful, could not conceal the new building's fundamental flaw: it lacked a large concert hall, which made student rehearsals difficult and left the Society's concert series without a permanent home. When the Society's efforts to acquire a former circus building as a concert hall met unexpected resistance from the St. Petersburg City Duma, one local paper used the occasion to attack the immaturity of Russian educated society. Praising music as a civilizing force, the author noted that all of the *civilized* capitals of Europe—Paris, Vienna, Brussels, London, Berlin, Milan, and so on—viewed a conservatory as a source of civic pride and provided it a correspondingly prominent place in the city center. With a caustic wit, the author wondered why the city's leaders seemed incapable of understanding the conservatory's cultural significance. The author sardonically imitated the line of reasoning he suggested the city's leaders must have followed in weighing the relative benefits of the circus and the conservatory:

> In 18** in the circus:
>
> The amazingly graceful lady rider Cherpito-Petipa first appeared, in an exceedingly short skirt. Every time she wiggled her little leg my heart went into spasms. Marvelous legs.
>
> In 18** in the conservatory:
>
> The violinist Tushilov graduated, whose hair is not jet black, as I prefer, but brownish. Tchaikovsky and Laroche also graduated from the conservatory, but they don't give me any pleasure and they don't wiggle their legs.[66]

By the mid-1880s, the St. Petersburg Conservatory's building was woefully inadequate. The student body had grown from less than two hundred students in 1862 to nearly eight hundred by the conservatory's twentieth anniversary. The building was cramped, dark, short of rehearsal and studio space, and, despite all efforts, still without a large concert hall. Efforts by the Society to use the conservatory's twenty-fifth anniversary to rectify the situation gained momentum early in 1888 when Anton Rubinstein, once again the director of the conservatory, brought its plight directly to Tsar

Alexander III's attention. Responding to Rubinstein's entreaties, the tsar visited the conservatory. His personal interest piqued, Alexander III bestowed the former Bolshoi Theater on the Society as a permanent home for the conservatory. The gift, however, came with strings attached: a supposedly strict proviso that no state funds be used for renovations or reconstruction. The tsar's admonition had little effect, however, as the Society used his generosity to manipulate the state into providing funds for the renovation. In the end, the state supplied nearly 2 million rubles for this project, covering the majority of its costs (see figure 3.3).

The cost of the reconstruction provoked consternation and outrage. *Syn otechestva* published a detailed—and damning—accounting of the construction costs. The leading music journal, *Russkaia muzykal'naia gazeta*, reprinted the report, drawing the musical community's attention to the threat implicit in the widening scandal. The St. Petersburg Conservatory, however, did not seem to understand the explosive situation. It attempted to use the project to stake a greater claim to state support, arguing that the maintenance of the new facility created expenses that its traditional sources of funding—tuition fees, modest subsidies, and so on—could not cover. Petitioning via the Main Directorate, the St. Petersburg branch demanded that the state accept its responsibility to adequately fund specialized music education. "Higher

FIGURE 3.3. "A. G. Rubinstein, V. A. Kologrivov, and A. F. Berngard at the Construction Site of the St. Petersburg Conservatory." Permission of the Russian Institute for the History of the Arts, St. Petersburg (fond 3, op. 4, no. 429)

musical educational institutions," it argued, "should be regarded as generally useful state institutions," noting that "similar institutions abroad, such as the Paris and Brussels conservatories," were fully supported by their governments. The branch requested a 100,000-ruble addition to the conservatory's annual subsidy of 15,000 rubles, justifying this dramatic increase by comparing it to state support for the Russian Academy of Arts (300,000 rubles annually) and the Paris Conservatory (1 million francs, or 250,000–375,000 rubles).[67] For its part, *Syn otechestva* doubted the conservatory's ability to save itself from its fiscal plight by persuading the state either to increase the subsidy or to accept it as a state institution. Citing the abundant circulation of "untrustworthy" information, *Syn otechestva* published a strict chronology of the project that emphasized its high cost and suggested the financial irresponsibility, if not outright dishonesty, of the Russian Musical Society.[68]

As *Syn otechestva* noted, it was the Society's request in 1897 for a final 505,000 rubles to complete the project that angered the State Council and prompted an official investigation. Only a year before, the state approved a 100,000-ruble appropriation on the condition that the Society submit no further funding requests. Although the new request was eventually approved, it provoked the ire of the Minister of Finance, Sergei Witte, who attempted to use the controversy to rescind the conservatory's annual state subsidy. Fortunately for the conservatory, the Ministry of Internal Affairs successfully resisted this proposal, arguing that the subsidy supported the Russian Musical Society's worthy educational efforts not the construction project.[69] The state, by repeatedly acquiescing to the conservatory's requests for construction funds, only encouraged further demands. In October 1897, the conservatory submitted yet another request, this time for nearly 50,000 rubles. Despite strong objections within the Ministry of Internal Affairs, the proposal was forwarded to the State Council on the grounds that Tsar Alexander III's support of the project created a moral obligation to see it through to completion. The State Council, however, had had its fill of the conservatory and the Russian Musical Society by this point. It rejected the petition, a decision upheld by the reigning tsar, Nicholas II.[70]

The controversy over the construction project notwithstanding, the new conservatory building figured prominently in St. Petersburg cultural life (see figure 3.4). A glittering public, including both Tsar Nicholas II and his wife Alexandra, attended its official opening on November 12, 1896. The list of dignitaries in attendance stretched for several column inches in *Novosti i birzhevaia gazeta*, including not only the imperial family but also leading government figures, such as the chair of the Committee of Ministers, I. N. Durnovo, and the Minister of Internal Affairs, N. L. Goremykin. Minister of

FIGURE 3.4. "The St. Petersburg Conservatory." Permission of the Prints Division, Russian National Library, St. Petersburg

Finance Witte was also in attendance, no doubt with mixed feelings. Once everyone was seated, guests were greeted by the ironic figure of Cesar Cui, once a diehard opponent of the Russian Musical Society, now delivering a celebratory speech as the chair of its St. Petersburg branch.[71]

In Moscow, the conservatory struggled in rented premises unintended for the needs of music study and rehearsal. Although the Moscow Conservatory grew more slowly than its counterpart in St. Petersburg did, by the mid-1880s it was almost literally bursting at the seams. Rather than relocate the conservatory, the Moscow branch decided to build a new, enlarged structure in the same location. Funds for this project came from a variety of sources that reflected both Moscow's secondary rank in Russia's cultural hierarchy and the conservatory's significance for local society. It was less easy for the Moscow Conservatory to lay claim to state support. As a result, the conservatory turned to Grand Duke Sergei Aleksandrovich, the appointed administrator of the city and an honorary member of the Moscow branch of the Society, whose personal intercession persuaded the tsar to release 400,000 rubles for the new building.[72] Gifts from private individuals, particularly the 200,000 rubles donated by G. G. Solodovnikov to the conservatory in 1891, played a larger role in Moscow than in the capital.[73] Nevertheless, state grants and private donations did not cover all the expenses, forcing the Moscow branch to assume a burdensome loan.

As in St. Petersburg, the opening of the new conservatory was celebrated with pomp, although the guest list reflected less the might of the empire and more the elite of Moscow. The official pamphlet commemorating the occasion included some thirty pages of celebratory greetings and congratulatory telegrams from a wide array of individuals and social organizations. Although the tsar sent only a formulaic statement of best wishes, the offerings of individuals and organizations more closely connected to the Moscow Conservatory reflected its centrality to local cultural life. The Russian Choral Society uniquely chose to pay tribute in song to those responsible for creating a "temple" that was both "new" and "pure."[74] Conservatory director V. I. Safonov highlighted the symbolism of the concert hall's decoration for the audience, noting that the images of the great symphonic composers that graced it "clearly" showed the "unity of our country with the entire educated world." Safonov also christened the hall as an incubator of the glory of Russian music, expressing the hope that the composers enshrined on its walls would "serve as examples for many generations." With such models to follow, Safonov suggested, perhaps it would be "our dear motherland" that would give "a new Beethoven to the world."[75]

Although the expense of these building projects aroused much criticism, the new conservatory buildings nevertheless successfully performed their practical and ideological functions. The conservatories now possessed both large and small concert halls, adequate rehearsal facilities, and interior layouts designed with the noise levels of musical instruction in mind. Although an efficient layout and a functional design were important, so was the embedding of a triumphant mythology of Russian musical culture. As ethnomusicologist Bruno Nettl has argued regarding twentieth-century American conservatories and university music schools, the physical structure and decoration of these institutions self-consciously reflect their artistic values and cultural ethos.[76] The newly finished Russian conservatories were intended, both figuratively and literally, to be temples of art. An appropriate pantheon of gods, saints, and martyrs adorned each building. Subsequent embellishments fleshed out the Society's narrative of Russian music and literally set it in stone.

The Small Hall of the Moscow Conservatory, because of its primary role as a space for student performances, was decorated in a didactic fashion. It was adorned with portraits of Alexander II, "under whom the Conservatory was founded," Alexander III, "who contributed the initial funds for the construction of the building," and Nicholas II, the reigning monarch. In short, the portraits were intended to remind students and audience members of the paternalistic benevolence of these rulers, emphasizing and exaggerating their role as patrons of Russian musical culture. Portraits of grand duchesses Elena Pavlovna and Alexandra Iosifovna, both important patrons of the Society, graced the foyer, again making explicit the indebtedness of the conservatory to the imperial family. A portrait of Grand Duke Konstantin Nikolaevich, as well as a bronze plaque noting the dates of the founding of the conservatory and the construction of the building, further linked the past, present, and future of the conservatory, the Russian Musical Society, and its imperial patrons. A marble plaque in the entry hall listed the names of students who had graduated with gold medals, while a bas-relief sculpture of Nikolai Rubinstein dignified the keystone arch of the stage, transforming him into an immortal observer of the concerts held there. The inaugural concert coincided with the fifth anniversary of the death of Tchaikovsky, which afforded a not-to-be-missed opportunity to stake a claim to the legacy of the composer who had "given his best years" to the conservatory. The opening concert consisted solely of works by Tchaikovsky, performed entirely by students.[77]

The large concert hall did not open until 1901. The gala inaugural concert highlighted the contributions of Russia's greatest composers, featuring works that remain central to the national canon, including Glinka's overture to *Ruslan and Ludmila*, Tchaikovsky's symphonic poem *Francesca de Rimini*, and Borodin's *On the Steppes of Central Asia*. A performance of the festive overture composed by Anton Rubinstein for the opening of the new St. Petersburg Conservatory building reminded the audience of the interconnectedness of the two institutions. The final work was Beethoven's Ninth Symphony, declared by Safonov "the greatest work in instrumental music."[78] Once again, the decoration of the hall reinforced the Russian Musical Society's preferred narrative of Russian musical development. The visual symbols they chose emphasized the emerging importance of Russian music in European culture. Fourteen portraits graced the hall—not simply of composers but of "the great creators of symphonic music." Only four of these titans were Russian: Glinka, Tchaikovsky, Anton Rubinstein, and Borodin. Glinka, of course, symbolized the beginnings of Russian symphonic music. Tchaikovsky's right to such honors was indisputable, but Rubinstein represented a choice that reflected less his ability as a symphonic composer than it did his importance as the founder of the Russian Musical Society. The four Russians joined the illustrious company of Bach, Handel, Haydn, Beethoven, Mozart, Schubert, Schumann, Mendelssohn, Gluck, and Wagner, while the "portraits were arranged so that the Russian composers were placed in the corners, framing the representations of the remaining composers." Glinka and Tchaikovsky held places of honor in the front of the hall flanking the stage; Borodin and Rubinstein presided over the rear. The "foreign" composers paraded in pairs on opposite sides of the hall in an order that reflected the "type and ... the character" of their creative work. Mozart and Handel, Haydn and Schubert, Mendelssohn and Schumann, Wagner and Gluck trailed Bach and Beethoven. The placement of the portraits reflected careful deliberations by the construction commission, who sought the advice of "competent persons from the musical world." As in the Small Hall, Nikolai Rubinstein watched over his heirs. His portrait graced the foyer, while a bas-relief medallion was again set in "the keystone of the arch." At the entrance to the hall itself, bronze busts of the "eternal custodians of pure art—Bach and Beethoven" reminded audience members of the significance of the experience they were about to share.[79] In both capitals and, as we shall see in chapter 5, in the provinces, the dedication of new buildings allowed the Society's branches to demonstrate their centrality to local cultural life. In Moscow, however, the construction commission used the elaborate symbolic representation of European music encoded in the design and decoration of the conservatory concert halls to reinforce the Society's claim to a formative role in Russian musical life.

The Temple and the Factory

Even before their foundation, the Russian conservatories were embroiled in debates over their place and purpose in society. Predictably, over the years this led to a number of efforts to reform these "temples of art," most of which revisited the same issues: the structure of the student body, the content of the curriculum, and the financial reliance on tuition fees. In the 1860s, disagreements over the curriculum, student body, and graduation standards prompted Anton Rubinstein's angry departure from the St. Petersburg Conservatory. In his absence, Grand Duchess Elena Pavlovna led an attempt to reshape the conservatory into a practical training ground for orchestral musicians. This rejection of Rubinstein's vision of an elite academy for artists provoked much resistance, however, and was implemented tentatively at best. Although some viewed such reforms as an attempt to divert the conservatories from their "true" task as higher musical educational institutions, such a reading oversimplified the situation. The proponents of a more practically oriented conservatory were not necessarily aesthetic philistines. They dedicated themselves to the transformation of Russian musical life through the training of a large cohort of rank-and-file musicians rather than a tiny number of elite composers and performers. One might argue that they were visionary reformers, who accurately assessed the cultural needs of the Russian Empire, rather than reactionaries. Moreover, a greater focus on the training of orchestral musicians would have more closely aligned the Russian conservatories with the Western European peer institutions they most frequently compared themselves to, particularly the Leipzig Conservatory. The persistent failure of their opponents to preserve the conservatory as a training ground for the musical elite only reinforced the validity of a practical or artisanal understanding of the conservatory. In any case, despite differences over the means, the goal was still the same: the creation of a class of Russian music professionals with the credentials and the training necessary to secure their position in society.

Conflicts over the purpose of the St. Petersburg Conservatory, for example, created "internal dissonance"—Evgeny Albrekht's term for contradictions in the structure and organization of the institution. More than twenty-five years after its founding, Albrekht charged, the conservatory still had "no clear understanding of what kind of people we educate, what role each of them should play in the musical profession," and had yet to even effectively consider the question of exactly how "to create *useful* musicians" out of the mass of unexceptional students. The result of this confusion was an indistinct and unfocused curriculum and instructional method, exacerbated by the tendency for internal "revolutions" every time a new conservatory director was appointed.[80] The conservatories, Albrekht charged, fundamentally failed Russian society by continually falling short in their social and artistic mission. Students enrolled for five or even ten years, but their employment prospects remained limited because their artistic education was based on elitist ideas of art. Consequently, naïve graduates rapidly grew disillusioned with the brutal realities of the musical profession. In response, Albrekht formulated an ambitious plan to convert the conservatories into practical training grounds for working musicians, while simultaneously advocating a wholesale transformation of Russian musical life. Rather than trying to meet *all* of Russia's musical needs, rather than trying to educate "both small children and adults," both "soldiers" and "little girls," both illiterates and university graduates under "one and the same roof," the reimagined Russian conservatories would copy the practices of some West European peer institutions, particularly the German conservatories, and focus solely on advanced professional training. The course of study would not exceed two or three years in length, with a curriculum that excluded all general education courses, basic theoretical musical subjects, and preparatory or intermediate instruction in applied music specialties.[81]

Mirroring the conflict that drove Anton Rubinstein from the St. Petersburg Conservatory in 1867, Albrekht rejected Rubinstein's elitist vision and rehabilitated the idea of a musical factory designed to train, polish, and send out into the world highly qualified and experienced musical artisans. Bewailing what he saw as a continued dependence on foreign musicians, Albrekht made the training of orchestral performers a matter of national pride. "Russia," he argued, "needs musicians of all categories. We need orchestras of various kinds, for artistic and celebratory goals, for theaters, for the circuses, for balls and (pleasure) gardens." Implicit in this was the threat that, if Russia did not respond by training more orchestral musicians, then the flood "of itinerant foreigners" would increase in response to the professional opportunities presented by "the continual development of social life." Instead of "Germans or Czechs," Albrekht wanted to see orchestras staffed by Russians. Unapologetically adopting the language of industry, Albrekht insisted that as the "only purveyor of professional musicians of all types," the Russian conservatories needed to accept their true role and "get started 'manufacturing' the materials we need."[82]

Albrekht's reform proposal was not simply a matter of restructuring the conservatory curriculum or rethinking admissions policies. The limited role of the West European conservatories that he so praised depended on the broad availability of elementary education, including orderly and effective instruction in singing and music, as well as a strong tradition of musical guilds, city orchestras, and theaters. Albrekht's proposal therefore called not only for a reconsideration of the role of the conservatory, but also for the broad musical education of society as a whole and the democratization of cultural life. Although this implied a dramatic increase in the Russian Musical Society's sphere of activity, Albrekht offered one final proposal that, if realized, would have fundamentally altered the relationship of the Society, its branches, and their educational institutions to each other, to the state, and to Russian society: the formal subordination of music education to state control.

Although Albrekht's pamphlet was intended to spark discussion within the musical world, the debate over the purpose of the conservatories attracted the attention of a broader public as well. Above all, the dominance of young female pianists drew the ire of social and cultural critics. Reviewing a student concert at the Moscow Conservatory in 1895, *Russkaia mysl'* revealed the truth behind the conservatory's façade: far from being a refuge for the cultivation of art and artists, the conservatory had become no better than any other private piano school in the city. Both this student concert and the conservatory as a whole displayed a chronic overabundance of pianists and a woeful lack of performers on orchestral instruments. The fault was not entirely the conservatory's, however. Society was blamed for its devotion to the "fad" of music education, which led inevitably to a glut of pianists as "even the deaf and blind" could master the instrument. Like Albrekht, this critic identified the crucial problem as a financial one: because the conservatory remained dependent on tuition payments, it was forced to encourage and enable the public's obsession with the piano.[83]

By the 1890s, the Russian Musical Society came under fire for its failure to maintain uniform standards in the St. Petersburg and Moscow conservatories. Eduard Napravnik, notably, highlighted the continuing disconnection between applied and theoretical subjects in the curriculum. Although "in the majority of cases" students achieved "fully satisfactory or even excellent," results in their applied performance subjects, their work in required subjects could not be regarded as either "brilliant or even satisfactory." The silently condoned devaluation of theoretical subjects, he argued, threatened the professional status of conservatory graduates. Because of their inadequate theoretical musical education, such individuals could not be considered "members of the musical intelligentsia." Napravnik noted that students themselves recognized and exploited the "condescending" attitude toward required theoretical subjects and rebuked the conservatory's administration for its hypocrisy in advertising that "it issues diplomas and attestats only to those who have passed exams in all applied and required subjects" while failing to address a situation where "huge numbers" of students studied for years while only the "smallest percentage" of students actually completed their training and graduated. Napravnik insisted "all those who do not wish or are unable to satisfactorily and successfully pass annual examinations in both applied and required subjects should be dismissed." Although he recognized that some would see this measure as too "strict," even "inhuman," he believed that it would benefit both the conservatories and society in the long term. In addition, he argued for a more streamlined and straightforward curriculum that would produce experienced and theoretically knowledgeable performers, arguing that "those who cannot use their theoretical knowledge in practice" are not true artists. The central issue, however, was the Society's ever-growing network of educational institutions and their ever-increasing student bodies. The Society, he noted, had a tendency to admit everyone, regardless of whether they had ability or not, in order to pay the bills, despite the fact that the majority of these students lacked "any potential for musical development" and therefore constituted nothing more than "an undesirable and harmful musical proletariat." Such practices, he insisted, contradicted the artistic goals of the Society and the purpose of its educational institutions, especially the conservatories. "Private schools and instructors," he argued, "may be served by the motto, Not Quality but Quantity, but the music classes, schools, and, in particular, the conservatories of the Imperial Russian Musical Society should be guided [by the motto] Not Quantity but Quality."[84]

Without question, many other musicians and cultural critics shared Napravnik's assessment of the detrimental effects of exponential growth. Few, however, offered practical solutions to alleviate the Society's dependence on student tuition payments. Whether favoring a vision of the conservatory as a temple or as a factory, musicians and cultural critics persisted in seeing the conservatory as a professional school and consequently failed to recognize its broader social and cultural functions. Still, the tremendous growth of the St. Petersburg and Moscow conservatories forced the Russian Musical Society to confront, once again, the conflict between the stated purpose of these "higher musical education institutions" and the ways they had been appropriated by the educated public. In 1907, A. I. Puzyrevsky argued for the reinvigoration of the St. Petersburg Conservatory, revisiting in the process the familiar debate over its professional and cultural purpose. Like Albrekht, Puzyrevsky argued that the conservatory should be a purely higher educational institution, offering "only professional courses" to students who already had acquired a basic musical education and who possessed adequate technical proficiency. Admission to the reorganized conservatory would be by competitive examination; students would also be subject to strict, and implicitly much narrower, age limitations at enrollment. Minor children would no longer study with adults, as Puzyrevsky hoped that the reorganized conservatory would admit only the "truly talented" (*deistvitel'no talantlivie litsa*). The success of his plan, however, hinged on better financing because, while advocating a substantial reduction in the student body, Puzyrevsky also called for a substantial increase in monetary support for successful applicants.[85]

The conservatory as both an institution and an idea remained the controversial focal point for debates on the structure and purpose of Russian musical life up until the revolutions of 1917 and, in fact, well beyond that point. In 1916, the debate over the purpose of the conservatory shaped E. Bogoslovsky's evaluation of the Moscow Conservatory's graduation examinations, which he attended on behalf of the Main Directorate. Bogoslovsky complained of a lack of rigor in instruction, the poor preparation of many students, and highly uneven repertoire. Bogoslovsky's comments, however, must be interpreted in light of his firm faith in the conservatory as a temple for the training of true artists. Intent on solidifying the conservatory's role as gatekeeper for the musical profession, Bogoslovsky advocated a clearer differentiation between those who graduated with a diploma and the title of free artist and those who graduated with an *attestat*.[86] The patron and chair of the Russian Musical Society, Elena Grigorievna Saksen-Altenburgskaia, shared Bogoslovsky's concerns. Nevertheless, the protests of elite musicians and cultural critics appeared to be futile. Music students, most of them pianists, most of them female, and most of them bourgeois, continued to enroll in the conservatories by the thousands. Both the temple of art and the musical factory were overwhelmed. Responding to Saksen-Altenburgskaia's proposal for a conference on the issue, M. M. Ippolitov-Ivanov, the director of the Moscow Conservatory, noted that his faculty council had frequently discussed but never successfully addressed the impact of growth on the quality of instruction. Although Ippolitov-Ivanov considered "the desire for knowledge completely natural" and therefore "not a threat" to Russian music, the conservatory faculty council believed that "the very organization of musical education" was "estranged from real life."[87]

When the proposed meeting finally took place, in January and March 1917, the greatest threat to the conservatories was increasingly the unsettled political situation rather than the student body. Nevertheless, the conservatory, in Russia and elsewhere, remained a poorly defined institution that, consequently, was open to constant renegotiation over its purpose. Throughout the nineteenth century and into the twentieth, conservatories struggled to reconcile the inherent tension between their avowedly professional goals and their broader role as incubators of more general cultural advancement. This was certainly the case in Russia. After more than fifty years, the Russian conservatories still struggled to define their institutional identity and their role in Russian society. Neither the "temple of art" envisaged by Anton Rubinstein nor the "musical factory" triumphed because educated society, despite the admonitions of critics, remained in a love affair with the piano and co-opted the conservatories for their own purposes.

CHAPTER 4

Conflicted Identities

The Professionalization of Russian Musical Life

IN A FAMOUS ARTICLE, ANTON Rubinstein argued that the absence of a musical profession in Russia was a consequence of musicians' failure to persuade the state to "give music . . . the same privileges accorded to the other arts" and to "give those involved in music the *civic status of artist*."[1] Rubinstein attacked Russia's dilettantes, insisting that "only amateurs are involved in music in Russia." For Rubinstein, the natural solution to this crisis was the establishment of an institution intended to foster, train, and legitimize a musical profession—the modern conservatory. Rubinstein's inflammatory statements, predictably, provoked a stormy, but surprisingly conflicted response. Most famously, the Balakirev Circle and its proponents tarred Rubinstein and the conservatory with the brush of "German pedantry," and lauded the creativity and originality of Russian "amateur" composers and musicians, all supposedly untainted by the heavy hand of German scholasticism.

The widely circulated daily newspaper *Nashe vremia* hinted at the broader intellectual resonance of the debate when it declared, "How can one not agree with [Rubinstein], that in music (and really just in music?), our scourge and curse is dilettantism. We are amateurs almost all, in almost everything, starting with playing at the piano, or the violin, and ending with playing at industry and science."[2] As this comment suggests, musical professionalization in Russia needs to be understood both as part of a broader process of social modernization, particularly the development of the professions and their role within the Russian and European middle classes, and as a reflection of anxieties latent in Russian cultural life, particularly the fear of inadequacy and inferiority vis-à-vis Western Europe.

During the nineteenth century, whether in Russia or in Western Europe, teachers, lawyers, university professors, pharmacists, and many others participated in complex negotiations with the state and educated society, seeking to securely establish the boundaries between themselves and dilettantes, amateurs, and lay practitioners, to establish recognized standards for entry into their profession, and to acquire the rights and privileges they felt appropriate to their corporate status. In Russia, professionals in general emerged slowly as a distinct social and political group. Indeed, scholars have argued that the Russian middle class, including members of the professions, developed their identity largely by defining what they were not: "They were not gentry, not *chinovniki*, not peasants."[3] At the same time, as Kendall Bailes has argued, Russian professionals as a group, although numerically small and lacking a strong corporate or political identity, played a critical role in the transformation of social and cultural life in the late imperial period. Although Bailes notes that the "record of Russian professions in effecting successful social change" was "much more mixed than in the case of Victorian Britain," he argues that "the frustration of professionals at the slowness of change and their anger at the bureaucratic obstacles to effective practice of their professions contributed considerably to the disillusionment of educated Russian society with the tsarist system." Yet, as Bailes notes, Russian professionals, despite their claims to "autonomy and self-regulation," constantly negotiated their status with an interventionist state that both "helped to bring into being most of the modern professional occupations" and sought to control and direct how those professions were practiced.[4]

Musicians, however, experienced particular difficulties in gaining recognition as a legitimate profession.[5] Throughout Europe, desire for professional legitimacy drove the institutionalization of music education during the nineteenth century; these new institutions could serve both as gatekeepers to the profession and as repositories of the expert and esoteric knowledge of the professional. Everywhere, conservatories reshaped not only musical training but also the status of musicians, now credentialed, certified, formally trained, and possessing, especially if they were the directors of these new institutions, an independent professional role and a prominent place in local society.[6] Yet, despite the rapid acceptance of conservatories, musicians frequently still relied on apprenticeship and other traditional forms of training, a practice that, however expedient for an individual musician, nevertheless undermined the claims of musicians as a class to professional standing. Moreover, not only did the working members of this would-be profession subvert the musical elite's agenda, amateur musicians refused to relinquish their place within musical life. Musicians across the continent fretted over the insidious influence of dilettantes, who remained unwilling to accept subordination to professionals. They worried about the dominance of foreigners who robbed native musicians of scarce jobs and opportunities and undermined the national character of musical life. The conflict was gendered as well, as male musicians debated the "problem" of excessive numbers of female pianists, their implications for professionalization, and the challenge of women's incursion into orchestral playing, previously a male preserve.[7]

If musical professionalization was a thorny problem throughout Europe, it was particularly difficult in the Russian Empire. Musicians struggled to define themselves as a professional group, a status that was fundamentally contingent on the dismantling of serfdom. Although musicians across Europe were engaged in an extended transformation from an artisan class into a profession, in Russia an outdated estate system and a tradition of serf musicians delayed this transition. At mid-century, gender, social status, and national origin divided musicians in Russia into discrete subsets: foreign artists, Russian artisans, and respectable dilettantes. In a society still legally dominated by social estates, Russian-born musicians, composers, and singers lacked any mechanism to secure official recognition of their professional abilities or even the credentials they had earned through study abroad. Consequently, the ability of the conservatory to convey both academic credentials and professional legitimacy was particularly important for Russian musicians.

Anton Rubinstein often related an anecdote purporting to illustrate his own vain attempts to secure official recognition of his professional status. In the anecdote, Rubinstein stymies a clerk at the Kazan Cathedral. Who, the clerk asks, is Rubinstein? Rubinstein replies that he is a musician—an artist. The clerk, seeking clarification, inquires whether Rubinstein serves in the Imperial Theaters. Rubinstein's negative response confuses the clerk, who repeatedly seeks to find the appropriate pigeonhole for the pianist. Finally, in exasperation, the clerk asks Rubinstein who his father was. The response: his father was a merchant of the second guild. Much relieved, the clerk is able to record Rubinstein in his "proper" place—the son of a merchant of the second guild.[8]

This often-repeated anecdote illustrates the professional aspirations of musicians and the inability of Russia's narrow estate categories to accommodate them. It also hints at the crucial role the state would play in the construction of a musical profession and the development of musical life. Through the pursuit of state recognition of its conservatories and music schools, the Russian Musical Society legitimized specialized music education and created the legal structure for the Russian musical profession.

Dividing Lines: Defining the Roles of Dilettantes and Professionals

The establishment of a Russian musical profession—at least from Rubinstein's point of view—required the elimination of dilettantism, which he equated with all that was vulgar and crass. Making no secret of his desire to force dilettantes and amateurs into what he saw as their rightful place—a seat in the audience—Rubinstein insisted that it was the prominence of dilettantes, as well as poor professional preparation, that had retarded the development of Russian musical life.[9] Rubinstein's determination to professionalize music promised to narrow the scope of amateur musical activity, prompting one of those much-reviled amateurs, Arkady Rakhmaninov, to defend the right of nonprofessionals to participate in public musical life. Rubinstein had "decided the fate of the amateur; if he must play, then he should only play for himself, for his own pleasure, as apparently amateurs had once been inclined to entertain the public for money!" Rubinstein belittled the salon romances and amateurish operas composed by dilettantes, insisting that they neither had nor could acquire the skill necessary to successfully create original works. Rubinstein, Rakhmaninov argued, fundamentally misunderstood the social function and emotional role of music. What did it matter if amateurs composed inadequate, ineffective, or even inartistic romances for their own enjoyment? For professionals, the theoretical aspects of music were crucial to the achievement of their larger professional and artistic goals and they gave these subjects serious and strict attention. For amateurs, music was not a trade or profession but a means of fruitfully occupying their free time. Although amateurs rarely had the time or inclination to seriously study the science of music, this did not, Rakhmaninov argued, eliminate the desire to compose and create. With some exasperation, Rakhmaninov insisted that amateurs who composed little pieces in "romantic" minor keys could not possibly pose the threat to the science and profession of music that Rubinstein seemed to imagine.[10]

Regardless of the polemical debates in the press, the real struggle for musical professionalization took place behind the scenes, as the Russian Musical Society negotiated with the state over the laws and regulations applicable to the conservatories, their faculty, and their graduates. The initial charter governing the St. Petersburg Conservatory, subsequently extended to the Moscow Conservatory, outlined the curriculum, entrance and graduation requirements, and the privileges attached to conservatory diplomas.[11] The 1861 charter awarded conservatory graduates the title of free artist (*svobodnyi khudozhnik*), a professional status similar to that awarded to graduates of the state-supported Academy of Arts. Graduation from the Academy of Arts entitled non-nobles to elevation to the social estate (*soslovie*) of honored citizen, which conferred personal respectability as well as professional recognition. For Jewish graduates, moreover, honored citizenship brought the right to reside outside the Pale of Settlement. By awarding honored citizenship to conservatory graduates, the state would recognize the conservatory and, by extension, the music profession as legitimate actors in Russian society.[12]

Although scholars have often seen the title of free artist as the major turning point in the professionalization of Russian music, the title itself was largely symbolic. It was the rights it conveyed, particularly elevation to the status of honored citizen, that gave the title practical significance. However, the proposal to extend honored citizenship to conservatory graduates provoked resistance among government ministers who were striving to limit pathways to higher social status for peasants and townspeople. Although the conservatory and the Russian Musical Society appeared to triumph when the Committee of Ministers ruled in 1876 that conservatory graduates were entitled to the same rights as their peers from the Academy of Arts, their victory turned out to be a hollow one as law codes and supporting legal documents were not amended to reflect this decision. Consequently, the rights of conservatory graduates long remained open to interpretation. Intriguingly, during the approval process for the conservatory charter, the Committee of Ministers had attempted to define the minimum qualifications that would entitle graduating students to inclusion in the ranks of credentialed, professional musicians. Only musicians with a sophisticated understanding of the theoretical basis of music, as well as technical facility on an instrument, would receive the title of free artist.[13]

This stricture, intended to limit the number of individuals advancing in social rank through a conservatory education, also fit neatly with Anton Rubinstein's ideal of the professional musician, who was distinguished from amateurs or artisans by the depth of his aesthetic and theoretical knowledge. The theoretical and aesthetic education of conservatory-trained professionals both provided a means to distinguish them from the technically adroit but theoretically unsophisticated artisanal class of working musicians and provided a rationale to insist on their inclusion in respectable, educated society alongside their less musically skilled but better educated amateur counterparts.[14] The changing status of V. V. Bessel, later a prominent music publisher, reveals both the significance and the practical limitations of acquiring professional standing via a conservatory education. In December 1865, Bessel graduated from the St. Petersburg Conservatory with a diploma and the title of free artist. Of the seven members of this first graduating class, three were listed as foreigners (Albrekht, Gommilius, and Reikhardt), two as members of the nobility (Tchaikovsky and Kross), one as the son of a Collegiate Secretary (Rybasov), and one—Bessel—as the son of a citizen of Riga.[15] In 1866, Grand Duchess Elena Pavlovna successfully petitioned to have Bessel removed from the tax registers. Bessel's petition for elevation to honored citizenship proved a far more protracted process; although submitted in 1868, it was approved only in 1871.[16]

Despite the delays, Bessel's elevation set a precedent for the approval of similar petitions by later graduates. Yet, the rights of conservatory graduates, and by extension the status of the musical profession, were far from secure. The expansion of the Russian Musical Society to Kiev, Kharkov, and other provincial cities generated a need to update the conservatory charter. The charter of 1878 codified elite musicians' assumptions that educational deficiencies prevented musicians from attaining a respectable position in society. In response, the new charter required students to supply proof of a secondary education before they could be awarded a conservatory diploma; to facilitate this, the charter mandated the inclusion of general education classes in the conservatory curriculum. Despite these changes meant to elevate the standing of conservatory graduates and the musical profession, the new charter worked against their interests because it inadvertently contained language restricting the rights of conservatory graduates. It failed to secure the right to the status of honored citizen, instead specifying only that graduates from the lower estates must petition for removal from the tax registers in order to be awarded the title of free artist. This attempt to clarify the rights of conservatory graduates effectively separated the title (*zvanie*) of free artist from the status (*soslovie*) of honored citizen.[17]

Similarly, the legal position of conservatory and music school faculty remained weak, an especially dangerous state of affairs as they were the elite of the Russian musical profession. Although the 1878 charter explicitly stated that conservatory professors were "considered to be in state service," their service rights were highly restricted.[18] Unlike other professionals, conservatory professors were not entitled to automatic promotion based on their time in service; advancement in rank required the personal request of the chair of the Society.[19] Sensitive to the ambiguous status of its faculty and graduates, the

Russian Musical Society attempted to use its achievements as a lever to extract concessions from the state. In 1883, in a memo to the tsar, Senator A. N. Markovich touted the Society's success in disseminating music education and enlightenment across Russia in an attempt to demonstrate the need for state recognition and financial support.[20] Just a few years later, in 1887, the Society seized the occasion of the twenty-fifth anniversary of the St. Petersburg Conservatory to petition for faculty pension rights. Borrowing liberally from Markovich's essay, the Society argued that it had created a Russian musical profession that was of service both to the state and to society. It enumerated the conservatory graduates who had gone on to careers as orchestral and operatic performers on the imperial stages and as instructors in the Society's educational institutions, state secondary schools, and private music schools. Little by little, they argued, Russian musicians, trained in Russian conservatories, were replacing foreigners as bandmasters, singers, orchestral musicians, and music teachers.[21] Despite the youth of the Russian conservatories in comparison to their Western European counterparts, they insisted, the results achieved by the St. Petersburg Conservatory in its first twenty-five years of existence proved the "enormous usefulness" of the "serious study of the musical arts." "Those who devote themselves to the peaceful study of music," they argued, "disseminate in society a love and taste for music," while the study of music "deflects many away from reprehensible ways of spending time" and, in general, "assists in elevating the moral spirit of society." Such moralistic arguments failed to convince the hard-nosed Ministry of Finance, which denied the petition; conservatory faculty received pension rights only in 1905.[22]

Despite official resistance, the Society continued to press for improvements in the status of conservatory faculty and graduates. During his second tenure as director of the St. Petersburg Conservatory (1887–1891), Anton Rubinstein pushed the Society's Main Directorate to address the issue of musicians' status. Despite the precedent set with Bessel's elevation to honored citizen, the Senate had recently denied similar petitions by conservatory graduates because the legal codes did not explicitly confer such rights. Rubinstein noted that the limited rights explicitly provided in the 1878 charter, particularly "removal from the tax registers," had lost their social significance and no longer "constitute[d] a privilege."[23] What was needed to guarantee recognition of professional standing was the state's explicit acceptance that a conservatory diploma conferred higher social status, through the unconditional awarding of the status of honored citizen to graduates from lower social estates. The state's reluctance to acquiesce reflects the provisional status of music as a profession. If, as Bailes has argued, "the dilemma" for most professional groups was how "to free themselves from the tutelage of the state, while still using the state for their own ends," musicians in Russia first needed to borrow the state's prestige to acquire even limited recognition as professionals.[24] Whereas better-established professions frequently balked at the state's intrusiveness into their internal affairs, the music profession struggled to attract the state's attention.

The role of the state, in some sense, in certifying professional status through the awarding of ranks and titles did provoke some controversy within the musical community. Although the state could confer legal rights and recognition, subordination to the state potentially threatened professional autonomy and institutional independence. In 1889, in a broad-ranging report on the status of the Russian Musical Society, conservatory professor Karl Zike mocked the notion that musicians' stature as artists would be threatened if they became *chinovniki* (bureaucrats); such recognition did not threaten the dignity of physicians or other recognized professionals. Lack of recognition, he suggested, threatened the material interests of musicians. Their insecure social position forced them to humiliate themselves and petition for ranks and awards. Diverging from the Society's focus on practical rights, Zike emphasized status, arguing that rank, *chin*, was the key to professional standing. Musicians employed by the imperial theaters, Zike noted, had rights to state pensions but not to *chin*. "Better they should award us *chin* without a pension," he insisted, as the government did for doctors, lawyers, and other independent professionals. The granting of rank would both "impart moral authority" and "improve the social position" of musicians.[25]

Yet, the value of *chin* for the musical profession was not universally recognized. In 1891, Anton Rubinstein proposed a series of changes to the Society's governing charters, including the incorporation of the St. Petersburg Conservatory into the state educational system and the transformation of the Kiev Music School into a second, state-run conservatory. In the face of resistance to his project from both the state and the Russian Musical Society, Rubinstein complained bitterly of the "fictitious" appointments of conservatory faculty to class rank. He claimed that if the conservatories remained private institutions "then the awarding of *chin*... is a joke, because [these rights] are fictitious, and neither in the eyes of the public, nor in the eyes of students, nor in the eyes of the state, do they have or can they have any significance whatsoever."[26] Despite Rubinstein's complaints, the Russian Musical Society remained convinced of the significance of *chin* and fought particularly hard for the appointment of conservatory graduates to class rank upon enrollment in state service. The Society's primary concern was to enhance the value of a conservatory education and to defend the interests of the musical profession. Rights in state service would convey an acceptance by the state, and particularly by the Ministry of Education, of the legitimacy of the Society's conservatories and music schools. Moreover, the attachment of service rights to conservatory diplomas would significantly enhance the economic and social value of a musical education. Until the turn of the century, the state and its ministries met these efforts with indifference, if not outright dismissal. The Ministry of Education objected particularly forcefully to the Society's request, arguing that the training offered by the conservatories and music schools did not meet its standards.[27]

For individual musicians, failure to secure legal recognition of professional status could have devastating consequences. Moreover, individuals were in no position to resist efforts by the state's representatives to encroach on or deny their rights. In 1893, in the context of a rising wave of officially tolerated anti-Semitism, ten Moscow professional musicians, all conservatory graduates and free artists, complained that the police had threatened to expel them from the city. In pleading their case, they cited the contradiction between the conservatory charter and the laws on social estates. Because conservatory graduates could petition for exclusion from the taxable estates, many of "those who receive the diploma of a free artist . . . are left without any estate." Yet, the law required all Russian subjects to belong to a definite estate: "Individuals who stand outside the *sosloviia* have no defined civil rights," the petitioners noted, and "the law ignores them." Free artists with origins in the taxable estates were vulnerable to persecution, including forcible reinscription in their natal estates. Moreover, the Moscow police had announced "all free artists in the capital [had] been deprived of residency rights." The musicians argued that it was illogical that the law that liberated free artists from the taxable estates should simultaneously demand that they immediately be reinscribed in these estates. They insisted that the intent of the conservatory charter was to remove graduates from the taxable estates in order to be inscribed in another, higher estate. The petitioners pointed out that graduates of the Academy of Arts acquired hereditary honored citizenship; graduates of other specialized educational institutions became personal honored citizens. The petitioners concluded that the absence of a specific law that defined musicians' social status based on their professional education compromised their legal rights. Frustrated by their powerlessness in dealing with the Moscow police and their inability to "personally struggle with this incomplete law," they appealed to the director of the Moscow Conservatory, asking him to petition on their behalf.[28]

In an effort to defend not only the rights of these conservatory graduates but also the status of the musical profession as a whole, the Russian Musical Society petitioned the State Council. Retracing the convoluted process of awarding civil status to musicians, the State Council noted the contradictory rulings made over the years. In the end, the authority of the tsar proved most persuasive. The Minister of Justice, N. V. Muravev, argued that individuals who had acquired the title of free artist by virtue of their musical education enjoyed rights to personal honored citizenship, basing his reasoning on the tsar's approval of the 1861 charter.[29] Ultimately, an amended statute on honored citizenship included a statement on the rights of conservatory graduates: "Persons who are awarded a diploma with the title of free artist by one of the conservatories of the Imperial Russian Musical Society are ranked as personal honored citizens if they do not belong to another, higher social estate."[30] Thirty-three years after the Russian Musical Society began its effort to secure a respectable social status for Russian musicians, the law codes finally acknowledged the rights of conservatory graduates to honored citizenship.

By 1902, the state had become noticeably more responsive to the Society's requests for additional rights for its graduates and for the legal codification of these measures. This was largely due to the increasing prestige and power of the Society and its network of educational institutions. Previously, the Society had based its requests for service rights on graduates' general educational credentials not their musical qualifications, irrespective of whether these individuals were expected to enroll in a specialized musical occupation, such as a music instructor in a state-supported secondary school, or in general state service. The final, successful attempt to secure service rights emphasized the intrinsic worth of a musical education. Increasingly self-confident, the Russian Musical Society presented its petition as an attempt to secure justice for its graduates by equalizing their rights with those of other specialized institutions.

Nevertheless, the decision to extend service rights to conservatory and music school graduates provoked controversy within the government. Although the Ministry of Internal Affairs strongly supported the petition, the fiscally conservative Minister of Finance, Sergei Witte, equally strongly opposed it. Witte acknowledged that the state recognized the "great significance of music education" and "continually aid[ed] its development" through "financial assistance to the Russian Musical Society," despite his own objections. But, Witte noted, if "the broadening of rights to class rank in general are not in accordance with the views of the government, how much less appropriate would it be to allow the awarding of these rights to persons who have dedicated themselves to a specialty... which has nothing in common with the structure of state administration?" Despite Witte's protests, the petition was approved. Male graduates of the Society's music schools and conservatories received the right to appointment at the lowest (fourteenth) class rank in general state service, while conservatory graduates hired by one of the Society's educational institutions would be appointed at the twelfth rank. Graduates hired as secondary school music teachers would receive the same rights, privileges, and rankings as faculty members teaching core academic subjects, rather than the provisional status normally awarded to music and singing instructors. Finally, all conservatory faculty, as well as the director and inspector of each of the Society's provincial music schools, were confirmed to be in state service and in class rank.[31]

Between 1862 and 1917, the Russian Musical Society slowly acquired professional rights and privileges for musicians. Because respectability meant formal rights and ranking in state service as well as professional titles, the rights conferred on the Society's graduates and faculty helped legitimize music as a profession. Moreover, because graduates of the Society's educational institutions enjoyed privileged access to these new markers of status, the prestige and dominance of the Society increased.[32] Yet, the symbolic importance of these rights did not necessarily make them a practical benefit to working musicians. Most of these rights applied only to individuals who graduated from the conservatories with a diploma and the title of free artist. A few, such as the right to state service, also applied to graduates of the Society's provincial music schools. For the small percentage of students who completed the musical curriculum and satisfied general education requirements, a music school certificate (*attestat*) or a conservatory diploma certified them as credentialed professionals. The overwhelming majority of students, however, never graduated and never received any of the professional benefits so painstakingly acquired from the state by the Russian Musical Society. Even many graduates completed only an abbreviated course of study and received second-rank credentials with far fewer formal rights. Consequently, the struggle for musical professionalization extended beyond the acquisition of legal privileges for the musical elite.

By the Numbers: The Demographics of Musical Training

In order to understand the emergence of the Russian musical profession, we must have at least some understanding of its composition. The statistical records of the Kiev Music School provide an opportunity to construct a composite social portrait of the complex institutions sponsored by the Russian Musical Society. These records, moreover, reflect the political, social, and cultural imperatives that strongly shaped the demographic structure not only of these institutions, but also of the music profession.

In 1890–1891, the Kiev Music School was a sizable institution, with more than three hundred students studying piano, voice, and orchestral instruments. Although almost one third of the students were Jewish, they made up the largest group in only two specialties, both in the lower status orchestral division. Most strikingly when compared to later patterns, Jews had yet to make significant inroads into the piano department, the largest division of the school. As table 4.1 shows, the school was clearly attractive to the city's rising middle classes, with the sons and daughters of the *meshchane* comprising almost a third of the school's students, although estate origins and religious confession interacted in complex ways to shape the student body. *Meshchane* origins were particularly frequent among Jewish violinists and cellists, as well as among both Orthodox and Jewish wind players. Although the piano was clearly the most popular specialty, especially among women, the voice department managed to be both relatively popular and elitist, with clear divisions of rank and religion noticeable among its students. The class differentiation among piano students was even more pronounced, with most of the Jewish students drawn from the merchantry and *meshchane*, while Catholic and Orthodox students were drawn primarily from the nobility and the *chinovniki*.

Twenty years later, a second statistical "snapshot" reveals how broad changes in Russian society intersected with the development of cultural institutions (see table 4.2). At the beginning of 1911, the majority of the Kiev Music School's more than 750 students were women, echoing a trend toward the increasing feminization of music schools and conservatories that accompanied the intense popularity of the piano in Russia. Whereas many continental European conservatories remained more balanced by performance specialty, with smaller piano departments and proportionally larger orchestral divisions, the Russian conservatories and music schools stretched to accommodate the feminine demand for the piano within their walls, a characteristic they shared with their British counterparts. The feminization of conservatory training in both empires had significant consequences for institutional identity as well as for the career opportunities of individual musicians. As Paula Gillett has argued in the British case, while the conservatories "offered women unprecedented opportunities for professional training, they also diminished, by their serious overproduction of aspiring entrants, the career prospects for many of those who sought to enter these already competitive and overcrowded professions.... The first and perhaps most unwelcome lesson for young female students of the 1890s and later was the existence of a serious and relentless glut of solo pianists and violinists."[33] The modest size of the voice department, also dominated by

TABLE 4.1. Students in the Kiev Music School, 1890–1891, by Gender, Social Status, Faith, and Applied Specialty

Specialization	Students	Gender		Social Estate					Religious Faith				
	Total	Female	Male	Priv	Urb	Rur	Cl	Other	Orth	Cath	Luth	Jew	Other
Piano	128	110	18	60*	56*	0	2	10	73	17	7	31	0
Voice	78	47	31	35	20	1	7	15	53	7	0	18	0
Violin	31	2	29	3	22	2	0	4	5	4	1	21	0
Winds/Bass/ Cello	48	2 (cello)	46	3	39	2	0	4	19	2	0	27	0
Total	285[1]	161 56%	124 44%	101 35%	137 48%	5	9	33	150 53%	30	8	97 34%	0

DAMK, fond 176, op. 1, d. 103, ll. 13–20

[1] In addition, some 30 or so students did not have any demographic data

* 24 Catholic and Lutheran students were not well differentiated by social estate and have been distributed equally between the privileged and urban estates

women, merely underscores the overwhelming popularity and importance of the piano.

Gender, however, was not the only determinant of musical specialization. Class, ethnicity, and religious affiliation further splintered the student body in Kiev and in the Society's other educational institutions. The female-dominated voice and piano departments attracted students of relatively high social status. In the piano department, nearly a third of students came from the ranks of the nobility and the *chinovniki* or their children, with only small minorities from the clerical and rural estates. Most notably, the substantial majority of piano students drawn from Kiev's urban middle classes reflected both their increasing social and economic weight and the importance they attached to music as a marker of status. Even in the vocal department, which tended to attract the highest status students, those from the privileged estates were nearly balanced by those from the urban estates. Specialized training in voice remained relatively elite in the Russian conservatories in part because of the intimate physicality of vocal training and the tendency to identify the performer with the performance, but also because of pedagogical practices that limited admission to the specialty to physically mature late adolescents and adults.

In Kiev, as in the rest of the Society's educational institutions, the orchestral division was overwhelmingly male. Among the violinists and the cellists, the highest status groups within the orchestral division, the vast majority of students belonged to the urban estates, although a substantial minority belonged to the nobility or *chinovniki*. Only a handful of the school's violinists were female, while, among the cellists, two women stand out as exceptions to the general exclusion of women from the orchestral specialty. The consequences of serfdom persisted in the low status of the brass, woodwind, and string bass specialties, which had difficulty attracting students at all, much less students from the nobility and *chinovniki:* only one trumpet player claimed membership in either of the higher social estates. Here, at last, one found a place for the peasantry; a third of orchestral wind and bass players had roots in the rural estates.

The social divisions that shaped the Society's educational institutions are most clearly revealed in the registration books for new students (see table 4.3). During the 1910–1911 academic year, 226 new piano students enrolled in the Kiev Music School, exactly half of whom were Jewish. Increasingly, one's identity determined one's musical specialty; gender, class, and religious fractures divided the student body.

Women utterly dominated this new class of pianists; the feminization of the piano division had become so pronounced that it seems likely that only

TABLE 4.2. Students in the Kiev Music School, 1911 by Gender, Social Status, Faith, and Applied Specialty

Specialization	Students	Gender		Social Estate					Religious Faith				
	Total	Female	Male	Priv	Urb	Rur	Cl	Other	Orth	Cath	Luth	Jew	Other
Piano	542	482	60	163	332	9	26	12	209	55	11	264	3
Voice	63	46	17	29	25	4	5	0	44	4	3	12	0
Violin	73	7	66	13	56	3	0	1	16	9	1	47	0
Cello	28	2	26	5	20	1	2	0	10	2	1	15	0
Winds/bass	42	0	42	1	26	13	0	2	25	2	0	15	0
Theory	10	1	9	3	4	2	1	0	6	0	0	4	0
Total	758	538 71%	220 29%	214 28%	463 61%	32	34	15	310 41%	72	16	357 47%	3

DAMK, fond 176, op. 1, d. 279, ll. 1–2

the most committed and confident of young men dared enroll in this specialty. However, this overwhelming statistic suggests a false uniformity that is complicated by examining class and religion as well as gender. In the piano department, class status seems to have trumped religious affiliation. Although Jewish students constituted almost half of the department, Orthodox students were close behind and Catholic students a sizeable minority. Among the Orthodox piano students, only five men enrolled, while among Jewish students men persisted as a significant minority. Although the *meshchane* were the largest group among the piano students as a whole, 90 percent of them were Jewish while nearly half of the Orthodox students were drawn from the ranks of the nobility and the *chinovniki*. Interestingly, the low status orchestral department and the high status voice department tended to attract the largest percentage of Orthodox students, reflecting once again the class divisions that pervaded the school.

For the students of the predominantly Orthodox voice department, class and religion seemed to combine to erect barriers against infiltration by either Jewish students or those from lower social estates (see table 4.4).

As table 4.5 illustrates, orchestral wind and low string specialists were divided roughly equally between Orthodox and Jewish students, but also between the *meshchane*, who comprised fully half of the new students, and a mix of other estates and social groups, with students with peasant backgrounds comprising the second largest group.

In contrast, as table 4.6 shows, although the relatively high status violin attracted a larger percentage of Jewish students, Orthodox students in this specialty, although less numerous, included a significant number drawn from the privileged social estates.

Thus, the Kiev Music School, like the Society's other educational institutions, was increasingly both highly feminized and structured along class and religious lines. From this point on, Jews were the largest group within the institution, increasing from 47 percent of the student body in 1910–1911 to a high of 55 percent in 1915–1916. Members of the urban estates strengthened their already dominant position at the expense of the nobility and *chinovniki*, whose representation in the student body slowly declined. The urban estates consistently comprised more than 60 percent of the student body, over twice the size of the next largest group.[34]

Similar demographic transformations occurred within most of the Society's institutions over the decades. These statistics emphasize the role that gender, class, ethnic, and religious identities played in determining an individual's educational and professional trajectory. Moreover, the class and gender divisions within these institutions—and within the musical profession—became

TABLE 4.3. New Piano Students, Kiev Music School, 1910–1911

Of 226 new enrollees:	Orthodox 90 (40%)		Jewish 113 (50%)		Other 23 (10%)	
Social Status	Males	Females	Males	Females	Males	Females
Nobility and Chinovniki	1	43	0	0	0	13*
Professionals, Honored Citizens, and University Students	1	13	2	14	1	1
Clerical Estates	0	14	0	1	0	0
Meshchane	2	4	14	60	0	2
Merchants	0	4	2	19	1	2
Peasants	1	1	0	0	0	0
Foreigners	0	2	0	1	0	2
Other	0	4	0	0	1	0
Total	5	85	18	95	3	20

DAMK, fond 176, op. 1, d. 238, ll. 107–151
* All Roman Catholic

TABLE 4.4. New Voice Students, Kiev Music School, 1910–1911

Of 51 New Enrollees:	Orthodox 32 (63%)		Jewish 13 (25%)		Other 6 (12%)	
Social Status	Males	Females	Males	Females	Males	Females
Nobility and Chinovniki	0	8	0	0	0	3
Professionals, Honored Citizens, and University Students	4	4	0	0	0	0
Clerical Estates	3	1	0	0	0	0
Meshchane	1	3	3	9	0	1
Merchants	0	2	1	0	0	0
Peasants	1	3	0	0	0	0
Other	0	2	0	0	0	2
Total	9	23	4	9	0	6

DAMK, fond 176, op. 1, d. 238, ll. 107–151

TABLE 4.5. New Orchestral Students, Kiev Music School, 1910–1911

Of 36 New Enrollees:	Orthodox 18 (50%)		Jewish 14 (39%)		Other 4 (11%)	
Social Status	Males	Females	Males	Females	Males	Females
Nobility and Chinovniki	1	0	0	0	0	0
Professionals, Honored Citizens, and University Students	1	0	0	0	0	0
Clerical Estates	0	0	0	0	0	0
Meshchane	7	0	13	0	1	0
Merchants	0	0	1	0	0	0
Peasants	5	0	0	0	2	0
Other	4	0	0	0	1	0
Total	18	0	14	0	4	0

DAMK, fond 176, op. 1, d. 238, ll. 107–51

TABLE 4.6. New Violin Students, Kiev Music School, 1910–1911

Of 38 new enrollees:	Orthodox 13 (34%)		Jewish 24 (63%)		Other 1 (3%)	
Social Status	Males	Females	Males	Females	Males	Females
Nobility and Chinovniki	5	1	0	0	0	0
Professionals, Honored Citizens, and University Students	0	0	2	0	0	0
Clerical Estates	0	0	0	0	0	0
Meshchane	1	0	19	1	0	1
Merchants	1	0	2	0	0	0
Peasants	4	0	0	0	0	0
Other	1	0	0	0	0	0
Total	12	1	23	1	0	1

DAMK, fond 176, op. 1, d. 238, ll. 107–151

more pronounced as the percentage of women and Jews increased. Women, in particular, were concentrated in piano and voice, the two specialties that conformed most closely to traditional gender expectations and which they increasingly dominated. The occasional female violinist or cellist was the exception that proved the rule, rather than an indication that it was becoming more socially acceptable for women to choose these specialties. As in other countries, societal norms for appropriate female behavior made it almost impossible for women to choose specialties that compromised their femininity (such as brass instruments) or good character (such as the cello, with its suggestive playing position, or the flute, oboe, or clarinet, with their phallic symbolism). Women's choice of performance specialty was further restricted by the resistance of male musicians to female encroachment on their territory. As a result, only piano, voice, and harp were freely available to women. The only significant penetration of women into "male" specialties was in violin and theory, where female students, although still a clear minority, had become a consistent presence by the end of the nineteenth century. Yet, although the orchestra remained a man's world, the conservatory increasingly belonged to women.

Female Musicians: Professionalization, Modernization, and the Piano

In April 1877, the popular journal *Strekoza* featured on its cover a detailed engraving of two flirtatious and fashionable young ladies, carefully coiffed, adorned with jewelry, and laced into elegant and décolleté dresses (figure 4.1).

Their sleeveless dresses emphasized the smooth skin of their bare arms. They sat, side-by-side, at the keyboard of a grand piano—*royal* in Russian—as richly ornamented as they were, accompanying themselves in a slightly suggestive duet, singing:

> We are two . . . girls . . . dark-eyed; we are two dark-browed gypsy lasses.
> In our dark eyes a fire glowed,
> In our hearts a passionate fire blazed up!
> A fire, a fire, a fire blazed up.
> A fire, a fire, a fire blazed up!!!

The illustration, entitled "A Domestic Concert in the Provinces (Duet)," provided a not altogether sympathetic portrait of the character and aspirations of the Russian variant of the "piano girl," a phenomenon familiar to European and American readers.[35] The girls used their "gypsy" romance to escape into a world more enticing than their own, where they were exotic, energetic, and alluring heroines. For the viewer, they were offered as a fantasy of young marriageable women, attractive, appealing, and more than a little naïve. Their fantasies of adventure, however, were implicitly disparaged as adolescent daydreams, while their dreams of musical artistry were subtly mocked. Although music might offer dreams of escape, it also helped define the boundaries of respectable young women's lives. Although they sang of adventure, the young women illustrated here were clearly on display. Moreover, the sexualized portrayal of their musical performance reduced their skills and abilities to accomplishments explicitly directed at the marriage market.[36]

Although the Russian Musical Society created an image of the ideal musician, most students fit uneasily into this mold. As we have seen, the majority of music students were female, most of them pianists. Some devoted years to study; others enrolled only briefly. Although most women, like most men, left the classes, schools, and conservatories never having completed the curriculum, a few completed their education, received their credentials, and went on to careers, modest or brilliant, as teachers and performers. The professional aspirations of women were limited by law and custom; most female music students could expect no more than honest employment as a music teacher or governess. The legal aspects of professionalization had different implications for female musicians as well. Although social estate applied to women as well as men, they did not hold service ranks and their social position was usually defined by their relationships to their fathers or their husbands rather than by any acquired, professional status. Both voice and piano were seen, in Russia as elsewhere, as feminine accomplishments; even if a young woman pursued her musical studies with excessive enthusiasm, she at most pushed the boundaries of appropriate female behavior, rather than violated accepted gender roles. In the 1870s, some still expressed their doubts about the feasibility and appropriateness of music instruction for girls. In Vladikavkaz, for example, the local newspaper debated the relative merits of piano versus violin instruction for female gymnasia students. Proponents of the violin emphasized the prohibitive cost of the piano; because few families could afford to purchase an instrument, and the gymnasia would only purchase a single piano, students would have almost no opportunity to practice. Other commentators, however, wondered whether it was appropriate for girls to play the violin or worried about the possible health consequences of music studies in general.[37]

By the late nineteenth century, piano instruction had been democratized. As Cyril Ehrlich has noted for the British case, the availability of "cheap, reliable

№ 14. ГОДЪ ВТОРОЙ. АПРѢЛЬ 4.

ЕЖЕНЕДѢЛЬНОЕ ИЗДАНІЕ.

Подписка принимается въ Конторѣ Редакціи, на углу Невскаго просп. и Михайловской улицы, въ зданіи Европейской гостинницы.

Цѣна отдѣльнаго номера 20 коп.

Цѣна за объявленія: 10 коп. за строку мелкаго шрифта.

СТРЕКОЗА

ХУДОЖЕСТВЕННО-ЮМОРИСТИЧЕСКІЙ ЖУРНАЛЪ.

Условія подписки:

въ С.-Петербургѣ:

безъ доставки на годъ . . 8 р.
» » на полгода . 4 р. 50 к.
съ доставкою на годъ . . 9 р.
» » на полгода . 5 р.

въ Москвѣ,

черезъ книжн. магаз. И. Г. Соловьева:
безъ доставки на годъ . . 8 р. 75 к.
» » на полгода . 5 р.
съ пересылкою, какъ въ Москву, такъ и въ другіе города Россійской Имперія: на годъ 9 р. 50 к., на ½-г. 5 р. 50 к.

Домашній концертъ въ провинціи.

(Дуэтъ).

„Мы двѣ... дѣвицы... черно-окія, мы двѣ цыганки чернобровыя;
„Въ глазахъ нашихъ черныхъ огонь заблисталъ,
„Въ сердцахъ-же страстныхъ огонь запылалъ!
„Огонь, огонь, огонь запылалъ,
„Ого-нь, ого-нь, огонь запы....лалъ!!!...

FIGURE 4.1. “Domestic Concert in the Provinces (Duet),” *Strekoza*, April 1877 pianos" beginning in the 1880s permitted the satisfaction of "a pent-up demand which was based upon increasing purchasing power, musical needs, and social emulation: possession symbolized respectability, achievement, and status."[38] Similarly, in Russia, as the price of a piano came down, and availability increased, the intensive study of music lost its elite character. As newly minted conservatory-trained pianists came "on the market" as teachers, the process accelerated as piano instruction became widely available and increasingly affordable. Girls' schools offered piano classes almost as a matter of course, and at a reasonable cost, while private piano teachers, small teaching studios, private music schools, and even mail order programs offered piano instruction to the masses. The mechanical nature of the modern, increasingly mass-produced, piano, led many to perceive it as an easy instrument. If the piano was difficult to truly master—to develop a deft touch and technical brilliance—it was easy to play in a pleasing manner. Consequently, relatively little was risked when a girl or young woman, a daughter, sister, or wife, pursued a musical education either haphazardly or with zeal. Should she fail in her studies, the damage would be diffused among the horde of other mediocre young pianists. Should she succeed, perhaps through an "unwomanly" devotion to hard work and technical development, she would enjoy, albeit most likely briefly, a degree of celebration of her individual brilliance before herself merging into the pianistic crowd. Moreover, it seems likely that for individual women and girls success and failure were difficult to differentiate. What mattered was not some objective demarcation of talent and artistry on a national scale, but local recognition and reward for achievement. Thus, for a young girl in Tomsk or Tambov, although she might dream of a career on the St. Petersburg stages, her most likely sources of a sense of artistic achievement and self-worth were to be found in the approval of her teachers and the recognition of her peers.

Through the piano, girls and young women could step onto the public stage without violating anyone's expectations. While the young women affiliated with the radical *intelligentsia* shocked and titillated educated society by their dress, behavior, comportment, and, most aggressively, their penetration of previously male bastions of power and enlightenment such as the medical school and the university, female musicians, especially piano students, only tentatively expanded women's public role. Indeed, because music was seen as a traditional feminine accomplishment, it took little to convince even the most conventional observers that women might legitimately pursue music in a professional capacity, in pursuit of "a crust of bread." In 1887, the governor of Kharkov framed his support for the local branch of the Russian Musical Society by arguing that nowhere did young women receive as complete an education as in the music school, which provided them with a marketable skill with which to make their way in the world.[39] Similarly, in 1885, the musician and educator K. Ed. Weber borrowed the language of maternal feminism to defend women's contributions to musical life. Weber argued that as "future mothers" women bore a responsibility to acquire useful knowledge to pass on to their children. Weber did not restrict women to domestic musical roles, however. Recognizing that many women supported themselves at some point in their lives, often working as governesses or teachers, he argued that a strong knowledge of music allowed them to command significantly higher wages.[40]

The willingness of educated society to accept women's pursuit of music as a profession of necessity helps to explain the hostility male musicians sometimes expressed toward their female counterparts; they perceived women as undermining the social standing of the profession by the very modesty of their claims. Yet, the radical *studentka* in the anatomy laboratory and the conventional young *pianistka* laboring at her scales and etudes complemented rather than contradicted each other. They represented two responses to a broader challenge to Russian (and for that matter, European) social conventions of gender. In many ways, and on many fronts, traditional understandings of the rights, responsibilities, and relationships of men and women were being questioned and renegotiated. Men debated the "woman question," uneasily considering the possibility of women's participation in public intellectual, economic, and political life. Under the pressure of both new ideas from the *intelligentsia*, such as Nikolai Chernyshevsky's radical reimaging of the proper relationship between men and women in *What Is to Be Done?* and new opportunities for legal redress against oppressive family circumstances, women at all levels of Russian society began to reconsider their place within the marital relationship, the family more broadly, and society as a whole.[41] Two paintings, both products of that last moment before the cataclysm of World War I, reflect the social and cultural ambiguities associated with women, and especially female musicians, in Russian society. S. A. Vinogradov's 1914 painting "At the Piano" tenderly portrays a young girl rather diffidently engaged in piano practice. The presence of the family dog as the girl's only audience both makes the scene more intimate and implicitly challenges the purpose and value of the family's investment in her musical training (figure 4.2). In direct challenge to Vinogradov's depiction of a quiet bourgeois home, with the piano providing both a pleasant accompaniment to domestic life and a source of hidden tension, Kazimir Malevich's "Woman at the Piano," despite focusing on the stereotypically conventional theme of female domestic music making, emphasizes in deep reds and sharp angles the disruption of gender expectations and traditional family life as a consequence of

FIGURE 4.2. *At the Piano* by Sergei Arsenevich Vinogradov, (1869–1938), Russia, 1914. State Art Museum of the Belorussian Republic, Minsk. Credit: culture-images/Lebrecht

the social chaos produced by rapid and profound social, economic, and cultural change (figure 4.3).

The periodical press alternately disparaged and defended women's participation in music. Women were seen either as a civilizing force for the enlightenment of the people or as a corrupting element undermining the cultural development of a masculinized "Russia." Predictably, one persistent target was the supposedly frivolous attitude of young women toward their piano

FIGURE 4.3. *A Woman at the Piano* by Kazimir Severinovich Malevich, (1878–1935), Russia, 1913. State V. Surikov Art Museum, Krasnoyarsk. Credit: culture-images/Lebrecht

studies. In 1866, the proposed opening of the Moscow Conservatory provoked comments on the sorry state of music education in Russia despite near universal "pounding on the piano," especially by young women. An ability to "play" the piano, *Russkie vedomosti* noted, was all but mandatory for Russian women who hoped to find a likely groom.[42] The critic Rostislav offered a similarly gendered evaluation of the Russian Musical Society's first five years. Although he praised the St. Petersburg Conservatory for training "educated" musicians, he nevertheless reinforced the stereotypical view of female music students, pronouncing the pianistic skills they acquired merely an effective "weapon" in any young woman's "arsenal."[43]

For some students and their parents, enrollment in a music school was merely the first stop on the road to what they hoped would be a brilliant career. In 1862, the popular newspaper *Syn otechestva* ridiculed such dreams in a caricature in which the sleep-deprived parents of a wailing child convince themselves that their daughter's impressive vocal "abilities" foretell a career as a *prima donna*. Her indulgent parents do everything they can to encourage her vocal gifts, a strategy that seems to pay off when she gains a place in the choir of a local theater. In the final frame, however, the dreams of the parents are brutally mocked: the girl has become a "popular" soloist, concertizing on the street corner accompanied by an organ grinder.[44]

Syn otechestva's cartoon figures had many real-life counterparts. The parents of Ksenia Liubochka, for example, worried that their daughter's talent might not be sufficient to support their dreams. In 1914, her father wrote the director of the Kiev Conservatory, demanding to know whether she studied diligently, was able or perhaps even gifted, and whether she had a strong voice that promised a career on the operatic stage or merely an ordinary one, "to which those complaining of boredom might listen." Ksenia's parents viewed her education as an investment from which they expected significant returns; in fact, the resources they devoted to her education were considerable. Her father noted that "in addition to the 175 rubles a year for tuition in the conservatory, we pay every month no less than 45–50 rubles for room, board, and miscellaneous (expenses)," leaving the rest of the family to subsist on only half of his monthly wages of 100 rubles. Although, unfortunately for her parents, Ksenia was not the brilliant singer they hoped for, neither was she without prospects. The conservatory inspector, K. Mikhailov, responded carefully to her parents concerns, although he deftly ignored her father's inquiries about scholarships or reduced tuition. Her voice was, in the words of her teacher, "not large, but not bad," she worked hard, and her parents could expect her to graduate with a diploma, the title of free artist, and the ability "to apply her knowledge in life." Her future career, however, was more likely to lead her to the teacher's studio than the stage.[45]

After the 1905 revolution, low graduation rates, extremely high levels of enrollment, and the high percentage of female students became a handy stick with which critics beat the Russian Musical Society and, especially, the conservatories. M. M. Ivanov, the longtime music critic for the conservative St. Petersburg daily newspaper, *Novoe vremia*, charged that the Society's leadership had succumbed to lazy bureaucratism.[46] Led, he claimed, by highly placed but professionally unqualified and organizationally inept individuals, the Society was utterly failing in its mission to aid the artistic and cultural development of Russia. In response, Prince A. D. Obolensky offered an eloquent defense of the importance of educating the sons and daughters of the bourgeoisie, not with professional careers in mind, but for their potential contribution to the broad cultural transformation of Russia. Obolensky flatly denied Ivanov's assertion that the sole purpose of specialized musical training was the preparation of professional musicians, although he grudgingly conceded "as far as the conservatories are concerned such views may be appropriate." Nevertheless, Obolensky argued, the Society's music classes and schools had "a broad mission." They were not just "institutions for the preparation of musical professionals and teachers," they were also the "transmitters of musical education and development to broad segments of society."[47]

Both Obolensky and Ivanov focused on the predominance of women in the Society's music schools and conservatories. Ivanov had damned women's enthusiasm for musical education, claiming that only five or six of the five thousand or more young women studying in the Society's institutions had real potential for professional careers. The musical education of the remaining 4,994, he maintained, was a waste of resources; they would simply abandon their musical activities on becoming wives and mothers. Obolensky dismissed this charge as irrelevant and turned Ivanov's argument on its head. The most important service of the Russian Musical Society, he insisted, was not that it had "educated many leading composers and artists" but that it had "enabled the musical education of our entire society, in both the capitals and the provinces through [the education of] these nonprofessional students." This, Obolensky concluded, "is worth the fifty thousand rubles that the government," according to Ivanov, "wastes on the Musical Society."[48] This exchange between Obolensky and Ivanov underscores the competing social and aesthetic conceptions of Russian musical culture. For the founders of the Russian Musical Society, the purpose of specialized music education had been clear: to create for Russia a new class of educated professional musicians.

However, the aesthetic and cultural ideologies initially advocated by Anton Rubinstein and his allies failed to satisfy the educational needs and aspirations of students or, indeed, of the growing number of specialists focusing on the broad transformation of Russian society through music.

The varied careers of the Society's former students illuminate the gradual transformation and invigoration of Russian cultural life during the second half of the nineteenth century. Our window into the lives of musicians is more transparent than one might expect. In addition to the predictable array of memoirs and biographies of famous composers and performers, more or less detailed accounts of the lives and careers of some of the most ordinary graduates of the Society's schools and conservatories survive. In 1895, the Russian Musical Society placed advertisements in a wide variety of newspapers and journals asking its former students to send in their biographical information.[49] These letters provide an unusually direct view into the personal aspirations and professional development of Russian musicians.

The experiences of Feofaniia Veliavskaia and Sofia Stremoukhova offer representative examples of the vagaries of women's musical careers. In 1883, at age nineteen, Veliavskaia enrolled in the conservatory, graduating three years later with an attestat and a large silver medal. Returning to her home town of Voronezh, she spent two years teaching piano at a private music school and to private students. Although the music school closed, a victim of a fragile cultural marketplace, she continued to teach uninterrupted even after her marriage to a teacher in the Voronezh Real School. Husband and wife continued to advance in their careers; in 1893, both accepted positions at the Poltava Institute for Noble Girls. Proud of her accomplishments as a teacher and professional, Veliavskaia noted "two of [my] former students from Voronezh have enrolled in the Warsaw conservatory [Warsaw Musical Institute] and two are currently studying in St. Petersburg." Ambitious and energetic, Veliavskaia declared that she was currently petitioning to open an independent music school in Poltava.[50] Stremoukhova's tale was similar. A noblewoman, born in 1868 in the village of Uspensky in Kursk province, she had completed the Moscow Alexandrovsky Institute in 1886, enrolled in the Moscow Conservatory in 1890, and graduated with an attestat in 1893. On the recommendation of conservatory director Safonov, she was hired as a teacher of music and singing at the Belostoksky Institute for Noble Girls with an annual salary of more than 1100 rubles.[51]

For the nascent music profession, women's prominence in music teaching created uncomfortable problems. Although numerous women with conservatory and music school credentials pursued active careers as music teachers and occasional performers, many more employed their skills and credentials on a casual basis. The career of Olga Ivanovna Andriukova provides a representative example. A noblewoman, Andriukova was born in 1858 in Sterlitamak, some 1500 kilometers from Moscow in the province of Ufa. Initially educated at home, she studied at the St. Petersburg Conservatory from 1874 until 1881 but did not graduate until 1882, when she took examinations as an extern and received an attestat. Since then, her musical career had been limited to "private piano lessons in the provincial capital of Ufa at various times, with significant interruptions," which did not, in her opinion "constitute a permanent and specialized occupation, like a profession." Although she may have refused to acknowledge herself as a "real" professional, she nevertheless is difficult to classify as a simple amateur; while her livelihood did not depend on her musical labors, she remained an active musician and had composed and published several songs.[52]

The complexity of female musicians' professional identities and the increasing importance of credentials emerge clearly in the almost stereotypical case of Aleksandra Nikolaevna Spanovskaia of Elisavetgrad. Spanovskaia studied music intermittently throughout the first half of the 1870s, first at the Kiev Music School and then at the St. Petersburg Conservatory. Financial difficulties forced her to abandon her studies in order to take a position as a governess. It was not until 1882, apparently, that she began to pursue music teaching as a career, eventually receiving an offer to teach at a women's gymnasia. Her new position, however, was contingent on her ability to provide formal credentials proving her legal right to teach music.[53] Spanovskaia was unusual in her ability to negotiate the transition back from a casual and highly feminized position as a governess to a formal professional position as a school music teacher. More frequently, women taught out of their homes, forced to fall back on their musical training after some domestic tragedy rather than making a conscious choice for a career, as was the case with Maria Stadlo-Sobeshchanskaia, who struggled to support three children on a small widow's pension and income from private music teaching. The increasing professionalization and institutionalization of music intruded even into her modest domestic studio. In 1903, after twenty years of teaching, she began to fear that she would soon be "banned" from giving private lessons because she lacked credentials. In all likelihood, she referred not to any real regulation against private music teaching but to her inability to compete after the impending opening of a new music school. Her request for some kind of certificate attesting to her studies at the Kiev Music School was abruptly denied. Ironically, Stadlo-Sobeshchanskaia was caught between the more casual expectations of her youth and the professionalizing ethos of her maturity. Her studies in Kiev twenty-seven years earlier had been characteristically sporadic. Not only had she never taken graduation examinations, but the school itself, then in its infancy, had lacked legitimacy and had been unable to grant any formal credentials.[54]

Even for the most ambitious women, the challenges to building a successful musical career were numerous and the path often circuitous, as can be seen in the career of Anna Iakovlevna Aleksandrova-Levenson. For a modest professional, Aleksandrova-Levenson remains unusually well documented in the historical record, a testament both to her own strong professional identity and the wide net cast around her sometime mentor, the composer Tchaikovsky. In addition to correspondence between her and Tchaikovsky, both the autobiographical letter she composed in 1895 for the Russian Musical Society and a series of letters, written in 1914, to her acquaintance and colleague, Alexander Ziloti, survive. These documents, in which she promoted her training, skills, experience, and devotion to the memory of Nikolai Rubinstein and Tchaikovsky, testify both to her commitment to her career and to the frustrations she experienced as she pursued her professional goals. Born in Odessa in 1856, she graduated from the Moscow Conservatory in 1877 with an attestat and specializations in theory and piano.[55] After beginning her pedagogical career in Moscow, she accepted a position in a private music school in Odessa in 1882, but departed after only a year because "the provinces offer musicians little in the way of nourishment." Her career, however, remained largely in a provincial orbit. Her marriage to a doctor of veterinary medicine, N. A. Aleksandrov, profoundly shaped her career. His employment at the Iurevsky Veterinary Institute reoriented her career initially to the Baltic states, where she concertized in support of local university students, and then to the Siberian city of Tomsk, where her husband was employed at the university.[56]

For Aleksandrova-Levenson, as for many graduates of the conservatory, a promising professional career degenerated into endless rounds of fruitless lessons with humble pupils. Her unimpressive career, especially according to the standards of a Moscow star such as Ziloti, required her to defend her abilities as a performer and her talent as a musician, even as she sought to trade on their earlier acquaintance:

> Supposing that you have not completely forgotten me, I am writing you about a question of great interest to me. In brief, I will tell you the following about myself: initially and for a rather protracted period after finishing the conservatory I was forced to give a mass of lessons, which I was never short of thanks to the support of N. G. Rubinstein and particularly P. I. Tchaikovsky.

Although Aleksandrova-Levenson never secured the position at the Moscow Conservatory that she coveted, with Tchaikovsky's help she secured an appointment as music teacher to the family of N. D. Kondratev, a position she held for seven years. In her worshipful recollection, it was this position that freed her from the most soul-destroying aspects of life as a music teacher:

> I constantly played for Tchaikovsky during this period and he always advised me to continually practice and . . . to devote myself to concertizing. . . . But, as I already said, giving lessons prevented me from performing, although I always practiced intensively.

Tchaikovsky's visits to the Kondratevs deepened their acquaintance and, she claimed, even gave her playing the imprimatur of Russia's greatest musical icon; she believed that Tchaikovsky himself had in some sense blessed her professional aspirations.[57]

> When our material position improved, I began to play publicly, concertizing in Kursk, Sumy, Orel, Kaluga, Astrakhan, Dorpat, and so on. My primary musical activities have taken place in Tomsk, where my husband was appointed a professor at the university. . . . The degree to which I have energetically worked here is displayed in the annual reports of the Tomsk branch of the IRMO. . . . [I]n general, I have performed a great deal the entire time [I've been] here.[58]

Invoking the names and the spirits of the departed heroes of Moscow musical life validated Aleksandrova-Levenson's claims to the stage. In any case, she refused to accept the modest professional role to which she seemed destined. She recounted her public performances as proof of the continuing viability of her artistic career. Although her concert appearances were restricted to second and third rank provincial cities, they nevertheless proved both her performing ability and her persistence. By Siberian standards at least, Aleksandrova-Levenson had managed a successful career, but she clearly still longed for fame if not fortune. She passionately hoped to reinvigorate her performing career and lay the groundwork for a triumphal return to the capital's stages after her husband's retirement from the university and the couple's relocation to St. Petersburg or Moscow. Yet, Aleksandrova-Levenson's career was clearly on the wane. She was, among other things, both physically and temporally far removed from the centers of Russian musical life. Her memories of her heady youthful relationships with Tchaikovsky and Rubinstein, and for that matter Ziloti, were decades old and she was now a mature woman nearing her sixtieth year:

> My oldest son is just finishing the Moscow Conservatory...he is a composer and a pianist. His wife, a student of [Emile Jaques-]Dalcroze, is a teacher of rhythmic gymnastics in the conservatory.... My younger son is finishing his studies for a doctorate in mathematics in Zurich.[59]

Unfortunately for Ziloti, her unrelenting desire to revive dreams of glory untarnished by years of lessons and unrewarding provincial concerts encouraged numerous letters to the hapless conductor. Dreams or desperation drove her to invoke tenuous bonds of friendship in an effort to persuade Ziloti to allow her to perform Tchaikovsky's piano trio—which to her was a "prayer"—at one of his concerts.[60] Beyond the confines of her own career, Aleksandrova-Levenson's example suggests the powerful appeal of professionalization. Her career was, quite simply, a continual struggle to avoid the typical fate of most conservatory and music school graduates: either a willing or a forced descent into the position of educated amateur. For women as well as men, a musical education offered an opportunity for individual achievement that demanded continued professional success for validation.

Jewish Musicians, Anti-Semitism, and the Musical Profession

The prominence of women in music sparked debate over women's roles in society and the structure of the musical profession. Such questions were controversial not only in Russia but also throughout Europe both in the context of the emerging musical profession and as part of the "Woman Question." For the Russian musical profession, however, the status of Jews presented an even more complex problem. Jews in the Russian Empire labored under a variety of social and economic restrictions.[61] The confinement of the majority of the Jewish population to the Pale of Settlement seriously limited the employment possibilities of musicians because it barred their access to most major cities, including Moscow and St. Petersburg. From November 1861, Jewish graduates of the universities and other designated higher educational institutions were exempt from this restriction, as were other Jews who enjoyed the status of honored citizen. As Benjamin Nathans has argued, the extension of rights to Jewish graduates of higher educational institutions, combined with a shift in Jewish attitudes in favor of secular education, spurred a rapid increase in Jewish enrollment. The conservatories, however, became particularly important for Jewish students after 1881, when the gradual introduction of the *numerus clausus* or quota system began to sharply limit the enrollment of Jewish students in higher education.[62] The conservatories, as private institutions, were not automatically subject to the same restrictions on Jewish enrollment. Their status as higher educational institutions, however, was long contested. For Jewish conservatory graduates, therefore, the conservatories' status as higher educational institutions and graduates' rights to the status of honored citizen had enormous implications for their careers.

In 1885, the St. Petersburg civil administration revoked the residency permit of a Jewish conservatory graduate by the name of Veinbren. This decision threatened not only Veinbren's career, but also the status of the conservatories, because the city administration justified its action on the basis that the conservatories were not included on the list of higher educational institutions whose Jewish graduates enjoyed the right to reside outside the Pale. After appeals to the Department of Police and the Ministry of Internal Affairs on Veinbren's behalf proved unsuccessful, the Society, recognizing the damage this case could do to the status of its educational institutions and to the stature of the musical profession, brought the case to the State Senate.

The Veinbren case is one of many examples where a defense of the rights of Jewish conservatory students and graduates turned into a broader defense of the rights of the conservatory and the music profession as a whole. The Society hoped to use the Veinbren case to settle not only the issue of a single graduate's residency rights, but also the larger question of the status of the conservatories as educational institutions. The representative for the Russian Musical Society, Senator Markovich, hoped for a ruling that would "secure for the conservatories the position" to which they were entitled "both by law and by their own educational significance." Marshalling a wide array of evidence to prove his point, Markovich persuaded the Senate to formally recognize the conservatories as higher educational institutions. Jewish graduates of the conservatories were consequently entitled to reside outside the Pale. Although this ruling seemed unambiguous, the status of the conservatories as higher educational institutions remained subject to conflicting interpretations until well after the turn of the century.[63] Moreover, despite the ruling in Veinbren's favor, Jewish musicians, including conservatory graduates, continued to experience significant social and legal obstacles in their professional lives.

By the last quarter of the nineteenth century, Jews were important both as producers and as consumers of Russian musical culture. Although the percentage varied widely from place to place, data collected for the Ministry of Internal Affairs shows that Jews accounted for approximately 25 percent of all students in the Society's educational institutions between 1907 and 1908. Branches with Jewish students constituting roughly a third or more of the student body included St. Petersburg, Kiev, Vilnius, Ekaterinoslav, Kishinev, Nikolaev, Odessa, Poltava, Rostov on Don, Zhitomir, Kherson, and Irkutsk.[64]

The presence of a large Jewish cohort had long colored public and official attitudes toward the Society's educational institutions. In 1887, critics celebrating the return of Anton Rubinstein as director of the St. Petersburg Conservatory bemoaned the "Jewification" of the conservatory student body under his predecessor Karl Davydov.[65] From the outset, the Society had enforced an egalitarian admissions policy: its educational institutions admitted students without regard to gender or social estate.[66] Although the conservatory charter did not explicitly mention religion, most of the Society's educational institutions admitted students without regard to faith. This frequently forced them to negotiate with state and local authorities over the status of Jewish students and, consequently, the status of the institutions themselves.

Jews enrolled in significant numbers in the conservatories and music schools not only because of their egalitarian admissions policies but also because of their peculiar institutional status. Although nominally under the jurisdiction of the Ministry of Internal Affairs, the Society's *private* classes, schools, and conservatories were not subject to quotas for Jewish students.[67] For music students of any faith, the St. Petersburg Conservatory represented the pinnacle of success. Securing a place in its student body always presented challenges for provincial youth. For young Jewish musicians, such as Aron Mikhailovich Goldshtein, a graduate of the Tomsk Music Classes, restrictions on Jewish residency made the prospect of traveling to the capital for examination especially daunting. The Tomsk branch approached the Main Directorate on Goldshtein's behalf, hoping, presumably, to prevent the young man from wasting his time and money if he would not be allowed to sit the entrance exams. Fortunately for Goldshtein, at that time the St. Petersburg Conservatory enjoyed an effective working relationship with the local police; applicants of Jewish descent were issued certificates for temporary residency in the city, while admitted students received extended residency rights.[68]

Scattered evidence suggests that the percentage of Jewish students in the conservatories and music schools was relatively low until the mid-1880s but grew rapidly thereafter in the wake of the establishment of the quota on Jewish enrollment in state-supported educational institutions. In 1881–1882, roughly 10 percent of the students in the Kiev Music School were Jewish.[69] By 1887–1888, the last year statistics on student religious affiliation were included in the branch's annual report, the percentage of Jewish students in the school had almost tripled.[70] In most cities, enrollment of Jewish students depended on the ability of the Russian Musical Society or the students themselves to secure residency permits from the local authorities. The ease with which such permits could be obtained varied enormously, determined primarily by the relationship between the director of the music school or conservatory, the local board of the Society, and local authorities. Thus, in the 1880s and early 1890s the percentage of Jewish students at the Moscow Conservatory ranged between 11 and 13 percent, significantly above the quota for Jewish enrollment at state-supported institutions of higher education.[71] As Ben Nathans has noted, the 1905 Revolution prompted higher educational institutions to ignore the prescribed quotas, leading to a dramatic increase in the enrollment of Jewish students. Predictably, such actions eventually prompted a repressive response by the autocracy, which effectively reinstated the quotas in 1907. The Russian Musical Society and its schools and conservatories were caught in this backlash, as Minister of Internal Affairs V. K. von Plehve attempted to extend quotas to private institutions. As Nathans has persuasively argued, "the numerus clausus set off multiple skirmishes over accreditation of entire institutions and their graduates, and more profoundly, over the boundary between state and private authority."[72] In general, the Society was able to resist pressure to impose quotas on its conservatories and music schools. In the case of the Moscow Conservatory, however, unofficial arrangements with the local governor-general ensured that Jewish enrollment echoed the quota established for the city's other higher educational institutions.[73] By 1910, the Moscow Conservatory strictly limited the enrollment of Jewish students, who represented just 6.5 percent of the student body (49/749 students). By September 1913, the representation of Jews in the conservatory had declined still further, to 3.66 percent (34/930 students). In St. Petersburg, more liberal arrangements ensured a much larger Jewish cohort, which constituted between 40 and 50 percent of the student body.[74] Because Kiev was, as John Klier has noted, "technically but not geographically outside the Pale," residency issues loomed especially large.[75] In Kiev, as in St. Petersburg, the enrollment of Jewish students depended in large part on the local governor's willingness to accept the music school as a legitimate educational endeavor.[76] Although arrangements changed over time, the Kiev branch of the Society was frequently able to secure residency permits for prospective students simply by attesting to their talent.[77] By 1912–1913, immediately prior to the Kiev Music School's reorganization into a conservatory, just under half of the student body was Jewish.[78]

Because of the presence of large numbers of Jewish students, anti-Semitism affected the Society in a variety of ways. When the composer A. S. Arensky inspected several provincial branches in 1904–1905, he noted the dominance of Jewish students in the Odessa Music School. Although expressing his general approval at the level of performance displayed by students, Arensky expressed his disappointment that, for example, one violin class had no Russian students at all, and that "seventy-five percent" of students in the school were Jews. Other members of the Main Directorate professed to find such statistics shocking, with one reader exclaiming "And this in the *Russian* Musical Society!" in the margins of Arensky's report.[79] At its most serious, anti-Semitism sparked waves of *pogroms* that threatened the safety of the Jewish population and the well-being of the Society's branches and educational institutions. The pogroms in Odessa in October 1905, for example, created "havoc" and led to a "stampede" of Jewish residents seeking shelter abroad. In the chaos, the Odessa Music School lost a third of its students, threatening its financial stability.[80] Less perilously, the high percentage of Jewish students in the Society's educational institutions provoked accusations both that they colluded in draft evasion schemes and that they unfairly favored Jewish students and faculty. Thus, in 1908, Nikolai Martsenko, a graduate of the Moscow Conservatory, wrote in protest to the Society's patron, Grand Duke Konstantin Konstantinovich, charging that the Odessa Music School hired only Jews and foreigners and actively discriminated against Russian musicians. Martsenko claimed that his application for a position as clarinet instructor was disregarded, despite his credentials, in favor of a Jewish candidate with "no education whatsoever." The Grand Duke read Martsenko's letter with some sympathy, noting that such a state of affairs would be "unbearable" if true. However, upon investigation, it emerged that the Odessa Music School had hired not an outsider or a Jew as its new clarinet instructor, but Pavel Antonovich Fidler, described as a Russian of Orthodox faith and a laureate of the St. Petersburg Conservatory who had been personally recommended by its director, Alexander Glazunov. The music school faculty, the branch also noted with some indignation, was hardly a preserve of local Jews. In the heart of the Pale, only six of thirty-two faculty members were Jews.[81]

Because Jewish musicians and music students were often the backbone of local cultural life, their uncertain legal status plagued the Society and its local branches. In 1910, the Stavropol branch wrote to both the Minister of Internal Affairs and Nikolai Findeizen, the editor of *Russkaia muzykal'naia gazeta* and a member of the Main Directorate, asking for assistance in negotiating with local authorities who had demanded that all Jewish musicians and actors return to the Pale of Settlement. The decree had decimated local musical life. The branch was threatened with the loss of an experienced piano instructor, Abram-Isaak Konstantinovsky (Shniperlman), while the town was on the verge of losing most of its instrumentalists. The town's theater and even its restaurant orchestras had disintegrated. The departure of more than twenty musicians had left the town "without music." Expecting the Ministry of Internal Affairs to refuse its petition, the branch hatched a plan to keep Konstantinovsky by declaring that he was a piano tuner with the right to reside in the city based on his artisanal skill. Through the intercession of the Main Directorate, Konstantinovsky received temporary residency rights, allowing him to finish the school year and buying the Stavropol branch time to find a more permanent solution.[82]

Despite anti-Semitism, restrictions on enrollment, residency, and other obstacles placed in the educational and professional paths of Jewish musicians, real opportunities did exist. Like other graduates of the Society's educational institutions, Jewish students could seek employment in orchestras, as singers, and as music teachers. A lucky few secured employment in the Society's music classes, schools, and conservatories. Others founded music schools and classes of their own, within or outside the Pale. Moreover, as James Loeffler has persuasively demonstrated in his study of the Society for Jewish Folk Music, musicians contributed significantly to the cultural and intellectual development of Russian Jewish society.[83] Yet, Jews faced more restrictions on their employment than did other members of the musical profession. Letters advertising available positions often declared that Jews were ineligible or, at the least, not preferred candidates. In September 1907, for example, the Commander of the 195th Dubensky Reserve Infantry Regiment wrote to the Kiev Music School seeking candidates to fill a position as military bandmaster. For annual wages of 600 rubles, the commander sought a young, but able and diligent man who "should be Russian in spirit, completely politically reliable, and if possible knowledgeable about the balalaika orchestra." Similarly, the 1st Black Sea Regiment of the Kuban Cossack Troop sought well-trained candidates able to serve both as bandmasters and as regents for the regimental chapel choir. "Conditions of service are: the bandmaster should be if possible (*po vozmozhnosti*) of Russian origins and without question not a Jew, wages are 100 rubles per month, the contract to begin from the 1st of June of this year."[84]

The frequency and strength of these demands indicates the prominence of Jewish musicians and their importance to sustaining the growth of Russian musical culture. Anti-Semites argued that Jews were chasing Russians out of the profession. The situation, some hysterically charged, had deteriorated to the point that Orthodox Church choirs were in danger of having to rely on Jewish regents.[85] Such accusations sometimes verged on the bizarre, as in one case in Odessa, where what was initially presented as an example of undue favoritism toward Jewish musicians turned out to be an attempt by a jealous woman to exact revenge on her personal and professional rivals. In pressing her case, Paula Nikolaevna Fomina appealed directly to Princess Elena

Georgievna Saksen-Altenburgskaia, then the Society's president and patron. Fomina borrowed liberally not only from paranoid theories of Jewish conspiracies but also from the emerging narrative of Russia's growing musical importance:

> Your Highness! it is very difficult for us, Russian musicians, to live in the south, which the Jews consider their own and they send us packing to the north.... Here Russian musicians are afraid and ashamed to call themselves Russians, because they laugh at us.... In the press, voices already proclaim that Russian music occupies the leading place in Europe and that among the names that it prides itself in, both in the present and in the recent past, there is not one Jewish name (Tchaikovsky, Rimsky-Korsakov, Balakirev, Serov, Musorgsky and only Rubinstein, a degenerate Russianized half-Jew). From Glinka to Glazunov—not one Jew. But here [in Odessa] they think that everything Russian is bad.... The chairman of [our local branch of] the IRMO is a wonderful man, but quite weak-willed, just like the director of the conservatory, and both are in the hands of the Jews. [86]

By 1905, the state was closely involved in the Society's music classes, schools, and conservatories, contributing subsidies, loans, and other material aid and conferring rights and privileges on students, graduates, and faculty. Eventually, some wondered whether these institutions had not already become *de facto* components of the state-supported educational system.[87] As the status of the Society's educational institutions grew increasingly unclear, high levels of Jewish enrollment gave the state cause for concern. If the Society's educational institutions were formally incorporated into the state system, quotas for Jewish enrollment would have to be enforced. At the same time, the state recognized an interest in music as a "natural" inclination of the Jewish people. Moreover, it believed this inclination to be socially and politically harmless, diverting Jews from other, potentially far more corrosive areas of activity.[88] Jewish musicians, then, paradoxically benefited both from the low status of music as a profession and from the low opinion that the tsarist regime had of its Jewish population. Despite efforts by the Russian Musical Society to improve the stature of music as a profession, most working musicians, particularly orchestral players, remained outsiders in Russian educated society. Music was a marginal profession and, as such, was relatively accessible to marginal groups within Russian society. Russian Jews also had a strong tradition of musicianship, which created a basis for inclusion in the musical profession. Jews were, by definition, already outsiders; employment as working musicians did not carry the stigma for Jews that it did for more respectable members of Russian society. At the same time, credentials from the Society's music schools and, especially, conservatories carried real social and legal privileges. Jews who enrolled in music schools or conservatories could obtain both a formal secondary education and a specialized music education at a time when the demand for spaces in the gymnasia and real schools far outstripped the quota for Jewish students. As a result, enrollment in one of these institutions held out the promise of social respectability and advancement. As Marion Kaplan has noted in the case of Germany, issues of social respectability and assimilation also likely explain the enthusiasm of young Jewish women for specialized music education.[89] Participation in shared cultural rituals, such as piano instruction, offered Jewish families a way to reduce the distance between themselves and their Gentile neighbors.

Becoming a Professional: Building Careers in Music

Musical professionalization in Russia differed most from similar processes elsewhere when it intersected with broader social changes resulting from the Great Reforms of the 1860s and 1870s. The Russian Musical Society initially encouraged the professionalization of composers, theorists, and virtuosi, rather than rank-and-file musicians. While novel in the Russian context, this process was directed at segments of society—the déclassé nobility, the intelligentsia, the *raznochintsy*, and the sons and daughters of an emerging professional middle class—that already enjoyed a relatively high social, if not necessarily economic, position. It was not until well into the 1880s that the first stirrings of professional consciousness began to infect a broad segment of working musicians. Beginning in the 1890s, both orchestral musicians and ordinary music teachers began to demand public recognition as professionals.

One such ordinary musician, Filipp Sergeevich Voskobainikov, was among those who submitted their biographies to the Russian Musical Society in the 1890s. Born a peasant in 1876, he enrolled in the Kharkov Music School at age eleven. In 1892, age sixteen, he graduated with a second-degree certificate that gave him the right to teach music or to conduct choirs. By August of that year, he became a string instrument and singing teacher in the Sumy Real School. We can judge the "fruitfulness of his labors" by the program from a student performance that he included with his biography. The sophistication of the concert suggests that both Voskobainikov and local society benefited from his education in the Kharkov Music School. The concert included choral works by Mozart, Bortniansky,

Tchaikovsky, and Voskobainikov himself, while the school's choir and orchestra combined to play excerpts from Mozart's *Requiem* and the Russian national hymn, "God Save the Tsar." Small mixed instrumental ensembles played pieces by Haydn and Kreutser, while the instructors, Voskobainikov on violin and Ia. I. Nurmik on French horn, performed solo works. The student string orchestra performed as well. Even the accompanists were students.[90]

The professional and personal possibilities provided by a musical education were extremely diverse. As we have seen, the conservatories and music schools attracted significant interest from the army and navy, who saw in these institutions an opportunity to train an elite cadre of Russian military musicians, thus eliminating dependency on foreign bandmasters and improving the quality of military bands. Military units sent apprentice musicians to study at the conservatories and music schools, while elite units, particularly the Preobrazhensky Guards Regiment, recruited graduating students, enticing them with the opportunity to fulfill their military service as musicians.[91] The conservatories and music schools responded to this interest by offering courses in military instrumentation, which enhanced the credentials of graduates, such as Nikolai Kazankov, as military bandmasters.[92] The son of a soldier, Kazankov completed his musical studies at the conservatory in 1892 and his general education courses in 1893, thereby earning a free artist's diploma. When he did not receive any offers for teaching positions, Kazankov took advantage of his course on military instrumentation and accepted a position as bandmaster with the Eighty-Seventh Infantry of the Neiligotsky Regiment.[93]

Other conservatory graduates employed more aggressive measures to secure their careers in an increasingly competitive environment. G. Ia. Fistulari, for example, resorted to blatant self-promotion, publishing a small pamphlet of reviews of his appearances as a conductor at the International Artistic-Industrial Exhibition in 1908. The pamphlet included a portrait and short biographical sketch that emphasized both his Russian origins and his professional training. Not the shy and retiring type, Fistulari described his appearances at the International Exhibition as a "colossal" success, an interpretation that was more or less sustained by the reviews included in the pamphlet. Fistulari left no opportunity for self-promotion untouched. He highlighted his abilities as a composer—with two symphonies, four overtures, two suites, and many romances to his credit—and as a public figure; he briefly served as the director of the Russian Musical Society's Orel branch and founded and directed the St. Petersburg Musical-Dramatic and Operatic Courses.[94]

The conservatory's existence was based on the premise that musicians can be made. Musicians can also be bred. In Russia, as everywhere, children of musicians often chose musical careers of their own after a childhood spent in an environment rich with music. The development of formal, institutionalized music education did not bring such informal avenues of entry to the profession to a halt, but it did alter them, as the educational and professional path of M. A. Bikhter, a pianist and conductor, demonstrates. Bikhter's incomplete memoirs cannot be trusted on the details—he wrote conflicting versions of some of the episodes of his life—but they serve as a narrative portrait of the family background, upbringing, education, and early career of a prototypical Russian professional musician before the revolution.

Bikhter was born in Moscow in 1881 to a cultured, if impoverished, Jewish family and raised largely by his grandparents. His grandfather had been a military cantonist during the reign of Nicholas I, a misfortune that he nevertheless credited with bringing music to the family; while in service, the grandfather learned to play and later found occasional employment as an orchestral musician. One evening, Bikhter accompanied him to "some popular theater or another" where his grandfather played in the orchestra, which made an enormous impression on the child.[95]

Bikhter's grandfather was not the only musician in the family. His father was a violinist, who is described at one point as a professional and at another as unskilled, and his mother a casual pianist; one of Bikhter's distant cousins was Sergei Koussevitzky. As a result, the family, at least as Bikhter recalled events, voiced no objections to his desire for a musical education. His first teachers were modest practitioners of the art; one was still a student, while another ran a small piano school out of her home. In this domestic setting, Bikhter first began to study music seriously, although his efforts were destined to be short-lived. The year was 1892, and the city administration proved determined to expel unwanted Jewish residents, an effort that disrupted the lives and careers of many musicians. This unanticipated departure from Moscow and his parents' subsequent search for work led the little family to Saratov. Although the results of this move were unhappy for the family—his parents separated—for Bikhter the move was an important step forward:

> We lived there for about a year.... The central event in my life was that I began to study at the Music School of the IRMO in the piano class of a teacher whose last name, I think, was Sheiberg. I also took a course in music theory.... I don't recall the lessons themselves... but I remember that one time I played Beethoven's Pathetique Sonata at an open ("public") student evening. My teacher sat beside me on the stage

and whenever I did not land on the proper note in my left hand, he played the correct one.[96]

Saratov also introduced Bikhter to the working world. Hired as the pianist for a restaurant orchestra, the young boy struggled to fit in among adult musicians with their coarse manners and impatience with neophytes. Still, the 20 rubles he earned each month were welcome. The always enthusiastic student attempted to seize every opportunity to sneak in a little more practice, playing quietly in the intermissions, until patrons suggested he stop tormenting them with his artless etudes and scales.[97]

By the fall of 1894, the family's fortunes had changed. Bikhter and his mother resettled in St. Petersburg, where he soon continued his musical training. Between 1894 and 1910, when he finally graduated, Bikhter was an intermittent conservatory student as he struggled to support his family. "I studied with Liadov and Esipova at the conservatory, while making my living with piano and music theory lessons and accompanying singers in their homes and in concert, [earning] between 60 and 120 rubles a month."[98] Bikhter's memory of his teaching career offers some insight into the complicated role of the piano instructor in the domestic and emotional lives of their clients. Bikhter recalled his acquaintanceship with a wealthy landlord, whose daughter became his piano student. "Elena, my piano student, was... talented in drawing and painting and studied music as a supplement to her elementary education. My constant presence... brought us together and colored our relationship. There is no doubt that we were in love with each other."[99] Predictably, the infatuation between the young piano teacher and his student did not end at the altar, but with her marriage to someone else. Bikhter, however, did marry and attempt to settle down. Although modest, Bikhter's wages allowed him to support himself, his wife, and his mother, but finances became more strained with the birth of a son, Vovochka, who completed their domestic "quartet."

Bikhter's professional ambitions soon led him to the conductor's podium:

> My first, unexpected conducting attempt was in Petersburg, in a small theater on Maksimilianov sidestreet, which, I think, was called the "Palm-tree Hall" (*Zal Pal'ma*).... One way or the other, I was in my [appointed] place at eight o'clock.... The small orchestra (16–18 men) had already made some noise "tuning up." When [the curtain] rose... I made all the proper gestures and managed not to hit anyone. But that night I learned how helpless a man with a little stick is when people with instruments don't want [to follow] that stick. The musicians... took pleasure in my helplessness. Later, I found out that this

was their protest in solidarity with their [former] director, who had been fired.[100]

Even this humiliating debut could not discourage Bikhter. In the spring of 1906 he joined a private opera troupe on a tour through the provinces. The birth of a second son had left his little family in dire financial straits and the tour promised both financial and psychic rewards; Bikhter was eager to see new and exotic locations. Although the tour did deliver both in modest terms—if dusty Tambov was neither exotic nor interesting, Turkestan was—the performances continued Bikhter's education as a conductor. Once again, however, he found himself facing a hostile orchestra. In this case, their resentment resulted from his innocent zeal to learn his job. An obvious and overeager novice, he scheduled numerous rehearsals, disrupting the relaxing "paid vacation" the experienced orchestra had been counting on. Nevertheless, by the end of the tour Bikhter had matured as a conductor. Returning to St. Petersburg, Bikhter, with his wife and sons in tow, soon departed for Tomsk, where the local branch of the Russian Musical Society had hired him as a piano teacher, a task he found both disheartening and dull. "My pedagogical work was of little interest. In the first place, I was quite young and lacked experience as a piano teacher; in the second place, I didn't much like this kind of work . . . ; in the third place, the students in my class were hopeless. Consequently, Tomsk was in no respect attractive to me. I already thought of returning to St. Petersburg after the examinations in the spring."[101]

Litanies of Victimization: The Rank-and-File and the "Musical Proletariat"

As the adventures of Bikhter and his colleagues suggest, the professionalization process of individuals was highly variable. Nevertheless, it is clear that orchestral musicians as a group lagged behind in developing a distinctive professional identity. Moreover, assertions of professional and corporative identity by orchestral musicians, unlike those by composers, virtuosi, and theorists, directly challenged assumptions about the place of music and musicians in Russian society. Because orchestral musicians were drawn primarily from the lower estates, they were far more difficult to integrate into the profession. They lacked not only the social status, but also the education, manners, and cultural capital essential to effective participation in educated society. An 1868 caricature in *Syn otechestva* emphasized this point. In it, a musician wheedles his friend, an orchestra manager, for a job. The pair's swollen and inflamed noses and slovenly appearance mark them as drunkards, while the details of the "contract" they work out casts doubt on the capabilities of the performing musician. Inquiring as to his friend's musical specialty, the manager is informed that, when sober, he plays the violin, but when drunk performs particularly "resonantly" on the trumpet. Considering his options, the musician suggests his manager friend sign him on as a trumpeter.[102] This caricature, by literally illustrating the degraded status of orchestral musicians in Russian society, hints at the problems orchestral musicians experienced in trying to assert their professional identity. Less mocking, but no less despairing depictions of the degraded social position and personal plight of instrumentalists can be seen in the work of more respectable artists, such as Nikolai Petrovich Petrov, whose 1876 painting, "A Musician," vividly depicted the exhaustion and poverty of the working Russian musician (figure 4.4). Even those with a conservatory diploma suffered from persistently low status within the expanding musical profession.

In 1886, Evgeny Albrekht penned a short book, best translated as *The Past and Present of the Orchestra (An Essay on the Social Position of Musicians)*, that examined the implications of the theatrical reforms of the early 1880s for the lives and careers of rank-and-file orchestral players. Albrekht clearly subscribed wholeheartedly to Romantic ideas of artistic genius and translated them into a moral demand for the elevation of musicians as both individuals and as a class. In an age when "music had become the property of the whole educated world," he found it difficult to comprehend that "great composers" once served "private individuals and frequently occupied the most humble positions." Although Albrekht acknowledged that "the position of musicians" in Western Europe had recently improved, he insisted that their "traditionally humiliating position in civic life (*grazhdanskii byt*)," isolated them "from the rest of society," while "their severe material insecurity" forced them to band together for survival. Concerned about their material well-being, Albrekht argued, they had begun to organize themselves in order to improve their social position.[103]

Russian musicians, he suggested, needed to borrow the strategies developed by their colleagues abroad. In this context, it was the legacies of serfdom that drew most of Albrekht's fire. He dwelt on the humiliating details of the lives of serf musicians. Lacking control over their professional lives, they were required to play when, where, and for how long the theatrical administration and their conductor demanded. Predictably enough, the result was a demoralized and undisciplined ensemble, staffed by musicians with little desire to perform accurately or diligently, much less artistically. Low wages forced them to search for employment in dance orchestras hired for balls. Exhaustion and overwork proved to be the death of artistic self-respect.[104]

These were the conditions Albrekht faced in 1877, when he was appointed the inspector of music for the Imperial Theaters. Dissatisfied with the quality of both musicians' working conditions and their performances, Albrekht helped introduce significant reforms that led, in 1882, to the establishment of the first formal wage scale for theater musicians. Decorum and discipline within the orchestras improved markedly, Albrekht asserted, because the musicians now felt that the administration recognized and valued their contributions. The result, thanks to the reforms and to the efforts of the ensemble's superlative conductor, Eduard Napravnik, was the creation of a model professional orchestra, with few if any equals on the European continent.[105] But Albrekht wanted to do more than simply raise wages and performance standards. He wanted to make orchestral musicians recognized and respectable professionals. Achieving respectability, Albrekht insisted, demanded the transformation of both musicians and society. Musicians needed to become educated and useful citizens instead of wandering players occupying the fringes of society. For Russian musicians, like their West European counterparts, education was the key to social advancement. A musician who "plays like a demigod... but is completely uneducated," Albrekht insisted, could play only "the most pitiable role," in educated society. Echoing Anton Rubinstein's rationale for the establishment of the Russian conservatories, Albrekht argued that, in order to raise orchestral musicians from their humiliating position, they needed to "receive an education no lower" than that typical "in the circles in which they move."[106]

Orchestral entrepreneurs and their restrictive employment contracts were among the favorite targets of Albrekht and other self-appointed spokesmen for working musicians. Although musicians viewed these contracts as little more than bald-faced attempts to cheat them of their full wages, orchestral entrepreneurs must surely have seen the contracts as an attempt to ensure the viability and stability of their ensemble. The contract drawn up by Nikolai Stepanovich Giarkin, who leased the Panaevsky Garden in Kazan during the 1880s, demanded that newly hired musicians agree to play their parts during all "rehearsals, theatrical performances, entr'acte, concerts, literary evenings, and other presentations given in the garden and theater of Mr. Giarkin by amateurs, artists, concert artists, conjuring shows (*fokusniki*), etc." The contract further obligated musicians to devote all of their energy and skill to the fulfillment of their duties, a stipulation that suggested musicians, feeling underpaid and badly treated, might retaliate with slack playing, chronic tardiness, and insubordinate behavior. The contract laid out the specifics of day-to-day employment, some of which must have been truly onerous for musicians struggling to get by on modest wages. In addition to supplying

FIGURE 4.4. *A Musician* by Nikolai Petrovich Petrov, (1834–1876), Russia, 1876. Regional A. Deineka Art Gallery, Kursk, oil on canvas. Credit: culture-images/Lebrecht

their own instrument and keeping it in working order, musicians had to appear for all performances in a black suit and its accoutrements. Failure to appear for a rehearsal or performance without a demonstrable, unavoidable reason resulted in fines of from 1 to 5 rubles for each offense. Should one of the other players fail to appear, fall ill, or be fired, the other musicians were required to fill his shoes if possible. Musicians were responsible for the music issued to them and required to reimburse the entrepreneur for its loss. Although the contract was written from the point of view of the entrepreneur and intended to protect him from the depredations of musicians who were clearly assumed to be both cunning and devious, the contract did provide some minimal legal protection for musicians as well. Wages were individually negotiated, as were penalties for breaking the contract early by either party. Musicians retained the right to perform at balls, weddings, dinners, and evening parties on their own time, an important supplement to their income. Conversely, Giarkin's contract carefully outlined the conditions under which he was no longer obligated to pay his employees. The closure of the pleasure garden and its theater, whether due to an official mourning period, a fire, the impoverishment of the region, or governmental decree, freed the entrepreneur of the need to pay wages from the day the theater closed. Finally, at the discretion of the entrepreneur, musicians who failed to meet the conditions of their contract could be fined from 1 to 10 rubles for each occurrence.[107]

The rules for orchestral musicians established by the Shelaputin Theater in Moscow in 1897 were a bit more rigid, perhaps due to the greater competition among theaters in the capital. They also suggest a greater degree of professionalization. On the one hand, the contract spelled out expectations for the appearance and cleanliness of musicians, who were obliged to appear for performances in a black suit with a clean shirt and white tie. On the other hand, musicians were expected to appear only ten minutes before the start of the performance and trusted to tune up under the leadership of the concertmaster. In the case of illness, musicians were required to notify the conductor or his assistant *in writing* in advance of the rehearsal or performance, a clear indication that musicians were assumed to be literate. Fines and wage deductions were still the blunt instrument used to control musicians' behavior. Failure to appear for a rehearsal resulted in the loss of half a day's wages; absence from a performance cost a musician a full day's wages. There were hints, however, that such draconian rules were necessary to rein in the behavior of musicians, who were forbidden to "smoke, snack, or chat loudly" during rehearsals, with fines at the discretion of the conductor for transgressions. Musicians were forbidden from complaining to the conductor or the administrator during rehearsals. The penalties for this sin were clearly spelled out, suggesting that orchestral musicians needed powerful incentives to dissuade them from expressing their displeasure. A first offense drew a fine of 5 rubles, but a second offense resulted in the termination of the musician's contract and his summary dismissal. Should the members of the orchestra legitimately need to consult with the administration, they were to select two of their number to represent them. Musicians clearly objected to fines for misbehavior. This set of rules stressed that fines, once levied, would not be refunded for any reason, a clear attempt to forestall arguments on this subject. To make such fines more tolerable, it was emphasized that the funds collected would not enrich the conductor or the administration, but would be deposited entirely in the account of the "Almshouse for Elderly Artists."[108]

By the 1890s, articles warning of a growing "musical proletariat" fed concerns about an increasingly overcrowded professional field. The somewhat hysterical battle cry seemed to be "There are too many musicians!" The proliferation of music schools, which had begun with the establishment of the St. Petersburg Conservatory, continued unabated and showed signs not of stopping but of further exponential growth. As conservatory graduates and former music students sought desperately to secure their livelihoods, they turned to music teaching. The unfortunate result, it was alleged, was the impoverishment of musicians and the degradation of music.

This gloomy view was expounded at length by A. Porten in his *Zaveshchanie muzykanta* (*Testament d'un musician*) of 1891. In more than two hundred pages of often purple prose, Porten strove tirelessly to dissuade the young from considering music as a career. Porten identified himself as a Russian citizen, but one with the confused antecedents that characterized so many "Russian" musicians. He was born in Lithuania into a noble family and educated in Germany and Belgium before returning to Russia for much of his career. Porten's *Testament* attempted to expose what he saw as a European-wide disaster in the making where alternately naïve and idealistic or lazy and greedy young people flooded the halls of the continent's conservatories.[109] Porten's arguments were hardly original. As Ehrlich has noted, many established musicians lamented the "damnable flood" of new competitors being unleashed from both well-established conservatories and from the ever increasing multitude of private music schools.[110]

Judging by his often confused and convoluted arguments, Porten was appalled at the changes in European musical life that he had witnessed over the course of his career. The professionalization and institutionalization of music advocated so forcefully by figures such as Anton Rubinstein just a few decades before had succeeded all too well; for Porten, the costs of musical modernization were too high and the social transformations that resulted represented a loss rather than a gain. Porten repeatedly complained about the "false adepts" of music whose lust for money and fame rather than a pure desire to serve music had drawn them to the stage. He bemoaned in this context not only the flooding of the concert and operatic stages with mediocrities, but also the commercialization and popularization of the arts.

Music was no longer the province of the elect, either on the stage or in the audience. Porten, unlike contemporaries who viewed the democratization of musical life as one of the keys to the cultural salvation of Russia, argued that the "dissemination of music to the masses" did not spring from any "real spiritual need." His complaints rested on a deeper disgust with the "practical and utilitarian" values of the age. Inspiration was subordinated to worldly considerations, Porten argued. "Art no longer stands apart from everyday life; it is initiating laymen (*profany*) into its mysteries and vulgarizing itself!" Porten's elitism rested on a nostalgia for a cultural past where art was a marker of real gentility that, in his mind, guaranteed the status of its adepts more than any diploma from an educational institution ever could. The conservatories and other musical institutions, whatever their intended goals, had not elevated music but had transformed it into a mere trade or handicraft (*remeslo*). The conservatories compounded their sins by admitting students of questionable ability, encouraging them in their delusions, and then being far too free with diplomas, setting these same mechanically trained but anti-artistic individuals loose on the streets of the city to either forge a career or starve.[111]

Throughout the *Testament*, Porten's driving concern was the low social status of the professional orchestral musician. He dreamed of the day when musicians would be as respectable in Russia as they already were in Germany, where musicians in the largest opera companies were able to "contemplate marriage with a young lady of a good family."[112] In Russia, he complained, the failure to make distinctions among musicians, in particular between members of the best orchestras of the Imperial Theaters and those of its more artistically insignificant ensembles, all of whom were styled "Artists of the Imperial Theaters," robbed the title of any real significance and thus musicians of any hope for a respectable social position.[113] Porten's complaint, and his implicit solution to the problem, echo the ways other professionalizing groups attempted to elevate their own status by denying professional recognition to less elite, or less skilled affiliate groups.[114]

Professionalization accelerated at the turn of the century as orchestral musicians borrowed the strategies of other would-be professional groups and began to establish mutual aid societies, voluntary associations, and specialized music journals devoted to their needs. They also laid claim to the idea of a musical proletariat, a term previously used to describe the hordes of underemployed pianists produced by the conservatories and music schools. Among those leading the charge into battle, so to speak, was the multitalented Ivan Lipaev, whose often-eloquent essays about the lives of orchestral musicians structured the debates over musical professionalization from the 1890s to the revolutions of 1917. Born in 1865, Lipaev pushed far beyond the career boundaries of a typical orchestral musician. After graduating from the Musical-Dramatic School of the Moscow Philharmonic Society in composition and trombone performance, Lipaev joined the Bolshoi Theater orchestra, performing with them from 1893 to 1912 and from 1924 to 1931. His multifaceted career included appearances as a conductor, lecturer, and actor, as well as social activist, prolific writer, and pedagogue. Among his other activities, he taught at the Saratov Conservatory from 1912 to 1921.[115] Lipaev's two books, *Essays on the Way of Life of Orchestral Musicians*, published in 1891, and *Orchestral Musicians*, published in 1904, sketched in dramatic and sometimes maudlin fashion the perilous and degrading day-to-day existence of orchestral musicians. Lipaev then inverted these criticisms into a manifesto for working musicians, a platform from which they might claim their rightful place in Russian society.

The front cover of *Essays on the Way of Life of Orchestral Musicians* trumpeted the burning issues that the book would address: education and training, wages, the length of the working day, lodging and living conditions, professional illnesses and life expectancy, and the appearance of "kulaks"—musical middlemen and entrepreneurs—and their characteristics. The tone of the table of contents, and of the book as a whole, is that of an expose, intended to reveal the "shocking facts" of the "life and work of a class of people almost completely unknown to society." Firmly convinced that orchestral musicians were a self-contained, identifiable group, a social "class," Lipaev went to some lengths to prove this assertion to his readers. Despite diverse origins, he insisted, musicians led similar lives and suffered in similar ways; factors that might seem to divide musicians from one another—such as nationality or religion—were insignificant in the face of larger challenges that all faced. Social diversity further weakened the hold of traditional ties and reinforced corporate identity as a musician. Children of the nobility sat beside the children of peasants, artisans, clerics, merchants, and musicians in the orchestras. Those with university educations shared music stands with those who could not even read. Their most identifiable characteristics, Lipaev asserted, were their ill health, poverty, and narrow social and intellectual development.[116]

Above all, Lipaev wanted to transform the way that orchestral musicians were trained. Those educated in the conservatories and private music schools that had appeared since the 1860s, rather than in a "brutal" apprenticeship or through rote learning in the army, were more skilled than their predecessors and less fortunate peers.[117] Improved training was only a part of the solution, however. Lipaev recognized the need to create a class of musicians whom society would willingly recognize as true professionals. The key to this transformation was not just education but also civilization, quite literally the domestication of musicians into productive and respectable members of the nascent middle class.

Lipaev presented a damning portrait of the daily lives and domestic situations of orchestral musicians. Most were not only poorly educated but also willfully ignorant, although he willingly made exception for the younger, conservatory-educated generation. They read newspapers, but only for their coverage of the arts. They moved often and earned relatively little, between 40 and 70 rubles per month, but only in the months that they were working. Uncertain employment led to disorder at home. They lived in uncomfortable apartments and rented rooms, spending their spare time doing "women's work" as few could support a family.[118] The depiction is one of meanness and squalor, rather than desperate poverty. The problem, for Lipaev and for orchestral musicians, was not that their working or living conditions differed so much from those of other semiprofessionals, low-ranking civil servants, or skilled workers, but that their expectations were so high. Nevertheless, the portrait that Lipaev paints of orchestral musicians in 1891 is that of the artisan or the skilled worker. His concerns—especially about working and living conditions—reflect broader social concerns about workers that emerged as Russia industrialized. Thus, workplace safety, the length of the working day, and the relationship of workers to management all play a major role in Lipaev's first book.

In the dozen years between Lipaev's two books, the position of orchestral musicians improved markedly. The self-righteous and inflammatory tone that made his first book such a compelling read was diluted in the second book every time Lipaev was forced to qualify his criticisms with acknowledgments of improving wages, working conditions, and, most important, the growing corporate consciousness of orchestral musicians. Nevertheless, the overriding issue in *Orchestral Musicians*, as in the first book, was the need to improve musicians' social status. Lipaev dwelt at length on the plight of serf musicians before 1861, including maudlin stories of their abuse by landowners. The effect, quite intentionally, was to both underscore the humiliating origins of Russian orchestral musicians as a social group and to build group solidarity. This rendered more plausible his assertion that the decree of 15 January 1839, which extended "the rights of artists," including personal honored citizenship and the title of "Artist of the Imperial Theaters," to orchestral musicians, was a predecessor to the Emancipation Manifesto of 1861.[119] For Russian musicians, the path to full civil rights led through serfdom, but for Lipaev, serfdom was merely an extreme example of the broader servitude of musicians to the wealthy and powerful. Freed from the legal bonds of serfdom, musicians still needed to break the moral chains that bound them, the traditions that encouraged them to accept their servile position and limited their ability to participate fully in educated society. Yet Lipaev was optimistic. With the disappearance and death of the older generation of "accidental musicians," serfs who had become musicians through no choice of their own, and through the educational opportunities created by the foundation of the conservatories, musical life had begun to change for the better. A new generation of educated musicians was emerging that possessed both the social prerequisites and the will to establish a corporate identity. Not only the former serf musicians, but also their culture, habits, and jargon were disappearing from the musical landscape.[120]

Lipaev's strategies would have been familiar to other professionalizing groups and to those striving to organize and assist workers. He proposed formal organizations for mutual aid and control of professional life, inspired primarily by such associations in Germany and France as well as models closer to home such as the mutual aid organizations of musicians in Moscow and Odessa. To help bring these dreams to reality, Lipaev proposed the establishment of professional journals able to give a voice to an emerging group.[121] Lipaev himself was hardly content to sit on the sidelines and complain about the status of musicians. After 1905, as editor and publisher of the self-consciously professional journals *Muzykal'nyi truzhenik* and *Orkestr*, Lipaev labored to provide orchestral players with a public forum for the symbolic construction and representation of their identity to the reading public. Yet, paradoxically, in attempting to encourage the development of professional identity among orchestral musicians, Lipaev obstructed the unification of musicians. His conception of professional orchestral musicians was limited to those who served in the orchestras of the Imperial Theaters and the most legitimate of private theaters. Specifically excluded were the members of military, factory, departmental, and private orchestras, all of whom he viewed as unfair competition for professionals.[122]

Until the revolution, internal diversity of education, social position, and working conditions limited the ability of musicians to coalesce as a professional group. Advocates of professionalization pursued a two-pronged strategy. In order for musicians to be accepted as professionals, they needed to conform more closely to educated society's image of "professionals." Proponents of professionalization advertised the educational, cultural, moral, and even physical transformation of musicians. Simultaneously, they encouraged musicians to demand inclusion in respectable society. Despite the torrent of books and articles on the subject, despite the efforts of musicians to organize in defense of their group interests, musicians remained as much artisan as artist up to the revolution.

CHAPTER 5

The Geography of Culture

The Expansion of Musical Life in the Provinces

Oh gentlemen who study the provinces and their way of life from far away: stop to visit and after three minutes of observation you will surely take away a more clearly defined idea of provincial life than all of your books could ever give you.

K.K. Zike, 1895 (TsGIA SPb, fond 361, op. 11, d. 221)

ALTHOUGH THE INITIAL CHARTER OF the Russian Musical Society spoke of a desire to disseminate music broadly throughout the empire, expansion took place slowly, with fits, starts, and dead ends. In the 1860s, the Society attempted to establish branches in Kiev, Kharkov, and Saratov, although only the branch in Kiev survived. In the 1870s, the Society successfully reestablished branches in Kharkov (1872) and Saratov (1873), and created new ones in Nizhnii Novgorod (1873), Pskov (1873), Omsk (1876), Tobolsk (1878), and Tomsk (1879). By the end of the 1880s, it boasted additional branches in Penza (1881), Tambov (1882), Tiflis (1883), and Odessa (1886). In the 1890s, the expansion of the Society gained significant momentum that accelerated rapidly after the turn of the century; of the fifty-six branches in existence in 1914, forty-one were founded after 1890.[1] As both Russia's population and its economy grew, small and isolated provincial towns emerged as new centers of commerce, administration, and culture. A map of the Society's branches highlights both the potential significance and the inherent limitations of expansion (figure 5.1).

FIGURE 5.1. Map of the branches of the Russian Musical Society, c. 1914

Because rapid urbanization created a need for new institutions to supply the cultural goods demanded by a larger educated population, the Russian Musical Society expanded in parallel with the growth of provincial cities. Unsurprisingly, most of the Society's branches, like most of the empire's population, were located west of the Ural Mountains, with the branches in Siberia and the Far East seemingly isolated and vulnerable in the vastness of the region. But as the map clearly shows, by the early twentieth century even these branches, and more broadly, these communities, were increasingly linked to the centers of Russian culture by the railroad. In European Russia and the Ukraine, conversely, larger populations and more dynamic local economies spurred the development of cultural life in second-rank towns; the branches of the Russian Musical Society established after 1900, in particular, were a key part of an ever-denser web of cultural institutions that reflected the growing demand for education, entertainment, and ideas in the provinces. If the earliest branches of the Society were, as they liked to consider themselves, oases in a cultural desert, by the outbreak of World War I, the Society's branches formed an archipelago of culture, linked by the railroad, the post, and the periodical press, that stretched from the Western Borderlands to the Sea of Japan.

Growing provincial cities pursued cultural institutions because they served as powerful symbols of civilization for residents and outsiders alike. For local residents, cultural institutions reinforced their often-tenuous claims to membership in the intelligentsia. Universities, schools, theaters, and music societies were badges of honor that could be displayed to prove the cultural sophistication of a city and its population. New branches of the Society, for example, were promoted by local cultural leaders who emphasized the civilizing potential of concert culture and music education. Predictably, however, the task of establishing a viable musical life in cities far from the geographical and intellectual centers of Imperial Russian culture proved complicated. The leaders of provincial branches of the Society, out of brutal necessity, improvised creative solutions to the obstacles they confronted as they sought to bring culture to the "wilderness."

Cultural Expansionism: New Branches, New Problems, New Solutions

The earliest and ultimately one of the most successful branches of the Russian Musical Society was founded in Kiev in 1863 when it was still just a provincial commercial center of some 70,000 inhabitants.[2] By 1910, the city had grown to more than 500,000 residents; the Russian Musical Society grew in strength and significance alongside it.[3] As the Kiev branch and its school grew stronger, it experimented with the curriculum, debated the purpose of music education, and struggled to develop a mutually beneficial relationship with local authorities, all of which provided a template for later branches to follow. When the branch was founded, no model existed for the establishment and maintenance of complex cultural institutions in the provinces. True, the St. Petersburg and Moscow conservatories provided some guidance, but the problems of day-to-day existence in the provinces were much different from the capitals. Yet, although it faced significant obstacles, the Kiev branch also enjoyed the support of local authorities, beginning with P. D. Seletsky, then the vice-governor. Subsequent general governors willingly collaborated with the Society, helping it secure permanent premises and, eventually, a state subsidy for its music school, thereby establishing a precedent for state funding that significantly reshaped the underlying assumptions of Russian musical life.[4]

The organizational, financial, and practical obstacles faced by the branch drew the attention of the critic for the newspaper *Kievlianin*, who used the occasion of the opening of the "long promised and much desired (if not by many)" music school in 1868 to reflect on its failure to win public support. Like similar critics in the capitals, he despaired over the supposed indifference of educated society, which he depicted as utterly lacking in both taste and cultural patriotism. Not only did Kiev's audiences still prefer Italian arias, he charged, they denied the very existence of worthwhile Russian music: "Really, does Russian art exist, can it really exist? Pah, peasants' concerts!" His descriptions of "respectable" concertgoers highlighted both their pretentiousness and the fragility of the status they sought to protect; he mocked those who professed to be appalled at the prospect of attending concerts side by side with "a coachman, who might be invited to perform on the accordion."[5] Societal resistance, the critic complained, sometimes degenerated into direct attack, as when concert posters were torn down or defaced with ethnic slurs, or when obscenities were appended to the family names of women.[6] Yet, these descriptions of the ignorance and backwardness of Kiev's audiences seem exaggerated, as educated society had long enjoyed a varied semipublic and domestic musical life. Less pejoratively, but probably more accurately, the critic for *Kievskii telegraf* noted persistent doubts about the appropriateness of the public performance of classical music; many potential audience members felt such music was only suitable in a more intimate setting. Such attitudes, of course, threatened the very existence of the Kiev branch as they rejected as futile any attempt to attract and educate a broader public.[7] Unfortunately, the Society's first, very unsuccessful local concerts seemed to support the opinion of such skeptics. Even the sympathetic critic for *Kievlianin* was forced to admit that they deserved only mockery.[8]

The struggles of the Kiev branch embodied the conflict implicit in the development of provincial cultural life. Proponents of a public musical life argued that complex modern works requiring large orchestras and sustained rehearsal time demanded the relocation of concert life from domestic settings to public ones.[9] Public cultural life, however, implied public expense, whereas domestic musical life was the financial responsibility of its direct participants. In calling for music to become a part of civic life, music critics and cultural leaders redefined it as a common good, a shared amenity that benefited the whole of society. Although even Kiev's music critics complained of the excessive expense of the Italian Opera, they nonetheless insisted that music per se was a real need. "Of course," they acknowledged, bridge improvements, a trade school, and a postal system were urgently needed, but "all the same, none of this is art, or public entertainment." The need for practical improvements did not negate the need to eliminate cultural inadequacies.[10]

To supporters of the Russian Musical Society, the indifference of the educated public reflected a broader cultural backwardness. Poor performances might explain the lack of interest in the Kiev branch's concerts, but not the public's coolness toward demanding, high-quality concert music in general.[11] The branch's struggle against public indifference met only limited success; in 1865–1866, its rolls included only twelve active and thirty attending members, although an additional forty individuals joined as performing members. The branch's weakness, however, reminded critics of the city's cultural weaknesses. Although the branch proved unable to attract enough members to staff an adequate orchestra, more dismaying still was the fact that the only available ensemble of note in the city was the remnant of Prince Lopukhin's serf orchestra. To local critics, the inability of a city the size and significance of Kiev to locate thirty capable musicians seemed both tragic and comic.[12]

The branch's educational endeavors got off to a similarly dismal start. The music school's miniscule first class consisted of ten students, two of whom were the children of the director, R. A. Pfenig, who achieved his position by virtue of his experience as a music teacher in the Kiev Institute for Noble Girls. By the third year, the school had tripled in size but remained vulnerable. Unfortunately for the Russian Musical Society, Pfenig's enthusiasm concealed his incompetence as an administrator and his inadequacy as an instructor. Although the faculty included skilled professionals, such as cello instructor M. G. Polianichevsky, a graduate of the St. Petersburg Conservatory, the school relied heavily on local amateur or semiprofessional musicians.[13] In 1875, the board of the Kiev branch, eager for an outside opinion and perhaps suspecting that all was not well, asked the Main Directorate for an evaluation.[14] The overwhelmingly negative assessment led to the unceremonious firing of Pfenig and his replacement by L. K. Albrekht, the man entrusted to perform the inspection.[15] Albrekht, scion of a prominent musical family, a fine cellist, and a student of Karl Davydov, was a member of the illustrious first graduating class of the St. Petersburg Conservatory in 1865. New leadership, unfortunately, did not improve matters much; Albrekht's authoritarian style soon led to scandal and, in 1877, he was dismissed.[16]

Ironically, the scandal proved to be the turning point for the Kiev Music School. In 1875, the branch hired the talented and energetic V. V. Pukhalsky, who had just graduated from the St. Petersburg Conservatory, as a piano instructor. In the wake of Albrekht's dismissal, Pukhalsky was appointed acting director of the school. He devoted his career to the school, shaping it into a robust and well-regarded cultural institution. Only in 1913, after overseeing its successful reorganization into the Kiev Conservatory, did he turn it over to his handpicked successor, the Kiev-born composer Reinhold Gliere. Under Pukhalsky's able leadership, the Kiev Music School thrived and attained a high degree of institutional stability and pedagogical excellence.[17] Pukhalsky inspired the loyalty of faculty and staff, whose commitment to the school's success fortified instructional standards and inspired public confidence. The school enjoyed a respected position among local educational institutions and the approval of local authorities for its orderly environment and well-defined curriculum.[18]

More than any other factor, the character of the director of the music classes or school determined the ultimate success or failure of a provincial branch. In addition to administrative and teaching responsibilities, the director usually planned and conducted the branch's concert series. If the director enjoyed professional credibility and wielded artistic authority, then he could usually establish a harmonious working relationship with the local board. In such conditions, the branch was likely to thrive, achieving, as in Kiev and Kharkov, a high standard in both music education and concert performance. If the director lacked appropriate credentials or a strong character, or, worst of all, if the local board refused to recognize the director as a legitimate professional, then matters often stagnated or degenerated to the detriment of music education, concert culture, and the reputation of the Russian Musical Society.

Pukhalsky worked in close cooperation with the board of the Kiev branch, whose members possessed an unusually high level of musical legitimacy. Longtime board member A. N. Vinogradsky, in particular, was an orchestral conductor whose work earned him respect and acclaim in Kiev, Saratov, Odessa, and other provincial cities.[19] Vinogradsky began his active involvement with the Russian Musical Society in the mid-1880s while serving as a functionary of the Ministry of Finance in Saratov. He joined the board of the Saratov branch, created a concert series for it, and served as its conductor. In 1887, he returned to his native Kiev, where he became an influential member of the local board, a frequent conductor of its concerts, and a benefactor of the Kiev Music School until his death in 1912.

Although the firing of two successive directors cost the Kiev branch public confidence in its early years, its school slowly gained institutional and educational stability, attracting ever-increasing numbers of students. By 1880–1881, the school enrolled two hundred students. Twenty years later, enrollment had roughly doubled. By 1912–1913, immediately prior to the school's reorganization into the Kiev Conservatory, enrollment stood at just under nine hundred students, larger than many West European conservatories.[20] Yet, despite its size, the Kiev Music School could not satisfy the local demand for music instruction. Private music courses and schools, often headed by graduates or former students of the Kiev Music School, competed for students and the public's attention. In 1904, the Kiev branch ridiculed a proposal by Nikolai Ikonnikov, a local nobleman, to establish a private musical-dramatic school because his explanations for the need for his new school were so patently ridiculous. According to Ikonnikov, Kiev was "extremely impoverished in artistic-educational institutions and, on the other hand, particularly rich in talented and able, but poor, musicians and actors," who had nowhere to turn for their artistic education. In fact, the branch argued, Kiev was particularly well endowed, providing a list of twelve substantial institutions, including the Kiev Music School as well as the Musical-Dramatic School established by the Ukrainian nationalist composer, N. V. Lysenko.[21] Institutionalized music education was no longer a novelty but an integral part of an increasingly sophisticated cultural network in the city.[22]

Kiev's story of rapid population growth, economic development, and social and cultural change were repeated in many other cities in the half century before World War I. For the Russian Musical Society, the growth of provincial cities provided both the justification and the opportunity for expansion. Yet, every new branch brought with it the risk of ignominious failure. Although the Kharkov branch, for example, ultimately became highly successful, boasting both significant concert series and a well-regarded music school, the initial attempt to establish it ended in disaster.[23] In Saratov, an important and rapidly growing regional center on the Volga River, the early days of the Society were similarly plagued by scandal. Interest in establishing a branch appeared as early as 1865, when M. P. Tuchkov, with the assistance of Anton Rubinstein, recruited local luminaries, including N. I. Ershov, a wealthy landowner, and Prince V. A. Shcherbatov to serve as members of the board. Predictions that merchants would provide financial support and that local amateurs would provide the resources for a passable orchestra proved overly optimistic. In 1872, the branch closed due to insufficient funding. The unexpected failure of the Saratov branch unnerved the leadership of the Society and forced it to confront its limitations as an engine of provincial cultural development. In order to prevent similar embarrassments, the Society's leadership resolved that new provincial branches would be approved only if they possessed adequate financial resources.[24]

Local leaders soon stepped forward to resuscitate the Russian Musical Society in Saratov. In August 1873, the local governor, M. N. Galkin-Vrasky, asked the Society to approve a new branch with music classes. Unanimously elected chair of the board, Galkin-Vrasky proved willing to wield his considerable authority in support of the Society.[25] He secured premises for the branch and its classes from the Nobles' Assembly and gained the active cooperation of local school officials, whom he personally encouraged to support the music classes.[26]

Whereas in Kiev Pukhalsky and Vinogradsky worked in tandem to establish a successful branch and music school, and in Saratov the local governor provided critical support, in Kharkov, I. I. Slatin found himself fighting the indifference of his branch's supposed leadership. In 1877, Slatin, then only six years into his tenure as director of the Kharkov Music School, complained bitterly of the unreliability of the chair of the board, Princess Kropotkina, and her husband, the local governor, neither of whom displayed any real interest in music. "If once in a while they do something in support of the society, then it is [only] thanks to its Imperial title."[27] Slatin's own commitment to music and to the Society can hardly be doubted. A former student of the St. Petersburg Conservatory, he would devote his entire career to the Kharkov branch and its music school. Thanks to his professional integrity and in large part due to his unremitting labor, the Society eventually acquired a respected role in the city (see figure 5.2).

Events in Saratov, however, emphasize the fragility of provincial cultural institutions. By the spring of 1883, the Saratov branch had once again fallen on hard times. Its board of directors evaporated after both Galkin-Vrasky and another influential member, F. Timiriazev, left the city. Because the branch had so few active members eligible to hold office, they could not be replaced. Finances had also reached the breaking point. The new provincial governor refused to allow the branch to raise funds through lotteries or street fairs, even though he admitted his own failure to persuade wealthy locals to patronize it. Nevertheless, educated society, in the form of the City Duma, clearly recognized the cultural significance of the branch. It approved a 1,000-ruble subsidy that allowed it to effectively assume the role of board of directors.[28] Although influential private citizens had launched the Russian Musical Society in Saratov, the crisis awakened the branch to the risks inherent in depending on the largesse of individuals. In the words of Liudvig Viniarsky, the acting director of the Saratov music classes, the branch needed to replace the support of individuals with that of society if it hoped to survive.[29]

The situation in Odessa, similarly, reminds us that provincial cultural life in the 1870s and 1880s remained dependent on the initiative of individuals rather than built on a robust institutional foundation. Highlighting the tenuous nature of provincial musical life, *Muzykal'noe obozrenie* noted that the temporary departure of pianist I. Tedesco, credited as the leading force behind the local Philharmonic Society, effectively meant the suspension of symphonic concerts in the city. As the journal reluctantly admitted, the closure of the Philharmonic Society did not leave the city entirely bereft of music, but the organizations that filled the void were seen as too unstable to sustain local musical life. An amateur musical circle dedicated to the promotion of Russian music had, by the 1880s, refashioned itself into the Odessa Musical Society, but had failed to move beyond its original, limited performance goals. The

FIGURE 5.2. "A. K. Glazunov and I. I. Slatin, Kharkov, 1899." Permission of the Russian Institute for the History of the Arts, St. Petersburg (fond 28, op. 1, no. 1245/4)

society was dominated by musical amateurs and so haunted by financial difficulties that it finally managed to open music classes only in 1885. Financial pressures, moreover, continued to threaten the Odessa Musical Society, prompting its board to seek reorganization and protection under the Russian Musical Society.[30]

This "rescue attempt" emphasizes both the increasing legitimacy of the Russian Musical Society and the practical difficulties faced by cultural associations in the provinces. Even the Odessa Society for the Fine Arts, which was subsidized by the city and owned its own building, found its attempt to expand beyond its traditional focus on the visual arts and establish a musical division too much of a strain.[31] Meanwhile, the Odessa Musical Society soon found it had a competitor for the favors of the Russian Musical Society. Another group of musical enthusiasts petitioned the Main Directorate for the right to open a branch but, although they elected a board of directors, they accomplished nothing of real significance. In the end, the Odessa Musical Society merged with this phantom branch to become the recognized leader of local musical life.[32]

Although the imprimatur of the Russian Musical Society provided provincial musical organizations with a degree of legitimacy, the need to maintain consistent policies between the Main Directorate, the large and relatively wealthy St. Petersburg and Moscow branches, and provincial branches created new challenges. Provincial branches struggled to adapt policies set in St. Petersburg to local social and economic realities. High membership dues, for example, enhanced the prestige of the Society by restricting access and lending the organization an air of social exclusivity. Such strategies were problematic in the capitals, where educated and wealthy society was concentrated, and disastrous in the provinces, where dues of 100 rubles for active members deterred membership.[33] In response, provincial branches adopted two strategies. Many lowered membership dues, hoping to create a more stable social and financial environment for the development of musical life. Other branches, notably the one in Kharkov, acted on the assumption that, regardless of the cost of membership, few people would ever step forward as leaders. The Kharkov branch opted to keep dues high and the administration of musical affairs "within the family."[34] Although exclusionary, this strategy rewarded longtime members for their leadership and encouraged them to identify with and financially support "their" society.

The need for prestige and access to the corridors of power prompted branches to recruit city and provincial governors, marshals of the nobility, and other prominent local figures, as well as their spouses, to serve on their boards. The consequences were mixed at best. Such recruitment efforts required an accurate understanding of local social divisions and their cultural implications. In Kiev, for example, one member attributed the branch's early difficulties to its failure to recognize the city's ethnic diversity and recruit Jewish and Polish members.[35] Similarly, the first Kharkov branch collapsed because the St. Petersburg leadership refused to allow "foreigners" to serve as plenipotentiaries, which alienated would-be supporters of the new society.[36] Moreover, as Slatin's complaint regarding the dubious commitment of the Kropotkins suggests, there were real risks as well as potential rewards inherent in recruiting socially prominent individuals. Many local notables enjoyed being courted, but their time and attention were likely to be scattered among their various interests, rather than focused on the Russian Musical Society. Nevertheless, the social prominence and personal wealth of board members frequently proved critical to the viability of a branch.

In general, however, the Society understood that provincial branches would be more successful if they were allowed to adapt to local social and economic conditions, unburdened by the biases and presumptions of the capitals. Although local branches remained quite closely tied to the Main Directorate, their governing boards handled day-to-day administration. Board members accepted both moral and financial responsibility for their branches and attached educational institutions. They often subsidized music education, covering not only operating deficits but also the tuition of talented but impoverished students. For example, when Pukhalsky threatened to resign as the director of the Kiev Music School in 1882, the acting chair of the Kiev branch dipped into his own pocket to increase Pukhalsky's salary from a paltry 600 rubles to a more respectable 1,500 rubles annually.[37] Similarly, in 1889, A. N. Vinogradsky supplemented a 1,000-ruble allocation to the Kiev Music School for the purchase of wind and percussion instruments with more than 700 rubles of his own funds.[38] Occasional gifts and subsidies by board members were the rule, rather than the exception, but civic leadership and a commitment to the Society sometimes crossed over into more substantial forms of patronage. Thus, the financial stability of the Kiev branch improved significantly in 1912 after it received large bequests, including 40,000 rubles from Vinogradsky's estate and 30,000 rubles from the widow of board member A. N. Tereshchenko. In both cases, the funds were dedicated to the support of student scholarships.[39] In Odessa, N. S. Shcherbinsky dedicated his brother Dmitry's 25,000-ruble estate toward the reorganization of the branch's classes into a music school; he wanted to memorialize his brother's love of music and honor their mutual membership in the Russian Musical Society.[40] Board members offered both civic leadership and financial support, but their prominence ensured that musical amateurs continued to play a guiding role in the Russian Musical Society. This practical reality became increasingly controversial as it contradicted the professionalizing ethos of the Society's educational institutions. In most branches, the only professional musician on the board was the head of the music school or classes. As we will see in the next chapter, this imbalance increasingly led to conflict between local boards and their music directors, and, more ominously, between the Society and the musical profession.

Supply and Demand: Orchestral Musicians and Concert Life

The innovations introduced by the Russian Musical Society to the concert life of the capitals eventually percolated to the provinces. Provincial concert life, however, continued to be episodic and opportunistic, dependent, as the example of Saratov shows, on both individual initiative and expertise and, most critically, on the availability of performers. After the City Duma's intervention in 1883, the Saratov branch began to establish a successful concert life as Vinogradsky worked "tirelessly, at significant cost to himself," to create "symphony concerts under his direction" in the city. While the public was cool at first, the concerts nevertheless soon enjoyed what the Society considered unprecedented success. But success remained dependent on the energy and enthusiasm of individuals. After Vinogradsky's departure for Kiev, concert life in Saratov became more sporadic and uneven. In 1897, the branch attempted to increase its visibility by creating concerts designed to both "popularize classical musical works" and "influence the musical development and understanding of the masses." In keeping with this goal, the branch established a symbiotic relationship with the Saratov Commercial Club. The branch acquired free use of the club hall for symphony and quartet concerts, while members of the club and their families were able to attend the concerts for a very modest fee. The arrangement proved effective and, at least according to the Saratov branch, concerts thereafter were frequently standing room only.[41]

In many ways, the cultural economy of provincial cities was characterized by persistent shortages, particularly of orchestral musicians and appropriate performance venues. Many branches were plagued by the unwillingness of local theatrical entrepreneurs to share their stages or their orchestral musicians. As late as 1905, when the composer and conductor A. S. Arensky toured the Society's provincial branches, the Kharkov branch still had difficulty sustaining its annual series of five symphony concerts.[42] When conditions were favorable, the larger branches could stage impressive concert seasons, as in 1892–1893 when the Odessa branch presented four symphony concerts, six chamber music evenings, and a special quartet concert featuring Leopold Auer. Tchaikovsky, moreover, directed two of the four symphony concerts; Auer conducted the remaining two. The repertoire performed was decidedly mixed: Tchaikovsky's concerts included the suite from his new ballet *The Nutcracker*, a Borodin symphony, and instrumental and vocal solo works by himself, Liszt, Ernst, Malchanov, and S. Menter. Auer's chosen repertoire proved more cosmopolitan: his first symphony concert included Beethoven's Seventh Symphony, melodies for string orchestra by Grieg, including "Anitra's Dance" from *Peer Gynt*, Borodin's *On the Steppes of Central Asia*, the Mendelssohn Violin Concerto with Auer as soloist, and Wagner's *Tannhaüser* overture.[43] By the 1890s, the inclusion of both significant Russian repertoire and recent works by foreign composers was a common expectation for concerts, even in provincial cities less sophisticated than Odessa.

However, while the capitals suffered from a perceived shortage of orchestral musicians, in the provinces the problem was very real.[44] The opera—if one existed—usually provided a city's only more or less competent ensemble, which could serve as the core of a concert orchestra filled out by local amateurs and students. Such orchestras produced disappointing results, due to poorly skilled performers (a charge leveled at the professionals as often as the amateurs), a shortage of rehearsal time, and a lack of group cohesiveness.[45] Short-term solutions proved elusive, but the Russian Musical Society and its educational institutions promised a more effective, permanent solution to the dearth of orchestral performers. The conservatories, the Society's proponents envisaged, would supply the St. Petersburg and Moscow orchestras, liberating Russia from enslavement to foreign performers. Provincial music schools and classes, similarly, would train performers for local orchestras, spreading European cultural ideals and artistic practices to Russia's periphery. However, the shortage of competent orchestral musicians meant that even half-trained former students of the Society's schools were extremely employable in Russia's ever-expanding musical marketplace, making it difficult to persuade students to stay in school long enough to graduate.[46]

The Kharkov branch was one of the first to attempt to find a practical solution to the perceived shortage of orchestral musicians. Like many of his colleagues, Slatin was convinced that a shortage of orchestral musicians was crippling Russia's musical advancement, especially in the provinces, where nonexistent, inadequate, or understaffed orchestras made it difficult if not impossible for provincial audiences to acquire the refined aesthetic taste that only acquaintance with the great works of the orchestral repertoire could instill. Slatin formulated a detailed plan for remedying this situation, in which he considered not only the question of hiring appropriate faculty, but also the problem of recruiting students and funding a comprehensive orchestral training program. He demanded an end to the traditional practice of simply hiring whoever happened to be in town as orchestral faculty, insisting instead on the recruitment of a full panel of specialists, ideally with conservatory credentials, including four woodwind and two brass teachers as well as violin, cello, and bass instructors. The instructors would also serve as principals in the orchestra, thereby revitalizing the branch's concert series. Modest salaries of 500 to 600 rubles for the academic year presumed that each instructor would have approximately six students, with each student taking lessons three times per week. Slatin had no illusions that such modest wages would persuade instructors to forgo additional employment in the local theaters, but he hoped that the prospect of a regular faculty appointment would ensure that their primary loyalty was to the music school.[47]

Slatin's proposal to train young peasants as orchestral players reflected both his awareness of the near impossibility of recruiting paying students for brass and woodwind instruments and the seriousness with which he regarded the orchestral musician crisis. Slatin suggested that the Kharkov Music School recruit adolescent singers from local church choirs. Although a child's recruitment into a choir could benefit a peasant family by both removing a mouth to feed and supplementing the family income, once the boy's voice broke his return home created new problems. Isolation within the church and a singular focus on choral music, Slatin charged, ruined these boys for peasant life. By enrolling their sons in the orchestral classes, Slatin optimistically predicted, parents could provide their children with a good education and upward mobility at a very low cost as the school would subsidize the boys' tuition. In turn, the school would gain students who, because of their prior musical training, would be likely to succeed in their studies. Slatin counted on the privileges that accrued to music school graduates to persuade students and their parents. Although he noted that outstanding students might hope to continue their educations at one of the conservatories, he clearly counted on more tangible privileges, particularly the right of music school students to draft deferments, to make enrollment attractive.[48]

Slatin planned to exploit the class differences of musical life to pay for his orchestral project. In Kharkov, as in nearly all of the Society's educational institutions, the tuition payments of piano students provided the primary source of income. Slatin proposed to triple the size of the school so that everyone wanting to study the piano could be accommodated; the excess funds generated by the tuition payments of well-off piano students would subsidize the musical educations of impoverished orchestral students. Although it is unclear how many former choristers enrolled in the Kharkov Music School, it clearly became an important training center for orchestral musicians. By 1888–1889, a quarter of the school's student body studied string or wind instruments.[49] Two years later, orchestral students made up almost a third of the student body—seventy-two students in the first semester—including a full complement of orchestral winds.[50] By consciously exploiting the bourgeois obsession with the piano, Slatin significantly advanced Russian orchestral training. Moreover, under Slatin's leadership, the Kharkov Music School was recognized as a model of effective music education.[51]

The Odessa branch also became known as an "orchestra school," playing a particularly prominent role in training violinists.[52] The focus on orchestral training in both schools altered their socioeconomic structure; in Odessa over 40 percent of the student body—including the majority of the orchestral students—studied on scholarships.[53] Although the strategies employed by both schools were expensive and risky, given that they lent support to the charge that the Society was willing to admit almost any student who could afford to pay, they were successful in creating provincial orchestral training centers. By 1908, the Odessa Music School boasted 159 graduates, including fifty wind players, thirty-five violinists, and a handful of cellists, bassists, and singers, in addition to forty-two pianists.[54] Another thirty students who had left without graduating, including the violinist Misha Elman, had nevertheless distinguished themselves and honored the school through their musical success.[55] Although luminaries such as Elman were, of course, rare exceptions, the Odessa and Kharkov music schools, through their concentrated efforts to build strong orchestral departments, made significant contributions to the development of a self-sustaining provincial cultural life.

By the turn of the twentieth century, the Society focused less on simply establishing provincial concert life and more on its proper conduct. The concert became more strictly defined, both in its repertoire and in its social practices. In April 1900, the Main Directorate, in an effort to establish uniform standards for concerts throughout the empire, condescendingly informed local branches that the "goal of the musical performances of the Imperial Russian Musical Society" was not just to attract a large audience but also to educate. A "significant portion" of the repertoire performed in any concert should consist of "models" of composition, whether Russian or foreign. Russian music, moreover, was not to be neglected. The guidelines mandated that "every program" must "include the work of at least one Russian composer." The performance of oratorios and other large-scale vocal and instrumental works was specifically encouraged, as was the establishment of separate concert series for vocal and instrumental chamber music. Despite the efforts of the Society's "orchestra schools," the ensemble as well as the repertoire demanded attention. Ideally, each branch would support its own permanent orchestra with a resident conductor. The Society's educational institutions and the orchestra as a civic institution were explicitly linked; branches were reminded of the need to "attract local conservatory . . . graduates to this orchestra." Yet, even the Main Directorate was forced to recognize that few provincial branches were likely to be able to establish and maintain symphony orchestras; instead, they remained dependent on local opera, military, and dance orchestras whose players, individually or as a group, might be co-opted or contracted to stand in as a concert orchestra for the Society.[56]

Building Culture in the Provinces: Property, Stability, and Status

The Saratov branch, despite its early troubles, eventually developed into a strong and ambitious organization that repeatedly sought to establish its dominance in local cultural life. In 1893, the branch, hoping to transform its music classes into a more prestigious school, petitioned the state for a 5,000-ruble subsidy. The branch wielded the Society's founding myth like a weapon as it tried to lay claim to the state's support. The branch sketched a portrait of local musical life as languishing in silence and mediocrity, with half-trained teachers who charged prohibitive fees the only source of music education, until the arrival of the Russian Musical Society. The branch, unsurprisingly, carefully sidestepped its own failures as well as its dependence on student fees, which were set at 50 rubles, a level guaranteed to exclude large sectors of the local population.[57]

In the subsidy request, the Saratov branch emphasized its intimate connection to the life of the city, arguing, for example, that the branch already enjoyed a "moral connection" of mutual assistance and support with the city's recently established opera company. It took pains to demonstrate that music education served the broader needs of society, not just the personal ambitions of students and their parents. The successes of a few student-performers in the branch's orchestra and chorus, as well as of a few graduates who served as music teachers or orchestra and choir leaders, bolstered the branch's assertions of its social utility.[58] Most boldly, the branch portrayed itself as the cultural center of the entire region, attracting students not only from the city of Saratov but also from surrounding towns, villages, and provinces. Accepting this representation, the Saratov governor argued that the branch's classes had already "acquired significance as a center of musical education for the entire

Volga region." The support of local society, meanwhile, was "proven" by its enthusiastic attendance at symphony and chamber music concerts.[59]

Such arguments failed to persuade Minister of Finance Witte, who insisted that the state had no funds to spare for cultural endeavors that were clearly beyond its purview. Witte's argument reflected one longstanding view within government circles, which held that cultural life and its institutions were the responsibility of local communities and society more generally, not the state. This viewpoint, however, was contradicted by the behavior of other governmental figures allied with the Russian Musical Society, who used their influence to extract financial support from state coffers. In this case, personal intervention by the founder of the Saratov branch, Galkin-Vrasky, and the staunch support of the Minister of Internal Affairs, I. N. Durnovo, persuaded the State Senate to award the branch an annual subsidy of 2,000 rubles, which was sufficient to allow it to pursue its ambitions.[60] Reorganization brought new opportunities but also new dangers. A music school required a more elaborate curriculum, additional faculty, and greater financial resources. Moreover, although the likely growth of the student body would signal public approval, it would bring problems of its own, specifically the need for larger and more elaborate premises.

Rents were a constant drain on the financially shaky branches of the Russian Musical Society.[61] Consequently, provincial branches viewed building ownership as the key to both financial stability and local prestige; real estate created the perception of a more viable and substantial institution. Very few branches, however, could muster the resources needed to purchase a building outright. They turned first to municipal or provincial authorities for assistance, but they also appealed to the Main Directorate, asking it to petition the state on their behalf for buildings, land, or loans. The active sympathy of local authorities helped provincial branches in Kiev, Odessa, Tambov, and Saratov, among others, acquire buildings either by transferring ownership or use of state property to the branch or by providing favorable purchase or lease terms, including no-interest, long-term loans. The construction of a more or less elaborate building designed for music enhanced the prestige of the local branch and emphasized the cultural sophistication of the city in which it was located.

In both Saratov and Tiflis, collaboration between local government officials, prominent members of educated society, and the local boards of the Society secured state financial assistance for the construction of purpose-built music schools. The construction and dedication of these buildings was a significant cultural event, replete with flowery speeches praising the Russian Musical Society's contributions to musical life. Local notables attended the celebrations with enthusiasm, while the presence of honored guests underscored the solemnity and importance of the occasion. In both cities, a festive cantata composed specifically for the occasion emphasized the Russian Musical Society's cultural contributions, while a ritualized reading of congratulatory telegrams reaffirmed the cohesion and common purpose of its disparate branches. This cultural ritual reached its culmination in the public celebrations of the jubilees of the Russian Musical Society and the St. Petersburg Conservatory.

The differences between the celebrations reflected the specific cultural and social roles of the Russian Musical Society in Saratov and Tiflis. The opening celebration of the new Saratov Music School focused on the building itself and its role in the city. Photographs of the building figured prominently in the commemorative pamphlet produced for the celebration, but a second photographic album entirely dedicated to the building and its construction was also published.[62] The building remains a focal point of cultural life in Saratov even today, a local landmark that anchors one end of the city's main street (figure 5.3). The crowd that gathered to dedicate the building in 1902 included Galkin-Vrasky, by then a member of the State Senate. Joining him in the seats reserved for honored guests were such local notables as the provincial governor, A. P. Engelgardt, the head of the city civil administration, A. O. Nemirovsky, and the chair of the provincial zemstvo board, Count [D. S.] Olsufev, among others.[63] The musical nobility of Russia was less well represented; guests included the former director of the Moscow Conservatory, V. I. Safonov, the Vice-Chair of the Moscow branch of the Society, S. P. Iakovlev, the composer A. S. Arensky, the director of the Tambov Music School, S. M. Starikov, and the inspector of that school, K. E. Weber. The only representative of the Main Directorate was its longtime secretary, V. E. Napravnik, son of the famed conductor.[64]

The telegrams and rescripts sent by the Society's Imperial Patron, Grand Duke Konstantin Konstantinovich, praised Galkin-Vrasky as well as the wife of the former governor, Princess M. A. Meshcherskaia, and Prince P. M. Volkonsky for their moral, organizational, and financial assistance. Such sentiments underscored the close relationship and identification of members of the nobility with the Russian Musical Society. The address of the mayor highlighted the usefulness and educational significance of the music school to the broader population of the city, while that of the Saratov Medical Society emphasized the importance of the Musical Society's self-imposed cultural mission and its commitment to the moral development of the populace. The Medical Society saw in the Musical Society a partner in its efforts to improve Russian social conditions. Similarly, addresses from other voluntary associations and the press

FIGURE 5.3. Postcard of the Saratov Conservatory, c. 1920s

suggest the symbolic importance of this event, of the new building as a cultural center, and of the Russian Musical Society in local cultural life.[65]

Like Saratov, Tiflis played an important role as a cultural center for its wider region. Tiflis, moreover, was unusually ethnically diverse; its population was composed primarily of Armenians, Georgians, and Russians, with smaller numbers of Jews, Germans, and other groups. As a consequence, the local branch of the *Russian* Musical Society, established in 1883, carried a special burden as it tried to negotiate the cultural boundaries not only between Russia and Europe, but also between the heartland of the empire and its non-Russian periphery.[66] Although concert offerings consisted primarily of works by major and minor Russian and European composers, ethnic divisions more strongly shaped educational affairs. The student body of the Tiflis Music School reflected the city's demographic and social barriers, enrolling mostly Armenians and Russians with small minorities of Jews, Georgians, and Germans.[67] While the curriculum of the music school differed little from that offered by the Society's other educational institutions, the branch expressed its desire to serve the whole of local society when it planned for general education classes in Georgian and Armenian as well as Russian.[68] Moreover, while the branch functioned to a degree as a mechanism for Russian cultural imperialism, the cosmopolitan nature of the city and the dense fabric of regional ethnic identities ensured that the local cultural situation was fluid and complex. Certainly, the leadership of the Russian Musical Society in St. Petersburg and Moscow viewed the Tiflis branch as uniquely located—culturally, as well as geographically—between Russia's cultivated Western (European) identity and its allegedly Eastern primordial self.

Perhaps because of Tiflis' position between these two worlds, those committed to the development of her musical life were truly committed. The board of the Tiflis branch of the Society was unusually stable, while its members worked hard and displayed significant initiative. At times, the branch seemed in danger of becoming a private club focused more on serving the desires of its members than on the broader cultural needs of the city and region.[69] Moreover, the Tiflis branch, like most provincial branches of the Society, struggled to meet its educational and concert obligations in the face of persistent financial difficulty. In 1896, V. D. Korganov used the branch's need for a permanent home for its music school to launch a broad critique of musical life in the city and in the empire. The inability to find funding for the Tiflis Music School, Korganov argued, revealed the city's lack of culture and civilization. Only in cities where people understood the importance of education, where they were able to "think and to feel" not just "to eat, sleep, and play cards" could one find generous and knowledgeable patrons for music and music education. In Tiflis, however, local patrons still could not tell the difference between real art—that of Beethoven, Raphael, and Shakespeare—and third-rate provincial artists. They lavished their money on useless projects while the music school, the city's most substantial cultural institution, languished. The school, meanwhile, struggled to combat the same cultural philistinism in its students that Korganov perceived in educated society. Although he recognized the public's right to complain when music students seemed unable to distinguish between the trivial pieces of minor composers and the works of Chopin or Beethoven, they were only guilty of the same light-minded attitude toward the arts that characterized local society, which preferred operettas and romances to Bach fugues, which gathered dust because they were "difficult to understand." The Russian Musical Society, he reminded the readers of the local newspaper, *Kavkaz*, had a broader responsibility to educate the public as well as its students, with the well-structured concert as the preferred mechanism for cultural enlightenment.[70]

Korganov did not paint an entirely dismal picture of musical life in the Caucasus. Tiflis, he suggested, was an unusually musical city, at least in terms of the number of inhabitants studying music. According to his calculations, one in every four hundred residents studied music, four times the percentage in St. Petersburg, Moscow, or Vienna. Like other cultural critics, however, Korganov complained that the city's musical enthusiasts focused their devotion only on the piano, that "contemporary instrument of torture." The piano's accessibility and ease of performance contributed to the "universal piano mania" that afflicted Tiflis as much as the rest of Europe, bringing, from his point of view, incalculable harm to art. The mechanical approach to music favored by many piano students, he argued, generated only ignorance. Unfortunately, Korganov complained, it was the judgment of such savages, such "Hottentots" of music that structured musical life in the provinces and, particularly, in Tiflis.[71]

Despite such blistering critiques, in 1905, when the Tiflis branch dedicated its newly constructed music school and concert hall, it offered a remarkably self-congratulatory history that emphasized the Russian Musical Society's critical role in unifying local cultural life. This version of the past required it to gloss over the fact that the educational institution in question preceded the establishment of the branch. In the early 1880s, the city's most prominent musical educational institution was a private music school established by conservatory-trained musicians. Despite their skill and society's clear willingness to support their endeavor, the school's owners struggled to overcome significant organizational and financial difficulties. The relative financial stability provided by a public subscription drive that yielded more than 5,000 rubles, as well as a city subsidy of 1,200 rubles annually, brought the school to the attention of the Russian Musical Society. In February 1883, the school was formally transformed into the music classes of the Society's newly established Tiflis branch. The branch's narrative of success highlighted its achievements in expanding local musical life through annual symphonic and string quartet series. Success followed success, in this version of events, and, in 1886, the classes were reorganized into the Tiflis Music School. According to the branch, its achievements won it the sympathy of local society, which demonstrated its approval by donating nearly 60,000 rubles for the construction of a new building.[72]

The dedication of the Tiflis branch's new building repeated many elements of the celebration in Saratov, but the dissimilar histories, constituencies, and local roles of the two branches led to different emphases in their rhetoric. The requisite festive cantata, composed by the director of the music school, N. D. Nikolaev, waxed poetic about the ability of music to bind together the disparate peoples of the Russian Empire:

> We will zealously work in the temple,
> That is dedicated only to music,
> That rose in the East.
> We will search for the echoes of paradise,

And the songs of the diverse peoples of the Caucasus,
Will stream together into one harmonious chord.[73]

Addresses and congratulatory telegrams highlighted the diversity of the city's population and the concern of educated society to achieve cultural harmony among the region's ethnic groups. The address of the Tiflis Artistic Society emphasized the importance of the music school and the Tiflis branch in developing "all aspects of the musical arts" in the region. Music possessed a unique ability to wordlessly "lead peoples to cultural unification and to Christian ideals." It therefore served as a "mighty weapon for progress" in the Caucasus, whose peoples spoke many languages, but were united in spirit.[74]

What Is to Be Done? The Piano, the Provinces, and the Limits of the Society's Authority

As the Russian Musical Society expanded, it became increasingly difficult for the St. Petersburg-based Main Directorate to coordinate the activities of the provincial branches. Annual reports and correspondence provided some idea of the difficulties provincial branches faced, but tended to minimize local conflicts, maximize achievements, and reduce every problem to one of inadequate financing. Nevertheless, certain patterns had emerged by the end of the 1880s. It was clear to the Main Directorate that in cities where the local administration and educated society "recognize[d] the usefulness of musical educational institutions for the younger generation" the Society's branches were comparatively secure and well financed, while those lacking such support languished.[75] Moreover, although musicians and cultural activists in the capitals and the provinces shared certain aesthetic values, pressing financial concerns frequently forced provincial branches to compromise their principles, particularly their ideological commitment to the orchestra as the focal point of musical life. The demand for piano instruction threatened the Society's ability to direct and control provincial musical life. For provincial cities and their inhabitants, however, the piano remained a marker of culture, civility, and status. During the nineteenth century, as prices came down and production increased, the piano became more accessible, although it remained far rarer in the provinces than in the capitals.[76] As one Soviet scholar has noted, well into the 1890s even provincial cities as large as Astrakhan, with over 100,000 inhabitants, generated only a handful of piano purchases annually. By 1900, however, the city boasted a thousand pianos, adding approximately fifty new instruments each year.[77]

In the provinces, even more than in the capitals, the daughters of Russia's nascent middle class captured the Society's educational institutions. This flood of young female piano students did little to secure the future of Russian music, at least according to conservatory professor K. K. Zike, who toured the Society's provincial branches in 1889 on behalf of the Main Directorate. He visited the Pskov, Vilnius, Smolensk, Kharkov, Kiev, Tiflis, Odessa, Penza, Tambov, Saratov, Samara, Kazan, and Nizhnii Novgorod branches but, unfortunately, time constraints made inspection of the Siberian branches impossible.[78] In his highly opinionated and biased report, Zike dwelt on the centrality of the piano to provincial musical life.[79] "The fortepiano," he admitted, was "the most suitable means for the dissemination of musicality to the masses and, God willing, in time all the people of the Earth will be able to play this instrument," but this did not mean that the masses should pursue the piano with "extreme fanaticism" as if they were all virtuosi. The cultivation of piano playing in this way, he argued, would only create a multitude of "disillusioned people, to put it bluntly, a pernicious proletariat... searching for a crust of bread."[80] Zike's disdain for the piano, however, warred with both its popularity and the Society's dependence on it.

By admitting so many piano students, he argued, the provincial branches of the Russian Musical Society undermined their primary goal, the establishment of a healthy musical life in their cities. The piano, Zike fumed, did not need the Russian Musical Society to spread its gospel across Russia: "Propaganda for piano playing [took] place all by itself... even in the most remote corners." The Society's educational institutions were supposed to be more than mere piano schools; they had a responsibility to further Russian cultural development by training amateur and professional performers on all instruments. Russia needed people who would not "discard all in music that is not connected with the piano." If only people would think of the larger purpose and their place in it—Zike used the choir and the orchestra as a metaphor for society in his argument—then Russia's musical development would soon be nothing short of spectacular. Not only cities, but also villages would boast choirs and orchestras that could perform large-scale works. Zike contrasted this idyllic picture with a dismal description of contemporary reality, in which even cities such as Kiev were dependent on itinerant musicians for their orchestras. Kiev, he noted morosely, was far superior to other cities, which could not even pull together a string quartet.[81]

Zike rather condescendingly implied that it was unfair to blame the provinces for their cultural backwardness. How could smaller provincial cities hope to establish a proper concert life when they often lacked even a single cellist or violinist? At the same time, he condemned provincial audiences for their futile adoration of touring stars, which caused them to overlook their own local performers. In part, as Zike recognized, touring performers attracted simply because of their novelty. Even a city fortunate enough to have skilled local musicians would likely tire of performances that constantly featured the same soloists. The key, Zike suggested, was to focus not on the individual but on the institution. As disdainful as audiences tended to be of local soloists, they were equally likely to appreciate local choirs and orchestras: "They not only listen to them, they care for them, cherish them, they are even proud of them as institutions which have emerged from the heart of their own home town."[82] Thus, the Russian Musical Society's essential task remained education, but the focus needed to shift away from the piano and toward the orchestra. An effective, rather than casual, local concert life would emerge only when the needed performers became readily available. Through music education, provincial towns could train enough skilled musicians to staff a competent string or symphonic orchestra, thus securing access to a broad repertoire.

The difficulties of provincial branches were due, in part, to the structure of the Russian Musical Society and its ambiguous legal and social position. Zike, it would seem, was unconvinced of the role of voluntary associations in Russian life. His comments suggest not so much a rejection of associational activity as a suspicion that Russians were not yet prepared to take part in civic life. The Society, Zike insisted, was not particularly well known or trusted in the provinces and it appeared insufficiently official to locals who distrusted the word "society." Provincials, he insisted, only trusted state power and authority. In the case of the Russian Musical Society, locals failed to understand the relationship of the provincial branches to the conservatories in St. Petersburg and Moscow. They wanted to deal with institutions directly, not through intermediaries. They understood "societies" as tools for exploitation, being neither one thing (the state) nor the other (the people). Zike's hostility toward voluntary associations reflects his deeper biases about Russian culture and society, particularly his discomfort with the Russian intelligentsia and its claims to cultural leadership. He contrasted the forced development of culture in Russia to what he saw as the more organic pattern established in the West, especially in Germany. There, he believed, the arts were rooted in the people themselves and matured alongside them, becoming part of the flesh and blood of the nation. In Russia, he complained, the intelligentsia artificially established "societies" to direct the light of art onto the masses below.[83] Zike's rather puzzling attack on associational activity, I would argue, was based in his own complex identity as both a "St. Petersburg German" and a Russian musician.[84] Although his education at the St. Petersburg Conservatory and his career in the two Russian capitals fully integrated him into Russian musical life, he seems to have struggled to accept intellectually the significant differences between Russian and Western European social structures and civic values.

Zike cast himself as something of a cultural radical, summarily dismissing the elitist attitude that "the music society doesn't exist for the rabble (*chernye*) but only for the educated classes." He blamed the low level of cultural and economic development in the Russian Empire for the unfortunate fact that "music, as an art form, had not yet reached the *narod*, or that the *narod* had not yet reached it."[85] In the highly romanticized and idealized Germany that Zike contrasted to Russia, even the poorest peasants knew of Beethoven and engaged in some form of music making. Interestingly, despite dismissing the interventionist attitudes of the Russian intelligentsia, Zike did not seek to limit the activities of the Russian Musical Society. Instead, he advocated their expansion, with the goal of creating a sustainable provincial musical life by training local performers on a range of instruments and providing broadly accessible music education.

A decade after Zike's report, the Poltava branch of the Russian Musical Society began to put some of his ideas into practice, constructing a unique civilizing mission for itself that hinged on the establishment of a large symphony orchestra that regularly toured provincial towns and cities. From its earliest moments, the Poltava branch was unusual. A local orchestral entrepreneur, D. Vl. Akhsharumov, established it in 1899, hoping to use it to support his ongoing concert activities.[86] Akhsharumov had the right social and musical qualifications to sponsor a new branch of the Society—he was the son of a local noble family, an educated musician, and a violin virtuoso in his own right—but his unwillingness to include broader circles of local educated society in the proposed branch's affairs raised the Main Directorate's suspicions. Concerned about Akhsharumov's motives, the Main Directorate demanded assurances that music classes would be established before it would grant permission to open the branch. Music classes opened in 1902 and within two years were reorganized into a music school. The school, however, remained more an appendage to concert activity than a focal point for a cultural voluntary association.[87]

The Poltava school taught music to a limited number of piano, voice, and orchestral students. The orchestra of the Poltava branch taught culture to a much broader public through its concert tours from 1903 to 1904 and from 1908 to 1919 (see figure 5.4). A well-qualified professional orchestra, a broad repertoire, and a schedule that included both major and minor provincial towns gave these tours significant cultural weight and attracted considerable public attention. The repertoire performed in the first few tours included more than seventy-five works by some thirty-seven Russian and foreign composers. The 1911 tour featured performances in thirty cities, beginning in Poltava and concluding in Elisavetgrad. In addition to entertaining and enlightening a broad public, the tours also recruited students for the Poltava Music School. Indeed, the detailed concert program for the branch's 1911 tour included a full-page announcement that both advertised the availability of tuition-free places in the orchestral division and cautioned "persons without any musical preparation are accepted for a period of study of no less than seven years."[88]

The tours represented a marked innovation in Russian musical life, as few ensembles of any size had toured the empire. The orchestra traveled by rail, disseminating and popularizing "serious" music to the *narod.* Some audiences were unprepared or unruly, as in Tambov in 1910, where Akhsharumov's "stern looks" and baton taps failed to quiet gossiping students. Losing patience, the conductor attempted to shame the audience into submission, warning them that if silence did not prevail then the performance would be cancelled. Akhsharumov's published and private commentaries on the tours highlight the complexities of moving a large ensemble and all of its baggage via a rail system still in development. The tours were also financially risky, as many concerts resulted in little or no net profit. Akhsharumov's tales are full of major and minor disasters—from imperious minor railway functionaries impeding travel to broken instrument cases and misplaced baggage—that emphasize the ways that cultural development in the provinces was tied quite literally to the industrial development of the empire as a whole.[89]

The energetic branch enjoyed an unusual array of financial support including, by 1914–1915, a 3,000-ruble annual state subsidy, 8,000 rubles from its local patron, Duke M. G. Meklenburg-Strelitsky, and 3,000 rubles from the Poltava provincial zemstvo, as well as smaller subsidies from local mutual aid societies and voluntary associations.[90] Such support signaled societal approval of the pedagogical and enlightenment activities of the branch, which, according to its advocates, had done so much to bring culture, civilization, and a developed musical life to a city that previously had virtually none.[91]

Like Odessa and Kharkov, the Poltava Music School emphasized the training of orchestral musicians. Largely prompted by the need to support its concerts, the branch opened classes on all woodwind and brass instruments immediately upon the establishment of the music classes in 1902. Orchestral students constituted an unusually high proportion of the student body; by

FIGURE 5.4. "D. V. Akhsharumov and the Touring Orchestra of the Poltava Branch of the Russian Musical Society." Permission of the Russian Institute for the History of the Arts, St. Petersburg (fond 21, op. 3, no. 19, l. 1.)

the 1904–1905 school year, piano students, although still the largest group, were no longer in the majority.[92] But Akhsharumov dreamed even greater dreams for the Poltava Music School, proposing, in 1908, a fundamental restructuring of the orchestral department. Playing on cultural anxieties already publicized by figures such as Lipaev, Akhsharumov cited foreigners' continued domination of the best St. Petersburg and Moscow orchestras and the ignorance of the "completely uneducated" native musicians who staffed the rest of the empire's orchestras as proof of the need to expand Poltava's orchestral program. A firm believer in the professionalization of musicians through formal education, Akhsharumov regarded the fact that many orchestral musicians still learned their trade on the job or through apprenticeships as archaic and abnormal. Nevertheless, he also wanted to update conservatory training and rid it of outdated practices that neglected ensemble playing. Echoing Zike's report, he argued that music schools and conservatories turned out too few orchestral musicians and too many unemployable soloists who quickly joined the ranks of the "musical proletariat."[93]

At the root of the problem lay the difficulty of funding music instruction. Like Slatin in Kharkov, Akhsharumov believed that it was unrealistic to rely on paying students to fill out the orchestral department. Akhsharumov hoped to provide orchestral training free of charge to boys between the ages of eleven and fourteen who possessed musical ability and, if possible, elementary music literacy. In order to "raise the general level of musical development in Russia," he argued, it was necessary to "cleanse" its musical educational institutions of paying but talentless students (implicitly female pianists) and replace them with theoretically more able (male) orchestral students. His plan called for admitting seventy-five orchestral students to the Poltava Music School every three years. Students would study free of charge for seven years; upon enrollment they or their sponsor would pay a 200-ruble fee that would be returned when they graduated. Once the plan was in place, it would produce a complete and fully prepared orchestra every three years. Akhsharumov requested an annual state subsidy of almost 30,000 rubles to support the project, but never received sufficient funding to implement the plan as proposed.[94] Nevertheless, the modest subsidies the branch received did allow it to substantially expand the orchestral department.

Akhsharumov correctly identified financial issues as the most pernicious problem facing the provincial branches of the Russian Musical Society. In addition to seeking support from the state, municipalities, and private individuals, provincial branches also courted district and provincial zemstva for support of their educational institutions. Zemstva support signaled the growing legitimacy of music education in the eyes of the provincial public. After 1900, the music classes of the Ekaterinoslav branch received an annual subsidy of 300 rubles from its provincial zemstvo, while both the district and the provincial zemstva supported the Tambov music classes with modest subsidies (200 and 500 rubles, respectively).[95] Competing artistic and social agendas remained difficult to reconcile, however, as the relationship of the Poltava branch with its provincial zemstvo clearly shows. The 3,000-ruble subsidy provided by the Poltava provincial zemstvo initially paid the tuition for thirty students, two from each of the province's districts. In theory, upon graduation these newly minted professionals would assume responsibility for choral and orchestral music and music education in their district.[96] This initial plan soon proved impractical; although students' tuition was paid they received no other financial support. Consequently, of the twenty-eight zemstvo students enrolled in the Poltava Music School in fall 1914, only six remained in August 1915. In response, the zemstvo halved the number of students it supported; it continued to pay tuition for fifteen students (at 100 rubles annually) but reserved the other half of the subsidy for their maintenance.[97] In retrospect, local society neither fully understood nor appreciated the professional agenda of the Poltava branch's orchestral program. Despite the care and attention lavished on orchestral students in the Poltava Music School, society continued to ascribe much higher status to bourgeois specialties, especially the piano. The revolutions of 1917 led to cultural as well as political confusion. In October 1917, the Poltava Soviet of Workers' and Soldiers' Deputies asked the Russian Musical Society to conduct a formal inspection of the Poltava branch. In addition to accusations of financial malfeasance, collusion in draft evasion schemes, and generally tyrannical conduct, the Soviet complained of Akhsharumov's attitude toward zemstva students. It was bad enough, from the Soviet's viewpoint, that they were treated coarsely, but it was completely unacceptable that zemstva students studied only low status orchestral instruments rather than more prestigious ones, such as the piano. This, the Soviet insisted, "could not be in accordance with the goals of the zemstvo."[98]

Hierarchy and Prestige: From Music Classes to Provincial Conservatories

As the Russian Musical Society grew, it developed a three-tiered educational structure. It was not until 1882, however, that the Society began to formalize the distinctions between its music classes (*muzykal'nye klassy*), music schools (*muzykal'nye uchilishcha*), and conservatories.[99] A new charter precisely defined the status of the Society's two higher musical educational institutions, the St. Petersburg and Moscow conservatories, and its two intermediate institutions, the Kiev and Kharkov music schools. All of the Society's other educational institutions were designated music classes, essentially musical primary schools. The reorganization of music classes into music schools was made contingent on evidence of financial resources sufficient to support an expanded educational institution.[100] The music classes lacked prestige and were largely neglected by the Society's leadership until the 1890s, when they began to attempt to standardize their curriculum and secure rights and privileges for their faculty.[101] Ironically, the Society's belated efforts to define the status and structure of its music classes grew out of its need to protect itself from competition from private music schools (*muzykal'nye shkoly*), many of which were established and staffed by the Society's own graduates.

If the Society's weakest music classes were little more than private piano studios, the largest and most successful music schools, especially those in Kiev, Kharkov, Odessa, Saratov, and Tiflis, rivaled the conservatories. Their curriculum was often very elaborate, distinguished from that of the conservatories by a smaller number of applied specialties and a more condensed theoretical curriculum. Music schools theoretically were also required to provide students with a general, albeit incomplete secondary education, although in practice many failed to do so.[102]

By the turn of the century, the difficulty of maintaining instructional standards among widely dispersed educational institutions had begun to worry the Society's leadership. In response, the Society brought the directors of its provincial music schools and classes together to create standard curricula, particularly for theoretical subjects. The proposed uniform curriculum would have mandated courses in music theory, including harmony and instrumentation, solfège, music history, and, for nonpianists, applied piano.[103] Efforts to devise a common curriculum and to enforce a shared set of educational standards, although only partially successful, illustrate the increasing self-awareness and assertiveness of educators within the Russian Musical Society. Nevertheless, students subverted attempts at standardization, taking idiosyncratic routes through the curriculum, depending on their goals, financial means, and abilities. Moreover, although the Society's educational institutions shared common ideals, they did not represent a coherent educational system. Attempts to transform this network of institutions into an educational ladder received only lukewarm support. Proposals to guarantee graduates of the provincial classes and schools privileged access to the conservatories foundered because of persistent doubts about the quality of instruction in the Society's less prestigious institutions.[104]

The rapid growth of provincial cities and their increasing cultural sophistication called the Society's institutional hierarchy into question. The most energetic provincial cities, such as Kiev, Odessa, and Saratov, grew less willing to accept their cultural subordination to the capitals. Echoing this cultural shift, the Russian Musical Society began to consider elevating at least one of its provincial music schools into a conservatory. In creating provincial conservatories, the Society sought to remind the public of its contribution to Russian cultural development. If before the advent of the Society even cities such as Kiev and Odessa lacked well-ordered music schools, now, thanks to the Society, they would boast elite institutions of higher musical education, placing these cities on the same cultural plane as not only the Russian capitals but also Paris, Berlin, Milan, London, and so on. More practically, the elevation of the Saratov, Kiev, and Odessa music schools into conservatories required a reconsideration of their curriculum, faculty, and student body that illuminated their inner workings and revealed the aesthetic and cultural ideologies shaping the Russian conservatories.

With the dedication of its impressive new building in 1902, the ambitious Saratov branch began to reach for a larger role in Russian musical life. Its concerted campaign to be the site of the first provincial conservatory, which began in late 1907, emphasized the inability of the St. Petersburg and Moscow conservatories to satisfy the entire empire's needs for higher musical education. A vibrant provincial cultural life, they argued, needed to be supported locally, not solely from the center. The branch's leadership envisioned Saratov as a regional cultural capital and the new conservatory as a musical hub for southeast Russia. Intent on selling the benefits of a provincial conservatory, they minimized the difficulties inherent in reorganization.[105]

The Main Directorate, although sympathetic to the idea in theory, was not easily convinced of the feasibility of provincial conservatories. In particular, they doubted both the Society's ability to secure additional state subsidies and the local branch's ability to financially support a larger institution. Other doubts lurked in the background. In December 1910, the Main Directorate dispatched the composer Sergei Rakhmaninov to Saratov for "familiarization" with the branch and its music school. Rakhmaninov's report, unfortunately, found little to recommend in the Saratov Music School beyond its impressive building. The faculty in particular seemed weak and ineffective. Rakhmaninov's doubts were shared by Alexander Glazunov, who compared students trained in Saratov unfavorably to those from the Society's other leading schools. Although Glazunov declared that students from the Kiev Music School "with rare exceptions" proved to be "very gifted," reflecting the "solid conduct of musical affairs" in that institution, he described students from Saratov as "individuals with average gifts," many of whom also suffered from a lack of systematic preparation.[106] Within an institution that prized talent above all else, to describe students as merely average was tantamount to damning them as dilettantes.

Despite these doubts, the project slowly moved forward, not least because the Saratov branch enjoyed the strong support and financial backing of local officials. With their assistance, the idea of a provincial conservatory won sympathy in the State Duma and State Council, which voted to release an additional subsidy. In the spring of 1912, as the project gained momentum, the Saratov branch attempted to address the Main Directorate's concerns about the faculty, revealing in the process the success of the professionalization project launched by Anton Rubinstein. Only faculty with credentials from peer institutions were accepted unquestioningly by the Main Directorate as fully qualified. While the Saratov branch argued somewhat defensively on behalf of several current instructors who lacked formal educational credentials, it emphasized that most were conservatory graduates.[107]

Perhaps because the proposed curriculum expanded rather than transformed the existing program of study, it drew criticism for its lack of depth.[108] In response, the Saratov branch insisted that its school had "significantly broadened instruction in theoretical subjects" in the past two years and had intensified ensemble classes, where "special attention" was now being paid to attendance. In short, the school was no longer complicit in students' attempts to turn the music school into a convenient location for private lessons in their chosen specialty. The Saratov branch presented the Main Directorate with a detailed curriculum that conformed to the underlying premises of a conservatory education as first articulated by Anton Rubinstein: that a professional musician must be an educated musician and that theoretical knowledge as well as applied skill distinguished the professional from the dilettante. Accordingly, the proposed curriculum for the Saratov Conservatory demanded five or six years of theoretical study. Instrumentalists and vocalists all pursued the same theoretical curriculum over five years, beginning with a year of elementary theory and preparatory solfège. In their second and third years, these students continued their study of solfège and added harmony. In their fourth year, music history and an "encyclopedic" course introduced performers to strict and free counterpoint and musical form. In their final year, performers studied instrumentation and aesthetics, which were considered advanced courses intended to prepare them both practically and intellectually for professional careers. Theoretical courses for composition and theory students provided appropriately greater intensity and depth. These students completed the entire course of harmony and solfège in their first year, moving on to counterpoint, harmonic analysis, and instrumentation in their second and third years. Music history, aesthetics, and homophonic form occupied their fourth and fifth years of study, followed by free composition in their final year. The detailed outline for the music history course followed those proposed by Sakketti for the St. Petersburg Conservatory in the 1880s. Like Sakketti's curriculum, the Saratov program reinforced a trajectory of musical development from primitive to modern that both celebrated Russia's musical achievements and reflected its cultural anxieties. Russian music still made its appearance only in the last section of the course, after the whole of West European operatic and symphonic music, including recent developments in programmatic music, had been discussed. Although this marginalized Russian music, the evolutionary trajectory of the course topics, from primitive to contemporary, also suggested that Russian music represented the most advanced development of European culture. This interpretation, perhaps, was reinforced in that the final topic was "Russian Secular Music" with "Independent Russian Music: Glinka and His Heirs" the last item to be addressed.[109]

In its first semester, the newly christened Saratov Conservatory enrolled just over 600 students, including 359 pianists. Fifty-four students, primarily poor boys studying brass and wind instruments, studied for free in a conscious effort to create the nucleus of a future symphony orchestra.[110] The new conservatory seemed a stunning success, with a robust curriculum and a well-qualified faculty. It was clearly a popular institution that responded to the cultural needs of the broader region, drawing nearly a third of its students from other cities and provinces. Yet, the director felt compelled to remind the Society's local leadership that the goals and purposes of a conservatory were more elevated and profound than those of a music school, although his explicitly professional vision of the conservatory emphasized the ordinary not the extraordinary, the factory not the temple. He insisted that the conservatory's mission was to "produce very good and already experienced teachers" trained in pedagogy and piano performance as well as orchestral musicians "able to take a place in any orchestra" and be welcomed there. Such modest professionals, he argued, were the real products of the conservatory, as "one cannot count on virtuosi: they are stars, who very rarely appear on the conservatory horizon."[111]

Despite the Saratov branch's assurances of instructional rigor, the Main Directorate clearly still feared that a failure to maintain artistic and educational standards in the provinces might undermine the authority of the Russian conservatory as an institution. In the spring of 1916, it dispatched the pianist and composer B. L. Iavorsky to Saratov to observe graduation examinations. Iavorsky was a good choice for the task. Trained in both the Kiev Music School and the Moscow Conservatory, he was one of the founders of the Moscow People's Conservatory. On his own initiative, Iavorsky expanded his mandate to include a broad investigation of the conservatory's curriculum and its implementation, including the degree to which students' training met the contemporary needs of musical life. Iavorsky's concerns about educational affairs in Saratov reflected his broader unease with the conservatory as a musical institution. He worried that conservatory students did not see themselves as students of a "higher educational institution" but as pupils of some "more or less gifted and experienced pedagogue." In this, he hastened to add, the Saratov Conservatory merely followed a pattern established by its elder siblings in St. Petersburg and Moscow.[112]

Iavorsky focused on the Saratov Conservatory's potential to foster provincial social and cultural development. The new conservatory, he hoped, would draw students from the entire region, including from the surrounding non-Slavic peoples whom he presumed to be particularly inclined and suited to the study of (low status) wind instruments. Iavorsky's understanding of the ethnographic significance of the Saratov Conservatory notwithstanding, he articulated a professional vision of its purpose quite at odds with that offered by its director. Conservatory graduates, he argued, should be "educated musical scholars" possessing an "exactly defined [body of] knowledge." The conservatory must graduate "not musically educated artisans but artistic public figures" whose activities radiated both "spirituality" and "artistry."[113] The ideological struggle between the temple and the factory had not lost any of its vehemence in its relocation to the provinces.

The Russian Musical Society and the Empire

Gradually, the Russian Musical Society expanded until its branches and educational institutions formed a cultural network that, although concentrated in European Russia, nevertheless extended across the length and breadth of the empire. In the process, the Society came to be accepted, for better or worse, as Russia's leading musical institution and, consequently, as the most likely guarantor of the success of local musical life. In Kazan, for example, local musicians clearly saw the Society as the best hope for the success of their private endeavors in music education. In 1873, G. Aristov's attempt to establish a branch of the Society to support his private music school failed, but Free Artists A. A. Orlov-Sokolovsky and R. A. Gummert, both owners of private music schools, revived this strategy in the late 1880s and early 1890s. Despite an energetic beginning, the branch established under Orlov-Sokolovsky proved financially and organizationally brittle. The branch benefited from its founder's energy and initiative but his financial adventures, particularly a turn as a theatrical entrepreneur, left it in a perilous state. It closed in 1891, before Orlov-Sokolovsky managed to incorporate his music school under its banner. Finally, in 1902, Gummert, an 1887 graduate of the St. Petersburg Conservatory, established a viable branch and succeeded in placing his successful private music school, which he had explicitly patterned after the Society's institutions, under its protection.[114]

The reopened Kazan branch pursued new goals that reflected educated society's increasing interest in the potential of the arts to civilize the Russian people.[115] Adopting this new aesthetic imperative, the Kazan branch engaged in an ambitious program of educational outreach designed to bridge the gap between the artistic life of the urban educated classes and that of peasants and workers. The branch offered classes for regents (choir directors) and orchestral musicians, which were initially subsidized by the local Temperance Committee. Only the regents' classes proved a success, attracting a range of mostly male students from among the educated peasantry and the lower urban estates. A few students even came from neighboring provinces. The classes promised marketable skills that might secure their graduates a position as a choir leader or school singing instructor, or enhance their qualifications as village schoolteachers.[116]

The Kazan regents' courses grew out of efforts by the Russian Musical Society to exploit a perceived connection between music and sobriety. Its interest in popular music education had increased substantially in March 1904 when the Ministry of Finance endorsed its active collaboration with the Guardianship for Popular Sobriety (*Popechitel'stvo o narodnoi trezvosti*), which the state funded as part of an effort to combat drunkenness and to encourage "healthy" forms of recreation among peasants and workers.[117] The guiding principles of the movement, as approved by the Ministry of Finance in 1897, emphasized the ennobling influence of music on the working classes and encouraged local committees to promote music through the establishment of choirs. Emphasis on church singing, it was suggested, would intensify the effectiveness of music as a moral counterweight to drunkenness and hooliganism. Local temperance committees, apparently, took this suggestion to heart; by 1898, they organized or subsidized nearly three hundred choirs. Only a year later, the number stood at almost eight hundred choirs.[118] In addition, some committees formed popular orchestras and even toured villages and towns, giving concerts. Peasants and workers responded with enthusiasm, but participants tended to be schoolchildren rather than adults.[119] In some cases, pleasure and enthusiasm quickly turned into resentment and heckling when organizers tried to lecture on the virtues of sobriety.[120]

The Russian Musical Society viewed all of this as both a threat and an opportunity. The musical activities of the temperance committees, if undirected, threatened the Society's leadership claims. At the same time, the well-funded committees represented a potentially significant source of funding. In response, the Main Directorate argued that "the dissemination of musical education" should be "entrusted to an institution sufficiently stable and competent in this specialty," in short, to the Russian Musical Society. The Society offered to open, with the financial support of the temperance committees, free orchestral and regents' courses and to assume the supervision of temperance choirs.[121] The two organizations proved unable to sustain a partnership. The Society was concentrated in regional centers and had few resources in smaller communities, where temperance societies focused their musical efforts. Conversely, when the Saratov branch proposed popular choral and instrumental classes and a school for regents, it was rebuffed because the local temperance committee was unwilling to divert funds for this purpose.[122] In addition, the goals of the two organizations sharply diverged. The temperance committees promoted popular music education as a means of reinforcing moral standards and maintaining social control over peasants and workers. The Russian Musical Society, while not denying the social benefits of popular music education, remained focused on the provision of more advanced, specialized musical training.

While the Kazan branch promoted broad cultural advancement, the Tomsk branch saw itself as an outpost of civilization on the frontier. Persistent efforts to establish and sustain a branch in Tomsk reflect a desire to transform the city into a cultural and intellectual center for all of Siberia.[123] Although the branch had been founded in 1879, its survival had been precarious, its leadership often inadequate, and its efforts to support music education and concert life generally unsuccessful. In the late 1880s, perhaps inspired by the rapid growth of the city's population, the Tomsk branch began to envision a greater cultural role for itself. The branch hoped to become a greenhouse for culture, nurturing musical life not only in this "future university city" but also in Siberia as a whole.[124]

Although it took five years just to establish music classes, which were merely the first stage of this dream, the leadership of the Tomsk branch remained enthusiastic. On the eve of the opening of the long-awaited classes, they painted a portrait of Tomsk as a city on the cusp of developing true cultural sophistication and a robust civic life. They emphasized the profound changes the city had experienced in just over a decade. In 1879, when the branch was founded, Tomsk had a population of barely 26,000 souls. With educated society consisting of a few civil servants and a handful of teachers, the branch remained moribund as few local citizens shared the interests of the branch's founder, Elizaveta Alekseevna Dmitrieva-Mamonova, a former student of Nikolai Rubinstein. By 1892, however, the city had become the administrative and scientific center of Siberia, while its population nearly doubled, to 45,000 inhabitants, creating a demand for a more vigorous cultural life. The institutions needed to support cultural life had yet to be developed, however. In the case of music, the branch estimated that nearly four hundred students suffered at the hands of self-taught music teachers, implicitly threatening not only their education but also the further improvement of the region's cultural life.[125]

Despite optimistic predictions about the Society's ability to foster cultural development, the Tomsk music classes barely clung to life, in part because of the obstacles inherent in establishing specialized institutions in remote locations. Finances were a constant problem, casting doubt on the supposed intensity of local demands for a cultured life. In 1891–1892, the Tomsk branch received just over 2,000 rubles from private donors, which was more than sufficient given that it had no expenses as it had done nothing. The establishment of music classes increased expenses but not, unfortunately, income. As the classes slowly grew, from 21 students in 1892–1893 to 117 students in 1897–1898, expenses grew as well. The branch took out its first loan, for slightly more than 2,000 rubles, in 1894. By 1898, not only was the branch almost 7,000 rubles in debt, but internal dissension had prompted many students to quit.[126] Moreover, despite improving transportation and communication links, Tomsk remained isolated and unattractive to musicians, who preferred to remain close to the capitals, the center of cultural life and the source of a prestigious career. Orchestral performers were scarce within the region and expensive to hire from outside. Experienced and credentialed instructors were unavailable locally and had to be recruited from European Russia. Not only did they demand premium wages and assistance with relocation costs, there was no way to guarantee their competence. Both the recruitment and retention of faculty presented a continual challenge for the Russian Musical Society in distant provincial cities.[127]

The Russian Musical Society and civic life expanded in the provinces in a kind of syncopated rhythm. Although most music school and conservatory students did not pursue professional careers, this did not mean that they abandoned their art, as the Society's critics often charged. Instead, they played key roles in developing local musical culture, sharing their performance skills, artistic knowledge, and cultural enthusiasm with like-minded compatriots. In small towns, in particular, educated musicians could have a lasting impact on local cultural life, even if the musical elite of the capitals might not recognize them as professionals. Women, in particular, sought ways to balance their familial responsibilities and their artistic aspirations. Although critics might see women such as Aleksandra Berndtovna Levshina and Anna Iosifovna Petropavlovskaia as damning examples of the frivolous attitude of women toward music education, their contributions to cultural development in the provinces were significant. After graduating from the St. Petersburg Conservatory in 1877, Levshina married and settled with her husband in the industrial town of Lugansk in the Donets coal basin, where she taught private piano lessons. As a student she had participated in charitable concerts, primarily as an accompanist; she enthusiastically continued this practice even after her marriage. Her involvement in local cultural life was not limited to teaching and accompanying, however. She was elected to the board of the local "Circle of Lovers of the Dramatic Arts, Music, and Singing," and served as its musical director. When she and her husband subsequently moved to Saratov, she continued to teach and perform in charitable concerts.[128] Petropavlovskaia lent her expertise to local cultural organizations even further afield. A native of Kharkov province, she completed the piano course of the Kharkov Music School in 1889, but, although she received a teaching invitation from the local Institute for Noble Girls, she chose marriage over a musical career. Her husband's career as an engineer took the couple to Vladivostok, in the Far East. Far from having abandoned music, Petropavlovskaia proudly noted that she performed in the musical evenings and concerts of her local musical circle.[129]

In part due to such individual and civic initiative, provincial concerts proliferated by the turn of the century. Branches of the Russian Musical Society and independent local musical circles offered serious quartet and solo-ensemble concerts, while other organizations promoted charitable concerts that combined agreeable musical performances with buffets, games, and dancing. As the new century took shape, provincial cultural life expanded still further, with People's Houses (*Narodnye doma*) serving as venues for edifying and accessible symphonic, choral, and chamber concerts. Choral societies, factory bands, military orchestras, operetta troupes, itinerant musicians, and touring ensembles performed at commercial and street fairs, summer gardens, and restaurants for the pleasure of consumers. Opinions, of course, differed as to the degree this array of musical offerings represented a qualitative improvement in Russian musical life, as opposed to simply a quantitative increase in its volume.[130]

In December 1906, the Main Directorate asked each of the Society's branches to complete a brief questionnaire regarding their financial status and educational and concert activities. The Russian Musical Society hoped to gather sufficient information to prove its effectiveness and to inspire "greater sympathy in Russian society toward its goals and mission."[131] Thirty-six branches responded with statistical information on concerts, audiences, concert receipts and expenses, the number of faculty, students, and graduates of their educational institutions, and the budgets of these schools and their sources of support. Most branches also provided information on the professional activity of former students and a brief narrative history.[132] Many of the complaints that appeared in these reports rang familiar: a shortage of qualified local performers, inadequate financing, and the need for permanent premises for educational and concert activities. There was one crucial change, however. The branches complaining of these problems were no longer those in major provincial centers such as Kiev, Odessa, Saratov, and Tiflis, but smaller cities such as Orel, Kishinev, Samara, and Irkutsk.[133]

Taken as a whole, these reports present an image of a successful, dynamic, and innovative organization that, despite obstacles and occasional failures, played a critical role in provincial cultural life. The Kiev branch, for example, provided career information for 99 of its 280 graduates.[134] Such lists emphasized the Russian Musical Society's role as an engine of musical development; its importance lay not only in its own efforts but in the successes of its students. Even the Kishinev Music School, in existence for only seven years, could boast of eighteen graduates who had continued their education at a conservatory or found employment either as music teachers or choir directors, or in orchestras and opera companies.[135] The report of the Samara branch, founded five years earlier by Ia. Ia. Karklin, a graduate of the St. Petersburg Conservatory, underscored the potential impact an individual graduate could have on provincial cultural life. The governor of Samara, A. S. Brianchaninov, served as the branch's first chairman, giving it a prominent position among local institutions. Yet, the branch's success was due primarily to Karklin, who not only willingly assumed the "lion's share" of the work but also covered much of the initial cost of establishing music classes and local concert life.[136]

The Nizhnii Novgorod branch complained that concert life in provincial cities still had little to do with music and much to do with creating opportunities for casual flirtation. Some twenty or more charitable concerts were held in the city every year, all of which offered dances, buffets, booths selling flowers and postcards, and, almost as an afterthought, musical performances featuring amateur female singers for the young men to fawn over. The serious concerts of the Russian Musical Society, the branch whined, could not compete.[137] Few other branches, however, viewed concert life so gloomily. In Rostov on Don, the local branch had benefited from the popularity of charitable concerts and helped to transform them into serious performances. "Not one charitable concert in Rostov on Don takes place without the participation of former students" or instructors of the branch's music school, they boasted. More important, they suggested that their efforts had improved the quality of these concerts, which began to attract a large audience once they "replaced amateurs with finished performers."[138] The Poltava branch of the Society, meanwhile, trumpeted the success of its first orchestra tour, which brought popular concert music, including Tchaikovsky's *1812 Overture* and Rubinstein's *Rossiia*, to the "working masses." Demand for tickets was so high that the orchestra had to add performances.[139]

The reports of the Kherson and Iaroslavl branches emphasized the new interest in popular music education. Both branches sought to broaden their base by offering both traditional music classes and courses for regents. In Kherson, the local temperance committee subsidized two highly successful popular concerts with ticket prices set at ten kopecks. The branch planned four similar concerts for the 1906–1907 season.[140] In Iaroslavl, it was the perceived inadequacy of local music teachers and the "complete absence of popular choirs" that fueled the decision to found a branch of the Society in 1903. Determined to control the aesthetic development of the *narod*, the branch vowed to maintain artistic standards by excluding "so-called factory songs and the performance of whole operas" from the repertoire of its choirs in favor of sacred music. The expressed goals of the Iaroslavl branch clearly attracted the sympathy of local authorities; in three years, the local temperance committee and the provincial zemstvo contributed more than 20,000 rubles for the branch's educational activities.[141]

In the tumultuous final years of the Russian Empire, the difficulties of a wartime economy as well as the more ordinary stresses of rapid industrialization and urbanization altered the social and cultural role of the Society. The industrial town of Ivanovo-Vosnesensk exemplifies the challenges and opportunities rapid social and economic change presented to the Russian Musical Society. The city, known as the "Russian Manchester," had grown from 10,547 inhabitants in 1871 to 31,056 in 1883, 54,208 at the time of the 1897 census, 108,033 in 1909, and 168,498 in 1914. The local branch of the Society, established in 1910, reached out to the working population, which seemed to hunger for musical instruction and entertainment.[142] The director of the music school noted that a "very large contingent" of its students were "either themselves workers or the children of workers." The branch struggled to support needy students, providing free tuition to 40 of the school's 172 students, with another 12 paying only half tuition. As usual, most of the free places went to orchestral students, enabling the school to sustain an orchestra of forty-five. The branch also supported a mixed choir of fifty voices "exclusively drawn from male and female factory workers," who also studied elementary theory, solfège, and even "an abbreviated course of harmony." For these singer-workers, music education might lead to social advancement; five students had completed the school's theory and composition curriculum, subsequently receiving offers to teach or serve as choral directors in local schools, factories, and churches.

The branch argued that although the school noticeably affected the lives of individuals it had transformed the life of the town. In its five years of activity, the Ivanovo-Vosnesensk Music School had exerted a "favorable influence" and brought "musical enlightenment" to the "simple people." The power of music combated fatigue; students worked in the factories all day, but devoted all of their remaining energy to music classes. To accommodate working students, the school held classes from seven until eleven o'clock in the evening. The branch was convinced that "musical education" was "one of the main factors in the cultural development of the people," especially in industrial centers such as Ivanovo-Vosnesensk, "where workers alone number seventy thousand" and "compulsory sobriety" imposed during the war had created a new demand for "cultural entertainments." It argued for increased state funding as well as public pressure on local governments, the zemstva, and factory owners in order to force them to provide moral and financial assistance to the Russian Musical Society as it attempted to meet the ever-growing need for music.[143]

A glance at a map makes clear why a conservatory or two in St. Petersburg and Moscow proved inadequate to meet the growing demand for music in the Russian Empire. In 1859, specialized musical instruction in a public, institutionalized setting was a novelty; by the outbreak of World War I, it had become a commonplace element of cultural and social life not only in the capitals, but also in many provincial cities. Over this same period, the Russian Musical Society firmly established itself as the dominant musical institution in the empire. As the Society began to expand rapidly after the 1890s, the Main Directorate attempted to assert its control over provincial branches, to establish uniform standards, and to provide administrative oversight, primarily through bureaucratic means: official memos and the control of the purse strings. Provincial branches may have operated independently, but they clearly looked to St. Petersburg and the Main Directorate for artistic, organizational, administrative, and financial support and guidance. Both the state and educated society perceived the Russian Musical Society as a single organization; nevertheless, one of the most frequent complaints directed at the Society was the Main Directorate's failure to exercise its oversight of provincial branches.

Although these criticisms were justified to some extent, the unique pattern of development of Russian musical life was due in part to the Society's administrative and organizational structure, which enabled Russian musicians to pursue, if not completely achieve, a common vision of the nature, purpose, and content of music education and local musical life. The Society's ambitions toward the centralization of musical life under its authority emerged quite clearly in the context of the first general conference of the directors of the Society's musical educational institutions, held in Moscow in May 1904. The topics proposed for discussion included not only a unified curriculum but also student uniforms, strategies for increasing cooperation between branches and improving concert life in the provinces, the rights of faculty in the music schools to state service, the legal status of music schools as secondary institutions, standardization of graduation certificates and diplomas, the establishment of a badge or medal for conservatory graduates, and the need to control the proliferation of private music schools. The last topic was of particular concern to many of the Society's weaker branches, which felt threatened by the proliferation of private music schools. In an ironic criticism, given the frequent attacks on the Society for its willingness to admit virtually anyone able to afford tuition, the Kherson branch damned private music schools as purely commercial ventures concerned only with attracting as many students as possible.[144] Well-established branches of the Society were less concerned. V. V. Pukhalsky, the director of the Kiev Music School, insisted that attempts to assert control over private institutions would only undermine the relationship between the Society and professional musicians, which might bring disaster in smaller provincial cities.[145] The Poltava branch did not share the caution of the Kiev branch, however. It argued that the Society played a role in musical life similar to that of the Ministry of Education; it therefore had the right to claim oversight of all musical educational institutions. Such claims to oversight were not accepted by the state, although it recognized the Society's legitimate expertise and even accorded it a consultative role in the approval process for private music schools.[146]

Still, the Russian Musical Society responded to the increasing demand for music education more effectively than its counterparts in other nations. Although critics complained that the state's failure to assume responsibility for specialized music education hampered the development of Russian musical culture, its unwillingness to incorporate music institutions into the state-supported educational network actually facilitated the creation of an effective system of specialized music education. Most European states boasted one or two state conservatories, or at most a scattering of city-supported conservatories, supplemented by a wide variety of private music schools.[147] Through the efforts of the Russian Musical Society, Russia acquired a network of cultural institutions increasingly conscious of their shared responsibility for the rational and systematic development of musical life. Nevertheless, in assessing the importance of the Russian Musical Society, one must weigh rhetoric against real achievements. The Society promoted itself as a seedbed for civilization, disseminating not only music but also European culture to the far reaches of the empire. The achievements of the Society in the provinces were truly impressive, although they never quite reached the grandiose proportions sometimes claimed. The Society did not create Russian musical culture, even in the provinces, out of a void but built upon a well-established foundation of domestic music instruction and music making. The Russian Musical Society, however, successfully relocated music from the private sphere of the home to the public sphere of the educational institution and the public concert. In many provincial cities, the Russian Musical Society served as the focal point for local concert culture. Its branches supplied provincial society with chamber music and symphony concerts, as well as numerous student recitals and performances. The Society, unsurprisingly, sometimes failed to live up to its promise. Too often, provincial branches were founded without adequate social support or financial backing. Both the St. Petersburg Conservatory, one of the finest in Europe, and the Omsk music classes were sheltered under the institutional umbrella of the Russian Musical Society. Nevertheless, the institutional strength and organizational flexibility of the Society allowed it to make a lasting contribution to the development of Russian culture.

CHAPTER 6 | Crisis, Celebration, and the Decline of the Old Cultural Order

FOR MORE THAN FIFTY YEARS, the conservatory was at the heart of a vigorous debate about the purpose of music in Russian society. These debates began when a Russian conservatory was still just an idea and continued into the first decades of Soviet power. At first glance, arguments over the structure, leadership, purpose, and social role of a specialized cultural institution appear marginal to broader social and political movements. Upon digging a little deeper, it becomes clear that the debates over the conservatories were chapters in a fiery struggle for Russia's cultural identity. The culmination of this struggle for cultural identity came, fittingly enough, with the publication of Lev Tolstoy's philosophical pamphlet *What is Art?* (*Chto takoe iskusstvo?*) in 1898. Despite the fact that, in many ways, Tolstoy and his family engaged with music in thoroughly conventional ways (see figure 6.1), his philosophical views challenged many of the most sacred beliefs of nineteenth-century musicians. Tolstoy rejected beauty as the definition of art, substituting instead a characterization that privileged feeling, especially religious feeling, and the communion of artist, musician, or writer with his or her audience. Art that did not generate an emotional or spiritual connection between creator and audience was not true art but merely a facsimile.

From this starting point, Tolstoy condemned much of the artistic heritage and contemporary brilliance of European art, up to and including Beethoven's Ninth Symphony and, in particular, the "Ode to Joy," a work all but fetishized by audiences of the nineteenth century. In rejecting Beethoven's symphony, Tolstoy applied criteria that demanded comprehensibility and accessibility to the whole of society. According to Tolstoy, if a painting, composition, dance, or story was incomprehensible to common laborers, peasants, or artisans it could not be true art.

FIGURE 6.1. "Leo Tolstoy and Daughter Alexandra at the Piano" by Sophia Andreevna Tolstaya (1844–1919), Russia, 1890. State Museum of Leo Tolstoy, Moscow. Credit: culture-images/Lebrecht

Tolstoy, of course, was not the only person at the turn of the century criticizing the inaccessibility of art to the lower classes. Many critics within the intelligentsia decried the high cost of concerts, plays, and ballet performances. They bemoaned the cultural gulf between the wealthy classes for whom these works were created and the broader mass, rural or urban, of Russian society. Strenuous efforts were made to bring art to the people. In music, popular and inexpensive (*obshchedostupnyi*) concerts were a regular feature of urban life. Even smaller provincial towns benefited from attempts, like those of the Poltava branch of the Society and its touring orchestra, to extend the reach of art and culture. Factory bands, village choirs, and inexpensive or free music lessons were all part of a broad attempt to enlighten, educate, and civilize the people.

Such well-meaning efforts served the upper classes as much or more as they did their intended beneficiaries. They assumed that "enlightened," "educated," and "civilized" peasants, workers, and artisans would be more useful and reliable members of Russian society. Of course, those promoting such cultural enlightenment efforts were pursuing a variety of agendas. The state supported some of these efforts in the hopes of quelling worker unrest, creating a more effective workforce, and a more stable political and economic situation. The need to retain control over the *narod* prompted the state and the church, in particular, to emphasize the moral enlightenment of the people in consonance with traditional assumptions about social hierarchies, religious belief, and the relationship of the tsar to the people. Factory owners and merchants shared similar goals, as well as, at least occasionally, a real desire for the betterment of those in their employ. Intelligentsia groups hoped to affect a broader transformation of Russian society by creating a *narod* willing and able to participate as an equal partner in Russia's social, political, and cultural advancement. In all of these cases, the driving motivation was the desire, or the need, to transform the *narod* into something resembling, at least in its cultural outlook, the urban upper and middle layers of Russian society.

Tolstoy denied any legitimacy to these initiatives. Echoing older intelligentsia ideas about the peasantry as the repository of Russian cultural traditions, Tolstoy insisted that it was not the *narod* that needed to be enlightened but the upper classes, who had lost any real understanding of the nature of art or its meaning. Instead of real art that created emotional or spiritual responses and was accessible to all, the upper classes had created an artificial art that rested on superficial definitions of beauty and pernicious ideas of pleasure and was accessible only to the elites:

> The art we possess is the whole of art, the true, the only art, and yet not only do two-thirds of the human race, all the peoples of Asia and Africa, live and die without knowing this only true art, but, furthermore, barely one per cent of all the people in our Christian society benefit from this art which we call the *whole* of art; the remaining ninety-nine per cent of our European people live and die by generations, working hard, without ever tasting this art, which besides is of such a kind that even if they could avail themselves of it, they would not understand anything.[1]

Tolstoy dismissed the rebuttal argument that "if not all benefit from existing art, it is not the art that is to blame, but the wrong organization of society," which served to justify the enlightenment campaigns outlined above. Mocking these ideas, he attacked the "slavery" required for the creation of "refined" art as well as the notion that art would become accessible to the people as they became more educated. Such would only be the case if in the process of educating the people the wealthy succeeded in perverting them, twisting them into adopting the values and habits of the corrupt and degenerate upper classes.

> For the vast majority of working people, our art, inaccessible to them because of its costliness, is also alien to them in its very content.... That

which constitutes pleasure for a man of the wealthy classes is not perceived as pleasure by a working man, and calls up in him either no feelings at all, or else feelings completely contrary to those it calls up in an idle and satiated man. Thus, for example, the feelings of honor, patriotism, and amorousness, which constitute the main content of present-day art, call up in a working man only perplexity, scorn or indignation. So that even if the majority of working people were given the opportunity...to see, to read, to hear...all that constitutes the flower of present-day art, these working people...would understand nothing..., and even if they did, the greater part of what they understood would not only not elevate their souls, but would corrupt them.[2]

The corrupt nature of contemporary art lay in its artificiality, in its lack of originality, and, especially, in its failure to call forth real emotion or a spiritual connection between artist, performer, and audience. This perversion of art, according to Tolstoy, rested on the increasing professionalization of musicians, painters, dancers, and writers. Artists no longer created out of the desire to share their joys and sorrows with their fellow men, but out of baser goals, such as financial gain, fame, and professional recognition. The process of professionalization, and, in particular, the creation of institutions for the training of artistic professionals, such as conservatories and academies of art, completed the distortion of true, spiritual, emotional art into a false, artificial art for the wealthy classes.

Professional schools, Tolstoy insisted, could do nothing but sustain an artificial and corrupt art. No school could teach the essence of true art, the "conveying to others of the special feeling experienced by an artist." Society should abandon the training of ever more technically adroit but spiritually empty performers and artists in conservatories and academies. Instead, Tolstoy advocated the broader education of the whole of society in the fundamentals of the arts. He wanted to create a society where "artistic activity will become accessible to all," one where the primary schools would teach "music and painting (singing and drawing), together with reading and writing, so that each person, could, if he felt...a calling for one of the arts, become perfected in it."[3]

Tolstoy's conception of artistic education, as well as his rejection of commonly accepted European artistic standards, jeopardized the gains musicians had made over the preceding decades in social status and professional recognition. Most profoundly, by rejecting professionalization and specialization, and by emphasizing the universality of artistic ability, Tolstoy undermined Romantic ideas of the artistic genius and the concept of talent. If the defining criteria of art was not beauty but feeling, and if the unrefined singing of untrained peasant women had more claim to being true art than did a skillful performance of a Beethoven sonata, then artists as an identifiable category dissolved into the broad mass of humanity.

Such a conclusion was not lost on professional musicians, such as V. G. Valter, a graduate of the St. Petersburg Conservatory and concertmaster of the Mariinsky Theater Orchestra. Valter reacted with horror to Tolstoy's philosophizing on the arts. He attempted to lessen the impact of Tolstoy's theories by producing a polemical pamphlet of his own, entitled *In Defense of Art*, in 1899. As a professional musician, Valter was most concerned about defending the social status and professional rights of both musicians and the institutions that trained and employed them. In many ways, Valter had the easier task. For all of Tolstoy's literary fame, he was nevertheless tilting at windmills in his attack on art. His arguments ran counter not only to mainstream critical and aesthetic opinion but also to the self-evident acceptance of the worth of the arts and of beauty as their defining characteristic in European society. Valter gave voice to musicians, writers, and artists outraged by Tolstoy's attacks. Speaking on behalf of humble artists and writers, he noted that while unbeknownst to themselves they had become "champions of evil" rather than laborers for the good of society, at least they found themselves in good company, lumped together with such dubious characters as Beethoven, Pushkin, and Tolstoy himself.[4]

Of all the issues raised by Tolstoy, the one that really threatened Valter, and the one to which he responded with the greatest vehemence, was the attempt to negate the role of talent in the artistic process. In defending talent, Valter denied the possibility that all people had the potential to be artists, to be creators of "true" art. Real art, Valter argued, reiterating Romantic and post-Romantic ideals of genius, was an activity for the elect, for those gifted by God, not for everyone. The broad masses were not creators of art but its recipients; they were moved to emotion or aesthetic pleasure by the work of the talented few.[5]

Tolstoy's critique of the arts, however, hinted at deeper levels of dissatisfaction with the musical status quo. Educators and musicians ever more frequently expressed their frustration with the provision of music education in the empire. Increasingly, they also expressed resentment at the Russian Musical Society's dominance over musical life. Paradoxically, the solution most frequently proposed to liberate the conservatories and music schools from the arbitrary control of the Russian Musical Society was to place them under the direct authority of the government. Would-be reformers looked with envy on the Paris Conservatory and other European conservatories for their apparently high level of state financial support. At a time when most Russian social organizations were agitating for less state control, many musicians were advocating closer ties between musical institutions and the state. Reformers perceived the Russian Musical Society as a block and hindrance to the further development of the musical arts and the musical profession in Russia. They disparaged the leadership of the Society as a group of wealthy and socially influential "dilettantes" and "amateurs" whose era had passed and who were unable to secure the further development of Russian music. They believed that by placing educational and cultural institutions directly under state authority they would garner greater prestige, secure control by qualified professionals, and, most important, acquire greater and more secure financing.

Paying the Piper: Patronage, the State, and the Society's Mission

The modernization of Russian musical culture inevitably altered the relationship between connoisseurs and patrons and musicians and composers. It created a new structure of support for the arts that depended on the cooperation of local educated society, voluntary associations, and local, provincial, and central government bodies. Scholarly interest in Russian artistic patronage has been directed primarily at the wealthy Moscow merchants who played such an important role in fostering Russian visual arts by creating both a market and, ultimately, mechanisms for the preservation and dissemination of Russian painting and sculpture.[6] Wealthy merchant *maecenases* certainly played a role in Russian music as well, and not only in Moscow. Merchant patronage was only one component of a large and complex set of relationships of mutual obligation and interest. Between 1859 and 1918, a broad spectrum of patronage and support mechanisms was employed to craft, stabilize, and invigorate Russian musical culture.[7] The traditional bonds between aristocratic patrons and artists grew increasingly thin, while a qualitatively different bourgeois patronage grew increasingly important. Anonymous support—through ticket sales, for example—began to emerge as a potent force further eroding any sense of the patron's entitlement to a guiding, much less a controlling, voice in the direction and content of musical production.[8] At the same time, the growing number of individuals involved in supporting the arts on a very small scale—through the purchase of individual or season tickets to concerts or through the payment of music school tuition fees—had the potential to create a sense of public ownership and responsibility for the arts.

New social and artistic ideologies privileged the artist at the expense of the dilettante. Aristocratic dilettantism, based in conceptions of innate moral superiority, gave way to bourgeois dilettantism, based in ideologies of effort, reason, and education. The combination of emerging professionalism, secured by academies and credentials, and the Romantic ideology of the artistic genius further undermined the position of the dilettante.[9] As one scholar has noted, "bourgeois artists reasserted—and inverted—the traditional unequal relationship between artist and dilettante. Now the artist took the role of the aristocrat. . . . Thus, the idea of aristocratic superiority came to be used against the dilettante by the 'innate genius,' the new aristocrat of culture: the artist. And so the dilettante sank from patron to supportive client to philistine."[10]

In order to succeed, the Russian Musical Society needed to attract patrons throughout its nearly sixty years of activity. But the patrons it attracted, and their roles, changed significantly over time, a consequence of the transformation of Russian society. In particular, the relationship of imperial patrons to the Russian Musical Society became increasingly complex, reflecting the changing position of music and musicians. The support of imperial patrons differed from that offered by other wealthy contributors because of their official role as chair of the society and the greater influence they were able to wield within official circles. But other patrons also played important roles in establishing and maintaining the Society. Among the most important of these was the state.

One of the primary functions of the leadership of the Russian Musical Society was to negotiate with the state on behalf of the local branches and educational institutions of the Society. Over time, the personal ties of its patrons, the imperial title it bore, and the tendency of the state to rely on the Society for expert advice on musical matters eroded the boundary between the voluntary association and the state. On one point, however, both parties were all too clear. The state never accepted responsibility for the financial support of the Society or its institutions.[11] Nevertheless, the state was occasionally willing to serve as a patron of the Society, primarily by providing modest subsidies to its educational institutions. These subsidies tied the Society to the state, compromising its independence in the eyes of the educated public. Moreover, although the state proved sympathetic to requests for funds to support educational endeavors, especially in the provinces, requests for funds for concert series, general support for the Society, or even subsidies for the conservatories usually fell on deaf ears. Indeed, despite several attempts by the Society, the initial subsidies awarded to the St. Petersburg (15,000 rubles) and Moscow (20,000 rubles) conservatories in 1869 and 1872, respectively, were never increased.[12]

By 1900, eight branches—in St. Petersburg, Moscow, Kiev, Kharkov, Odessa, Saratov, Tiflis, and Tomsk—were receiving a total of 62,000 rubles annually. More than half this amount—35,000 rubles—consisted of the subsidies to the two conservatories.[13] Rapid expansion after 1900 prompted the Society to pursue more robust and consistent state support for its provincial institutions. In 1902, it petitioned the state for 5,000-ruble subsidies for its six recently established music schools in Astrakhan, Ekaterinoslav, Kishinev, Nikolaev, Rostov on Don, and Tambov, as well as a renewal of funding to the Kiev and Kharkov music schools. The strong support of the Ministry of Internal Affairs barely sufficed to overcome the objections of Minister of Finance Witte or of the State Comptroller. Disagreeing with Witte, the State Council ruled in favor of the Russian Musical Society, although the funds allocated fell short of the Society's hopes. Ultimately, the Society received a subsidy of 33,000 rubles for the eight institutions listed above, that, combined with subsidies committed to the St. Petersburg and Moscow conservatories as well as the 17,000 rubles already assigned to the Tiflis, Odessa, and Saratov music schools and the Tomsk music classes, brought the total amount of state funding to 75,000 rubles. Most important, the subsidies were now made permanent, rather than being subject to renewal every five years. At the same time, however, the Council's ruling placed severe limits on the state's responsibility for musical life, reiterating the expectation that support for music should come from educated society.[14]

The state subsidies were symbolically important but they covered just a fraction of the Society's costs. On average, between 1906 and 1914, state subsidies covered less than 10 percent of the expenses for the five Russian conservatories. Funds were unequally distributed, however, with the Moscow and Saratov conservatories receiving proportionally larger subsidies (12.5 percent and 19.6 percent of annual expenses, respectively) and the St. Petersburg and Kiev conservatories receiving relatively insignificant amounts (in both cases amounting to 6.3 percent of annual expenses). Support for the Society's twenty-two music schools was somewhat more robust, with all but two schools receiving subsidies (although these ranged from 132 rubles in Zhitomir to 5,125 rubles in Kharkov and Tiflis). The Society's music classes were consciously neglected, with only seven of nineteen awarded subsidies, which ranged from 250 rubles (Vladivostok) to 625 rubles (Orel) and covered a mere 1.7 percent of their expenses.[15]

By 1908, the Russian Musical Society had renewed its efforts to secure greater state funding, this time provoking a response from the press as well as debates within the State Duma. In the pages of *Novoe vremia*, M. M. Ivanov voiced his opposition to any state aid for provincial musical life. Subsidies,

Ivanov noted sardonically, were wonderful things; everyone seemed to want one. Ivanov criticized the pretensions of the St. Petersburg Conservatory and other artistic institutions as they attempted to stake their claim to the state's limited financial resources. In particular he attacked the conservatory, charging that although it possessed a veritable palace paid for with state funds, its achievements had failed to keep pace with its institutional aggrandizement. Insisting that talent was a rare commodity, Ivanov portrayed the Society's provincial educational institutions as frivolous endeavors that merely satisfied the vanity of provincial cities. The state's failure to support artistic education in the provinces, he insisted, would not damage Russian culture; it might, however, reduce the number of mediocre musicians.[16] Fortunately for the Russian Musical Society, this dismissive attitude was not universal. *Muzykal'nyi truzhenik* noted that its current subsidy barely equaled that for *one* secondary school. Despite such meager support, the Society had proven itself an extremely useful institution. Although its flaws were numerous, it had accomplished the "musical education and enlightenment" of the empire; the "entire musical life of Russia" revolved around it.[17]

The rhetorical strategies employed by the Society in presenting its funding petition, particularly an emphasis not only on the Society's achievements but also on the "absence" of musical life before its establishment, proved effective enough that they were redeployed when the Society celebrated its jubilee in 1909 and that of the St. Petersburg Conservatory in 1912. Sensing that simple assertions of success would not be enough to persuade the Duma to greater generosity, the Society attempted to prove its success in bringing music, education, and the light of culture and civilization to the empire through numbers. The growth of its branches and institutions, the Society insisted, demonstrated popular approval. In 1872, only 644 students studied in the Society's conservatories and schools. By 1905, the Society's educational institutions enrolled nearly seven thousand students and boasted nearly three thousand graduates. Statistics gave weight to the Society's claims that its efforts had allowed native composers, bandmasters, opera singers, orchestral musicians, and music teachers to displace the foreigners who had previously dominated Russian musical life. Moreover, the Society insisted, it brought enlightenment to a broad provincial audience; it had presented some six thousand musical performances over the course of forty-seven concert seasons. It educated the public taste. It encouraged Russian music. Its activities, the Society insisted, were *the* crucial element in Russian musical life. Even the appearance of private opera theaters, the inclusion of provincial cities in the itineraries of touring concert artists, and the appearance of smaller musical-amateur circles and societies were all claimed as direct results of the

Society's civilizing project. The Society had transformed backward Russia, the petition claimed. Thanks to its efforts, Russian music seemed assured of a great future, perhaps even a preeminent position in European musical culture.[18] Now it was owed something in return.

Although the petition highlighted the state's prior generosity, it simultaneously emphasized the inadequacy of this support. Russian music, the Society insisted, was obliged to it for its "elevated position," both in Russia and abroad. If Russia, they argued, "is presently able to take pride in anything before Europe in a cultural or artistic sense, it is, of course, in our music. Everyone knows the kind of success Russian music has met abroad, especially recently, and the honorable reputation our composers, singers, and artists enjoy with [foreign] audiences." Most of these proselytizers of Russian culture abroad were products of the conservatories, indebted to the Russian Musical Society for the development of their musical talents. Given the Society's service to Russian culture, the state could neither deny its significance nor refuse its claim to state support. The petition demanded, at the very least, parity in state support for the visual arts and music.[19]

In concluding its arguments, the Society offered the state two alternatives to secure Russian musical life. The state could assume direct control of the Society's institutions. Such an action, the Society acknowledged, would lead to its liquidation as an organization but might finally lead to financial security. The Society did not, however, actually expect this outcome. Instead, it offered this alternative in an effort to make its request to increase its total subsidy to 235,000 rubles appear both reasonable and attractive, anticipating the resistance that it indeed provoked from the Ministry of Finance.[20] Responding to the Ministry's counterproposal, the Society insisted that a request for 115,000 rubles to support both the St. Petersburg and Moscow conservatories could hardly be considered unreasonable given that the state provided 400,000 rubles annually to the Academy of Arts. In an effort to pressure the Ministry, the Russian Musical Society provided an unflattering comparison of Russia to its European cultural and political competitors. All eight French conservatories and the four Belgian conservatories, it alleged, were supported entirely by the state. The Paris Conservatory alone received the equivalent of 110,000 rubles annually in state appropriations.[21] Under pressure from the Ministry of Internal Affairs, the Society reluctantly agreed to trim its request to 210,500 rubles, which was further reduced to 200,000 rubles by the time it reached the State Duma.[22] The Duma, however, only approved an increase of 37,500 rubles to the existing subsidy, which brought the total to 112,500 rubles, less than half of what had been initially requested. Moreover, the additional allocation was directed entirely toward the maintenance and improvement of the

Society's provincial educational institutions; neither the Moscow nor the St. Petersburg conservatory received any additional funds from the state. Yet, this should not be interpreted to mean that the Duma was hostile to the goals of the Russian Musical Society. They particularly approved of the Society's efforts to expand in the provinces, which they saw as an essential step toward a desirable decentralization of Russian cultural life. To that end, requests for supplementary funding for the reorganization of the Saratov Music School into the Saratov Conservatory passed easily, in part due to the eloquent support of A. M. Maslennikov, a Duma representative from the city.[23]

Throughout its existence, the Society struggled to balance its expansive tendencies with the limitations of its resources. In 1902, the conductor Eduard Napravnik once again voiced his frustration with the status quo in an extended memo to the Main Directorate. Napravnik expressed his admiration for the organizers of the Society, with whom he had long been affiliated, and emphasized his appreciation for the growth of local branches and educational institutions, which now included "28 branches, 2 conservatories, 11 music schools, and 7 music classes, in which...about 5,000 students study under 400 specialist instructors." Praise was only the precursor to serious criticism, however. Napravnik noted the debilitating effects of the constant worry over finances. Although he absolved the Society of most responsibility, he once again argued that the results of its labors had been "expressed more in terms of *quantity* than *quality*." The Society's branches, he complained, were forced to admit "a huge number of paying but ungifted students" as soon as they stepped beyond limited concert activity. Branches that were content to conform to older patterns for local music societies, with only a few casual concerts a year and no music classes of any kind, easily met their expenses. Branches that took seriously their responsibility to develop local cultural life jeopardized their financial health and even their survival.

For Napravnik, the solution was to persuade the state to accept its cultural responsibilities. State support to the Russian Musical Society and to musical life more generally had been "more than meager," he argued. Instead of limited state subsidies, he advocated "an annual outlay from the treasury" that would provide the Society with sufficient funds to distribute in support not only of its "needy educational institutions" but also for the establishment of new music classes, the reorganization of existing classes into music schools, the issuance of loans or grants for the support of concert activity in the provinces, and grants to musicians and music teachers. Thus, for Napravnik, the state held the key to the successful reorientation of Russian musical life. With its willing assistance, the "musical educational institutions" of the Society would be able to "embark on normal conditions of existence" by limiting the size of the student body to a "relatively small" number of "really talented youth" sufficient to meet the "contemporary needs of musical Russia." Without such aid, Napravnik implied, Russian musical life would continue to be distorted, as the nascent middle and professional classes appropriated the conservatories, schools, and classes of the Society for their own social and status needs.[24]

Napravnik's letter reflected the unease of a considerable number of leading musicians and cultural critics, who viewed the existence of a network of educational institutions under the authority of a private organization, administered by dilettantes, and only nominally supervised by the state as an anomaly. They believed that the state had a responsibility for music education. The state, they argued, was not meeting its cultural obligations, relying instead on the Russian Musical Society because it offered a cheaper alternative to direct state support. The transfer to the state of both fiscal responsibility and effective oversight for specialized music education was part of a broader campaign to transform the relationship of the state to Russian culture. As Katerina Clark has noted, the turn of the century witnessed calls within many artistic fields for the creation of a Ministry of the Arts.[25] In music, calls for such a Ministry or, at the very least, for a Department of the Arts within the Ministry of Education date back much further.[26] From the 1890s, calls for a Ministry of the Arts appeared with greater frequency and met with increasing approval in musical circles. Only institutionalized state support, proponents of an arts ministry argued, could provide a stable financial foundation to allow Russian music to advance beyond the heights already achieved through private efforts. Only state support would ensure the safe removal of Russian music education from the hands of the amateurs and allow the professionals to develop music education—at all levels—according to a rational plan.[27]

In part, this debate responded to what musicians perceived as the inappropriate jurisdiction of the Ministry of Internal Affairs over specialized music education and, in particular, the expanding educational network of the Russian Musical Society. The Ministry oversaw the establishment and approved the charters of private social organizations.[28] Musical, dramatic, and artistic societies of all stripes fell under its authority. The Russian Musical Society, at its inception, scarcely differed from the myriad of small artistic societies that both preceded and followed it. Most of these societies provided a modest level of concert and social activity for their members; their rhetorical size within the cultural public sphere was minor. The Russian Musical Society, however, ultimately eclipsed its predecessors and competitors, developing into a robust and influential cultural institution. In the process, the inclusion of the Society's educational institutions under the

Ministry's umbrella became a problem. As long as authority over the Society's educational institutions remained outside the Ministry of Education, their status was insecure.

The Conservatory Revolution and the Rimsky-Korsakov Scandal

In 1905, longstanding tensions within Russian society exploded. The Bloody Sunday massacre of January 9 horrified educated society. Popular faith in the tsar was fatally shaken; disillusionment with the government seemed almost universal. As the revolution gathered steam, strikes spread across Russia. Widespread peasant unrest and rebellion followed urban disorders in which students struck in solidarity with workers. The universities and most other higher educational institutions suspended classes until the fall. The liberal opposition gained strength and confidence, openly demanding fundamental changes to the political structure.

The revolution shook Russia's musical world as well. The Rimsky-Korsakov scandal, the crucial event of the so-called conservatory revolution, overlapped broader social and political events in 1905. The revolution engulfed the Russian Musical Society because it, like the autocracy, had difficulty accommodating new social aspirations and a changing cultural hierarchy. The hybrid structure of the Society gave it something of a split personality. Socially prominent musical amateurs provided leadership for the voluntary association, while its educational institutions provided the basis for an emerging musical profession.

The complicated question of musicians' professional and social status flavored their response to the 1905 revolution. As Harley Balzer has argued, most professions struggled to reduce the authority of the state over professional, social, and political life.[29] Musicians, however, struggled to reduce the authority of a voluntary association over musical life and increase the authority of the state in music and music education, in order to raise the status and security of their profession and its institutions. The coincidence of the height of this process with the 1905 Revolution turned the Russian Musical Society into an unexpected villain. The educated public, in the context of the 1905 Revolution, identified the conservatories with the liberal ideas usually associated with voluntary associations and regarded the Society as a tool of the state rather than an expression of Russia's nascent civil society.

Scattered evidence suggests that the leadership of the Russian Musical Society and its provincial branches may have been more politically diverse than the leadership of other voluntary associations due to the persistence of older, aristocratic patterns of artistic patronage. Nevertheless, the Russian Musical Society did not differ markedly from other voluntary associations in terms of its structure, membership, or broad social goals. The virulently negative reaction of the liberal public toward the Society during the 1905 Revolution is not a commentary on the personal politics of the Society's leadership. Rather, it is a reflection of the willingness of educated society to transfer its anger at the tsarist regime onto an available and appropriate bureaucratic scapegoat.

In the St. Petersburg Conservatory, a foolish boast sparked the flame of revolution. A military musician whose regiment subsidized his studies claimed that he had shot several workers during the Bloody Sunday massacre. Although, according to memoirists, "the only weapon in [his] possession on January 9 was undoubtedly his cornet," outraged students demanded the braggart's expulsion.[30] Conservatory director A. R. Berngard's refusal alienated the student body.[31] The revolutionary flame did not burn particularly brightly in the conservatories, however. Conservatory students were arguably more tractable than university students. The social composition of the conservatories—distinctly different from that of other higher educational institutions in the capitals—clearly shaped its political dynamics.[32] Not only did women comprise a majority of the student body, but both the St. Petersburg and Moscow conservatories also enrolled a significant number of children and mature adults. Social class disparities, particularly between well-to-do female pianists and vocalists and often-impoverished male orchestral musicians, as well as a large Jewish cohort in St. Petersburg, created tensions within the student body.

Even before the protests in the conservatories, Russia's musical world was already in upheaval. In early February, leading Moscow musicians, including A. Grechaninov, S. Taneev, S. Rakhmaninov, F. Chaliapin, R. Gliere, A. Gedike, K. Igumnov, and N. Kashkin, published a resolution in *Nashi dni* that demanded political reform and proclaimed support for the "eleven theses" drafted at the Zemstvo Congress of November 1904. "We are not free artists," they declared, "but like all other Russian citizens, the disenfranchised victims of today's abnormal social conditions. It is our conviction that there is only one solution: Russia must at last embark on a road to radical reforms."[33] From St. Petersburg, Rimsky-Korsakov and several other conservatory professors added their names to the resolution.[34] The musicians' resolution affirmed their support for the *Declaration of the 342*, published on January 18 in *Nashi dni*, which had declared the opposition of academics to the autocratic system.[35] Yet, this statement, like so many others made by musicians during 1905, responded both to the escalating political crisis and to conflicts within the musical community. Prominent musicians publicly declared their support for the liberation movement, but did so by venting their resentment at the hollow privileges and uncertain status accorded to professional musicians.

In St. Petersburg, some six hundred conservatory students assembled on February 10, 1905 in an unprecedented meeting.[36] Citing recent shocking events and declaring their support for the liberation movement, the students proclaimed: "We, both as citizens and as artistic individuals, are unable to ignore the general call to protest and to quietly continue our studies given the current conditions of Russian life." By a vote of 451 to 146, the students added their names to the resolution of the Moscow musicians and called for the cessation of conservatory classes until September 1. The students' demands focused on artistic, pedagogical, and professional issues. Chief among their concerns were greater opportunities for students to perform and to attend concerts, the improvement of instruction in music history, and the expansion of the course in ensemble playing. They declared their intention to petition the State Council for a larger subsidy to the conservatory "in view of the great significance of music to the cultural development of the country."[37] The meeting was not wholly devoted to professional concerns, however; a police report emphasized the inflammatory political nature of several students' speeches.[38] The conservatory students were hardly alone in their unrest; in a very real sense, they were mimicking the behaviors and the rhetoric of their more politically engaged peers at the universities. Conservatory students had never really belonged to the *studenchestvo*, the "student corporation" that formed the heart of the "imagined community" of university life. As Susan Morrissey has argued, *studenchestvo* can best be understood "as a phenomenon analogous to both class and nation, because, like these other categories of identity," it "existed through the consciousness of its members." If, as Morrissey argues, "cultural identity was paramount" for members of the *studenchestvo*, it is hardly surprising that conservatory students stood apart, except at times of crisis.[39] Their identity as musicians and would-be artists prevailed over their identity as students. In the forge of revolution, however, conservatory students began to acknowledge their common interests with counterparts at the universities and other higher educational institutions. Equally important, their peers and, eventually, educated society, began to accord them membership in the *studenchestvo* (see figure 6.2).

In response to the students' protests, the faculty council considered suspending classes until the middle of March. Some faculty members, including

Rimsky-Korsakov, sided with the students and demanded the cessation of classes until September, which would have brought the conservatory into line with most other higher educational institutions. The faculty, however, failed to agree on a course of action. In any case, the St. Petersburg branch of the Russian Musical Society preempted any faculty decision and suspended classes until March 15.

Moscow Conservatory students protested in support of their colleagues in St. Petersburg and in their own political and professional interests. A meeting on March 4 attracted over half of the conservatory's six hundred students. Like their counterparts in St. Petersburg, the overwhelming majority of students present voted to adopt the resolution of the Moscow musicians. The question of a strike proved more divisive. Approximately two-thirds of students at the meeting voted for a strike, but less than half of these voted for a strike on exclusively political grounds. A few supported a strike purely on academic grounds, while most argued for a combined political and academic protest. The strike was to begin the following day and continue until September.[40] Although expressing their "complete sympathy to the liberation movement," Moscow Conservatory students also focused on internal issues.

FIGURE 6.2. "Committee of St. Petersburg Conservatory Students in 1905." Permission of the Russian Institute for the History of the Arts, St. Petersburg (fond 3, op. 4, no. 336)

As in St. Petersburg, their most political demands included the right to hold meetings and establish student organizations such as a student aid fund, a student court, a reading room, an employment bureau, a cafeteria, and a boarding house. Throughout the spring and fall of 1905, conservatory students' demands consistently focused on curricular issues, relationships between students and faculty, and the cost of tuition.[41]

Conservatory students were clearly politically inexperienced, but were they less radical than their compatriots in the universities? Many of the demands voiced by conservatory students were similar or identical to those of students in other types of institutions. As Abraham Ascher has argued, students in many institutions "demanded changes in the educational structure, the curriculum, and pedagogy," that did not necessarily require or imply radical political views. Whatever the political motivations of student protests, he concludes, they can also be seen as an attempt to force significant cultural changes.[42] Susan Morrissey counters this interpretation, arguing that "students rarely made such rigorous distinctions between their 'objectively' academic and political goals."[43] Nevertheless, the supposed political immaturity of conservatory students persisted in the interpretation of the conservatory revolution, not only in its immediate aftermath, but also well into the Soviet period as these institutions struggled to recast their histories in the context of the revolutions of 1917.

Initially, conservatory student protests barely registered in the public arena. The satirical journal *Budil'nik* ridiculed conservatory students in one caricature, "Anti-Musical Pupils" (see figure 6.3). The conservatory "choir" of wild-eyed men and women bawled the words "We also don't want to stu-u-udy," to which their disconcerted conductor, the conservatory—portrayed as a classical goddess—responded with puns, "This is a false step ladies and gentlemen! With such plans you will never get on in art." [44]

Mildly amusing anecdotes in the same publication took aim both at conservatory students and at the broader musical community:

— Did you hear? Our future singers and musicians are on strike!
— It would make more sense if many of our current singers and musicians went on strike.
— What, exactly do the striking conservatory students want?
— They've simply gotten carried away by the current "popular aria," when what they really need is to study some more.[45]

In St. Petersburg, despite continuing student protests, the Russian Musical Society reopened the conservatory on March 16. Striking students attempted to block access to the building. The administration

FIGURE 6.3. "Anti-Musical Pupils (On the Cessation of Studies in the Conservatory)," *Budil'nik*, 6 March 1905

called the police, who forcefully broke up the demonstration. The next day, students redoubled their efforts. While one group of students protested at the conservatory's main entrance, a smaller group entered via the box office. Once inside, protesters vandalized classrooms, broke windows and doors, and set off a stink bomb that drove professors and their remaining students from the building. Police arrested more than one hundred students.[46]

That same day, *Russkie vedomosti* published a letter by Rimsky-Korsakov addressed to conservatory director Berngard. In the letter, and in the scandal that followed, professional, artistic, and political issues intertwined. Rimsky-Korsakov protested the St. Petersburg branch's unwillingness to suspend classes until September, thereby leaving the conservatory and its students vulnerable to police repression. The decision of the St. Petersburg branch to reopen the conservatory over the objections of many of its faculty and in opposition to other educational institutions left the conservatory isolated. The consequences were painful for a man who had devoted more than thirty years to the institution. "Today, after 11 a.m., the conservatory found itself surrounded by a cordon of mounted and foot police. The striking pupils have been left to the tender mercies of the police, while those who have not gone on strike are guarded by the same police." The St. Petersburg branch, it seemed, was not "disconcerted by things that make the government itself stop to think." The composer publicly rebuked the members of the board and questioned their competence to direct the St. Petersburg Conservatory or any other musical institution. He wondered whether change was even possible at the conservatory, where "musical artists" were subordinated to "a circle of dilettantes." The conservatory, he feared, had become "utterly indifferent to the fate of its pupils."[47]

On March 19, the faculty council of the St. Petersburg Conservatory met to consider the culpability of student protesters. Disagreements among the faculty and hostility toward conservatory director Berngard led to calls for his resignation and the suspension of the meeting with these issues unresolved.[48] The board of the St. Petersburg branch, meeting that same day, accepted Berngard's resignation. The board also expelled student protesters, citing the apparent unwillingness of the faculty council to accept this responsibility as justification for its usurpation of this duty.[49] The main item on the agenda, however, was Rimsky-Korsakov's provocative letter. Most unwisely, as subsequent events would prove, the board voted to dismiss the composer from his post at the conservatory.[50]

Kashchei the Immortal: Performing Politics and the Politics of Performance

On March 27, 1905, Alexander Glazunov conducted the St. Petersburg premier of Rimsky-Korsakov's one-act opera "Kashchei the Immortal" (*Kashchei bezsmertnyi*) in the private theater of V. F. Komissarzhevskaia.[51] The plot of the opera was fairy-tale simple, but in the context of the 1905 Revolution its political overtones were readily apparent. In a dark kingdom, condemned to an endless autumn, the sorcerous despot Kashchei holds a beautiful princess captive. Her true love, Ivan Korolevich, searches desperately for her, hoping to win her freedom. In his fortress, Kashchei mocks the recalcitrant princess's hopes for rescue. In an attempt to subdue her, the despot shows her an image of her forlorn lover in his magic mirror. Unexpectedly, the mirror shows Kashchei his daughter Kashcheevna's growing affection for Ivan Korolevich. Kashchei fears the image foretells his demise, for he will remain immortal only as long as his daughter feels no love and weeps for no man. Intent on preserving his power, Kashchei releases another of his captives, the Storm Knight, charging him to ensure that his daughter safeguards his immortality. The Storm Knight takes his revenge on his captor and gives Ivan Korolevich news of his beloved. In the end, good triumphs over evil. The lovers are reunited, but Kashcheevna has fallen in love with Ivan Korolevich. Weeping bitterly from the pain of her unrequited love, Kashcheevna is magically transformed into a weeping willow. Kashchei's spell is broken! Spring arrives at last. The people join in a joyous hymn: "Go in freedom! The storm has opened the doors for you! Go in freedom! Oh, beautiful sun, freedom, springtime, and love!"[52]

An unusually diverse audience filled Komissarzhevskaia's theater for the matinee performance. The draw was neither the novelty of the opera nor the quality of the performance. The spectacle, as anticipated by the audience, proved far more significant as a political occasion than as an artistic event. Gossip circulated regarding the political connotations of the opera, including the rumor that Kashchei was a portrait of the reactionary Procurator of the Holy Synod, Konstantin Pobedonostsev.[53] The public's attention focused on the composer, recently dismissed from the conservatory. More poignant still, the cast and orchestra consisted primarily of students who had resigned or been expelled from the conservatory in the wake of student demonstrations. The audience, and subsequently liberal educated society, used the operatic performance as an opportunity to demonstrate its support for the composer and its disdain for the repressiveness and rigidity of not only the Russian Musical Society but of the autocracy itself. Rimsky-Korsakov recalled the event in his memoirs: "At the conclusion of Kashchei, something unprecedented took place: I was called before the curtain, addresses from various societies and unions were read to me, and inflammatory speeches were delivered. It is said that someone in the uppermost tier shouted: 'Down with autocracy!' The din and hubbub after each address and speech were indescribable. The police ordered the . . . curtain to be lowered and thereby stopped further excitement."[54]

The circumstances of the premiere encouraged critics to devote their attention to its political implications, rather than its artistic resonance. Most reviewers were more interested in the audience, which they described in detail, than in the music, which they generally ignored.[55] Students, professors, artists, and writers filled the hall to overflowing. Following the opera, a series of speakers took the stage. They presented Rimsky-Korsakov with seven wreaths, including one from Komissarzhevskaia's theater inscribed "To a Fighter," while another read "To a Great Artist and Citizen."[56] Notable among the speakers was the elderly Vladimir Stasov, the fierce cultural critic, promoter of the Balakirev Circle, and opponent of the Russian Musical Society from the 1860s whose unrelenting support for Russian cultural nationalism was now passé. Typically, Stasov interpreted the public's outrage as the ultimate vindication of his own aesthetic principles.[57]

For some observers, Stasov's presence indicated the ability of the event to bring together all of Russian society—young and old, men and women, Russians and non-Russians, the past and the future—to honor and defend

Russian culture.[58] Delegations from professional unions made a profound impression on observers, such as the young M. F. Gnesin, then a composition student at the conservatory. Gnesin had recently replaced professor L. A. Sakketti as the representative of the proposed Union of Musicians.[59] Delegates from trade unions, women's groups, and a Ukrainian-speaking "Little Russian" proclaimed their unconditional devotion to Rimsky-Korsakov as a symbol of liberty and a bringer of culture to the masses.[60] "The performance," according to Gnesin, "turned into a completely unprecedented" demonstration for Rimsky-Korsakov and "against the government."[61]

The press quickly grasped the political implications of the performance. In addition to written reviews and commentary, caricatures emphasized the farcical nature of the developing scandal. In one of these, *Teatral'naia rossiia* recast the roles of Kashchei. The board of the St. Petersburg branch starred as a decrepit, debased, and malevolent Kashchei, hoisted by the collar by a muscular and boisterous Public Opinion, in the role of the Storm Knight. The intervention of Public Opinion/the Storm Knight saved the hero, Ivan Korolevich, an improbably cast Rimsky-Korsakov with flowing cape and sword at his side, from the vicious attacks of the now ineffectual and pathetic sorcerer.[62]

Other politicized performances of Rimsky-Korsakov's works followed. In Voronezh, a concert turned into a demonstration when supporters demanded that the audience stand during the performance of the composer's works and followed them with shouts of "Long Live Rimsky-Korsakov!"[63] As a consequence of such public demonstrations, Rimsky-Korsakov's compositions were banned, at least informally, adding yet another layer of political symbolism to the conflict. "The police issued orders forbidding the performance of my compositions in St. Petersburg," Rimsky-Korsakov later remarked in his memoirs. "Some of the crotchety provincial governors also issued similar orders in their domains.... Toward summer the force of this absurd prohibition began to weaken little by little, and, owing to my being in fashion, my compositions came to figure with considerable frequency on the summer programs of out-of-town orchestras. Only in the provinces did the zealous martinets persist in considering them revolutionary for some time longer."[64]

The reading public was more than willing to extrapolate a broad condemnation of Russian society from the scandal. Doggerel verses published in *Peterburgskii listok* explicitly compared the conflict between Rimsky-Korsakov and the Russian Musical Society to that between educated society and the state. The allegedly stifling bureaucratic hand of the Russian Musical Society on cultural life was portrayed as one example of a pervasive disease afflicting all of Russian society. The poem took the character of Kashchei and transposed it into a characteristic flaw in Russian life.

Immortal Kashcheis
Here and there and everywhere Kashcheis
There is no end to their cruel fame
They live in our Duma and prosper in office.
According to their own whims
They ruin every living thing
No one knows for whom
They pile up their fabled riches.

If Russia's lack of "civilization" and failure to develop along "normal" European lines was attributed to its plethora of petty Kashcheis, the verses nevertheless placed much of the blame for Russia's social and political failures on the willingness of educated society to tolerate petty tyrants and their passivity before them.

Everything is hidden from prying eyes
All the squabbling of our capital
While around us
Orphanages, schools, and hospitals decay.

The poem offered few solutions. Far from being a call to arms, the overall tone of the piece was self-pitying. It absolved the reader, and by extension all ordinary members of educated society, of responsibility.

We are living in trying times
Vicious snakes suck at our heart
And the only ones who flourish
Alas, are the immortal Kashcheis.
A series of unfortunate incidents
Pave the way for a general failure.
They are everywhere: In the courts
And backstage at the theaters.
What does it matter to them—
The despair and bitterness of our life?
Their motto unites them
"Backwardness, Stagnation, and Routine..."
They are everywhere: Now they are
Even a force in the musical world...
They have even "gobbled up"
The creator of "Immortal Kashchei."[65]

These verses portrayed the Rimsky-Korsakov scandal as the ultimate example of the repressiveness that was choking Russia. Not everyone shared these sentiments, however. *Novoe vremia* mocked the public's outrage over Rimsky-Korsakov's dismissal in an installment of its feuilleton-in-verse, "Woe from Stupidity" (*Gore ot gluposti*), a parody of Griboedov's famous *Woe from Wit*.

Pardon me, the other day in the papers
I read the following fact:
In imitation of the strikes and boycotts
Of students, who avoid science
A riot suddenly broke out at the conservatory
And they all got warmed up.

In Russian, puns and turns of phrase undermined the significance of the Rimsky-Korsakov scandal. The students' outrage is depicted with the phrase *razygrat'sia kak po notam*, which means both to get carried away by your feelings or, in the case of musicians, to warm up. Moreover, musicians here do not play or sing, they wail (*vopit'*), strike up a tune (*zatianut'*), and whistle (*svistet'*). The verses also savagely mocked the public's desire to transform Rimsky-Korsakov into a political martyr. Exasperated at the commotion, the author objected to what he saw as the unsavory willingness of Rimsky-Korsakov, conservatory students, and other musicians to secure free publicity and inject glamour into their careers by jumping on the liberal political bandwagon.

Boy-singers, girl-singers, tenors,
Basses, sopranos, baritones,
Pianists, violinists, et cetera,
Suddenly began to wail:
Time to overthrow all obstacles to freedom!
One cannot sing fa-sol-si
While absolutism has not been abolished
It's impossible to toot on a horn
Until a parliament drones on in Russia
It's impossible to take violin lessons
Or whistle into a pipe,
While in the Far East
Hostilities with Japan have not ceased.
Well in a word, they decided everything in an uproar:

Put an end to runs, trills, and scales,
They had to put a stop to the study of music,
For the victory of a free regime.

The piece continued with a barbed commentary on educated society's manipulation of the premiere of Kashchei to create a political martyr out of Rimsky-Korsakov. Anti-Semitism and anti-intelligentsia bias colored the scornful account of these events. The high-minded intelligentsia was portrayed as mindlessly gushing over the star of the hour.

Well, it's all foolish, but what can you do—
Aspiration to stupidity is now unrestrained,
All the same, there is a limit to foolish words and deeds,
A musical priest has been found,
Who crossed that line:
Carried away by the [glory of a scandal],
This decrepit old man began to sing riot in harmony,
And because of this was fired from his professor's chair.
My God, what happened here! They sounded the alarm,
Rang a cacophony of bells!
He was proclaimed a great citizen
To all of Russia,
A mighty genius, a fighter against violence;
And as if from the horn of plenty,
Dozens of addresses were showered upon him, —
Protests—all hell simply broke loose!
They honored the creator of "wonderful Russian opera"
With sentiments of flattering nonsense,
Led first and foremost by the Yids ...
Then, burning with a fiery delight,
Chemists, pharmacists, workers from the brick factory,
Students, house painters, "Ukrainians," and tramps,
And others of that ilk,
A sonata, a symphony of experts.

Withering criticism of the overblown praise of the composer highlighted his inadequacy as a hero of the intelligentsia. Newspaper commentators were castigated for exploiting the scandal for their own purposes. Newspaper readers were attacked for their willingness to believe whatever lies they were told, as long as they made scandalous reading.

Well, here is the situation: although there is a little something new in it,
Its main characteristic,
As always
Is that society is forever ready
To lend support to an uprising.[66]

Liberal Politics and the Rimsky-Korsakov Scandal

The furor surrounding the St. Petersburg premiere of Kashchei was merely the most public performance of the conflict between the Russian Musical Society, musicians, and the public. With the dismissal of Rimsky-Korsakov, voices calling for the reform of the Society grew stronger and more passionate. Musicians, cultural critics, and journalists portrayed the Society as a retrograde, bureaucratic force delaying Russia's cultural development. Some of the most vicious criticism appeared in the pages of Russia's leading music journal, *Russkaia muzykal'naia gazeta*, where calls for the radical reorganization of the Society contrasted oddly with extensive reporting on the activities of its numerous branches and educational institutions.

In 1905, Rimsky-Korsakov was a beloved professor to several generations of students and the dean of Russian composers. Although popular and critical response to his most recent operas had been uneven, Rimsky-Korsakov remained an active and respected composer. In addition, he was a living reminder of the Balakirev Circle and the beginnings of the Russian national school. He still attracted brilliant students, including not only Glazunov but also Igor Stravinsky and Sergei Prokofiev; through his teaching, Rimsky-Korsakov ensured the future dynamism of Russian music.[67]

Politically, Rimsky-Korsakov was a true *shestidesiatnik*—a man of the sixties. Born in 1844 to a family of old nobility, the future composer's parents set him on a course for a respectable naval career. Enrollment in the Naval College brought him to St. Petersburg, where he soon became involved in local musical life. His acquaintance with Mili Balakirev in 1861 drew the budding composer into the Balakirev Circle. Mounting hopes of a musical career had to be postponed, however; Rimsky-Korsakov graduated from the Naval College in 1862 as a midshipman and embarked on an extended voyage.[68]

Like many other young noblemen of his generation and family standing, Rimsky-Korsakov held liberal political sympathies. The composer flirted with more radical views during his youth, exhibiting enthusiasm for

Alexander Herzen and sympathy for the rebellious Poles.[69] As an adult, despite occasional battles with the censors over the libretti of his operas, the composer lived a comfortable, quiet, and apolitical life. The stunning events of 1905, however, stirred many members of liberal educated society to greater activity, and Rimsky-Korsakov was no exception. In his recollections of the composer, V. V. Iastrebtsev suggests that Rimsky-Korsakov became a "vivid red" in 1905 and sympathized with the ideals of the Social Democrats.[70] Rimsky-Korsakov's actions, nevertheless, are more consistent with the ideals of a member of the liberal intelligentsia. His concern surprised protesting conservatory students, given his reputation for discipline and hard work. Remembering the events of 1905, M. F. Gnesin argued that the composer's general sympathy for the liberation movement translated into support for the striking students.[71] If Rimsky-Korsakov's support for the students and his criticism of the decision to reopen the conservatory grew out of his liberal concern for individual rights, his objections to the powerful role of the "dilettante" leadership of the Russian Musical Society were rooted not in his political views but in an increasingly influential artistic ideology that insisted on professional control of cultural life.

The conflict between the Russian Musical Society and Rimsky-Korsakov was the culmination of years of frustration. The Russian musical profession was slow to emerge, but as it gained strength, it struggled to wrest control of musical life from its amateur patrons. For Russian educated society, such concerns were of secondary importance. Public response to the firing of Rimsky-Korsakov was immediate and dramatic. The composer quickly became a cause célèbre. His treatment by the Russian Musical Society symbolized the suffering of educated society at the hands of the repressive Russian state. The supposed inability of the Society to recognize and honor artistic genius was implicitly compared to the state's inability to recognize the right of educated society to participate in politics and the conduct of social affairs.

The board of the St. Petersburg branch, although cast as villains in the Rimsky-Korsakov scandal, were the elected leaders of a well-established and highly successful voluntary association. In another context, rather than opponents of liberalism, democracy, and civil society, they might have appeared as its champions. In the context of the 1905 Revolution, however, attempts by the board to justify its actions only exposed it to ridicule. Its legalistic explanations only provoked further attacks on its artistic and administrative legitimacy. For educated society, the fundamental question was what moral, rather than legal, rights the Russian Musical Society retained over the profession it had done so much to establish, but which had outgrown its parent organization.

The decision to fire the Grand Old Man of Russian music made the board of the St. Petersburg branch an easy target for its critics. Board members included chair P. N. Cheremisinov, vice-chair A. M. Klimchenko, Princess A. A. Obolenskaia, A. S. Taneev, and I. A. Persiani, who resigned in a gesture of protest. Moreover, the resignation of conservatory director Berngard left the board without a working professional musician. Criticism that portrayed the board as pathetically incompetent to direct the musical affairs of the capital did them a disservice, however. A. S. Taneev, although a high government official, was also a prominent amateur composer. Other members of the board, such as Persiani, were well-trained amateur musicians. Social prominence and enthusiasm, not artistic training, moreover, truly was the greatest contribution of board members to the Society. Board members oversaw financial and administrative affairs and promoted concert activities. Responsibility for the artistic quality of concerts and the educational affairs of the conservatory lay with its director, Berngard, and the faculty council. Nevertheless, because of the associational structure of the Russian Musical Society, ultimate authority—including the hiring, firing, and disciplining of faculty—rested with local boards and the Main Directorate of the Society as a whole.

A flurry of editorials and letters to the editor protested the decision of the St. Petersburg board. Newspapers covering the scandal included *Rus'*, *Peterburgskaia gazeta*, *Peterburgskii listok*, *Russkie vedomosti*, *Svet*, *Zaria*, *Syn otechestva*, *Slovo*, *Budil'nik*, and *Novosti i birzhevaia gazeta*. The composer's faculty colleagues objected in print; the resignation of leading professors, including Glazunov, Anatoly Liadov, and Felix Blumenfeld jeopardized the continued functioning of the conservatory, as did the threat to organize a competing, "truly free" conservatory.[72] Several graduating composition students refused to complete their final examinations.[73] Students resigned en masse, publicizing their actions with bitter letters to the press.[74] When conductor A. B. Khessin refused to honor his contract for the Society's final symphony concert of the season, the last-minute cancellation emphasized the seriousness of the rift between professional musicians and the Russian Musical Society.[75] As the scandal dragged on, additional professors, including the star of the piano department, Anna Esipova, threatened to resign if their colleagues did not return to the conservatory.[76]

Many others also voiced their outrage in the press. University professors, students, professional groups, and workers trumpeted their support for Rimsky-Korsakov in collective letters that vilified the Russian Musical Society and sanctified Rimsky-Korsakov as a martyr of the repressive Russian bureaucracy. The collective address of more than 130 professors from higher educational institutions in the capital prompted the editors of *Slovo* to highlight for its readers the "general social significance of the disgraceful events in our musical life."[77] Fearing demonstrations, the administration of the St. Petersburg Hall of the Nobility canceled a concert featuring works by Rimsky-Korsakov. Students, who had planned to present an address to the composer at the concert, went to his home to honor him. Students from the technical institute lauded the composer as a "fighter for truth and light, who openly and bravely declared his protest against the existing arbitrary rule." Students from other St. Petersburg higher educational institutions issued a joint address, celebrating Rimsky-Korsakov's "struggle with tsarist darkness, routine, and arbitrariness."[78] Educated society enthusiastically adopted the dispute between the Russian Musical Society and Rimsky-Korsakov and transformed it into a commentary on the state of Russian society.

The St. Petersburg branch's claim that Rimsky-Korsakov's letter libeled them provoked derision. How, the critic for *Slovo* wondered, could they have been offended, much less libeled, by Rimsky-Korsakov's accusation of dilettantism, when their actions proved the charge was accurate?[79] In a sardonic commentary on the Society's leadership, *Peterburgskaia gazeta* provided a portrait of one of "Our Musical Public Figures." Instead of featuring a composer, conductor, or prominent musician, it presented a full-length sketch of... the treasurer of the St. Petersburg branch, V. A. Ture.[80]

Peterburgskaia gazeta sent its critic, perhaps in the interests of fairness, to interview Klimchenko, vice-chair of the St. Petersburg board. Klimchenko defended the right of amateurs to participate in the governance of cultural life. Those who labeled the composer's "judges" mere "talentless bureaucrats," who expressed surprise that the local boards of the Russian Musical Society consisted of *chinovniki*, had conveniently forgotten that similar *chinovniki* founded the society in the first place. Rejecting the right of professionals to primacy in musical life, Klimchenko defended the board's musical authority by noting that its members were amateur musicians and composers.[81] Klimchenko was particularly critical of the pianist and conductor Alexander Ziloti, a brutal opponent of the St. Petersburg board. Klimchenko mounted an energetic defense of his "dilettante" contributions to Russian music, angrily noting that he had worked for the success of the conservatory for nearly forty years. Ziloti had taken no part in managing its affairs and therefore had no right to discredit Klimchenko's relationship to the institution. Ziloti's dismissive response reveals the irreconcilable gulf between the two sides. He mocked Klimchenko's "service" to the conservatory in firing its most noted professor.[82]

The conflict between the Russian Musical Society and the music profession attracted the sustained attention of two of the most prominent Russian arts journals. In *Russkaia muzykal'naia gazeta*, A. Livin tendentiously described the important, but dangerous role of the Society in musical life. Although the cultural level of the country had continued to advance since the 1860s, music had failed to keep pace. It remained under the control of a "society of amateurs" that was plagued by its hybrid, "mongrel" organizational structure. Worse still, it was led by a handful of unqualified individuals, its "board members," who were merely "capitalists (lovers of singers' high notes, of the pretty students of the school, or of ranks and awards, and only sometimes [lovers] of serious music)." Not only did these artistic philistines decide policy for the Russian Musical Society, Livin warned, the decisions made by the Society directed the tastes of the masses.[83]

Teatr i iskusstvo similarly denounced the existing order. Perhaps, it editorialized, when Anton Rubinstein first formulated his plan for the development of Russian music a "social-dilettante" administration was appropriate. At the time, Russian music was in its infancy. Rubinstein dreamed of a "free academy of art, a holy temple of sound, completely independent and self-governing." After Rubinstein's death, bureaucracy got its "bony hands" on Rubinstein's dream. Casual dilettantes, products of officious St. Petersburg, "became the managers of the fate of musical Russia." Little by little, the free academy of art turned into a musical bureaucracy, leading to the artistic bankruptcy of the Russian Musical Society and the conservatories. The conservatory faculty councils were impotent, subordinated as they were to local boards, which had authority to make artistic decisions for which they lacked professional competence. This curious duality revealed the underlying problem. "What, in actuality, is the Musical Society?" the journal asked. If it really was a voluntary association, the editorial continued, it should act like one and not like an agent of the repressive state police apparatus. If it was a state institution, then why retain the outward characteristics of a social organization? Music could not serve two masters simultaneously.[84]

The conservative newspaper *Zaria*, conversely, forthrightly criticized public support for the composer. It compared the protesting conservatory students to the hooligans and drunken crowds that wrecked the gardens and factories of landowners and industrialists. Praise for the composer would be appropriate, it editorialized, if Rimsky-Korsakov led the students continuing their studies, rather than supporting the strikers.[85] *Zaria's* stance was unusual, however, as most papers unabashedly championed the composer. *Novosti i birzhevaia gazeta* used the Russian Musical Society's own charter to convict it of crimes against Russian culture. The directory *All St. Petersburg* (*Ves Peterburg*) listed "the encouragement of talented Russian artists" as one of the Society's goals. It was so simple and clear, *Novosti* mocked. The Society encouraged Russian music by firing its most notable composer. Rimsky-Korsakov, the paper pointed out, was unlikely to suffer from the loss of his post. His reputation was unstained. His talent demonstrated to a doubting world Russia's creative vigor and potential. The scandal tarnished the reputation of the conservatory, for it had lost its genius.[86] Even *Novoe vremia* rebuked the St. Petersburg branch, an editorial stance that seemingly conflicted with the conservative slant of the newspaper but coincided nicely with the deep-seated hostility of the paper's music critic, M. M. Ivanov, toward the Russian Musical Society and its institutions.[87]

The scandal, another article suggested, humiliated Russia before peoples who properly honored their artists: Wagner in Germany, Verdi in Italy, or Gounod in France. Russia was "shamed before the whole civilized world," which would not distinguish who was or was not guilty in the affair. Such shameful treatment of creative geniuses promised to make Russia the laughingstock of European culture. The "genius, dismissed on the basis of point 5, paragraph 14 [of the conservatory charter], remains a genius. The *chinovniki*... remain *chinovniki*. And the good name of Russia is once again subject to ridicule... the nation (*narod*) of Goethe, the nation of Voltaire, and the nation of Shakespeare are all laughing derisively at the nation of Pushkin."[88]

Another writer compared the Russian Musical Society's dismissal of Rimsky-Korsakov to Pushkin's death at the hands of d'Anthès and the excommunication of Tolstoy by the Russian Orthodox Church. All three were martyrs for Russian culture.[89] Newspapers and popular journals mocked the Society's presumption. One particularly pointed caricature, "In the Conservatory," lampooned the board's musical judgment. A bald-headed, long-bearded, rake-thin man, carrying a folder titled "conservatory bureaucrat," scratched his head with one long finger. In bewilderment, he confronted three empty chairs bearing the names of Rimsky-Korsakov, Glazunov, and Liadov: "Hmm... so who in the world will teach music? Bah! Eureka! Stepan the watchman said that our senior yardman is not too bad on the balalaika."[90] Another caricature depicted the relative harm the Society could do to Rimsky-Korsakov and to itself. The shrunken, insignificant leaders of the St. Petersburg branch, demonstrating their musical prowess on the accordion, the barrel organ, and a tin whistle, show the monumental composer the door. The composer departed, with the top of the conservatory tucked safely under one arm and his operas under the other.[91] In "The Conservatory in the Near Future," a caricature appearing in *Teatr i iskusstvo*, M. Demianov explored the possible consequences of Rimsky-Korsakov's departure. Utter chaos reigned as the police seized control. One portly policeman sawed away at a cello or string bass with a fire hose, his ample hindquarters threatening the structural integrity of the bass drum he was using for a chair. Mice ate the strings of a violin, while a cat seemed to be intending to take a nap in its case. Another corpulent policeman thumped away at a grand piano, while others played cards in the back of the room. Watching over it all was a portrait of five corks, symbolizing the five "dumbbells" on the board of the St. Petersburg branch, who allowed this disaster. Hanging beside it was a portrait of Anton Rubinstein, with a pained expression on his face. Rimsky-Korsakov, meanwhile, fled the scene in disgust.[92]

Novosti i birzhevaia gazeta commented on the widening scandal: students and faculty were abandoning the conservatory, foreign honorary members of the Society were apparently resigning in protest, and letters and addresses from all sorts of organizations were appearing in the press, all supporting Rimsky-Korsakov. Only the *chinovniki* of the Society did not seem to be taking any notice. The problem, arguably, was not the existence of a musical bureaucracy per se but that Russian society had only just noticed it. Society, lulled to sleep "by the cradle-songs of [its] bureaucrat-nannies," had only recently awakened from its slumber. Now nothing prevented Russian society from liberating art. Willing patrons—in the best sense of that word—still existed. Educated society might establish a free conservatory and a free musical society. The bureaucrats would be able to go on about their business. "The musical bureaucracy can set *chinovniki* to play the piano, violin, and flute," the article predicted, "...and we, perhaps, will attend a symphony concert of musical *chinovniki*, all ranked according to *chin*: musical registrar, musical assessor, musical councilor, etc. Directing the orchestra of musical *chinovniki* will be the director of the musical department himself, privy musical councilor, Disciplinov."[93]

During 1905, musicians got caught up in the revolutionary movement, adopting the rhetoric of liberal politics to wage a struggle that was at heart a professional dispute over the control of Russian musical life. Although musicians may have believed that their struggle was one of liberation from repressive authority—of the tsarist regime or of the Russian Musical Society—and however much later writers have viewed the conflict as the political awakening of musicians as a social group, the issues raised by the conservatory revolution and the Rimsky-Korsakov scandal were fundamentally products of the process of professionalization and institutionalization of Russian musical life that occurred over the course of the nineteenth century. At the same time, liberal educated society found itself captivated by the conservatory revolution and, especially, the Rimsky-Korsakov scandal. Rimsky-Korsakov's struggle with the Russian Musical Society was read by the educated public as a script of its own struggle with the tsarist regime. The professional dispute at the heart of the Rimsky-Korsakov scandal (who should control musical life) functioned as a symbolic substitute for the dispute at the heart of the 1905 revolution (who should control Russia's political life).

The Struggle for Control: Institutional Autonomy and the Structure of the Society

Newspaper coverage, protests at concerts, and celebrations of the martyred composer constituted the public face of the scandal. Behind the scenes, the Society's Main Directorate, the St. Petersburg branch, and leading musicians struggled to negotiate a solution to the crisis. In early April, a delegation of conservatory professors offered to mediate between the St. Petersburg board and Rimsky-Korsakov, Glazunov, and Liadov. The delegation hoped to discover a compromise that would preserve the dignity and mollify the wounded pride of all parties. They believed it their moral duty to persuade Rimsky-Korsakov to reconcile with the Society and return to the conservatory.[94]

Hopes for a compromise solution rested on the close personal and professional relationship between Glazunov and Rimsky-Korsakov. The conservatory faculty overwhelmingly favored Glazunov for the director's post. If Glazunov returned to the conservatory, Rimsky-Korsakov might be willing to return at his invitation. All attempts to negotiate a solution throughout the spring and summer failed as Glazunov and Liadov adopted more intransigent positions. They demanded a public apology to Rimsky-Korsakov, the return of all expelled students, and greater independence for the faculty council and the conservatory director as conditions for their return.[95] Calls for greater independence soon metamorphosed into demands for autonomy, while Rimsky-Korsakov insisted that he would not return to the conservatory until it was liberated from the dilettante leadership of the St. Petersburg branch.[96]

On August 27, 1905, the state issued new rules governing its relationship with the universities, reinstating the autonomy that had been abolished in 1884. The universities reacquired both the right to elect their rectors and a greater degree of academic freedom and administrative control for the faculty, although, as Samuel Kassow has noted, the "legal ambiguities" of university autonomy complicated their relationship to the state for the next decade.[97] However, when classes resumed in September, students quickly attempted to turn the newly autonomous universities into a public platform for their political views. As David Wartenweiler has shown, the universities were caught between the demands of students and junior faculty for a firm political stand, sure to provoke the state's anger, and the likelihood of intense confrontations with the student body if they insisted on maintaining the universities' neutrality. Waves of student meetings and protests ultimately resulted, on October 15, in the forced closure of most higher educational institutions. The universities would not reopen until the fall of 1906.[98]

Conservatory students imitated their counterparts in the universities. In St. Petersburg, they held numerous public political meetings in late September, which the temporary faculty committee viewed with dismay. The conservatory closed on October 1 and then briefly reopened in mid-October before closing for the rest of the semester, although some professors continued to teach lessons in their homes. Throughout October and November, conservatory students in St. Petersburg continued to hold meetings, debating both the internal affairs of the conservatory and broader political issues. The press regularly reported on events in the conservatories, discussing student meetings in the context of similar events in other higher educational institutions.[99] In Moscow, student participation in meetings and political protests led to the closure of the conservatory on November 4.[100] Neither institution would reopen until after the question of the conservatories' relationship to the Russian Musical Society was resolved, at least temporarily.

Negotiations between the Main Directorate and the Ministry of Internal Affairs, as well as between the conservatory faculty and the boards of the St. Petersburg and Moscow branches of the Society, eventually resulted in the extension of autonomy to the conservatories on November 17, 1905. Amendments to the conservatory charter stipulated that the faculty councils would elect the director from among the faculty for a three-year term. Moreover, the faculty councils acquired greater authority over academic affairs and student discipline.[101] While these changes greatly reduced the authority of local boards over the conservatories, they failed to sever their institutional ties with the Society. The Main Directorate replaced the local boards as the body ultimately responsible for educational affairs in the conservatories, while the chair and "August Patron" of the Society now confirmed the elected conservatory directors in their duties.

Conservatory autonomy allowed a resolution of the immediate crisis. For the public, the return of Rimsky-Korsakov to his post and the election of Glazunov as the director of the St. Petersburg Conservatory represented a clear victory for educated society over a repressive bureaucracy. Indeed, Glazunov and his counterpart at the Moscow Conservatory, M. M. Ippolitov-Ivanov, successfully reestablished an effective working atmosphere in the conservatories. However, the implications of the conservatories' supposed victory in securing autonomy were far from clear.

Because the universities were state institutions, the autonomy they received represented a significant concession that eroded the state's control over the public sphere and symbolically acknowledged the legitimacy of educated society's demands for an independent role in public life. The conservatories, however, were private educational institutions. For the conservatories, autonomy was not about eliminating state interference in educational affairs and offenses against academic freedom, but about reducing the meddling of dilettantes in cultural life. "Autonomy," moreover, failed to liberate the conservatories from the Russian Musical Society as the St. Petersburg and Moscow branches remained responsible for their financial affairs and assets. Local boards also retained their control over the administration of provincial music classes and schools. Organizationally, financially, and administratively the Russian Musical Society and its educational institutions, including the conservatories, remained intertwined. The 1905 Revolution brought longstanding issues to a crisis level but their immediate resolution did not fundamentally restructure the relationship between the Society and its educational institutions. Yet, the events of 1905 did force the Society to reexamine its organizational structure and educational rationale. Between 1905 and 1917, the Russian Musical Society and its educational institutions attempted to rewrite the charters that governed their relationship and, implicitly, the relationship of the state to musical life in the Russian Empire. The inability of the conservatories and the Society to reach a compromise on a new charter prevented any fundamental alteration of the administrative relationship between the educational and the organizational structures of the Society.

After 1905, debates about the composition of both local boards and the Main Directorate became increasingly frequent and bitter. Many professional musicians and music critics strongly believed that only qualified specialists should direct cultural affairs. The leading members of the Society, unsurprisingly, resisted efforts to undermine their authority and insisted on their right, as patrons and civic leaders, to participate actively in Russian musical life. Nevertheless, the Society was slowly forced to renegotiate the distribution of power and authority as it confronted increasing professionalization, the growth of a Russian middle class, and a pronounced decline in the prestige of the aristocracy. The conflict over the governance of the Society was a microcosm of a much larger conflict over political power and social hierarchies.

The autonomy awarded to the conservatories failed to satisfy the expectations of either the conservatory faculty or the broader musical community. An elected director and increased independence for the faculty council did not transform the conservatories into fully independent educational institutions.

Not only did they remain under the jurisdiction of the Russian Musical Society, but the state also showed no inclination to incorporate the conservatories into its educational system. The conservatories, music schools, and classes of the Society remained under the purview of the Ministry of Internal Affairs. The increasingly obvious need to transform the large and dynamic music schools in Saratov, Odessa, and Kiev into provincial conservatories further exposed the inadequacy of the new arrangement as the extension of autonomy to the provinces would unsettle the relationship between the Society's branches and their educational institutions. The continued existence of the Russian Musical Society as a voluntary association was at stake.

Some evidence suggests that the scandals of the 1905 Revolution made the boards of the Society's local branches more reluctant to intervene in educational affairs than they should have been. In Saratov, for example, the newly reorganized conservatory attracted negative attention in the local press when both students and faculty began to attend courses irregularly. Although the faculty council and the conservatory director addressed these problems, they failed to take effective action, particularly with regard to students' indifferent attendance of classes in theoretical subjects. Only belatedly did the board confess to the chair and patron of the Society, Elena Grigorievna Saksen-Altenburgskaia, that "all of these facts were known to the board but, unfortunately" it had "mistakenly quite narrowly interpreted" its rights and responsibilities to "intervene in the conduct of instructional affairs" because it feared to "infringe on the prerogatives of the faculty council." The unfortunate public attention to the conservatory's internal disorganization, however, proved that "sometimes such intervention is extremely necessary." The situation in Saratov was resolved only after repeated communication with the Main Directorate. Following a diplomatic proposal by Saksen-Altenburgskaia, the Saratov board arranged a joint meeting with the conservatory faculty council. In a "prolonged discussion," the board explained its "categorical decision" not to allow such irresponsible behavior to continue. The faculty, perhaps, took the rebuke to heart as, at least according to the Saratov board, they redoubled their efforts to prepare students for their examinations, even putting in extra hours to do so. Despite the relatively successful results of the graduation examinations in 1916, however, the relationship between conservatory director Slivinsky, the faculty, and the local board remained stormy. In April 1917, Slivinsky resigned.[102]

From 1905 to 1918, the charters governing the Russian Musical Society and its conservatories became an arena for open conflict as the two sides struggled to renegotiate their relationship. Increasingly, the conservatories sought complete independence from their parent organization. The multiple projects for new charters compiled by faculty committees and the Society's leadership after 1905 indicate the deep rift between the two parties and their inability to resolve the situation satisfactorily. One early draft charter, for example, highlighted the resistance of many professors toward the Society's continued control of the conservatories. Prepared by a St. Petersburg Conservatory faculty committee that included Glazunov, Rimsky-Korsakov, and Liadov, it insisted that higher music education be placed under the control of responsible authorities.[103] Responsible authorities, the drafting committee clearly implied, did not include the dilettante leadership of the Society or its local boards. Their proposal emphasized that the "conservatory is an autonomous institution, which, except in those cases specifically noted in the charter, is completely independent, both in its musical-pedagogical and in its administrative and economic affairs."[104] Such uncompromising language obscured the practical difficulties of severing ties between the Russian Musical Society and the conservatories. The Society's leadership, of course, had a stake in maintaining the status quo; if they allowed the conservatories to emerge as fully independent entities it would probably lead to the collapse of the voluntary association. The conservatories, however, despite their artistic prominence and institutional strength, depended on the Society to secure state financial assistance. Both legally and practically the conservatories were unable to declare their independence and strike out on their own.

This first draft charter still presumed that supervision of the conservatories would remain with the Ministry of Internal Affairs. Another faculty project took autonomy a step further and proposed the Ministry of Education as the appropriate supervisory body.[105] Leopold Auer, a member of the faculty committee drafting this charter proposal, wondered to whom the project could be submitted, given that the conservatories were already subject to the authority of both the Russian Musical Society and the Ministry of Internal Affairs.[106] This and similar projects proved untenable as they demanded that the conservatories seek their independence and incorporation into the state educational system by persuading their current governing body and the imperial patron of a private voluntary association to petition the state on their behalf. The Moscow Conservatory, in its attempt to devise a new charter, explicitly addressed the impossibility of resolving this conflict of interest. For an entire year, from April 1906 to April 1907, a committee consisting of professors Kashkin, Ippolitov-Ivanov, von Glen, Gubert, and Morozov labored over a draft charter. Unable to resolve the question of who should have jurisdiction, they produced a document that they claimed would be functional irrespective of whether the conservatory remained under the authority of the Society, came under the administration of a government department, or became completely independent.[107]

Despite the efforts of faculty from both conservatories and the strongly voiced opinions of many music journalists, the draft charter that the Main Directorate ultimately submitted to the Ministry of Internal Affairs in December 1911 failed to mention the conservatories as autonomous institutions. Neither did this draft include any provision for an administrative relationship with the Ministry of Education. The submitted draft, moreover, reinforced the jurisdiction of the Russian Musical Society over the conservatories. The chair of the Society (also the chair of the Main Directorate) remained the patron of the conservatories and honorary chair of their artistic councils. Local boards retained control over decisions regarding finances and real estate.[108] The draft charter stalled in the approval process and was not implemented. A satisfactory compromise remained elusive.

The struggle for control, formalized in attempts to rewrite the Society's charters, can be read on two levels. On the practical level, professionalized musicians attempted to wrest control of specialized music education away from the leadership of a voluntary association, the Russian Musical Society. The leaders of the Society were castigated as both dilettantes and members of a social elite that had long since outlived its usefulness. Their critics condemned them for seeking to retain administrative authority and financial control over the Society's educational institutions, the conservatories in particular. Viewed objectively, however, the expectations of the local and central leadership of the Society seem reasonable. Local boards continued to fund, subsidize, and secure financing not only for concert life but also for their affiliated educational institutions. The conservatories had developed into significant cultural institutions. As such, they demanded the opportunity to negotiate directly with the state and educated society for financial support. The same cannot be said for the provincial branches and educational institutions that comprised the Russian Musical Society as a social organization. Nor should the leadership of the Society be tarred uniformly with the brush of dilettantism. Professional musicians did occasionally participate in the governance of local branches, as did educated amateurs and cultural philanthropists. Even those whose musical participation was limited to a seat in the concert hall played an important and characteristic role as well-placed patrons whose financial contributions and social and political connections ensured the continuing existence of the Society.

On the rhetorical level, the struggle for control of the Russian Musical Society, played out as it was on the public stage of the concert hall, journal article, and newspaper page, reflected the ongoing conflict between the autocratic state and Russian educated society over popular participation in political and social life. The parallels between the stifling bureaucracy of the Society and that of the autocracy were clearly drawn. The primary sin of the Main Directorate, and of the Society as a whole, was that it functioned effectively within the restrictive Russian political and social context; it had achieved a successful accommodation with the autocracy.

After 1905, the Russian Musical Society struggled to resolve multiple tensions: between professional and patron, professional and dilettante, voluntary association and the state, the provinces and the capitals, and, finally, the autocratic state and educated society. At the height of the Society's success as a voluntary association, the ideological and artistic conflicts between its administrative and artistic leadership began to tear it apart. The Main Directorate was well aware of the possible consequences of the loss of public confidence in the Society as a leading force in Russian musical life. After 1905, the Society struggled to recapture public support by demonstrating its continuing effectiveness as an artistic and educational organization. Moreover, the memory of the conservatory revolution remained an important subtext in public discussions of the Russian Musical Society and its educational institutions.

Calls for Celebration: The Conservatory and Society Jubilees

The fiftieth anniversaries of the Russian Musical Society in December 1909 and the St. Petersburg Conservatory in December 1912, celebrated with great fanfare, offered both the Society and its critics opportunities to reevaluate the organization, its achievements, and its failures. Newspapers and journals covering the jubilee celebrations ranged from specialized music and arts periodicals such as *Russkaia muzykal'naia gazeta* and *Teatr i iskusstvo* to the daily newspapers and the boulevard press. Even *Sel'skii vestnik* commented on the 1912 conservatory celebrations.[109] Both celebrations included several days of formal presentations by delegations, festive banquets, chamber music and symphonic concerts, and opera performances. The celebrations attracted attention as much for the glittering public in attendance as out of recognition of the importance of the Society and the conservatory.[110]

These jubilee celebrations were, in part, attempts to replace the negative image generated by the scandalous events of 1905 with a carefully constructed master narrative of Russian musical development that highlighted the indispensable role of the Society. The need to reinforce the importance of the Society in Russian musical life was particularly important in 1909, when the memory of the conservatory revolution was still fresh and public sentiment ran against the organization. The jubilee festivities took care to celebrate Russian cultural heritage and establish a Russian artistic lineage. Not only was Anton Rubinstein lauded for his role in establishing the Society and the conservatory, he was also actually present at the celebrations, despite having died in 1894. An enormous bust of Rubinstein, placed carefully on the official dais, watched over the affair with paternal pride (see figure 6.4).

The procession of delegates and the reading of congratulatory speeches and telegrams, although formulaic and undoubtedly tedious, insistently reminded observers of the achievements of the Russian Musical Society. Provincial delegations usually consisted of members of the local board or faculty of its music school or classes. The most important provincial branches, such as those in Kiev, Kharkov, and Odessa, enjoyed prominent places in the festivities as their success reinforced the Society's claims to having transformed Russian musical culture. Those branches unable to afford the expense of sending a delegation sent congratulatory telegrams. Individuals also sent telegrams and letters, praising the Society for the transformation it had accomplished in their own lives and in the lives of the Russian people through the dissemination of music into the provinces. The universities, the Public Library, the Academy of Sciences, and other leading cultural and intellectual institutions sent delegations and telegrams as well, bestowing their recognition on the Society and the conservatory.[111]

The festivities were exciting and energizing, especially for provincial delegates, despite the seemingly endless procession of speeches and telegrams. Many attendees were graduates of the St. Petersburg or Moscow conservatories, so a celebration of the Russian Musical Society legitimated their own professional and artistic identities. The recognition of provincial delegates, even just the invitation to attend the festivities in the capital, conveyed cultural legitimacy on the often-struggling provincial branches. Press coverage of these events transmitted and interpreted the Society's narrative for the reading public. Despite the celebratory atmosphere, not all of musical St. Petersburg valued the "services of the honoree," as *Peterburgskaia gazeta* noted.[112] Still, these complaints did not spoil the celebration. Rather, they highlighted what was at stake: the Russian Musical Society's claim to leadership and its ability to attract the loyalty and support of both musicians and the public.

Similarly, in 1912, the gala performances and festive dinners that marked the fiftieth anniversary of the St. Petersburg Conservatory drew a crowd that included many of Russia's most famous musicians, artists, and public figures. Faculty members and former students, including such luminaries as violinist Leopold Auer and the tenor Nikolai Figner, supplemented the conservatory's own orchestra and choir. Delegations and congratulatory telegrams arrived from most of the Russian Musical Society's then fifty-three local branches, numerous other educational and cultural institutions in Russia and abroad, as well as from private individuals, many of whom had received their education in the conservatory. The festivities once again caught the eye of local newspapers, as well as the musical periodical press. Coverage included reviews and society-page narratives of the banquets and performances complete with descriptions of the women's ball gowns.

Beyond the glitter, the fiftieth-anniversary celebrations of the St. Petersburg Conservatory prompted a reassessment of it as an educational and social institution. "The history of the Petersburg Conservatory," according to the newspaper *Kievskaia mysl'*, was "the history of the struggle for knowledge, the struggle for the liberation of Russian music from the yoke of foreign influence and enslavement."[113] Instead of "dilettantes" and "foreigners," Russia now had its own "army" of music professionals, which included not only ordinary musicians and "officers," but also a few "generals."[114] Most journalists singled out

FIGURE 6.4. "Celebratory Concert of the Student Orchestra and Choir of the Conservatory in Connection with the 50th Anniversary of the Imperial Russian Musical Society, St. Petersburg, 1909." Permission of the Central State Archive of Documentary Films, Photographs, and Sound Recordings, St. Petersburg

Anton Rubinstein for his leadership of the Russian Musical Society and the St. Petersburg Conservatory. Lauded as the father of Russian music education and its "Peter the Great," Rubinstein was celebrated in particular for securing civil rights for Russian musicians and for creating a new class of people: the educated, expertly trained, professional musician.[115] Ironically, given the bitter public feuds of the recent past, commentators noted with particular pride that the St. Petersburg Conservatory was the achievement of a private organization. More than modest at its founding in 1862, the conservatory had grown to accommodate more than two thousand students. It had produced thousands of musicians and singers and had "dealt dilettantism a fatal blow."[116] Certainly, commentators acknowledged, the conservatory had its faults, but most of these were shared by conservatories across Europe, particularly the tendency to confuse the quantity of students with their quality. Yet, even its critics conceded that the conservatory both ably served Russian culture and demonstrated the potential of private initiative.[117]

The Society's sometimes grandiose assertions of its significance did not go unchallenged. In 1909, some critics complained about the Russian Musical Society's tendency to exaggerate its own importance and achievements, singling out the commemorative history of the St. Petersburg branch compiled by A. I. Puzyrevsky as a particularly egregious example of this unfortunate tendency. Grigory Timofeev, an ally and confidante of Balakirev and Stasov, took considerable offense at its tendency, "from the very first line," to treat the Society "as if it was the institution 'thanks to which the musical arts were created and developed.'" Such an interpretation, Timofeev argued, was not in accordance with what he saw as the facts. Echoing the attacks on the Society from the 1860s and 1870s, Timofeev accused it of possessing "a conservative-bureaucratic character with clearly expressed German tendencies" that "prevented it from serving the true progress of Russian national music."[118] Similarly, many of the reviews of the symphonic, chamber music, and operatic concerts held as part of the 1912 conservatory celebration were less than glowing, casting doubt on the conservatory's claims to artistic eminence.[119]

Yet, many critics were clearly partisans of the Russian Musical Society, praising it and its flagship institution in the most extravagant terms. As Timofeev's article makes clear, the conflict between the Society and the Balakirev Circle resurfaced, but now the nationalist views of the 1860s seemed archaic and immature. One commentator noted that there was once a time when a "cult of ignorance" flourished in Russian musical life, when the misled "evilly laughed off" any attempt to subordinate their "native talent to the 'German science' of music."[120] Still, other commentators, while lauding the achievements of the Russian Musical Society and the St. Petersburg

Conservatory in developing Russian musical culture, noted their shortcomings as well. *Vechernyi peterburg*, for example, praised the Society's "colossal" influence on the development of Russian musical life but identified its most grievous sins. In particular, the newspaper noted, tuition fees at the conservatories were too high and entrance requirements too liberal, while repertoire selection for the Society's concerts continued to conform to narrow, partisan criteria.[121] Still other writers complained of the leading role of dilettantes in the Society and of the failure to bring music education to the lower classes.[122]

The Russian Musical Society used the festivities to both celebrate its achievements and lay the groundwork for the continued survival of its institutions. The master narrative reinforced by the commemorative histories published for these occasions highlighted the transformatory power of the Society in Russian cultural life, its effectiveness as a civilizing tool, and its practical achievements in disseminating education and enlightenment. The narratives celebrated the patronage of the imperial family and other highly placed persons, and trumpeted the support received from the state, while simultaneously insisting on the need for further, greater support. Successes achieved had been realized against great odds and only with the cooperation and assistance of the state and society. The founders of the Russian Musical Society and the directors of the conservatories were singled out for their moral and artistic leadership. The students, for the most part, were absent from these narratives, except for those who had already gone on to glorious achievements. The narrative minimized the struggles and defeats that the Society faced in achieving its goals, establishing its institutions, and securing rights and recognition for its students, faculty, and graduates. Rarely was there any suggestion that the Society and its educational institutions were anything other than a complete and unqualified success. The Russian Musical Society was presented as having single-handedly slain the dragon of resistance to the development of European musical culture in Russia. It was credited with having created, from a complete void, a musical profession and a musical infrastructure capable of bringing the light of art to the darkest and most forsaken corners of the empire.[123] Nevertheless, although the master narrative was surprisingly persuasive, it was not strong enough to deter the growing demand for professional control of musical life that, in effect, called for the disbanding of the Society. In essence, the Society succeeded in convincing the Russian public of its instrumental role in creating Russian musical culture but not in persuading educated society or the musical community of its continuing vitality or future effectiveness.

CHAPTER 7

Conclusion

Everything Old Is New Again

DURING THE 1912 CONSERVATORY JUBILEE, *Russkaia molva* published Iuliia Veisberg's remembrances of the conservatory revolution, protecting her identity with the pseudonym "X."[1] In 1905, she had been a student at both the St. Petersburg Conservatory and the Bestuzhevsky Higher Courses for Women; she later went on to a successful professional career.[2] In interpreting the results of the conservatory revolution, Veisberg noted the failure of the reform projects it inspired but nonetheless offered the memory of 1905 as a critical affirmation of the artistic and civic identity of the student-artists who took part. In particular, the performance of *Kashchei* testified to the "fervor and artistic enthusiasm" of the young musicians during the social and political crisis. Having been tested by the fires of revolutionary politics, she insisted "in that memorable year" they "deserved their title of 'free artist' in the best and highest sense of that phrase!"[3] Thus, although critical of the Russian Musical Society, even Veisberg had internalized the professional ethos and artistic identity promoted by its flagship institutions.

Between 1859 and 1918, the Russian Musical Society led a remarkable transformation of Russian musical life. At the time of its inception, Russian musical culture unquestionably lagged behind many of its European neighbors. Not only had serfdom and the estate system prevented the establishment of a Russian musical profession, but Russia also lacked many of the institutional structures that were then modernizing European musical life. By the outbreak of World War I, however, Russia had emerged as one of Europe's musical leaders. An increasingly assertive and robust Russian musical profession sought a leadership role in musical life. In addition to the imperial theaters, Russia now boasted innovative private opera theaters. Permanent concert orchestras were also beginning to emerge, while an increasingly wide variety of professional performers and soloists circulated between the capitals and provincial cities. Three generations of Russian composers had appeared since the 1860s. The first generation had struggled to prove itself on both Russian stages and in European musical circles. The latest generation, including Prokofiev, Stravinsky, and Scriabin, no longer had to struggle against perceived Russian cultural inferiority. Musically, Russia was no longer racing to catch up, now it was racing ahead of its European competitors.

The achievements of the Russian Musical Society were considerable. It had created not only a Russian conservatory, but also an entire network of specialized musical educational institutions. It had trained tens of thousands of musicians, among whom were both highly qualified professionals, whose careers would have national or international repercussions for Russian music, and innumerable amateur musicians, whose lives shaped Russia's cultural infrastructure by providing the educated audience and enthusiastic consumers needed to drive the engine of cultural development. The Society's local branches and their educational institutions created cultural centers of gravity that, especially in the provinces, provided the needed resources and legitimacy for the development of local cultural life. Eventually, they became nodes in Russia's increasingly dense web of cultural interchange. The concerts sponsored by provincial branches provided job opportunities for touring soloists, private orchestras, rank-and-file musicians, and novice and veteran conductors. Such concerts, especially as programming grew more self-consciously coherent at the end of the nineteenth century, allowed residents of provincial cities to participate in the blossoming of Russian musical life. The Society's provincial music classes and schools, whatever their faults, provided jobs for conservatory graduates and a focal point for the bourgeois aspirations of local society through the cultural education of their sons and, especially, daughters. Like ripples in a pond, the impact of the Russian Musical Society expanded in concentric circles as its local branches grew in number and became more substantial and significant. The growth of supporting industries—music publishing, instrument manufacturing, sales, and repair, for example—as well as the growth of competing musical associations and schools can be attributed to the success of the Society as well. By creating a successful model of cultural development, by finding an appropriate mixture of education, performance, and associational initiative, the Russian Musical Society provided a pattern that its competitors could follow, adding further density and complexity to the expanding web of cultural life.

In short, the Russian Musical Society was instrumental in accomplishing the fundamental transformation of Russian cultural life during the second half of the nineteenth century. The cultural infrastructure developed under the Society's leadership proved to be so stable and well-structured that even the vicissitudes of early Soviet cultural life were not able to fundamentally disrupt it. Despite the profound ideological differences between the Bolshevik cultural leadership and that of the tsarist era, in music at least the new regime had little choice but to build on the foundation already established by the Russian Musical Society.

From War to Revolution: 1914–1917

As the Russian Musical Society celebrated the jubilee of its flagship institution, it had no way of predicting the chaos that would soon engulf it and the whole of Russian society. During World War I, the Society's public image took yet another blow as it was repeatedly accused of collusion in draft evasion schemes. The Society, critics claimed, charged masses of supposedly talentless musicians, primarily Jews, extortionate fees for enrollment in its music schools and conservatories. Allegations that young men enrolled in the educational institutions of the Society solely in order to evade military service were not new; the authorities had long been suspicious of the musical interests of young men of draft age. In 1874, military service became universal for males, regardless of social estate, with a complicated system of exemptions, deferments, and reductions in service based on educational qualifications and family status.[4] Students in the Society's music schools and conservatories were eventually considered eligible for deferments while they completed their educations and for reductions in the term of service upon graduation. However, the rights of music students to privileged status in military service were controversial and frequently contested by the state and questioned by society.[5] In 1875, the satirical journal *Maliar* remarked on the sudden attractiveness of a musical education in a caricature that depicted a crowd of determined young artists clutching a motley assortment of instruments. Their talent, newly discovered in the face of universal military service, had them clamoring for entrance into the conservatory.[6] This caricature, however, made no explicit mention of Jews, probably because Jewish enrollment in the conservatories and music schools remained low. Specific accusations of Jewish evasion of military service through enrollment in music education institutions did not surface until some ten years later. During World War I, however, such accusations became increasingly frequent and brought unwelcome scrutiny to the Society's educational institutions.[7] As the rhetoric grew more heated, *Muzyka* reprinted a vicious satire that all but damned the Samara Music School, and by extension the Russian Musical Society, for treason. An "epidemic" of music had infected the city, where the war had transformed the city's inhabitants into "Italians" virtually overnight. The music school's director, Ia. Ia. Karklin, was portrayed as a ruthless opportunist, who demanded that would-be students study everything from the piano to the phonograph at inflated prices in order to line his own pockets. Such high fees, it was insinuated, were seen as no obstacle by those fleeing call-up to active service. The war, it seemed, "gave birth not only to heroes, but also to musical talents."[8]

Although this satire was grossly exaggerated, it is nonetheless clear that the Russian Musical Society did foster draft evasion, at least inadvertently. Both Jewish and non-Jewish draft-age males viewed enrollment in music schools as a relatively easy means to avoid military service, but Jewish youths had fewer alternatives.[9] University students also received deferments, but quotas on Jewish enrollment were strictly enforced. Suspicion of student draft evasion strained the Society's working relationship with central and local authorities, who demanded that the Society's educational institutions make clearer distinctions about the enrollment status of their students. Increasingly, those who did not meet general education requirements or enroll in the full course of study were properly identified as auditors, who were ineligible for military deferments.[10] Although this classification scheme partially satisfied demands for greater vigilance against draft evasion, it also allowed the music schools and conservatories to manipulate the statistical representation of their student body. By counting only official students and excluding auditors, for example, the Kiev branch of the Society was able to significantly undercount the number of Jews enrolled in its music school.

During the war, the percentage of Jewish students in the Moscow Conservatory slowly rose, although it remained far lower than in the Society's other conservatories.[11] Such statistics, of course, fail to illuminate the human consequences of efforts to restrict Jewish enrollment, whether in adherence to anti-Semitic policies or in response to charges of draft evasion. For Sholom Berkov Goldin, restrictions on Jewish enrollment meant the death of his hopes for his son's career. Goldin's son was denied admission to the Moscow Conservatory in part because he had failed to present documents proving his current military status or his right to residency. All of these documents, Goldin argued, were held by the Warsaw Musical Institute, where his son was currently enrolled and were therefore unavailable until he transferred. Yet, Goldin's objections ring rather hollow as he admitted that his primary motivation was to preserve his son's safety. He begged the conservatory to accept his son as a student at least until "the complete victory of Russian arms over the conceited enemy Germans," a declaration sure to provoke suspicion that a desire to avoid military service, not a love of art, had prompted the decision to pursue a musical education. Goldin, however, couched his petition in flowery patriotic prose, emphasizing not only his own military service in the 1870s against Turkey, but also the death of another of his sons on the field of battle in Prussia in 1914. How cruel then to deny his other son the opportunity to "dedicate his entire life to art for the glory of himself and his native land" simply because of his faith, while still expecting him to take up arms in its defense. In protesting the Moscow Conservatory's admission decision, Goldin threw himself into a frontal attack on the anti-Semitic beliefs and practices of the Russian people. If Russian society, and the Moscow branch, hoped to distinguish themselves from the "Teutonic barbarians," then they needed to accept Jews as equally loyal subjects of "our dear fatherland Russia" and its "Great Tsar." Goldin's petition, however, fell on deaf bureaucratic ears. The director of the Moscow Conservatory, M. M. Ippolitov-Ivanov, reminded Goldin that, since 1906, only Jews with residency rights were accepted as applicants. Moreover, no Jews whatsoever would be admitted because the current percentage of Jewish students exceeded the established norms for higher educational institutions.[12]

Despite such occasional diligence, the Ministry of Internal Affairs clearly feared that the Society's educational institutions harbored Jewish youth intent on avoiding the draft.[13] Because the Society's institutions lacked the strict age limits, educational qualifications, and caps on Jewish enrollment characteristic of other higher educational institutions, the ministry viewed them as particularly vulnerable to abuse. In addition, several of the Society's largest and most active educational institutions, including the Odessa Conservatory and the Poltava Music School, were located within the Pale of Settlement. Under pressure, the Society responded by putting new barriers in place to guard against frivolous enrollment. Statistics, however, make clear that some men did seek refuge from military service in the Society's schools and conservatories. In September 1913, for example, the Odessa Conservatory enrolled 393 new students (136 men, 276 women). Three-quarters of the men and almost 80 percent of the women were Jewish. By September 1915, however, the proportions of male and female students had reversed; the conservatory admitted 268 men and 137 women. The proportion of Jewish students, moreover, had significantly increased, including more than 95 percent of the male students. The proportion of Jewish female students, however, had decreased somewhat, to 73 percent.[14] Still, the Society strenuously denied accusations that it colluded in draft evasion schemes and made every effort to demonstrate their cooperation with the state in rigidly enforcing entrance and graduation requirements.[15]

Worsening economic conditions complicated the already difficult relationship between the Main Directorate and the Society's educational institutions. The Society's rapid expansion into the provinces in the previous decade had attracted increased state subsidies, but the finances of the provincial classes, schools, and conservatories remained precarious. Unexpected problems, such as the requisitioning of some provincial music schools by local military authorities threatened the continuing existence of these branches.[16] Faculty as well as students were vulnerable to call-up to military service, which disrupted academic life and shrank the student body. Because the Society's educational institutions were tuition dependent, any decline in enrollment imperiled struggling branches.[17] Even the most successful branches were undermined by the exigencies of the war. In Kiev, the conservatory's evacuation to Rostov on Don in August 1915 nearly bankrupted it when enrollment dropped by more than two-thirds. Faced with financial catastrophe, the conservatory petitioned to return to Kiev, where enrollment soon returned to more normal levels. The Kiev branch estimated its total losses in the adventure at more than 80,000 rubles.[18] Rather optimistically, the Kiev branch requested that it be reimbursed for its troubles by the Ministry of Internal Affairs. Neither such special requests nor petitions for increased state subsidies appeared likely to succeed in wartime conditions.[19]

Despite these difficulties, however, the Society and its branches continued to function and satisfy the educational and cultural needs of their local communities. Nevertheless, the tensions between the Society and its conservatories, masked by the granting of autonomy after 1905, grew stronger as the goals of the two institutions increasingly diverged. Concerns about artistic standards prompted the Society's patron and president, Saksen-Altenburgskaia, to call a meeting of the five conservatory directors in January 1917.[20] Almost immediately, the relationship of the conservatories to the Society, although not intended to be the focus of the meeting, became the central issue. The Moscow Conservatory faculty council insisted that the "first and most basic question" was the "position of the conservatories compared to other higher educational institutions in Russia as well as ... to other institutions of the Imperial Russian Musical Society."[21] Saksen-Altenburgskaia eventually lost control of the meeting's agenda. By the final day of the conference, issues that strayed significantly beyond her original agenda reached the floor; most important, the question of the financial stability of the conservatories and their relationship to both the Society and to the state. G. P. Prokofiev, representative of the Moscow Conservatory's faculty, reported on the conservatories' inadequate financing, a chronic problem that prevented them from creating new courses or departments, providing better wages, or more strictly evaluating the abilities of enrolling students. According to Prokofiev, "only by placing the conservatories under the protection of the State, in line with all other educational institutions," and by ensuring their "complete independence from the casual generosity of local boards," would music education be raised to the appropriate level. This basic position was warmly supported by all representatives from the conservatories, who advocated petitioning the state for significantly increased funding. In response, the vice chair of the Society, V. I. Timiriazev, reminded delegates of the Society's long struggle to secure even limited state subsidies and warned them that additional requests were unlikely to be realized, especially in wartime. While Timiriazev advocated the mobilization of local resources, the delegates from the Moscow and Odessa conservatories explicitly raised the idea of transferring the Society's educational institutions to government authority. In response, Timiriazev warned against counting on the generosity of the state and counseled, rather prophetically as it turned out, that incorporation into the state system might have unintended consequences; the state, once obligated to provide financial support, would feel entitled to meddle in musical affairs.[22]

From Revolution to Revolution: February to October 1917

In the aftermath of the February Revolution, the conservatories began in earnest to renegotiate their relationship with the Russian Musical Society, while the Society itself also began to cast about for a new role. To most observers, it appeared increasingly likely that the conservatories would secure real independence in the near future. At the same time, the unstable political and social situation caused anxiety, especially about the future of the Society's far-flung provincial branches. The collapse of the tsarist regime unsettled the Russian Musical Society, which struggled, between February and October 1917, to renegotiate the relationship between its constituent branches and institutions and its central leadership. Recognizing the urgency of the situation, the Main Directorate announced that "the great events, which have placed Russia on the path to freedom and broad social initiative" had created an urgent need "to discuss ... the further direction of affairs of the [Society] and the conservatories, music schools, and music classes under its supervision."[23]

The Society planned a conference in Petrograd in May 1917 to discuss the future. Each branch sent three delegates, including one member of the local board, the director of the musical educational institution, and a representative of the faculty. In March, the five conservatory directors preempted the planned conference, meeting in Moscow to draft a new charter that quickly became a determined bid for institutional independence. Although the second article of the proposed charter boldly declared that "the conservatories" were "autonomous institutions" entitled to "completely independently organize their educational-artistic and financial affairs," these brash statements were still little more than dreams. The directors hoped that the Ministry of Education would accept oversight of the conservatories; even more ambitiously, they promoted the conservatories as public institutions "supported on sums issued by the state" as well as by tuition payments, interest paid on invested capital of stipends, receipts from property, and gifts.[24] Yet this final attempt to restructure the conservatory charter was no more successful than previous ones. In any case, political events soon overtook both the conservatories and the Society as a whole.

The Main Directorate simultaneously created a commission of its own that, while it reaffirmed its faith in the viability of the Society, also insisted that the charter must govern any restructuring. Above all, they questioned the desirability and utility of the "separation from the Russian Musical Society" of its conservatories and other educational institutions, expressing their dismay at this assault on the integrity of the organization they credited with the solid foundation of music education and concert life across the empire. Unanimity on this question, however, was impossible due to the presence of professor L. Nikolaev, who brought the views of musical professionals into the commission's deliberations. Nikolaev acknowledged the "legal and financial difficulties of separating the musical-educational institutions ... from the Society," but stated flatly "although such a separation is not in the interests of the Russian Musical Society, it is in the interests of its educational institutions and also of musical-educational affairs in Russia. Music education should be the business of the state, not of private society. Accordingly, the musical-educational institutions of the country should be state [institutions] and, as such, should receive from the government" adequate financial support in proportion to their financial needs.[25] Nevertheless, the commission did what it could to subvert the breakaway tendencies of the conservatories and music schools, promising them complete artistic autonomy. Clearly sensing that this offer might not satisfy musical professionals, they also attempted to craft a new role for the Society. They outlined an ambitious but vague plan to transform the Russian Musical Society into a coordinating council for the myriad musical organizations of the country. They further suggested that the Society might find a new purpose in bringing music to the broad working masses.[26]

In the provinces, the success of the new conservatories in Kiev, Saratov, and Odessa encouraged the Kharkov and Tiflis branches to pursue the elevation of their music schools. War and revolution, however, interfered with their ability to accomplish these transformations. When, in April 1917, the Kharkov branch advanced the idea of reorganizing its music school into a conservatory, it relied on still simmering debates on the purpose of the conservatory and access to music education to frame its proposal. "The growing flood of students in recent years" had allowed the branch to demand better preparation from prospective students and, in effect, to select a student body that mirrored that of the conservatories in terms of talent and skill. The discrepancy between the abilities of students and the privileges available to them in a music school, as opposed to a conservatory, posed a real threat to the long-term viability of the school. Without conservatory status, the Kharkov branch feared its most able students and faculty would eventually depart for more prestigious institutions.[27] Despite the unsettled political situation, the Main Directorate supported the reorganization of the Kharkov Music School, although, as with the earlier case of the Saratov Conservatory, it wanted guarantees that the faculty would possess appropriate professional credentials. The ability of the Kharkov Conservatory to attract professors with conservatory diplomas underscores the distance between Russian musical life in the early 1860s, when the newborn St. Petersburg Conservatory recruited most of its faculty abroad, and the early twentieth century, when even provincial conservatories and music schools could retain well-qualified musical professionals, credentialed primarily by Russian institutions.[28]

As winter wore on into spring, the Russian Musical Society struggled to cope with the shifting political terrain. The decision to reorganize the Tiflis Music School into a conservatory, approved by the Main Directorate in January 1917, suddenly became more complicated as the interests of the faculty, the director, the branch, the Society, and local authorities collided. In a volatile political climate, the faculty council pressed ahead with reorganization, approaching neither the Main Directorate nor the local board, but the new local authorities, the *Osobyi Zakavkazskii Komitet*, for approval. Despite the protests of the Tiflis branch, which demanded that reorganization be delayed while it awaited new guidelines from Petrograd, the request was approved by local authorities and grudgingly accepted as a fait accompli by the Main Directorate. The actions of the Tiflis faculty threatened the integrity of the Society and, in particular, the supervisory authority of provincial branches toward their educational institutions. The Tiflis faculty justified their actions by emphasizing the unstable revolutionary political situation, but their rhetoric belied behavior that reflected not the short-term disruptions of the

February Revolution but longstanding tensions between professional musicians and amateur board members. The Tiflis faculty council had asked the local authorities to confirm it as an "independent, autonomous, and representative organ which directs the musical, administrative, and financial affairs" of the new conservatory. The *Osobyi Zakavkazskii Komitet* expressed concerns over the legality of these demands for complete autonomy, which forced the faculty council to modify its proposal to fit within the existing charters of the Society and the conservatories. The limited autonomy granted to the faculty council in these charters hardly satisfied them; they hoped that a new charter would give them complete autonomy so that they could work to benefit a "Free Russia." The future role of the Russian Musical Society in this new "Free Russia" remained uncertain and of little interest to the Tiflis faculty. In a letter full of disappointment and bitterness, the director of the newly rechristened Tiflis Conservatory, N. Nikolaev, wrote to V. E. Napravnik regarding his fears for his institution and the Society as a whole. Politics, he noted sadly, had touched even their "little musical world." Caught up in the excitement of revolutionary events, the music school's faculty council joined "the revolutionary movement so as not to be left behind everyone else." The faculty, he complained bitterly, felt the need to "perform a revolution so as to demonstrate their participation in the general liberation movement." Only the needs of the institution he loved persuaded Nikolaev to remain at his director's post; he had signed the request for reorganization only after a unanimous vote of the faculty council. Tired and dispirited, he feared for the survival of the Tiflis Conservatory.[29]

Events soon overtook internal efforts at restructuring. By late spring, virtually everyone understood that the conservatories would soon secure their independence from the Society. Negotiations over autonomy, property, and inventory were well under way by the end of April 1917. Rather than a coup d'état, the final split between the Moscow and Petrograd conservatories and the Russian Musical Society was more of an amicable if protracted divorce. In Moscow, the conservatory and the Society negotiated the transfer of assets, while in Petrograd the local board expressed its "complete sympathy" under "these conditions" for the separation of the conservatories from the Society, provided the government accepted them as state institutions. Although the Society clearly understood that it had already effectively lost the conservatories, the Petrograd branch insisted that the Society still had a "wide field" of activity open to it. Just as the Society "brought to life the first Russian Conservatory and covered Russia with a network of musical-educational institutions," it might continue to serve the nation's maturing cultural needs.[30]

After October: The Birth of Soviet Music

The Society had hardly come to grips with the February Revolution when it was overtaken by the Bolshevik seizure of power. When, in July 1918, the Bolsheviks nationalized the Moscow and Petrograd conservatories, they put an end to all attempts to restructure the Russian Musical Society. Although the Society might have survived the loss of the conservatories, the loss of its provincial educational institutions led inevitably to its disintegration. By October 1918, Narkompros, the People's Commissariat of Enlightenment, had assumed administrative control of all of the Society's branches.[31]

The nationalization of the Society's conservatories, schools, and classes fulfilled the desires of many musicians and cultural critics; incorporation into the state-run educational system liberated these institutions from the supposedly pernicious control of amateurs and allegedly delivered their long-sought autonomy. Music and music education, it was believed, were finally being recognized for their important contributions to the development of Russian society. Most important, the state assumed direct responsibility for the financial support, administration, and continued productivity of institutions that now formed the core of the Soviet system of specialized music education. Even Narkompros was a reasonable facsimile of the Ministry of the Arts so desperately desired by musicians and cultural critics under the old regime.[32]

To its credit, Narkompros, under the leadership of Anatoly Lunacharsky, did its best to support the conservatories financially and materially.[33] Narkompros's best, however, was severely limited in the context of the civil war that devastated Russia from 1918 to 1921. Although Lunacharsky tried hard to find funds for the conservatories and protect their premises, personnel, libraries, and instrument collections from requisition, he could not prevent their decline. Moreover, the sudden rise of Moscow as the Bolshevik capital had significant consequences for the Petrograd Conservatory. Accustomed to its exalted position as the preeminent musical educational institution in Russia, the Petrograd Conservatory struggled to accommodate itself to a new reality in which Moscow now occupied the dominant position and could claim the largest share of resources and attention from the state. The conservatories lost faculty as many leading artists fled the country for calmer conditions and more lucrative positions abroad. Enrollments contracted as provincial students returned home or were prevented from enrolling due to the disruption caused by the war. In the provinces, conditions were even more desperate. In Ukraine, political instability gave the Kiev branch and its conservatory new authority;

branches within the region increasingly looked to Kiev, rather than to Petrograd or Moscow, for guidance.[34]

The collapse of the Russian Musical Society forced its former institutions to negotiate a new relationship with the state and society. For the conservatories in particular, this process was often painful as they struggled to accommodate themselves to the new political reality while securing, insofar as possible, the resources and support needed to maintain their artistic and educational integrity. As Amy Nelson has conclusively shown, between 1917 and 1932 the Moscow and Leningrad conservatories were socially, musically, and politically divided. Factions and interest groups struggled for dominance, attempting to shape the conservatories both as musical and as Soviet institutions. Party and Komsomol cells formed in the two conservatories early in the 1920s and quickly became involved in academic governance as well as ideological agitation and education. Activist students of Moscow's composition department created PROKOLL, the Proletarian Composers' Collective, while faculty members formed the Faction of the Red Professors. Organizations such as the Association for Contemporary Music (ASM), the Russian Association of Proletarian Musicians (RAPM), and its splinter group the Organization of Revolutionary Composers and Music Workers (ORK) had deep roots in the conservatories.[35] Disparities in the social status of students in different performance specialties remained from the prerevolutionary conservatory, but now they took on new, ideologically driven, meanings. Rivalries were particularly deep between the prestige specialties (piano, violin, operatic voice) and the workhorse ones (brass, winds, percussion, low strings, and choral singing).[36] Teachers argued among themselves over the creation of new departments and faculties and the adoption of new methodologies.[37] Within departments, controversies arose over pedagogical methods; according to one former student, the composition faculty of the Leningrad Conservatory was polarized between the traditionalist Maximillian Steinberg, Rimsky-Korsakov's son-in-law, and Vladimir Shcherbachev, a charismatic young composer of the modernist school.[38] Incorporation into the state educational system, of course, brought with it the close involvement of both Narkompros and Glavprofobr (Department of Professional Education) in conservatory affairs.

With the end of the civil war, musical life began to settle into a more familiar routine. In the conservatories, familiar issues such as student recruitment, admissions standards, the composition of the student body, the components of the curriculum, and graduation standards resurfaced, albeit with a new, Bolshevik coloring. The bourgeois origins and ethos of the conservatories made it both difficult and imperative that they find a revolutionary purpose and socialist structure. Defining that new purpose and creating that new structure, however, proved to be a complicated and dangerous task. The 1920s were a time of conflict, negotiation, and compromise. Institutions strove to retain power, influence, and privileges while the Soviet state attempted to retain the more-or-less willing services of "bourgeois specialists." As scholars have shown, throughout the 1920s the Bolshevik state pursued a shifting but relatively tolerant and pluralistic approach to the professions and the arts. Recognizing both the abilities of artists, intellectuals, and technical professionals and the continuing need for their services, the Bolsheviks provided financial and administrative support to cultural and educational institutions. Narkompros in particular encouraged artists and intellectuals to respond creatively to the revolution, while striving to maintain relative neutrality in the consequent skirmishes between artistic and intellectual factions.[39]

The conservatories, although subject to Bolshevik educational and cultural policies, were of relatively little concern to the state, which remained focused on the universities and technical institutions.[40] If the arts in general were peripheral to the concerns of the Soviet leadership, music in particular was even further out on the fringes. Russian literature had always been highly politicized. The graphic arts possessed clear possibilities as propaganda tools. Classical music, however, was perceived as abstract and apolitical, which created problems for musicians struggling for support in a revolutionary society. Conservatory musicians attempted to justify themselves and their institutions, acquire status, and gain material support by crafting a revolutionary legitimacy that emphasized music's closeness to the proletariat. At the same time, even the most revolutionary students and teachers within the conservatories expressed concern about musical and professional standards. They struggled to preserve the artistic integrity of music in general, and the conservatories in particular, under the new, revolutionary regime.

The pressures brought to bear on the universities had their echoes in the conservatories as well. The new, socialist society demanded the proletarianization of the conservatories and the democratization of musical life. More specifically, the Bolsheviks insisted on improved access to higher education for working-class students. New enrollment policies demanded that admissions decisions be based on social and political criteria and that "professional students," those with inadequate academic records, and those with suspect social backgrounds be purged from the student body.[41] Such ideological needs, however, conflicted with strong cultural traditions and musical practices. The desire to open the conservatories to the working classes, by eliminating admissions examinations for example, quickly foundered because of the "obvious" need for talent and the resulting need for diagnostic testing.[42] Even Soviet cultural authorities subscribed to traditional ideas about the nurturing of talent. As a result, the problem soon became how to identify, foster, and cultivate talent among the workers and peasants.

Simultaneously, the existing student body of the conservatories came under scrutiny, particularly during the 1924 student purge.[43] Throughout the 1920s, music journals complained of the weaknesses of the student body and the failures of the admissions process. Too many applicants were pianists and singers; too few of these had proletarian antecedents. Few applicants chose to study orchestral wind instruments; the Soviet musical press brooded about a looming crisis in the supply of orchestral musicians, echoing similar complaints from the nineteenth century.[44] Those intent on a radical restructuring of the conservatory revived old accusations that the conservatories harbored hordes of "untalented" young, bourgeois, piano-playing women who threatened to infect the new proletarian students with their pernicious cultural ethos. Unfortunately, scholars have often repeated these charges at face value, underestimating the social complexity of the conservatories and music schools, as well as the musical profession as a whole, before 1917.[45] In practice, proletarianizing the conservatory meant reducing the piano and vocal departments, strengthening the orchestral, composition and theory, and conducting departments, and creating a new instructional-pedagogical department.[46] In an effort to boost the conservatories' revolutionary legitimacy, doubtful efforts at proletarianization were declared great successes, as in 1924 when *Muzykal'naia nov'* reported on the preliminary results of the Moscow Conservatory's entrance examinations. The conservatory planned to admit only one hundred new students; their allocation by department clearly reflected the imperative to create a more proletarian student body. Thirty spaces were allocated to orchestral instruments, twenty spaces for pedagogical students, and eighteen for choral students. Thus, the least prestigious prerevolutionary specialties were targeted to become the core of a new, proletarian student body. Conversely, the piano department was allotted a mere twelve new students in an effort to reduce the influence of this suddenly shameful bourgeois specialty. The remaining twenty places were divided between the vocal performance (10), composition-theory (8), and conducting (2) departments.[47]

The results of these examinations cast doubt on the success of proletarianization. Not only did roughly 60 percent of applicants fail their examinations, their social and employment profiles did not really conform to the proletarian ideal. Although nearly a quarter of the applicants were sponsored by local Party, Komsomol, or trade union organizations, the conservatory was forced to count all applicants *twice*, once in their own social position and once in their parents' social category, in order to create the impression that applicants of proletarian origin predominated. In actuality, the applicant pool was overwhelmingly nonparty and white collar. Although Party and Komsomol members, as well as workers, children of workers, peasants, and children of peasants were more likely to be admitted than were students from other, less politically desirable groups, a significant percentage of these applicants failed their exams. More than 80 percent of newly admitted students had bourgeois origins. In short, a traditional result was camouflaged by distorting the social origins of applicants and new students.[48]

The attack on the piano and voice departments had one clear consequence: a significant shift in the gender structure of the conservatory student body. While young women dominated the tsarist-era conservatory, new admissions policies and pedagogical emphases privileged young men. Women were heavily concentrated in the most bourgeois departments, piano and voice, and virtually absent from the most proletarian department, orchestral instruments. Discriminatory admissions policies that limited entrance to arguably overloaded specialties, such as piano performance, had the effect of limiting female access to the conservatory, at least in the short term. In 1924, not only were nearly 60 percent of applicants male, but men also were somewhat less likely to fail their examinations. The newly admitted class reversed the traditional gender structure of the student body; for the first time since its founding in 1866, the Moscow Conservatory was on track to become a male-dominated institution.[49] The professionalizing ethos of early Soviet cultural policy, which included a sharp dismissal of the kinds of informal employment in music more frequently practiced by women than men, simply recast longstanding male fears of the threat posed by amateur or semiprofessional female musicians into an acceptable socialist framework.

At the very same time, however, opposition to the ideal of a leaner, more professional conservatory arose within musical and educational circles. To be sure, no one argued for the retention of the bourgeois, dilettante "ballast" of the prerevolutionary conservatory. Instead, reiterating arguments dating back to the 1870s, they advocated a broader definition of musical professional and, as a consequence, a broader interpretation of the mission of the conservatory. Instead of an institution devoted to the training of a narrow cadre of specialists, the conservatories, they argued, should train a broad array of ordinary musicians, pedagogues, music teachers, and leaders for clubs, circles, and factories, as well as composers, conductors, and virtuosi. Borrowing the language of proletarianization, they defended a vision of the conservatory that emphasized the acculturation and aesthetic education of the whole Soviet/Russian people. Indeed, two of the most prominent voices in these debates were Nadezhda Briusova and Boleslav Iavorský, both of whom had been leaders of the People's Conservatory movement that emerged in the aftermath of the 1905 Revolution.[50]

In any case, the Soviet conservatories proved as resistant to change as their tsarist predecessors. Despite the concerted efforts of reformers, the Moscow and Leningrad conservatories possessed a degree of institutional conservatism and an artistic identity that limited the ability of ideologically driven reform to encroach on their activities. As scholars have shown, musical institutions possess clear, if often unspoken, status hierarchies that shape their institutional practices. Thus, musicians and music students tend to rank themselves by specialty, with composers and virtuosi on solo instruments—especially piano and violin—ranked highest and singers and pedagogues ranked lowest.[51] The strength of these internal artistic hierarchies is revealed by the failure of the Soviet regime to substitute a more ideologically appropriate sociopolitical hierarchy, despite sustained efforts throughout the 1920s and 1930s. As a result, in the aftermath of the October Revolution, the conservatory held on to its old bourgeois flavor. It was demonstrably not a revolutionary institution, and it had difficulty attracting students hoping for quick success and promotion in the new political context. Instead, it continued to attract the same kind of students it had attracted prior to the revolution.

In an attempt to distance themselves from their bourgeois origins, the Leningrad and Moscow conservatories not only attempted to reshape their student bodies, they also attempted to reshape their pasts, particularly the memory of 1905. Revolutionary credentials and demonstrated political activism were crucial components of personal and institutional credibility in the Soviet era. Over time, 1905 became an ideological turning point that demonstrated the possibility of transforming an intensely bourgeois institution into a proletarian one. The Leningrad and Moscow conservatories enlarged on the memory of their participation in the 1905 Revolution in order to bolster their shaky revolutionary legitimacy, but the memory eventually grew into a myth that distorted the actual events and real significance of the conservatory revolution. By the centenary celebrations of the Leningrad and Moscow conservatories in 1962 and 1966, the myth of the conservatory revolution was a fundamental component of the identity of both institutions. The year 1905 became a dividing line in the emerging Soviet narrative of Russian musical life. In the commemorative history published for the centenary of the Moscow Conservatory, the 1905 Revolution received unprecedented attention, occupying an entire chapter and serving to separate the main narrative of the prerevolutionary conservatory from that of its Soviet successor. The construction of 1905 as a founding myth of the Soviet conservatory is revealed most clearly, however, in early post-Soviet commentaries on these institutions, which avoid mention of 1905 and ignore the conservatory revolution entirely.[52]

In the 1920s, however, the memoirs of conservatory student activists highlighted the importance of the conservatory revolution for the political and social maturation of the student body. *Krasnaia gazeta* republished Iuliia Veisberg's reminiscences, which had first appeared in 1912, with alterations and additions that self-consciously merged the myth and the memory of 1905. Veisberg shifted the focus of her narrative, emphasizing the growing political awareness of conservatory students as they participated in meetings and demonstrations. In this revised narrative, the conservatory revolution proved a success; demands for the "emancipation" of the conservatory were realized and the "conservatory entered a new phase of its existence."[53] Similarly, the reminiscences of Anatoly Drozdov, first published in *Muzyka i revoliutsiia* in 1926, highlighted the importance of 1905 as a turning point in the social and political life of the St. Petersburg Conservatory. Unusually politically active, Drozdov had greeted the sudden appearance of revolutionary sentiments among his fellow students with skepticism.[54]

Longer and more detailed than other memoirs, Drozdov's first-person account of the political awakening of music students cemented the Soviet narrative of the conservatories and justified the proletarianization campaigns of the 1920s. Although he blamed students' lack of social awareness on the preponderance of "young ladies and golden youths" in the student body, he also emphasized the conservatory's hidden potential for transformation into a truly proletarian institution. If the bourgeoisie determined the conservatory's overall character before 1905, they nevertheless did not completely dominate it; both the "democratic intelligentsia," clustered in the composition department, and the "musical proletariat" of orchestral students and singers, competed with the bourgeoisie for the conservatory's soul. Their presence nevertheless hinted at the possibility that the conservatory itself might be redeemed if only these progressive elements could be nurtured and politically awakened.[55]

Narkompros had sufficient resources to attempt innovative solutions to the problem of proletarianizing and democratizing musical life. In concert with sympathetic groups within the conservatories (groups that were, however, often at odds with each other), Soviet cultural agencies created alternative mechanisms intended to develop a cadre of socialist musicians drawn from the working classes and the peasantry. The most publicized of these was the musical Rabfak, an artistic offshoot of the worker's faculty (*Rabochii fakul'tet* or Rabfak) system that provided a remedial secondary education for adults preparing for higher education. Because the Rabfak system was intended to quickly create new professional cadres with both political loyalty to the Bolshevik regime and technical skills, Rabfak graduates were exempt from admissions exams for higher educational institutions, including the conservatories.[56] From its opening in Moscow in 1923, the musical Rabfak was loudly proclaimed as the key to overcoming the narrow professionalism and conservatism that had heretofore undermined attempts to proletarianize the conservatory.[57]

Those promoting the Rabfak often saw it as the antithesis of the conservatory, which they castigated for its apoliticism, bourgeois nature, and overspecialization. As articulated by E. Vilkovir in the pages of *Muzykal'naia nov'*, only the Rabfak could salvage the conservatory by infusing it with new blood, with the energy and enthusiasm of workers and peasants. Rejecting the need for technique, training, or even talent, Vilkovir suggested that normal physical and psychological development, as well as a strong attraction to music, were the only criteria that should be required for admission to the musical Rabfak.[58] Yet, despite liberal admissions policies, the Rabfak had little impact on the conservatories. Not only was the artistic Rabfak a minor part of the broader system, it was also plagued by such low graduation rates that it was unable to supply even the Moscow Conservatory with graduates in any significant number.[59] The Leningrad Conservatory drew little if any benefit from its activities. In 1928, *Muzyka i revoliutsiia* complained that the Rabfak was a well-kept secret even among the musicians of Moscow and was almost wholly unknown in the provinces. The late appearance of the conservatory Rabfaks, the low numbers of graduates, and the abysmal levels of achievement demonstrated by their music students suggests that the Rabfak failed to further the cause of musical proletarianization and democratization. Underfunded and deprived of resources, the musical Rabfaks subsisted largely on the enthusiasm of their instructors, primarily conservatory students. Only a handful of Rabfak students enrolled in the conservatories; most of those who enrolled failed to graduate, further undermining the position of proletarian students.[60]

Like the musical Rabfak, the Sunday Workers' Conservatory (*Voskresnaia Rabochaia Konservatoriia*) was publicly promoted as a mechanism for the proletarianization of the conservatory. Founded in Moscow in 1927, similar institutions were soon established in Leningrad, Saratov, Kiev, and other cities. Despite the wishful thinking of propagandists, in actuality the Workers' Conservatory was neither intended nor did it function as a preparatory school for conservatory-bound musicians. It was conceived and conducted as an amateur musical academy, offering small group and ensemble classes on popular instruments such as the accordion and the domra as well as on brass and woodwind instruments, piano, violin, and singing. The Workers' Conservatory, by all accounts, proved extremely popular; many times more people applied than could be admitted.[61] As a means to provide workers with basic music education and satisfying recreation, the Workers' Conservatory was a success. As an attempt to identify and prepare musically gifted workers and peasants for professional musical training, it was a failure. The Workers' Conservatory was directed at adults who were active members of the labor force; the interests of its students, as demonstrated by their course preferences, were not those of conservatory-bound musicians. Domra, balalaika, and accordion were popular choices, as were the choir and the wind orchestra. Least popular were the prestigious conservatory instruments: piano and violin. Workers were apparently extremely interested in pursuing music as an attractive hobby, not as the beginnings of a professional career. Indeed, students at the Workers' Conservatory appear to have been disturbed by their teachers "bias towards professional daydreams."[62]

Moreover, despite their Bolshevik trappings, neither the Rabfak nor the Workers' Conservatory represented a break with prerevolutionary musical or educational traditions. The institutions and structures created by Narkompros to provide cultural education to workers, including outreach programs into the factories and villages, were reworkings and restructurings of prerevolutionary institutions and programs. The Workers' Conservatories in particular were a resurrection of the People's Conservatories of the early twentieth century.[63] Before the revolution, factory owners sponsored choirs, wind bands, and orchestras for their workers, primarily as a means of social control and moral hygiene, but also in the hopes of elevating the taste, and the mores, of their employees. The musician-specialists who guided these efforts, along with those who guided the related efforts of temperance societies to establish choral groups in the villages, were motivated by deeply held beliefs about the need to provide the toiling masses with access to, and the means to understand, the rich cultural and musical heritage of Russia and of Western Europe. As utopian and idealistic as their Soviet counterparts, these would-be culture-bringers hoped to transform Russia by transforming Russians. The October Revolution, one could argue, merely gave these enthusiastic cultural missionaries official sanction and support, as well as an ideology that justified their efforts to remake the world.

Upheaval, Resilience, and the Reemergence of Tradition

Although turbulent and disruptive, even the Cultural Revolution of 1928–1932 proved, in the end, unable to fundamentally transform the Russian conservatories.[64] Unquestionably, debates about the proletarianization of the conservatories and the democratization of music took on new virulence. Students and faculty judged ideologically or socially inappropriate were purged and pushed out of the conservatories. In Moscow, the new Communist rector, B. Pshibyshevsky, called boldly for a radical transformation of the ethos of the conservatory. A renewed campaign to recruit proletarian and peasant students and suppress the bourgeois elements within the student body emboldened socialist organizations within the conservatories, such as Prokoll and the Association of Red Professors, which pushed for still more radical restructuring. Conflicts over revolutionary and bourgeois repertoire reached new heights, encouraging the Russian Association of Proletarian Musicians (RAPM) to demand adherence to a narrowly defined conception of socialist repertoire and performance while simultaneously condemning those, such as the Association for Contemporary Music, who insisted on the need for experimentation, innovation, and the exchange of ideas with the centers of contemporary music in Western Europe and North America.[65]

Yet, even at the height of the Cultural Revolution, the issues were still ones that echoed from the prerevolutionary past, indeed from as far back as the 1860s and the early days of the Russian Musical Society. Once again, musicians proclaimed the need to uplift and enlighten the backward masses. Yet again they debated the purpose of music education, arguing vociferously about who should be trained at the conservatory and to what end. The identity of conservatory students once again came under close scrutiny. The core problem remained the difficulty of ensuring a student body that would produce true professionals, albeit now with a new emphasis on socially useful specialties, such as orchestral performance or music teaching. Despite the determined efforts of Nadezhda Briusova and her colleagues in the pedagogical division (Pedfak), music teaching, especially in the schools and in the workers clubs, still lacked status among musicians. Indeed, the existence of the pedagogical division in the conservatories remained precarious, as many musicians viewed it as a threat to high standards of professional training. Even the renewed effort to proselytize music to the masses reflected earlier intelligentsia values as much as they did a commitment to socialist ideology.

Pshibyshevsky weighed in on these issues in the pages of *Muzykal'noe obrazovanie*. He argued that, despite the conservatory's socialist achievements in creating the musical Rabfak and the Sunday Workers' Conservatory, the Moscow Conservatory had not changed its basic personality but remained set in its old, bourgeois ways. The composition of the student body was of particular concern to the new director. Not only was the absolute number of proletarian students in the conservatory insufficient but they were also in danger of losing their proletarian characteristics. "The insignificant group of workers and communists is daily, hourly exposed to the influence of the petty bourgeois mass who populate the halls."[66]

Accusations began to appear in the musical press. Both the conservatories and Glavprofobr were charged with negligence in their attempt to improve the social composition of the conservatory student body. One leading music journal professed shock that only 12 percent of conservatory students were workers and peasants. Decisive improvements were demanded, including a quota of 50 percent workers and peasants among the next group of new students. Yet, even the propagandists of proletarianization clearly had their doubts about the likelihood of success. They accompanied their demands for quotas with proposals for remedial programs designed to "facilitate the entrance into the conservatory of weakly prepared, but talented persons of worker and peasant origins." At the same time, they insisted that the requirements for admission to "currently overloaded virtuoso-performance specialties" be sharply increased. Would-be composers and musicologists, moreover, were to be subjected to increased ideological scrutiny. Most ominous of all were the calls for a much stricter academic, ideological, and social selection of nonproletarian students and a radical purge of the student body.[67]

The effectiveness of this sharply accelerated drive to proletarianize the conservatory remains doubtful. Yuri Elagin's memoir *Taming of the Arts* provides an evocative if impressionistic portrait of the Moscow Conservatory that gives depth and personality to the insults suffered by that venerable institution. "The Moscow Conservatory went through the dark days of a musical inquisition. With the students, the new director [Pshibyshevsky] took a line of ruthless class discrimination. Irrefutable proletarian antecedents became the sole basis for admission. All students who could be classified as class enemies, including those who were in their last year, were expelled. The requirements were lowered and all forms of evaluating a student's progress were abolished."[68] Yet, as Elagin notes, although the Cultural Revolution had severe consequences, lowering musical and academic standards and stifling creative individuality, it did not permanently scar the conservatory. "The restoration of everything that had been demolished ... was not a formidable task, because the core of the organization remained. The faculty was unchanged.... The system of evaluating a student's progress and of examinations was reinstated." By the time Elagin entered the conservatory in 1934, peace and quiet had been restored and the troublesome Russian Association for Proletarian Musicians disbanded.[69] The traditional musical values of the Moscow Conservatory had been carefully preserved and continued to be passed on from faculty to students. Standards of performance were exceedingly high and failure in an examination resulted in automatic expulsion. Moreover, efforts to artificially proletarianize the conservatory had fallen into such disrepute that the Rabfak closed in 1936.

By 1932, the Cultural Revolution had spent itself in the Russian conservatories. The excesses of the previous five years were slowly remedied. Students with sterling proletarian credentials but dubious musical abilities gradually disappeared from the student body under the pressure of a renewed commitment to maintaining high, i.e., traditional, artistic standards. With encouragement from the Soviet state, the so-called Great Retreat brought a renewed effort to sustain the institutional and personal strengths of Russian music. The best traditions and greatest heroes of nineteenth-century Russian music were revived, while the structures, institutions, and principles developed by the Russian Musical Society were reclaimed to serve as the foundation for Soviet musical culture.[70]

In tracing the rise and fall of the Russian Musical Society, one glimpses the transformation of Russian musical culture from anxiously self-conscious of its status as an outpost of Western European artistic life to independent and self-confident, a full participant in some of the boldest musical experiments of the early twentieth century. Although the maturation of Russian composition is clearly important, it was the establishment of a broad network of institutions, associations, legal precedents, and social behaviors that created the infrastructure necessary to sustain and nurture an independent cultural life, first in the Russian Empire and subsequently in its successor state, the Soviet Union. The transformation of musical life, moreover, had its counterparts in other areas, such as theater and education. These processes, taken together, encouraged the circulation of ideas, the growth of a civic space, if not, perhaps, a civil society, and the development of a modern Russian cultural identity.

So strong was the cultural infrastructure and cultural identity created during the nineteenth century that the upheavals of revolution and civil war failed to disrupt it. The structures created by the Russian Musical Society and its counterparts provided the early Bolshevik state with a foundation from which to build the edifice of Soviet culture with its state-supported, "empire"-wide network of arts schools, theaters, performance halls, and publishing houses. The values promoted by the Society, of artistic professionalism and the broad cultivation of taste, resurfaced with a vengeance in the Soviet period as well. The Moscow and Leningrad conservatories and their provincial counterparts, all direct heirs of the institutions of the Russian

Musical Society, provided thousands of dedicated young musicians with explicitly professional training and virtually guaranteed employment. Ironically, it was in their Soviet incarnation that the Russian conservatories came closest to achieving the ideal of the nineteenth-century conservatory: a training school for truly professional musicians, not a finishing school for the bourgeoisie. Yet, the conservatism and resilience of the conservatories made the proletarianization or Sovietization of these institutions difficult and complex.

The network of educational institutions created by the Russian Musical Society thus displayed substantial internal stability in the face of politically motivated attempts to restructure them. Inevitably, Soviet conservatory and music school faculty, well into the 1930s, were the products of the Russian Musical Society's educational institutions. As these quintessentially bourgeois institutions attempted to redefine themselves in socialist terms, old debates reemerged. New Soviet music journals addressed an old question: for what purpose were musicians being trained? Despite strenuous attempts to proletarianize the student body, the conservatories remained bastions of the middle class. Eventually, even the female piano student reinsinuated herself into the conservatories. If the proletarians of the orchestral division now had increased political influence outside the conservatories, attempts to artificially enlarge that cohort had only eroded their musical authority within them. The musical elite remained, as before, concentrated in the bourgeois composition and piano departments. Efforts to enhance the social utility of the conservatories through the creation of teacher training programs fell short because of their low artistic prestige. Even the new initiatives for popular music education were not new at all; they merely continued or expanded on prerevolutionary formulas. Despite the gloss of radicalism offered by avant-garde experiments in both musical composition and institution-building during the 1920s and early 1930s, artistic traditions and institutional conservatism had preserved most of the prerevolutionary artistic heritage intact. The educational institutions of the Russian Musical Society had survived, albeit under new management. They survive to this day.

ABBREVIATIONS

DAMK	Derzhavnyi arkhiv mista Kyiva (State Archive of the city of Kiev)
RGALI	Rossiiskii gosudarstvennyi arkhiv literatury i iskusstva (Russian State Archive of Literature and Art)
RGIA	Rossiiskii gosudarstvennyi istoricheskii arkhiv (Russian State Historical Archive)
RIII	Rossiiskii institut istorii iskusstv (Russian Institute for the History of the Arts)
TsDAMLM	Tsentral'nyi derzhavnyi arkhiv-muzei literatury i mistestva (Central State Archive-Museum for Literature and Art)
TsGIA SPb	Tsentral'nyi gosudarstvennyi istoricheskii arkhiv Sankt-Peterburga (Central State Historical Archive of St. Petersburg)
TsGMMK	Tsentral'nyi gosudarstvennyi muzei muzykal'noi kul'tury im. M. I. Glinki (M. I. Glinka Central State Museum of Musical Culture)
DZh	*Damskii zhurnal*
MO	*Muzykal'noe obozrenie*
NV	*Novoe vremia*

RI	*Russkii invalid*
RMG	*Russkaia muzykal'naia gazeta*
SPV	*S.-Peterburgskie vedomosti*

NOTES

Introduction

1. P. Bebutov, "Piatidesiatiletie S.-Peterburgskoi konservatorii (putevyia zametki i lichnyia vpechatleniia)," *Kavkaz*, 29 December 1912.

2. Ibid.

3. On the impact of the Great Reforms, see Ben Eklof, John Bushnell, and Larissa Zakharova, eds., *Russia's Great Reforms, 1855–1881* (Bloomington, Ind., 1994); and Bruce Lincoln, *The Great Reforms: Autocracy, Bureaucracy, and the Politics of Change in Imperial Russia* (DeKalb, Ill., 1990).

4. I. F. Petrovskaia, "Metodologiia izucheniia istorii muzykal'noi kul'tury," in her *Muzykal'noe obrazovanie i muzykal'nye obshchestvennye organizatsii v Peterburge 1801–1917: entsiklopediia* (St. Petersburg, 1999), 353–57.

5. Louise McReynolds, *The News under Russia's Old Regime: The Development of a Mass Circulation Press* (Princeton, N.J., 1991); and Jeffrey Brooks, *When Russia Learned to Read: Literacy and Popular Literature, 1861–1917* (Princeton, N.J., 1985).

6. Leopold Haimson, "The Problem of Social Stability in Urban Russia, 1905–1917," parts 1 and 2, *Slavic Review* 23 (1964): 619–42; 24 (1965): 1–22.

7. Gregory L. Freeze, "The *Soslovie* (Estate) Paradigm and Russian Social History," *American Historical Review* 91 (1986): 11–36.

8. Elise Kimmerling Wirtschafter, *Social Identity in Imperial Russia* (DeKalb, Ill., 1997). See also her earlier study, *Structures of Society: Imperial Russia's "People of Various Ranks"* (DeKalb, 1994).

9. That historians in general have struggled with the Habermasian concept of the public sphere can be seen from their numerous attempts to define its parameters. See in particular Andrej Pinter, "Public Sphere and History: Historians' Response to Habermas on the 'Worth' of the Past," *Journal of Communication Inquiry* 28, no. 3 (July 2004): 217–32; Andreas Gestrich, "The Public Sphere and the Habermas Debate, *German History* 24, no. 3 (2006): 413–30; Dena Goodman, "Public Sphere and Private Life: Toward a Synthesis of Current Historiographical Approaches to the Old Regime," *History and*

Theory 31, no. 1 (February 1992): 1–20; and Harold Mah, "Phantasies of the Public Sphere: Rethinking the Habermas of Historians," *The Journal of Modern History* 72, no. 1 (March 2000): 153–82.

10. For recent examples of historians still-evolving efforts to grapple with the Russian public, see Thomas Porter and Thomas Pearson, "Historical Legacies and Democratic Prospects: The Emergence of a Civil Society in Twentieth-Century Russia," *The Soviet and Post-Soviet Review* 23, no. 1 (1996): 51–66; Michael C. Hickey, "Discourses of Public Identity and Liberalism in the February Revolution: Smolensk, Spring 1917," *Russian Review* 55, no. 4 (October 1996): 615–37; and Elizabeth A. Hachten, "In Service to Science and Society: Scientists and the Public in Late-Nineteenth-Century Russia," *Osiris*, 2nd Series, 17, Science and Civil Society (2002): 171–209.

11. See in particular Adele Lindenmeyr, *Poverty Is Not a Vice: Charity, Society, and the State in Imperial Russia* (Princeton, N.J., 1996); and Joseph Bradley, "Subjects into Citizens: Societies, Civil Society, and Autocracy in Tsarist Russia," *American Historical Review* 107 (2002): 1119, 1121–22.

12. Joseph Bradley, "Voluntary Associations, Civic Culture, and *Obshchestvennost'* in Moscow," in *Between Tsar and People: Educated Society and the Quest for Public Identity in Late Imperial Russia*, ed. Samuel D. Kassow, James L. West, and Edith W. Clowes (Princeton, N.J., 1991), 148.

13. Bradley, "Subjects into Citizens, 1119, 1121–22.

14. William Weber, "Toward a Dialogue between Historians and Musicologists," *Musica e storia* 1, no. 1 (1993): 7.

15. Julia L. Foulkes, "Review Essay: Social History and the Arts," *Journal of Social History* 39, no. 4 (Summer 2006): 1177.

16. Murray Frame, *School for Citizens: Theatre and Civil Society in Imperial Russia* (New Haven, Conn., 2006).

17. *Almanakh-Spravochnik: vsia teatral'no-muzykal'naia Rossiia, 1914–1915* (Petrograd, 1914), 56–62.

18. On class and modern concert culture, see William Weber, *Music and the Middle Class: The Social Structure of Concert Life in London, Paris, and Vienna* (New York, 1975).

19. See the classic study by Arthur Loesser, *Men, Women, and Pianos: A Social History* (New York, 1951). Also useful are Richard Leppert, *Music and Image: Domesticity, Ideology, and Socio-Cultural Formation in Eighteenth-Century England* (New York, 1988); and James Parakilas et al., *Piano Roles: Three Hundred Years of Life with the Piano* (New Haven, Conn., 2000). See also Cyril Ehrlich, *The Piano: A History*, rev. ed. (New York, 1990); and Dieter Hildebrandt, *Pianoforte: A Social History of the Piano*, trans. Harriet Goodman (New York, 1988).

20. The most important prerevolutionary commemorative histories of the RMO and its institutions are N. Kashkin, *Pervoe dvadtsatipiatiletie Moskovskoi konservatorii: istoricheskii ocherk* (Moscow, 1891); Nikolai Findeizen, *Ocherk deiatel'nosti S.-Peterburgskogo otdeleniia IRMO (1859–1909)* (St. Petersburg, 1909); A. I. Puzyrevskii, *Imperatorskoe russkoe muzykal'noe obshchestvo v pervye 50 let ego deiatel'nosti (1859–1909)* (St. Petersburg, 1909); N. D. Kashkin, *Moskovskoe otdelenie Imperatorskogo russkogo muzykal'nogo obshchestva: ocherk deiatel'nosti za piatidesiatiletie 1860–1910* (Moscow, 1910); and A. I. Puzyrevskii and L. A. Sakketti, *Ocherk piatidesiatiletiia deiatel'nosti S.-Peterburgskoi konservatorii* (St. Petersburg, 1912).

21. The lives and careers of Mikhail Glinka and Alexander Dargomyzhsky have been the subject of numerous scholarly studies. English-language scholarship includes, in addition to biographical works such as David Brown's *Mikhail Glinka: A Biographical and Critical Study* (New York, 1985 [1973]), a variety of specialized studies, such as Robert W. Oldani's "Sing Me Some Glinka or Dargomyzhsky," *History of European Ideas* 16, no. 4–6 (1993): 713–19; and Jennifer Baker's "Glinka's *A Life for the Tsar* and 'Official Nationality,'" *Renaissance and Modern Studies* 24 (1980): 92–114.

22. Puzyrevskii, *IRMO v pervye* 50 *let*, 3–6 and 45.

23. Yuri Olkhovsky, *Vladimir Stasov and Russian National Culture* (Ann Arbor, Mich., 1983). See also Elizabeth Valkenier, *Russian Realist Art: The State and Society; The Peredvizhniki and Their Tradition* (New York, 1989).

24. Richard Taruskin, "Others: A Mythology and a Demurrer (By Way of a Preface)," in his *Defining Russia Musically: Historical and Hermeneutical Essays* (Princeton, N.J., 1997), xiii–xiv.

25. Compare, for example, David Brown, *Musorgsky: His Life and Works* (New York, 2002); Caryl Emersen, *The Life of Musorgsky* (New York, 1999); and Richard Taruskin, *Musorgsky: Eight Essays and an Epilogue* (Princeton, N.J., 1993); Robert C. Ridenour, *Nationalism, Modernism, and Personal Rivalry in Nineteenth-Century Russian Music* (Ann Arbor, Mich., 1981).

26. A few examples will have to suffice. For the Imperial period, see Julie Buckler, *The Literary Lorgnette: Attending Opera in Imperial Russia* (Stanford, Calif., 2000); and Carolyn C. Dunlop, *The Russian Court Chapel Choir, 1767–1917*, Music Archive Publication, Series F, vol. 1 (Amsterdam, 2000). For the Soviet period, see Amy Nelson, *Music for the Revolution: Musicians and Power in Early Soviet Russia* (University Park, Pa., 2004); Kiril Tomoff, *Creative Union: The Professional Organization of Soviet Composers, 1939–1953* (Ithaca, N.Y., 2006); and Neil Edmunds, ed., *Soviet Music and Society under Lenin and Stalin: The Baton and the Sickle* (New York, 2004), as well as his earlier volume *The Soviet Proletarian Music Movement* (New York, 2000).

27. W. Bruce Lincoln, *Between Heaven and Hell: The Story of a Thousand Years of Artistic Life in Russia* (New York, 1998); Boris Gasparov, *Five Operas and a Symphony: Word and Music in Russian Culture* (New Haven, Conn., 2005). For another popular interpretation of Russian musical development, see Francis Maes, *A History of Russian Music from Kamarinskaya to Babi Yar* (Berkeley and Los Angeles, 2002).

28. Denis Lomtev, *Nemetskie muzykanty v Rossii: k istorii stanovleniia russkikh konservatorii* (Moscow, 1999); S. V. Belov, *Muzykal'noe izdatel'stvo P. I. Iurgensona* (St. Petersburg, 2001).

29. D. L. Lokshin, *Khorovoe penie v russkoe dorevoliutsionnoi i sovetskoi shkole* (Moscow, 1957); K. I. Shamaeva, *Muzykal'noe obrazovanie na Ukraine v pervoi polovine XIX veka* (Kiev, 1991); V. I. Adishchev, *Muzykal'noe vospitanie v kadetskikkh korpusakh Rossii (konets XIX—nachalo XX veka)* (Perm, 2000); and *Muzyka v zhenskikh institutakh Rossii kontsa XIX—nachala XX veka: teoriia i praktika obrazovaniia*; G. M. Kantor, L. V. Brazhnik, and V. I. Iakovlev, *Iz istorii muzykal'noi kul'tury i obrazovaniia v Kazani* (Kazan, 1993).

30. Key Soviet and post-Soviet studies of the conservatories include B. I. Zagurskii, *Kratkii ocherk istorii Leningradskoi konservatorii* (Leningrad, 1933); Iu. Kremlev, *Leningradskaia gosudarstvennaia konservatoriia, 1862–1937* (Moscow, 1938); L. S. Ginzburg, et al., eds., *Moskovskaia konservatoriia, 1866–1966* (Moscow, 1966); G. A. Pribegina, ed. and comp.,

Moskovskaia konservatoriia, 1866–1991 (Moscow, 1991); N. A. Mironova, *Moskovskaia konservatoriia: istoki (vospominaniia i dokumenty, fakty i kommentarii)* (Moscow, 1995). The celebratory tendencies of such publications are continued in more recent volumes, including E. S. Barutcheva, et al., comps., *Sankt-Peterburgskaia konservatoriia: dokumenty i materialy na fondov biblioteki i muzeia* (St. Petersburg, 2002); E. G. Sorokina, et al., eds., *Moskovskaia konservatoriia: materialy i dokumenty iz fondov MGK imeni P. I. Chaikovskogo i GTsMMK imeni M. I. Glinki* (Moscow, 2006); N. A. Mironova, ed., *Moskovskaia konservatoriia: ot istokov do nashikh dnei; istoriko-biograficheskii spravochnik* (Moscow, 2005); and M. S. Starcheus, *Moskovskaia konservatoriia: traditsii muzykal'nogo obrazovaniia, iskusstva i nauki, 1866–2006* (Moscow, 2006); as well as E. D. Ershova, et al., eds., *Iz istorii Saratovskoi konservatorii* (Saratov, 2004).

31. See, for example, N. N. Emelianova, *Muzykal'nye vechera: khronika muzykal'noi zhizni Tambovskogo kraia za 100 let* (Voronezh, 1977); B. S. Shteinpress, ed., *Iz muzykal'nogo proshlogo: sbornik statei*, vols. 1–2 (Moscow, 1965). More recent, and more theoretically sophisticated work includes G. P. Borisov, "Muzykal'naia kul'tura Ekaterinodara s nachala XIX veka po 1920 god" (Ph.D. diss., Rossiiskii institut iskusstvoznaniia, 1992); and M. P. Chernykh, "Muzykal'naia zhizn' Rostova-na-donu ot serediny XVIII do 20-kh godov XX stoletiia: puti razvitiia, osobennosti muzykal'nogo oklada" (Ph.D. diss., Rossiiskii institut iskusstvoznaniia, 1991). On *kraevedenie* as a discipline, see Emily D. Johnson, *How St. Petersburg Learned to Study Itself: The Russian Idea of Kraevedenie*, Studies of the Harriman Institute (University Park, Pa., 2006).

32. Michael Fend and Michel Noiray, eds., *Musical Education in Europe (1790–1914): Compositional, Institutional, and Political Challenges*, vol. 1 (Musical Life in Europe 1600–1900 Circulation, Institutions, Representation), (Berlin, 2005), 1.

33. Richard Stites, *Serfdom, Society, and the Arts in Imperial Russia: The Pleasure and the Power* (New Haven, 2005), esp. chaps. 2 and 3. See also Iu. Vl. Savel'eva's theoretically sophisticated study of music in St. Petersburg's cultural life, "Muzyka v prazdnichno-razvlekatel'noi kul'ture Peterburga pervoi treti XIX veka," (Kand. diss., Rossiiskii gosudarstvennyi universitet im. A. I. Gertsen, 2003).

34. The indispensible guide remains T. N. Livanova, *Muzykal'naia bibliografiia russkoi periodicheskoi pechati XIX veka*, vols. 1–6 (Moscow, 1960–1963). See also Gerald Seaman, "Contemporary Music as Revealed in Nineteenth-Century Russian Periodicals," *Revista de Musicología* 16, no. 3 (1993): 54–62; and "Nineteenth-Century Italian Opera as Seen in the Contemporary Russian Press," *Periodica musica: Newsletter of the Répertoire international de la presse musicale du XIX siècle* 6 (1988): 21–24.

Chapter One

1. See A. I. Puzyrevskii's claim that "in the first half of the nineteenth century, we hardly had music at all" in his commemorative history *IRMO v pervye 50 let*, 3–6.

2. I. F. Petrovskaia, *Kontsertnaia zhizn' Peterburga: muzyka v obshchestvennom i domashnem bytu; materialy dlia entsiklopedii "Muzykal'nyi Peterburg"* (St. Petersburg, 2000), 3. This short encyclopedia, along with Petrovskaia's earlier *Muzykal'noe obrazovanie i muzykal'nye obshchestvennye organizatsii v Peterburge 1801–1917: entsiklopediia* (St. Petersburg, 1999), provides an indispensible guide to musical life in late imperial St. Petersburg.

3. *Moskovskie vedomosti*, 26 February 1802.

4. On Russian theatrical life, see Murray Frame, *School for Citizens: Theatre and Civil Society in Imperial Russia* (New Haven, Conn., 2006); and Richard Stites, *Serfdom, Society, and the Arts in Imperial Russia: The Pleasure and the Power* (New Haven, 2005), esp. chap. 4.

5. On the role of serf musicians and actors, see Stites, *Serfdom, Society, and the Arts*, 71–84 and 238–43, and Priscilla Roosevelt, *Life on the Russian Country Estate: A Social and Cultural History* (New Haven, 1995), esp. 130–53.

6. *Moskovskie vedomosti*, 17 March 1806.

7. See E. K. Al'brekht, *Proshloe i nastoiashchee orkestra: ocherk sotsial'nogo polozheniia muzykantov* (St. Petersburg, 1886).

8. For a Russian view of the long-term consequences of enserfed musicians, see N. Findeizen, "Krepostnye muzykanty," *RMG*, no. 7 (1911): 177–81.

9. "Izvestiia vnutrenniia: iz Ufy, ot 10 fevralia," *Severnaia pochta*, 8 March 1811.

10. *Literaturnaia gazeta*, "Smes': Peterburgskaia khronika," 11 January 1845, 38.

11. Stites, *Serfdom, Society, and the Arts*, 57–63. See also an earlier version of this material in "The Domestic Muse: Music at Home in the Twilight of Serfdom," in *Intersections and Transpositions: Russian Music, Literature, and Society*, ed. Andrew Baruch Wachtel (Evanston, Ill., 1998), 187–205.

12. Iu. B. Aliev, "Muzykal'noe vospitanie," and L. A. Barenboim, "Muzykal'noe obrazovanie," in *Sovetskaia muzykal'naia entsiklopediia* (Moscow, 1976), 9: 755–58, 776–81.

13. For a detailed examination of the role of music in the formal education of the wellborn, see Shamaeva, *Muzykal'noe obrazovanie na Ukraine*, 82–164.

14. "Izvestiia vnutrenniia: iz Vladimira, ot 19 noiabria," *Severnaia pochta*, 4 December 1809.

15. "Iz Kazani, ot 14 iiunia," *SPV*, 4 August 1803. See also "Iz Penzy," *SPV*, 22 December 1803.

16. "Smes': muzykal'naia shkola," *SPV*, 20 October 1837.

17. Dobrozhelatel'nyi muzykant, "Kak u nas obuchaiut devits muzyke," *Literaturnoe pribavlenie k Nuvellistu*, no. 4 (1844): 2.

18. Carolyn C. Dunlop, *The Russian Court Chapel Choir, 1767–1917*, Music Archive Publication, Series F, vol. 1 (Amsterdam, 2000), 5–26.

19. Anton Rubinstein, *Literaturnoe nasledie*, ed. L.A. Barenboim (Moscow: Muzyka, 1983), 1: 70.

20. [A. F. L'vov], "Zapiski Alekseia Fedorovicha Lvova," *Russkii arkhiv* 4 (1884): 225–60 and 5 (1884): 65–114, referenced in Stites, "The Domestic Muse," 190.

21. Petrovskaia, *Kontsertnaia zhizn' Peterburga*, 73–74; Stites, *Serfdom, Society, and the Arts*, 58–59.

22. Stites, *Serfdom, Society, and the Arts*, 60.

23. A. M. Sokolova, "Kontsertnaia zhizn'," in Iu. V. Keldysh, et al., *Istoriia russkoi muzyki*, vol. 4 (Moscow, 1986), 276–80. See also Petrovskaia, *Kontsertnaia zhizn' Peterburga*, 58–60; L. V. Beliakaeva-Kazanskaia, *Siluety muzykal'nogo Peterburga* (St. Petersburg, 2001), 172–85; Iu. Kremlev, *Russkaia mysl' o muzyke: ocherki istorii russkoi muzykal'noi kritiki i estetiki v XIX veke*, vol. 1, *1825–1860* (Leningrad, 1954), 14–18; and Stites, *Serfdom, Society, and the Arts*, 63–71.

24. See T. Shcherbakova, *Mikhail i Matvei Viel'gorskie: ispolniteli, prosvetiteli, metsenaty* (Moscow, 1990), as well as Neil Cornwell, *V. F. Odoyevsky: His Life, Times, and Milieu* (Athens, Ohio, 1986), esp. 7–10 and 121–59; and Stuart Campbell, *V. F. Odoevsky and the*

Formation of Russian Musical Taste in the Nineteenth Century, Outstanding Dissertations in Music from British Universities (New York, 1989). On Odoevsky and the Wisdom-Lovers, see Andrzej Walicki, *A History of Russian Thought: From the Enlightenment to Marxism*, trans. Hilda Andrews-Rusiecka (Stanford, Calif., 1979), 74–80.

25. Eleonora Fradkina, *Zal dvorianskogo sobraniia: zametki o kontsertnoi zhizni Sankt-Peterburga* (St. Petersburg, 1994), 11.

26. P. Stolpianskii, *Muzyka i muzitsirovanie v starom Peterburge*, 2d ed. (Leningrad, 1989), 23, citing *Severnaia pchela*, 1848. Ironically, the hall, after extensive renovations over the years, is now praised for its superb acoustics. Fradkina, *Zal dvorianskogo sobraniia*, 16–17.

27. Beliakaeva-Kazanskaia, *Siluety muzykal'nogo Peterburga*, 125–28.

28. A. A. Gozenpud, *Dom Engel'gardta: iz istorii kontsertnoi zhizni Peterburga pervoi poloviny XIX veka* (St. Petersburg, 1992), 231–32.

29. N. V. Kukolnik, *Illiustratsiia*, 1846, vol. 2, no. 30, 474. Cited in Gozenpud, *Dom Engel'gardta*, 233.

30. *100-letnyi iubilei S.-Peterburgskogo filarmonicheskogo obshchestva, 1802–1902* (St. Petersburg, 1902), 10.

31. Boris Berezovskii, *Filarmonicheskoe obshchestvo Sankt-Peterburga: istoriia i sovremennost'* (St. Petersburg, 2002), 94–102, 113–28.

32. See Joseph Bradley, "Subjects into Citizens: Societies, Civil Society, and Autocracy in Tsarist Russia," *American Historical Review* 107 (2002): 1108–9.

33. Ilrn Vsl'eve, "O muzykal'noi akademii v Sankt-Peterburge," *DZh*, part 22, no. 10 (May 1828): 155. See also "Muzykal'naia akademiia," in Petrovskaia, *Muzykal'noe obrazovanie i muzykal'nye obshchestvennye organizatsii*, 172–73; and N. Findeizen, "Muzyka v Rus. obshchestv. zhizni nach. XIX v.," *RMG*, no. 48 (1900): 1177–78.

34. A. V. Nikitenko, "Dnevnik, 1826–1860," in *Moia povest' o samom sebe*, vol. 1 (St. Petersburg, 1904), 182–83.

35. Kh. G. [Modest Rezvoi], "Smes': bibliograficheskiia izvestiia," reprinted from *Khudozhestvennaia gazeta*, no. 10 (1841), in *SPV*, 4 July 1841.

36. D. V. Stasov, "Muzykal'nye vospominanii," *RMG*, 1909, no. 11: 291–92; no. 12: 325.

37. [Modest Rezvoi], "Smes': bibliograficheskiia izvestiia," *SPV*, 4 July 1841.

38. Pl[aton] Sm[irnovskii], "Peterburgskaia pis'ma," *Literaturnaia gazeta*, 17 February 1849, 112.

39. Nikolai Findeizen, *Ocherk deiatel'nosti S.-Peterburgskogo otdeleniia IRMO (1859–1909)* (St. Petersburg, 1909), 7.

40. Petrovskaia, *Muzykal'noe obrazovanie i muzykal'nye obshchestvennye organizatsii*, 134–36.

41. See A. S. Rozanov, *Muzykal'nyi Pavlovsk* (Leningrad, 1978), esp. 24–62; and N. F. Findeizen, *Pavlovskii muzykal'nyi vokzal: istoricheskii ocherk 1838–1912*, reprint ed. (St. Petersburg, 2005 [1912]), esp. 35–41.

42. "Kontserty," *Russkii pustynnik*, part 1, no. 9 (1817): 180–81. Emphasis in original.

43. Iu. Vl. Savel'eva, "Muzyka v prazdnichno-razvlekatel'noi kul'ture Peterburga pervoi treti XIX veka," (Kand. diss., Rossiiskii gosudarstvennyi universitet im. A. I. Gertsen, 2003), 124–25.

44. "Rossiia: bol'shoi kontsert v pol'zu invalidov," *RI*, 8 November 1813.

45. *Pribavlenie k zhurnalia Russkogo invalida*, 12 November 1813.

46. *RI*, 15 November 1813.

47. The concert collected 5,465 rubles, including 2,965 rubles in charitable donations. *RI*, "Rossiia: podrobnoe izchislenie dokhoda s kontserta dannogo zdes' v pol'zu invalidov," 22 November 1813.

48. "Smes': Kontserty," *Biblioteka dlia chteniia* 124 (April 1854): 221–22. On the Russian national anthem, see N. A. Soboleva, "Sozdanie gosudarstvennykh gimnov Rossiiskoi imperii i Sovetskogo soiuza," *Voprosy istorii* no. 2 (2005): 25–41, esp. 27–31; and "Iz istorii otechestvennykh gosudarstvennykh gimnov," *Otechestvennaia istoriia* no. 1 (2005): 3–21.

49. "O muzykal'nom vechere v dome gospozhi Annenkovoi i o kontserte v Blagorodnom sobranii, 9 i 13 aprelia," *DZh*, part 1, no. 5 (May 1823): 209–10.

50. "O blagotvoritel'nom kontserte v pol'zu postradavshikh ot navodneniia, dannom v dome Moskovskogo blagorodnogo sobraniia 7-go dekabria 1824," *DZh*, part 9, no. 1 (January 1825): 34, 36–37, 38–39.

51. "O muzykal'nom vechere v dome Eia P-va, Mar'i Ivanovny R.-Korsakovoi, 12 marta," *DZh*, part 18, no. 7 (April 1827): 43.

52. "O drugom muzykal'nom vechere dome Eia P-va, Mar'i Ivanovny R.-Korsakovoi, 27 Marta," *DZh*, part 18, no. 8 (April 1827): 101.

53. Liubitel' muzyki, "Moskovskie kontserty," *Moskovskii telegraf* 20, no. 8 (April 1828): 526.

54. "Muzykal'nye vechera v Blagorodnom sobranii," *DZh*, part 21, no. 5 (March 1828): 273–74.

55. Ab. Ir. [V. F. Odoevsky], "Muzykal'nyia nadezhdy," *Literaturnoe pribavlenie k russkomu invalidu*, 6 March 1837, 97.

56. Ab. Ir. [V. F. Odoevsky], "Smes': kontserty," *Literaturnoe pribavlenie k russkomu invalidu*, 20 March 1837, 118.

57. W. W. [V. F. Odoevsky], "Pis'ma v Moskvu o peterburgskikh kontsertakh, VII," *SPV*, 30 March 1839.

58. "Moskovskaia letopis': zhizn' v Moskve v fevrale 1846 goda," part 2, *Moskvitianin*, no. 3 (1846): 277.

59. X. X. [V. F. Odoevsky], "Fel'eton: peterburgskaia letopis'," *SPV*, 15 March 1850.

60. Stites, *Serfdom, Society, and the Arts*, 104–5.

61. V. G[aevskii]., "Fel'eton: Muzyka i blagotvoritel'nost'," *SPV*, 15 March 1850.

62. X. X. [V. F. Odoevsky], "Fel'eton: peterburgskaia letopis'," *SPV*, 14 March 1850. On *Kamarinskaia*, see Richard Taruskin, "How the Acorn Took Root: A Tale of Russia," *Nineteenth-Century Music* 6, no. 3 (Spring 1983): 189–212.

63. G[aevskii]., "Fel'eton," *SPV*, 15 March 1850.

64. Prokhozhii [V. F. Odoevsky?], "Fel'eton: O russkikh kontsertakh obshchestva poseshcheniia bednykh v muzykal'nom otnoshenii," *SPV*, 8 April 1850; and I. M[ann], "Fel'eton: peterburgskaia letopis'," *SPV*, 11 April 1850.

65. I. M[ann], "Peterburgskaia letopis'," *SPV*, 28 March 1850.

66. R., "Fel'eton: peterburgskaia letopis'," *SPV*, 2 April 1853.

67. [V. Timmom], "Peterburgskii kontsertnyi sezon 1853 goda," *Russkii khudozhestvennyi listok*, 1 May 1853.

68. "Smes': Kontserty," *Biblioteka dlia chteniia*, vol. 124 (April 1854): 212–15.

69. K. V., "Pis'ma dilletanta," *Severnyi tsvetok*, no. 1 (January 1857): 29–30.

70. "Fel'eton: peterburgskaia letopis'," *SPV*, 17 March 1857.

71. "Pis'mo iz Tobolska," *Moskovskii telegraf* 29, no. 20 (October 1829): 540–45.

72. N. Batalin, "Voronezh v muzykal'nom otnoshenii," *Moskvitianin*, part 4, no. 7 (1844): 183–85.

73. K-skii, "Kontserty v Kieve," *Literaturnaia gazeta*, 9 March 1844, 184, as well as ***, "Pis'mo k redaktoru (Kiev, 5 oktiabria)," *SPV*, 12 November 1843.

74. K-skii, "Kontserty v Kieve," 183–84.

75. "Fel'eton: muzykal'nyia novosti v Kieve (Pis'mo v redaktoru *Russkogo invalida*)," *RI*, 1 March 1847.

76. Ibid.

77. Ibid.

78. X., "Neskol'ko slov o kontsertakh," *Odesskii vestnik*, 25 March 1844.

79. R., "Smes': kontsert 16-go marta," *Odesskii vestnik*, 24 March 1845.

80. On the meaning of Beethoven in Russian cultural life, see Frederick W. Skinner, "A Shakespeare of the Masses: Beethoven and the Russian Intelligentsia, 1830–1914," *Canadian-American Slavic Studies/Revue canadienne-américaine d'etudes slaves* 38, no. 4 (Winter 2004): 409–29. See also Alessandra Comini, *The Changing Image of Beethoven: A Study in Mythmaking* (New York, 1987).

81. R., "Smes': kontsert 16-go marta."

82. Chuzhbinskii, "Fel'eton: dorozhnyia zapiski," *RI*, 16 July 1847.

83. "Vnutrenniia izvestiia: kazanskiia novosti," *Moskvitianin*, part 2, no. 4 (1848): 25–26.

84. Liubitel' muzyki, "Kazanskaia khronika: kontsert v zale universiteta, dannyi v pol'zu bednykh," *Kazanskie gubernskie vedomosti*, no. 12 (1846): chast' neoffitsial'naia.

85. See Lindenmeyr, *Poverty Is Not a Vice*, esp. chap. 5, "From Charity to Philanthropy: Private Charitable Associations and the Origins of Civil Society, 1762–1856," 99–119. On Odoevsky's charitable activities, see Cornwell, *V. F. Odoevsky*, 169–73.

86. Aleksandr Iablonskii suggests as much in his essay, "List v Rossii," *Sovetskaia muzyka* 50, no. 12 (1986): 99.

87. On the development of Russian music criticism, see Kremlev, *Russkaia mysl' o muzyke*, vol. 1.

88. See *SPV*, 31 January, 21 February, 1 March, 5 March, 10 March, 12 March, and 30 March 1839.

89. I. [A.] M[ann], "Fel'eton: peterburgskaia letopis'," *SPV*, 21 October 1851.

90. M. M. Ivanov, *Istoricheskii ocherk 50-letnei deiatel'nosti muzykal'nogo zhurnala "Nuvellist"* (St. Petersburg, 1889), 19–20, 27.

91. I. M., "Fel'eton: peterburgskaia letopis'," *SPV*, 31 January 1850. On the musical exercises at Moscow University, see I. M., "Fel'eton: pis'mo iz Moskvy," *SPV*, 17 March 1850.

92. "Peterburgskii vestnik," *Panteon* 25, book 1 (1856): 8.

93. A. Serov, "Kontsert Filarmonicheskogo obshchestva (9 dekabria)," *Muzykal'nyi i teatral'nyi vestnik*, 16 December 1856, 511.

Chapter Two

1. M. S. Starcheus, "Ob odnoi probleme istorii muzykal'nogo obrazovaniia i kul'tury Rossii kontsa XIX—nachala XX v.," in *Muzykal'noe obrazovanie: uroki istorii*, ed. V. V. Medushevskii, et al., (Moscow, 1991), 50–63.

2. RMO, *Proekt ustava Russkogo muzykal'nogo obshchestvo* (St. Petersburg, 1869), article 1.

3. See, for example, Philip S. Taylor, *Anton Rubinstein: A Life in Music* (Bloomington, Ind., 2007), esp. chap. 4, "The Founding of the Russian Musical Society and Russia's First Conservatory, 1859–67."

4. Dmitrii Stasov is the least well known of these figures. For a brief introduction to his life and legal career, see D. M. Legkii, "Dmitrii Vasil'evich Stasov," *Voprosy istorii*, no. 7 (2003): 54–73.

5. A. P. Shestopalov, "Velikaia kniaginia Elena Pavlovna," *Voprosy istorii*, no. 5 (2001): 73–94. See also Anna Schwarz (A. Shvarts), "Pokrovitel'stvo sem'i romanovykh muzykal'noi kul'ture Rossii v kontse XVIII—seredine XIX veka," *Novaia i noveishaia istoriia*, no. 6 (2001): 191–92. On the Obolensky family, see Dimitri Obolensky, *Bread of Exile: A Russian Family* (London, 1999).

6. Prince Dm. A. Obolensky, *Moi vospominaniia o velikoi kniagine Elene Pavlovne* (St. Petersburg, 1909), 58.

7. TsGIA SPb, fond 361, op. 11, d. 1, ll. 38–39 (*c.* 1872). On the state subsidy for the St. Petersburg Conservatory, see RGIA, fond 1152, op. 7, 1868, d. 877, ll. 2–6 and 10.

8. Rostislav [F. M. Tolstoy], "Po povodu vypusknykh ekzamenov proiskhodivshikh v dekabre 1866 g. v Sanktpeterburgskoi konservatorii," *Golos*, 25 January 1867.

9. RGIA, fond 1152, op. 7, 1868, d. 877, ll. 2–6; TsGIA SPb, fond 408, op. 1, d. 154, ll. 5–8 and 15–15v.

10. N. Kashkin, *Pervoe dvadtsatipiatiletie Moskovskoi konservatorii: istoricheskii ocherk* (Moscow, 1891), 24–25. See also A. I. Puzyrevskii and L. A. Sakketti, *Ocherk piatidesiatiletiia deiatel'nosti S.-Peterburgskoi konservatorii* (St. Petersburg, 1912), 40–42, as well as TsGIA SPb, fond 408, op. 1, d. 154, ll. 5–8 and 15–15v.

11. Joseph Bradley, "Subjects into Citizens: Societies, Civil Society, and Autocracy in Tsarist Russia," *American Historical Review* 107 (2002): 1110.

12. Robert C. Ridenour, *Nationalism, Modernism, and Personal Rivalry in Nineteenth-Century Russian Music* (Ann Arbor, Mich., 1981), 217. See also, George G. Weickhardt, "Music and Society in Russia, 1860s–1890s," *Canadian-American Slavic Studies/Revue canadienne-américaine d'etudes slaves* 30, no. 1 (1996): 57.

13. S.-Peterburgskoe otdelenie IRMO, *Otchet S.-Peterburgskogo otdeleniia IRMO za 1872/73 god* (St. Petersburg, 1874), 3.

14. TsGIA SPb, fond 361, op. 11, d. 75.

15. Obolensky, *Moi vospominaniia*, 71.

16. Anton Rubinstein, "Vospominaniia A. G. Rubinshteina," *Russkaia starina*, November 1889, 553.

17. Ibid., 553–54.

18. Ibid., 559.

19. Ibid., 557–58.

20. See Gregory L. Freeze, "The *Soslovie* (Estate) Paradigm and Russian Social History," *American Historical Review* 91 (1986), 14, 23, 26, 28–30, and Elise Kimmerling Wirtschafter, *Social Identity in Imperial Russia* (DeKalb, Ill., 1997), 169–71.

21. On Nikolai Rubinstein, see Lev Barenboim, *Nikolai Grigor'evich Rubenshtein: istoriia zhizni i deiatel'nosti* (Moscow, 1982). Gordon D. McQuere provides a useful introduction to

his educational and organizational roles in, "The Moscow Conservatory, 1866–1889: Nikolai Rubinstein and Sergei Taneev," *Canadian-American Slavic Studies/Revue canadienne-américaine d'etudes slaves* 34, no. 1 (Spring 2000): 36–49. Particularly interesting is the warm biographical sketch of the younger Rubinstein in N. A. Mironova, ed., *Moskovskaia konservatoriia: ot istokov do nashikh dnei; istoriko-biograficheskii spravochnik* (Moscow, 2005), 516–20.

22. S. P., "Moskovskaia letopis'," *SPV*, 21 December 1860.

23. *Zapiska direktorov Russkogo muzykal'nogo obshchestva v Moskve o neobkhodimosti obezpechit' prochnost' sushchestvovaniia sostoiashchei pri obshchestve konservatorii* (Moscow, 1870), 3.

24. By 1869–1870, membership levels stood at 1,093. *Zapiska direktorov RMO v Moskve*, 2–3.

25. On this issue, see William Weber, *Music and the Middle Class: The Social Structure of Concert Life in London, Paris, and Vienna* (New York, 1975). See also Elaine Leung-Wolf, "Women, Music, and the Salon Tradition: Its Cultural and Historical Significance in Parisian Musical Society" (DMA diss., University of Cincinnati, 1996).

26. Rostislav, "Po povodu vypusknykh ekzamenov," *Golos*, 25 January 1867.

27. V. D., "O deiatel'nosti otdelenii IRMO," *NV*, 4 July 1883.

28. RMO, *Proekt ustava RMO*, 1869, articles 4, 17–18, 20, 23–24, 25–39. The Main Directorate had begun to function somewhat earlier, in 1865, but the precise relationship of the Main Directorate to the branches, in particular to the St. Petersburg RMO, remained ill-defined. It was only with the new charter that the structure of the Society was finalized. See, Ridenour, *Nationalism, Modernism, and Personal Rivalry*, 51 and Taylor, *Anton Rubinstein*, 112–13.

29. RMO, *Proekt ustava Russkogo muzykal'nogo obshchestva* (St. Petersburg, 1873), chap. 1, arts. 2 and 12, chap. 5, art. 64.

30. RMO, *Ustav Imperatorskogo russkogo muzykal'nogo obshchestva* ([St. Petersburg], 1873), articles 1–2.

31. T. Vladimirov, "Neskol'ko slov po sluchaiu otkrytiia Russkogo muzykal'nogo obshchestva v S. Peterburge," *Severnyi tsvetok*, no. 28 (11 July 1859): 22–24.

32. A. Serov, "Pervyi vecher Russkogo muzykal'nogo obshchestva (23 noiabria)," *Teatral'nyi i muzykal'nyi vestnik*, no. 47 (29 November 1859): 463–65.

33. T. Vladimirov, "Pis'ma v provintsiiu," *Severnyi tsvetok*, no. 50 (12 December 1859): 382–83.

34. See Marina Frolova-Walker, *Russian Music and Nationalism: From Glinka to Stalin* (New Haven, Conn., 2007); and Richard Taruskin, "Some Thoughts on the History and Historiography of Russian Music," *The Journal of Musicology* 3, no. 4 (Autumn 1984): 329–37.

35. James H. Johnson, *Listening in Paris: A Cultural History* (Berkeley and Los Angeles, 1995), 230–32. On the difficulty of disciplining Russian audiences, see Ella Fradkina, "Zal Dvorianskogo sobraniia: zametki o kontsertnoi zhizni S.-Peterburga 1839–1914 gg.," *Muzykal'naia akademiia* no. 2 (1994): 212–14.

36. Nekto, "Fel'eton: i to i se," *RI*, 13 December 1859.

37. Ridenour, *Nationalism, Modernism, and Personal Rivalry*, 81–85.

38. "Fel'eton: peterburgskaia letopis," *SPV*, 20 December 1859.

39. P-Na, "Peterburgskie zametki," *Severnyi tsvetok*, no. 1 (2 January 1860): 3.

40. On the Slavophile-Westernizer debates, see Andrzej Walicki, *The Slavophile Controversy: History of a Conservative Utopia in Nineteenth-Century Russia*, trans. Hilda

Andrews-Rusiecka (New York, 1975); and Susanna Rabow-Edling, *Slavophile Thought and the Politics of Cultural Nationalism* (Albany, N.Y., 2006). See also Ridenour, *Nationalism, Modernism, and Personal Rivalry*, 79–80, on the Slavophile overtones of Balakirev's nationalism, as well as Frolova-Walker, *Russian Music and Nationalism*, esp. 11–18 and 42–46.

41. "Liubitelia muzyki," *Iskra*, 8 January 1860, 20.

42. "Smes': obshchestvennaia zhizn' v Peterburge," *Russkoe slovo*, no. 1 (January 1860): 115–16.

43. Ibid.

44. "Sovremennoe obozrenie: peterburgskaia letopis'," *Svetoch*, book 1 (1860): 93–94. Emphasis in original.

45. Ridenour, *Nationalism, Modernism, and Personal Rivalry*, 81–85.

46. Rubinstein, "Vospominaniia," 555, 559–60.

47. "Fel'eton: peterburgskaia letopis'," *SPV*, 29 December 1859.

48. See, for example, A. Sas, "Za i protiv: S.-Peterburgskaia muzykal'naia konservatoriia," *Golos*, 27 July 1864; and "Publichnyi vecher uchashchikhsia muzykal'nykh klassov Odesskogo otdeleniia IRMO," *Novorossiiskii telegraf*, 3 May 1893.

49. "Smes': obshchestvennaia zhizn' v Peterburge," *Russkoe slovo*, no. 2 (February 1859): 26–27.

50. Korrespondent, "Fel'eton: moskovskaia khronika," *RI*, 19 March 1860.

51. Nekto, "Fel'eton: i to i se," *RI*, 1860, no. 64, 22 March, 253–54.

52. "Domashnyi kontsert," *Syn otechestva*, 31 May 1864, no. 22, 356.

53. E. Moller, "Smes': obshchestvennaia zhizn' v Peterburge," *Russkoe slovo*, no. 4 (April 1860): 154.

54. Ridenour, *Nationalism, Modernism, and Personal Rivalry*, 76–80.

55. "Pis'ma iz Peterburga," *Illiustratsiia*, 11 February 1860, 91.

56. The two most prominent musical publishing houses, those of P. I. Iurgenson in Moscow and V. V. Bessel and Co. in St. Petersburg, were both connected to the Russian Musical Society. Vasilii Vasilievich Bessel, cofounder of the Bessel publishing empire, was a member of the first graduating class of the St. Petersburg Conservatory. Iurgenson enjoyed a particular closeness with Nikolai Rubinstein and served as a member of the board of the Moscow branch for more than thirty years. S. V. Belov, *Muzykal'noe izdatel'stvo P.I. Iurgensona* (St. Petersburg, 2001), 22–23. See also N. F. Findeizen, *Vasilii Vasil'evich Bessel': ocherk ego muzykal'no-obshchestvennoi deiatel'nosti* (St. Petersburg, 1909).

57. V. Bessel, "Po povodu otcheta S.-Peterburgskogo otdeleniia Imperatorskogo russkogo muzykal'nogo obshchestva za 1884/5 g.," *MO*, no. 14 (4 January 1886): 110–12.

58. TsGIA SPb, fond 408, op. 1, d. 538, ll. 9–16v.

Chapter 3

1. See, for example, Tim Hays, "Development of the Music Conservatory in Europe and the United States," *Journal of the Midwest History of Education Society* 23 (1996): esp. 4 and 8; and David Wright, "The South Kensington Music Schools and the Development of the British Conservatoire in the Late Nineteenth Century," *Journal of the Royal Musical Association* 130, no. 2 (2005): 236–82.

2. Compare traditional studies such as George M. Logan, *The Indiana University School of Music: A History* (Bloomington, Ind., 2000) with recent dissertations by Maria

M. Chow, "Representing China Musically: A Chinese Conservatory and China's Musical Modernity, 1900–1937" (Ph.D. diss., University of Chicago, 2005); and Emmanuel Hondré, "L'établissement des succursales du Conservatoire de musique de Paris, de la Restauration à la Monarchie de Juillet: un exemple de decentralization artistique" (Ph.D. diss., Université de Tours, 2001), as well as works more broadly interested in the conservatory as a social institution, such as Jane Fulcher's *French Cultural Politics and Music: From the Dreyfuss Affair to the First World War* (New York, 1999).

3. A. Rubinstein, "O muzyke v Rossii," *Vek*, no. 1 (1861): 33–37.

4. As will be discussed in chapter 6, state subsidies covered only a small portion of the conservatories' operating budgets. TsGIA SPb, fond 361, op. 11, d. 618.

5. Robert C. Ridenour, *Nationalism, Modernism, and Personal Rivalry in Nineteenth-Century Russian Music* (Ann Arbor, Mich., 1981), 36. Anton Rubinstein, "Vospominaniia A. G. Rubinshteina," *Russkaia starina*, November 1889.

6. Anton Rubinstein, "Vospominaniia A. G. Rubinshteina," *Russkaia starina*, November 1889, 558.

7. On the Leipzig Conservatory and Mendelssohn's complex role within it, see Leonard M. Phillips, "The Leipzig Conservatory, 1843–1881" (Ph.D. diss., Indiana University, 1979) 77–80, 84–89, 103–7, 109–16.

8. Rubinstein, "Vospominaniia," 560–61.

9. See Philip S. Taylor, *Anton Rubinstein: A Life in Music* (Bloomington, Ind., 2007), chap. 4, "The Founding of the Russian Musical Society and Russia's First Conservatory, 1859–67, 82–122.

10. K., "Russkaia konservatoriia," *Russkii listok*, 5 August 1862.

11. *Syn otechestva*, "Listok," 9 May 1862 and 21 July 1862.

12. K., "Russkaia konservatoriia," *Russkii listok*, 5 August 1862, no. 30, 258.

13. Ibid.

14. "Fel'eton," *Russkii mir*, no. 44 (10 November 1862): 812.

15. On Russian Germans in Russian musical life, see Denis Lomtev, *Nemetskie muzykanty v Rossii: k istorii stanovleniia russkikh konservatorii* (Moscow, 1999), esp. chaps. 3–4, 98–163, as well as his illustrated popular volume, *U istokov nemetskie muzykanty v Rossii: k istorii stanovleniia rossiiskikh konservatorii* (St. Petersburg, 1999).

16. Auer's autobiography is an indispensable if not entirely trustworthy account of Russian musical life. Leopold Auer, *My Long Life in Music* (New York, 1923).

17. N. Mel'gunov, "Iz kakikh sredstv uchredit russkuiu konservatoriiu muzyki?" *Nashe vremia*, 22 January 1861.

18. N., "Otkrytie Moskovskoi konservatorii," *Sovremennaia letopis'*, no. 30 (4 September 1866): 2–4. On the opening festivities of the Moscow Conservatory see also Omega, "Pis'mo iz Moskvy," *RI*, no. 226, 1866.

19. Ridenour, *Nationalism, Modernism, and Personal Rivalry*, 214–18.

20. *Moskovskie vedomosti*, "Moskva, 22-go fevralia," 23 February 1872.

21. M. R[appaport]., "Teatral'naia letopis'," *Syn otechestva*, 22 November 1862.

22. TsGIA SPb, fond 361, op. 11, d. 4, 27 December 1864–15 June 1869, ll. 43–47, November 1868. The dominance of female students in the Moscow Conservatory was even more striking, accounting for roughly two-thirds of the student body at its opening in 1866. TsGIA SPb, fond 408, op. 1, d. 538, ll. 26v–28, 32v–33, and 251–56. In Stockholm, by contrast, the conservatory had approximately 180 students in 1900, of

which 110 were male and 70 female.). Margaret Myers, "Blowing Her Own Trumpet: European Ladies' Orchestras and Other Women Musicians 1870–1950 in Sweden" (Ph.D. diss., Göteborg University, 1993), 60, table 3.

23. "Vsednevnaia zhizn'," *Golos*, 8 September 1863.

24. TsGIA SPb, fond 361, op. 11, d. 4, ll. 95–100.

25. V. A., "Iz vospominanii o N. G. Rubinshteine," *Russkii arkhiv*, book 3, no. 11 (1897): 441.

26. Ibid., 442.

27. A. Nezhdanova, "Konservatoriia," in *Vospominaniia o Moskovskoi konservatorii*, comps. E. N. Alekseeva and G. A. Pribegina (Moscow, 1966), 159–63.

28. RMO, *Ustav muzykal'nogo uchilishcha pri Russkom muzykal'nom obshchestve* ([St. Petersburg], 1861), article 9.

29. RMO, *Ustav konservatorii RMO* (St. Petersburg, 1878), chapter 4, article 56. On the 1878 charter, see also RGIA, fond 1149, op. 9, 1878, d. 133 and fond 1284, op. 223, d. 4a, l. 73.

30. See, for example, Moskovskoe otdelenie IRMO, *Usloviia dlia priema i pravila dlia postupleniia v Moskovskuiu konservatoriiu* (Moscow, 1886).

31. Ibid., 8–9.

32. See "Khronika muzykal'no-uchebnykh zavedenii," *RMG*, no. 43 (1907): 981, on the news that the Moscow Conservatory would not be allowed to admit any Jews that year.

33. Application and admissions data for the Moscow Conservatory, TsGIA SPb, f. 408, op. 1, d. 559, ll. 97–98 and 410–12:

1910–1911 acad. year (applied/admitted)		1913–1914 acad. year (applied/took exam/admitted)	
Piano	170/82	Piano	226/182/88
Voice	130/39	Voice	188/154/48
Theory	8/4	Theory	8/6/3
Strings	46/26	Strings	63/47/29
Winds	24/16	Winds	40/32/17
Harp	3/2	Harp	1/1/1
TOTAL	381/169	TOTAL	524/422/186

34. S.-Peterburgskoe otdelenie IRMO, *Usloviia priema v S.-Peterburgskuiu konservatoriiu Imperatorskogo russkogo muzykal'nogo obshchestva i izvlechenie iz pravil konservatorii* (St. Petersburg, 1908), 9–10.

35. Ibid., 10–11.

36. Ia. Vitol, "Gody ucheniia," in *Leningradskaia konservatoriia v vospominaniiakh*, 2d ed., vol. 1., eds. G. G. Tigranov, et al. (Leningrad, 1987), 24–25.

37. TsGIA SPb, fond 361, op. 11, d. 167, ll. 12, 13, 14–15.

38. Henry Kingsbury, *Music, Talent, and Performance: A Conservatory Cultural System* (Philadelphia, 1988), 76–80.

39. "Muzykal'nye zametki," *SPV*, 20 December 1866.

40. "Peterburgskiia pis'ma: pervyi vstupitel'nyi pansion g-zhi Petrovoi," *Illiustrirovannaia gazeta*, 15 June 1872, 362–63. See also "Teatral'noe ekho," *Peterburgskaia gazeta*, 31 August 1879.

41. S.-Peterburgskoe otdelenie IRMO, *Usloviia priema v S.-Peterburgskuiu konservatoriiu* (1908), 12–16.

42. For a representative example of such criticisms, see M. R., "Ekzameny v S.-Peterburgskoi konservatorii," *Russkii mir*, 8 May 1872.

43. TsGIA fond 361, op. 11, d. 618, ll. 58–59 and 60–61. This document includes data on the new provincial conservatories in Odessa, Saratov, and Kiev, as well as the St. Petersburg and Moscow conservatories.

44. S.-Peterburgskoe otdelenie IRMO, *Usloviia priema*, 12–16. Both auditors and probationary students were normally excluded from consideration for either half or full scholarships. Foreign citizens were excluded and women who married lost their eligibility.

45. Peterburgskaia konservatoriia, *Polozheniia po Sanktpeterburgskoi konservatorii RMO* (St. Petersburg, 1887), article 33, as well as RGIA, fond 1284, op. 223, d. 115, 1889, and TsGIA SPb, fond 361, op. 11, d. 217.

46. See for example, TsGIA SPb, fond 408, op. 1, d. 328, l. 133.

47. S.-Peterburgskoe otdelenie IRMO, *Usloviia priema*, 3, 5–6.

48. A. N. Amfiteatrova-Levitskaia, "Vospominaniia," in Alekseeva and Pribegina, *Vospominaniia o Moskovskoi konservatorii*, 82, 86–87.

49. S.-Peterburgskoe otdelenie IRMO, *Usloviia priema*, 4–5. See also *Usloviia priema v Saratovskuiu konservatoriiu IRMO i izvlechenie iz pravil konservatorii* (Saratov, 1912), 4–5.

50. The Ministry of Education, however, did not recognize these "scientific" classes as equivalent to a regular secondary education. TsGIA SPb, fond 361, op. 11, d. 174, ll. 1–2, and 5. See also, "Iz instruktsii ili polozhenii po Peterburgskoi konservatorii, sostavlennykh dlia rukovodstva uchebnoi i khoziaistvennoi zhizn'iu, 1865–1866 gg; o vydavaemykh konservatorieiu diplomakh, attestatakh i medalakh," esp. article 1, in A. L. Birkengof, et al., compilers, *Iz istorii Leningradskoi konservatorii: materialy i dokumenty,* 1862–1917 (Leningrad, 1964), 36–37.

51. "Programma obiazatel'nogo kursa istorii muzyki, sostavlennaia L. A. Sakketti," (1883–1884) and "Programma spetsial'nogo dvukhgodichnogo kursa istorii muzyki, sostavlennaia L.A. Sakketti," (1885–1886), both in Birkengof, et al., *Iz istorii Leningradskoi konservatorii*, 109–10 and 111–16.

52. TsGIA SPb, fond 408, op. 1, d. 137, l. 9, cited in Birkengof, et al., *Iz istorii Leningradskoi konservatorii*, 161. On conservatory student evenings in St. Petersburg, see "Kontserty uchashchikhsia i opernye postanovki," in ibid., 158–98.

53. "Iz protokola zasedaniia soveta professorov o poriadke provedeniia ekzamenov," (1862); "Iz protokola zasedaniia soveta professorov ob ekzamenatsionnykh trebovaniiakh dlia okanchivaiushchikh v sviazi s pervym vypuskom," (18 September 1865); and "Iz protokola zasedaniia soveta professorov o poriadke provedeniia vypusknogo publichnogo ekzamena," (7 September 1866) in Birkengof, et al., *Iz istorii Leningradskoi konservatorii*, 128–39.

54. Rostislav [F. M. Tolstoy], "Po povodu vypusknykh ekzamenov proiskhodivshikh v dekabre 1866 g. v Sanktpeterburgskoi konservatorii," *Golos*, 25 January 1867.

55. "Ekzameny v S.-Peterburgskoi konservatorii," *Literaturnoe pribavlenie k Nuvellistu*, March 1867, 20–21.

56. *** [Cesar Cui], "Muzykal'nyia zametki," *SPV*, 6 October 1870.

57. *** [Cesar Cui], *SPV*, 22 September 1871.

58. Aleksandr Famintsyn, "Sanktpeterburgskaia konservatoriia i g. Zaremba," *Golos*, 2 October 1871.

59. Amfiteatrova-Levitskaia, "Vospominaniia," 109.

60. Birkengof, et al., *Iz istorii Leningradskoi konservatorii*, 163, citing S.-Peterburgskoe otdelenie RMO, *Otchet... za 1876/77 g.*, (St. Petersburg, [1877]), xi, 101.

61. *Golos*, "Muzykal'nye zametki," 10 February 1880.

62. ***, "Khronika: publichnyi vecher uchenikov konservatorii," *MO*, no. 6 (31 October 1885): 41–42.

63. Programs of student performances of the St. Petersburg Conservatory are collected in Birkengof, et al., *Iz istorii Leningradskoi konservatorii*, 158–87. For graduation requirements, see, in the same volume, "Iz protokola zasedaniia spetsial'noi komissii po otdelu igry na fortepiano o trebovaniiakh dlia okanchivaiushchikh," (18 October 1912), 155–56 (derived from TsGIA SPb, fond 361, op. 11, d. 498, ll. 30–31v). On concerns about the student repertoire, see TsGIA SPb, fond 408, op. 1, d. 833, ll. 10–14 and d. 710, ll. 46–46v, 47–55, and 20–36.

64. ***, "Khronika: publichnyi vecher uchenikov konservatorii," *MO*, no. 6 (31 October 1885): 41–42.

65. TsGIA SPb, fond 361, op. 11, d. 5, ll. 12–12v, 13–14, 15–16, 22–22v, and 23–24. See also A. I. Puzyrevskii and L. A. Sakketti, *Ocherk piatidesiatiletiia deiatel'nosti S.-Peterburgskoi konservatorii* (St. Petersburg, 1912), 30–32.

66. L'homme qui rit, "Voskresnaia beseda (gorod i konservatoriia)," *SPV*, 6 November 1877.

67. TsGIA SPb, fond 361, op. 11, d. 346, ll. 1–2.

68. "Istoriia postroiki S.-Peterburgskoi konservatorii," *RMG* 1897 (December): 1797–1799.

69. RGIA, fond 1152, op. 12, 1897, d. 55, ll. 41–52.

70. RGIA fond 1152, op. 12, no. 489, esp. ll. 13–14 and 24–27.

71. "Otkrytie konservatorii," *Novosti i birzhevaia gazeta*, 13 November 1896. On Cui's ironic presence, see V. Baskin, "Razmyshlenie u paradnogo pod'ezda novoi konservatorii," *Teatr i iskusstvo*, no. 2 (1897): 24–25.

72. RGIA, fond 1152, op. 11, 1894, d. 202, esp. ll. 36–38.

73. Kashkin, *Moskovskoe otdelenie IRMO*, 60–63. See also Moskovskoe otdelenie IRMO, *Ocherk po postroike i torzhestvennomu otkrytiiu zdaniia konservatorii* (Moscow, 1905).

74. Moskovskoe otdelenie IRMO, *Ocherk po postroike*, appendix, 7.

75. Ibid., 15–16.

76. Bruno Nettl, *Heartland Excursions: Ethnomusicological Reflections on Schools of Music*, Music in American Life (Champaign, Ill., 1995), 16–19.

77. Moskovskoe otdelenie IRMO, *Ocherk po postroike*, 8–9.

78. Ibid., 16 and 23.

79. Ibid., 10.

80. Evgenii Al'brekht, *S.-Peterburgskaia konservatoriia* (St. Petersburg, 1891), 3–4. See also an earlier version, E. Al'brekht, "Neskol'ko slov o nashikh konservatoriiakh," *Sufler*, no. 31 (1882).

81. Al'brekht, *S.-Peterburgskaia konservatoriia*, 10–11.

82. Ibid., esp. 14, 18–20.
83. "Sovremennoe iskusstvo," *Russkaia mysl'*, book 3 (1895): 231–32.
84. TsGIA SPb, fond 408, op. 1, d. 356, ll. 216–18.
85. TsGIA SPb, fond 408, op. 1, d. 538, ll. 288–90.
86. TsGIA SPb, fond 408, op. 1, d. 833, ll. 10–14.
87. TsGIA SPb, fond 408, op. 1, d. 824, ll. 3–3v and 6–6v.

Chapter 4

1. A. Rubinstein, "O muzyke v Rossii," *Vek*, no. 1 (1861).

2. N. Melgunov, "Iz kakikh sredstv uchredit' russkuiu konservatoriiu muzyki," *Nashe vremia*, 22 January 1861.

3. Samuel D. Kassow, James L. West, and Edith W. Clowes, "Introduction: The Problem of the Middle in Late Imperial Russian Society," in *Between Tsar and People: Educated Society and the Quest for Public Identity in Late Imperial Russia* (Princeton, N.J., 1991), 4–5.

4. Kendall E. Bailes, "Reflections on Russian Professions," in *Russia's Missing Middle Class: The Professions in Russian History*, ed. Harley Balzer (Armonk, N.Y., 1996), 42–43.

5. On the European musical profession, see in particular: Cyril Ehrlich, *The Music Profession in Britain since the Eighteenth Century: A Social History* (Oxford, UK, 1985); Deborah Adams Rohr, "A Profession of Artisans: The Careers and Social Status of British Musicians, 1750–1850" (Ph.D. diss., University of Pennsylvania, 1983); Paula Gillett, *Musical Women in England, 1870–1914: "Encroaching on All Man's Privileges"* (New York, 2000); and Helen H. Metzelaar, *From Private to Public Spheres: Exploring Women's Role in Dutch Musical Life from c. 1700 to c. 1800 and Three Case Studies* (Utrecht, 1999).

6. See, for example, Leonard Phillips, "The Leipzig Conservatory, 1843–1881" (Ph.D. diss., Indiana University, 1979), esp. 24–25, 31–35, 101, and 221–26.

7. See for example, Fanny Raymond Ritter, *Woman as a Musician: An Art-Historical Study* (London, 1877); John Towers, *Woman in Music* (Winchester, Va., 1918); George P. Upton, *Woman in Music*, 4th ed. (Chicago, 1892 [1886]); and Arthur Elson, *Woman's Work in Music: Being an Account of Her Influence...* (Boston, 1904).

8. Anton Rubinstein, *Autobiography of Anton Rubinstein, 1829–1889*, trans. Aline Delano (Boston, 1890), 90–93.

9. Rubinstein, "O muzyke v Rossii."

10. Ark. R-kh-m-n-v, "Stepnoi otgolosok na stat'iu g. Rubinshteina 'O muzyke v Rossii,'" *Russkii mir*, no. 56 (1861): 956–57. Rakhmaninov was a particularly brilliant example of the noble amateur; he was a student of John Field, a collector of folk songs, and, eventually, the grandfather of Sergei Rakhmaninov.

11. RMO, *Ustav muzykal'nogo uchilishcha pri Russkom muzykal'nom obshchestve.*

12. Elizabeth Valkenier, *Russian Realist Art: The State and Society; The Peredvizhniki and Their Tradition* (New York, 1989), 3–10.

13. RGIA, fond 1149, op. 11, 1894, d. 5, l. 2 (p. 1).

14. Rubinstein, "O muzyke v Rossii."

15. TsGIA SPb, fond 361, op. 11, d. 5, l. 51. An additional five students graduated with a certificate (*attestat*) in their applied subject only.

16. TsGIA SPb, fond 361, op. 11, d. 5, ll. 54 and 77. RGIA, fond 1149, op. 11, 1894, d. 5, ll. 4–8.

17. RGIA, fond 1284, op. 223, d. 4a, ll. 71–84, 127–28.

18. RGIA, fond 1149, op. 9, 1878, d. 133 and fond 1284, op. 223, d. 4a, l. 73.

19. RMO, *Ustav konservatorii RMO* (St. Petersburg, 1878), article 9.

20. RGIA, fond 1284, op. 223, 1883, d. 29, ll. 2–15.

21. Peterburgskaia konservatoriia, *Polozheniia po Sanktpeterburgskoi konservatorii RMO* (St. Petersburg, 1887).

22. TsGIA SPb, fond 361, op. 11, d. 204, ll. 1–6, 9–10, and 22–23.

23. TsGIA SPb, fond 361, op. 11, d. 237, ll. 1–2.

24. Bailes, "Reflections on Russian Professions," 44–45.

25. TsGIA SPb, fond 361, op. 11, d. 221, l. 21v–22v.

26. TsGIA SPb, fond 361, op. 11, d. 217, ll. 8–24 and 46–79. Citation is from margin comments on l. 77v.

27. TsGIA SPb, fond 361, op. 11, d. 174, ll. 1–2, 5. See also RGIA, fond 1284, op. 223, 1897, group A, d. 23, ll. 1–5.

28. TsGIA SPb, fond 408, op. 1, d. 311, ll. 38–39v.

29. RGIA, fond 1149, op. 11, 1894, d. 5, l. 2v–3.

30. Ibid., l. 12 v.

31. RGIA, fond 1149, op. 13, 1902, d. 165, l. 7–7v, 10–11, and 21–24v.

32. The School of the Moscow Philharmonic Society also was able to award its students and graduates some of these rights.

33. Gillett, *Musical Women in England*, 190–91.

34. DAMK fond 176, op. 1, d. 238, ll. 107–151. DAMK fond 297, op. 1, d. 10, ll. 2 and 4, d. 78, ll. 3–5, d. 106, ll. 3–4, and d. 107, ll. 1–2.

35. On the "piano girl," see Judith Tick, "Passed Away Is the Piano Girl: Changes in American Musical Life, 1870–1900," in *Women Making Music: The Western Art Tradition, 1150–1950*, eds. Jane M. Bowers and Judith Tick (Urbana, Ill., 1986), 325–48.

36. On the visual representation of the sexual anxieties attached to young women's music making, see Richard Leppert, *The Sight of Sound: Music, Representation, and the History of the Body* (Berkeley and Los Angeles, 1993), 119–87.

37. *Terskiia vedomosti*, "Kopii s protokolov popechitel'nogo soveta Vladikavkazskoi Ol'ginskoi zhenskoi gimnazii," 5 March 1875; B., "Po povodu obucheniia muzyke v Vladikavkazskoi Ol'ginskoi zhenskoi gimnazii," *Terskiia vedomosti*, 12 March 1875; Announcement from head of women's gymnasia, *Terskiia vedomosti*, 19 March 1875; D., "Neskol'ko slov o vvedenii igry na skripke v Vladikavkazskoi Ol'ginskoi zhenskoi gimnazii," *Terskiia vedomosti*, 9 April 1875; Editorial, *Terskiia vedomosti*, 9 April 1875; and B. "Eshche po povodu skripki," *Terskiia vedomosti*, 16 April 1875.

38. Ehrlich, *The Music Profession in Britain*, 102.

39. TsGIA SPb, fond 408, op. 1, d. 263, ll. 35–39.

40. K. Ed. Veber, *Kratkii ocherk sovremennogo sostoianiia muzykal'nogo obrazovaniia v Rossii* (Moscow, 1885), 6.

41. Nikolai Chernyshevsky, *What Is to Be Done?* trans. Michael R. Katz, annotated by William G. Wagner (Ithaca, N.Y., 1989). On women's exploitation of the changing power dynamics within the family, see Beatrice Farnsworth, "The Litigious Daughter-in-Law: Family Relations in Rural Russia in the Second Half of the

Nineteenth Century," *Slavic Review* 45, no. 1 (Spring 1986): 49–64. The classic study of the changing role of women in Russian society is Richard Stites, *The Women's Liberation Movement in Russia: Feminism, Nihilism, and Bolshevism, 1860–1930* (Princeton, N.J., 1978). See also Barbara Alpern Engel, *Mothers and Daughters: Women of the Intelligentsia in Nineteenth Century Russia* (Evanston, Ill., 2000). On women's desire for education, see Christine Johanson's *Women's Struggle for Higher Education in Russia, 1855–1900* (Montreal, 1987). For a more intimate portrait of the experiences of Russian women during this period of change, see Praskovia Tatlina, "Reminiscences," in Toby W. Clyman and Judith Vowles, eds., *Russia through Women's Eyes: Autobiographies from Tsarist Russia* (New Haven, Conn., 1996), esp. 260–70 for a decidedly negative view of the influence of music education.

42. *Russkie vedomosti*, "Muzykal'noe uchilishche v Moskve," 3 February 1866.

43. Rostislav, "Kratkii obzor piatiletnei deiatel'nosti Russkogo muzykal'nogo obshchestva," *Golos*, 17 February 1865.

44. *Syn otechestva*, "Doch' okonchila svoe vokal'noe obrazovanie," 20 May 1862, no. 20, 476.

45. DAMK, fond 297, op. 1, d. 70, ll. 2–4.

46. M. M. Ivanov, "Muzykal'nye nabroski: polozhenie RMO," *NV*, 22 October 1907.

47. DAMK fond 176, op. 1, d. 239, ll. 45, 46, and 82.

48. Ibid., ll. 46 and 82.

49. TsGIA SPb, fond 408, op. 1, d. 362 and TsGIA fond 408, op. 1, d. 363. The two collections hold approximately seventy letters.

50. TsGIA SPb, fond 408, op. 1, d. 362, ll. 12–13v.

51. Ibid., ll. 61–61v.

52. Ibid., ll. 8–8v. Her composition, "Three Children's Songs," was published by Iogansen in 1890.

53. DAMK, fond 176, op. 1, d. 56, ll. 8–9 and 10–11.

54. TsDAMLM, fond 646, op. 1, d. 146, ll. 29, 30, 31, 32.

55. This is according to her recollections. According to the published records of the Moscow Conservatory, she enrolled at the conservatory in 1872, studied primarily with professor K. K. Klindvort, and graduated in 1878 with an *attestat* in piano.

56. TsGIA SPb, fond 408, op. 1, d. 362, ll. 6–7v. Iur'ev is known today as Tartu, Estonia.

57. RIII, fond 17, op. 1, d. 18, l. 1. Letter to Aleksandr Ziloti from Anna Iakovlevna Aleksandrova-Levenson, (no later than May, 1914).

58. Ibid., l. 1v–2.

59. Ibid., ll. 2–3.

60. Ibid., ll. 3–3v.

61. On the complex position of Jews in Russia, see Zvi Y. Gitelman, *A Century of Ambivalence: The Jews of Russia and the Soviet Union, 1881 to the Present* (Bloomington, Ind., 2001); John Klier, *Imperial Russia's Jewish Question* (New York, 1995); and Benjamin Nathans, *Beyond the Pale: The Jewish Encounter with Late Imperial Russia* (Berkeley and Los Angeles, 2002). See also Steven G. Rappaport, "Jewish Education and Jewish Culture in the Russian Empire, 1880–1914" (Ph.D. diss., Stanford University, 2000).

62. Nathans, *Beyond the Pale*, 215–20, 222–25.

63. TsGIA SPb, fond 361, op. 11, d. 161, 5–6, 9–10, 13–14.

64. "Dannye ob obuchaiushchikhsia v 1907–1908 uchebnom godu v muzykal'no-uchebnykh zavedeniiakh RMO," in *Materialy po voprosy o prieme evreev v sredniia i vysshiia uchebnyia zavedeniia* (St. Petersburg, [*c.* 1908]), 21–22 (Harvard Pre-Soviet law preservation microfilm project, 03975).

65. "Teatr i muzyka," *NV*, 10 January 1887; 11 January 1887.

66. RMO, *Ustav muzykal'nogo uchilishcha pri Russkom muzykal'nom obshchestve*, article 9.

67. *Materialy po voprosy o prieme evreev*, 16–18. (Memo, S. Kryzhanovskii to N. V. Pleve, 28 March 1908.)

68. TsGIA SPb, fond 408, op. 1, d. 472, ll. 16–16v.

69. Kievskoe otdelenie RMO, *Otchet... za 1881–1882*, 15. The student body by faith and social estate:

Religious affiliation:		Social Status:	
Orthodox	154	Nobles and State Servitors	141
Catholic	33	Clerical estates	15
Lutheran	11	Urban estates	54
Jewish	26	Peasants	4
Other	2	Foreigners	12

70. Kievskoe otdelenie RMO, *Otchet... za 1887–1888*, 12. The student body by faith and social estate:

Religious affiliation:		Social Status:	
Orthodox	155	Nobles and State Servitors	123
Catholic	35	Clerical estates	15
Lutheran	8	Merchants	48
Jewish	88	Other urban and rural estates	93
Other	0	Foreigners	12

71. See the *otchety* of the Moscow RMO for 1884–1885, 1885–1886, 1887–1888, 1888–1889, 1890–1891, and 1891–1892.

72. Nathans, *Beyond the Pale*, 298–301; quotation is from page 300.

73. *Materialy po voprosy o prieme evreev*, 18. For statistics on the Moscow Conservatory see TsGIA SPb, fond 408, op. 1, d. 559, ll. 97–98, 114–14v, 143–44, 223–24, 282–83, 304–5, 345–46, 410–12.

74. TsGIA SPb, fond 361, op. 11, d. 595, l. 26.

75. Klier, *Imperial Russia's Jewish Question*, 199. On the position of Jews in Kiev more generally, see pp. 182–221.

76. DAMK, fond 176, op. 1, d. 85 (1886–1887), ll. 13–13v and d. 300 (1912–1913), l. 55.

77. DAMK, fond 176, op. 1, d. 486, Minutes of the meetings of the Faculty Council of the Kiev Music School for 1887–1901.

78. DAMK, fond 297, op. 1, d. 10, l. 2. Composition of the student body:

Religious affiliation		Social Estate	
Orthodox	351	Nobles and State Servitors	253
Catholic	73	Clerical estates	38
Lutheran	20	Urban estates	544
Jewish	445	Rural estates	41
Other	6	Other	19

79. TsGIA SPb, fond 408, op. 1, d. 511, l. 20v.

80. TsGIA SPb, fond 408, op. 1, d. 544, ll. 1–2. Of the 360 students enrolled at the Odessa Music School in September 1905, only 245 remained in January 1906.

81. It is possible that Fidler was a Jewish convert to Orthodoxy. TsGIA SPb, fond 408, op. 1, d. 544, ll. 40–40v, 41, 42–42v, 43.

82. TsGIA SPb, fond 408, op. 1, d. 401, ll. 46–47, 48–49, 52, 53.

83. James Loeffler, " 'The Most Musical Nation': Jews, Culture, and Nationalism in the Late Russian Empire" (Ph.D. diss., Columbia University, 2006), esp. chaps. 3 and 4. See also G. V. Kopytova, "Evraiskaia muzyka v Peterburge—Petrograde," *Muzykal'naia akademiia*, no. 3 (1993): 156–59.

84. DAMK, fond 176, op. 1, d. 239, ll. 119, 124, 175, and d. 123, l. 58. See also TsDAMLM, fond 406, op. 1, d. 146, ll. 61–62.

85. "Nashi konservatorii," *NV*, 7 July 1889. See also TsGIA SPb, fond 408, op. 1, d. 363, ll. 5–7 (biographical letter of Ivan Vasil'evich Pokhvalinskii, a.k.a. Alinskii).

86. TsGIA SPb, fond 408, op. 1, d. 775, ll. 5–6, 7–8v. See also the anti-Semitic tracts, also likely the work of Fomina, *Odesskaia konservatoriia* ([1914]), *Voinskaia povinnost' i konservatoriia*, and *Odesskaia konservatoriia* ([1916]).

87. TsGIA SPb, fond 361, op. 11, d. 577, l. 9–9v.

88. *Materialy po voprosy o prieme evreev*, 19–20.

89. Marion Kaplan, *The Making of the Jewish Middle Class: Women, Family, and Identity in Imperial Germany* (New York, 1991), 121.

90. TsGIA SPb, fond 408, op. 1, d. 362, ll. 16–17.

91. DAMK, fond 176, op. 1, d. 254, esp. ll. 2, 3, 16, and 19, and TsDAMLM, fond 646, op. 1, d. 124, ll. 42–42v. See also DAMK fond 176, op. 1, d. 123, l. 108.

92. See, for example, TsGIA SPb, fond 408, op. 1, d. 461, ll. 38–39 and 43–43v.

93. TsGIA SPb, fond 408, op. 1, d. 362, ll. 30–31v. See also TsGIA SPb, fond 408, op. 1, d. 362, ll. 4–5 (Maxim Osipovich Agninskii) and d. 363, ll. 8–9v (Aleksei Vladimirovich Pernits), and 17–17v (Dmitrii Vasil'evich Popov).

94. *Otzyvy bol'shogo simfonicheskogo orkestra (70 chelovek) pod upravleniem dirizhera i kompozitora G. Ia. Fistulari, v S.-Peterburge, na Mezhdunarodnoi khudozhestvenno-promyshlennoi vystavke v Mikhailovskom manezhe s 31-go avgusta po 19-e oktiabria 1908 goda* (St. Petersburg, 1908), esp. 1–2.

95. RIII, fond 96, op. 1, no. 4, M. A. Bikhter, ll. 2–5.

96. Ibid., l. 19.

97. Ibid., ll. 11, 17, 19–20, 30v–31v.

98. Ibid., ll. 55v–56.

99. Ibid., ll. 57–58.

100. Ibid., ll. 61–62v.

101. Ibid., ll. 84v–86.

102. *Syn otechestva*, no. 25 (1868): (addendum).

103. E. K. Al'brekht, *Proshloe i nastoiashchee orkestra: ocherk sotsial'nogo polozheniia muzykantov* (St. Petersburg, 1886), 16–23, 26–31.

104. Ibid., 38–44, 59–67.

105. Ibid., 69–74. The salary scale for the opera orchestra ranged from 720 to 1500 rubles for violinists. Wind instrument players generally received 1200 rubles for first chairs and 960 rubles for those in the second chair.

106. Ibid., 32.

107. *Uslovie* (Kazan, 1886).

108. *Obiazatel'nyia pravila dlia orkestrovykh muzykantov, sluzhashikh v teatre Shelaputina* (Moscow, 1897).

109. A. Porten, *Zaveshchanie muzykanta (Testament d'un musician)* (St. Petersburg, 1891), 50.

110. Ehrlich, *The Music Profession in Britain*, 123–26.

111. A. Porten, *Zaveshchanie muzykanta,* 2–5, 7–12, 15–25, 182–86, and 187–89.

112. Ibid., 86–87.

113. Ibid., 91–92.

114. See on this issue with regard to the medical profession, Samuel C. Ramer, "Professionalism and Politics: The Russian Feldsher Movement, 1891–1918," in *Russia's Missing Middle Class*, 117–42.

115. G. B. Bernandt and I. M. Iampol'skii, *Kto pisal o muzyke: bio-bibliograficheskii slovar' muzykal'nykh kritikov i lits, pisavshikh o muzyke v dorevoliutsionnoi Rossii i SSSR*, vol. 2 (Moscow, 1974), 150–51.

116. I. Lipaev, *Ocherki byta orkestrovykh muzykantov* (Moscow, 1891), 1–3.

117. Ibid., 4–7.

118. Ibid., 7–18.

119. Iv. Lipaev, *Orkestrovye muzykanty* (*istoricheskie i bytovye ocherki*) (St. Petersburg, 1904), 64–69, 79–89.

120. Ibid., 120–21.

121. Ibid., 149–54.

122. Ibid., 145–49.

Chapter Five

1. TsGIA SPb, f. 361, op. 11, d. 618, ll. 58–59 and 60–61. See also *Doklad v Glavnuiu direktsiiu Imperatorskogo russkogo muzykal'nogo obshchestva obrazovannoi po postanovleniiu Glavnoi direktsii 13 Dekabria 1915 g. komissii po raspredeleniiu posobii na 1915/1916 uchebnyi god* (Petrograd, 1916).

2. Michael F. Hamm, *Kiev, a Portrait, 1800–1917* (Princeton, N.J., 1993), 25.

3. Thomas Stanley Fedor, *Patterns of Urban Growth in the Russian Empire* (Chicago, 1975), 183–214, cited in Hamm, *Kiev, a Portrait*, 42.

4. Some, such as Prince A. M. Dondukov-Korsakov, continued to support the RMO even after they left Kiev for other posts. See Ios. Miklashevskii, *Ocherk deiatel'nosti Kievskogo otdeleniia Imperatorskogo russkogo muzykal'nogo obshchestva* (Kiev, 1913), 32. See also TsDAMLM fond 646, op. 1, d. 20, l. 3v, and d. 31, ll. 3–3v, 4–5v, 7–8v. On Tiflis, see

RGIA, fond 1152, op. 10, 1885, d. 629, ll. 20–23, as well as fond 1152, op. 9, 1882, d. 482 and op. 10, 1885, d. 629.

5. O. R[omer], "Novoe delo (o muzykal'noi shkole)," *Kievlianin*, 16 June 1868.

6. Khokhlomany—pejorative for Ukrainian—from khokhol (crest, topknot). R[omer], "Novoe delo."

7. Chlen posetitel', "Fel'eton: Russkoe muzykal'noe obshchestvo v g. Kieve," *Kievskii telegraf*, 4 January 1867.

8. R[omer], "Novoe delo."

9. Chlen posetitel', "Fel'eton."

10. M. "Muzykal'noe obozrenie," parts 1 and 2, *Kievlianin*, 26 November 1866; 29 November 1866.

11. O. Romer, "Tochno-li my liubim muzyku?" *Kievlianin*, 27 October 1864.

12. El'der, "Kievskoe muzykal'noe obshchestvo v 1865–66 godu," *Kievlianin*, 1 September 1866.

13. Miklashevskii, *Ocherk deiatel'nosti Kievskogo otdeleniia IRMO*, 13, 26–27.

14. TsDAMLM, fond 646, op. 1, d. 39, ll. 9–16.

15. TsDAMLM fond 646, op. 1, d. 50, ll. 2 and 5.

16. TsDAMLM fond 646, op. 1, d. 48a, ll. 28–29v and d. 38, ll. 2–3v.

17. On the qualifications and reputations of Kiev faculty, see TsDAMLM, fond 646, op. 1, d. 112b, ll. 140v–144v (1909). On the general quality of instruction, see TsGIA SPb, fond 361, op. 11, d. 221, ll. 53v–55.

18. DAMK, fond 176, op. 1, d. 85, ll. 13–13v.

19. Miklashevskii, *Ocherk deiatel'nosti Kievskogo otdeleniia IRMO*, 64–65.

20. TsGIA SPb, fond 408, op. 1, d. 328, ll. 40–41. For the later period, see DAMK, fond 176, op. 1, d. 252, ll. 3 and 7, and DAMK, fond 297, op. 1, d. 10, l. 2.

21. DAMK fond 176, op 1, d. 217, ll. 41–43. For the Kiev branch's view on the rapid increase in the number of private music schools, see TsDAMLM, fond 646, op. 1, d. 170. For an overview of private musical and theatrical schools in Kiev, see O. J. Koreniuk, "Iz istorii muzykal'nogo obrazovaniia v Kieve (XIX– nach. XX st.)" (Kievskaia gosudarstvennaia konservatoriia, 1972), 182–215. On Lysenko and his school, see Taras Filenko, "Ethnic Identity, Music, and Politics in Nineteenth-Century Ukraine: The World of Mykola Lysenko" (Ph.D. diss., University of Pittsburgh, 1998).

22. For a more complete description of social and cultural life in Kiev, see Hamm, *Kiev, a Portrait*, 135–72.

23. TsGIA SPb, fond 408, op. 1, d. 17, and d. 73, ll. 3–4.

24. TsGIA SPb, fond 408, op. 1, d. 57, ll. 1–2, 3–4, 44, and 45–45v. See also TsGIA SPb, fond 408, op. 1, d. 190, ll. 60–61 on the critical position of the first Saratov branch of the RMO because of its failure to attract active members.

25. TsGIA SPb, fond 408, op. 1, d. 57, ll. 48–51.

26. TsGIA SPb, fond 408, op. 1, d. 190, ll. 1–5v.

27. TsGIA SPb, fond 408, op. 1, d. 191, ll. 36v. For a charitable view of the Kropotkins' role, see Khar'kovskoe otdelenie RMO, *Otchet direktsi Khar'kovskogo otdeleniia IRMO za 1878–79 g.* (Khar'kov, 1879), 3–4, which laments his untimely death and her departure from the city as significant losses for the branch.

28. TsGIA SPb, fond 408, op. 1, d. 190, ll. 60–62v. Saratov was only one of a number of cities where the local duma awarded a subsidy; however, such funding was unstable,

generally being approved on an annual basis. See RGIA, fond 1152, op. 12, 1899, d. 306, ll. 2–2v. In 1884, Kharkov's budget deficit endangered a 1,000-ruble city subsidy to the Music School. In Moscow, the city's subsidy supported the studies of orchestral students rather than the conservatory per se. TsGIA SPb, fond 408, op. 1, d. 263, ll. 1–2v.

29. TsGIA SPb, fond 408, op. 1, d. 190, ll. 71–72v.

30. P. P. S., "Korrespondentsii: Odessa," *MO* 1887, no. 16: 126.

31. Obshchestvo iziashchikh iskusstv, *Doklad kommissii, izbrannoi obshchim sobraniem Obshchestva iziashchikh iskusstv* 18 *maia* 1886 *goda, po delu o muzykal'noi shkole obshchestva* (Odessa, [1886]), 1–2.

32. P. P. S., "Korrespondentsii: Odessa," 125–26; V. I. Malishevskii, *Kratkii istoricheskii ocherk deiatel'nosti Odesskogo otdeleniia Imperatorskogo russkogo muzykal'nogo obshchestva i sostoiashchego pri nem muzykal'nogo uchilishcha za dvadtsat' piat' let (1886–1911)* (Odessa, 1911), 3–4.

33. See, for example, V. D., "O deiatel'nosti otdelenii Imperatorskogo russkogo muzykal'nogo obshchestva," *NV*, 4 July 1883.

34. TsGIA SPb, fond 361, op. 11, d. 221, ll. 41v–42v.

35. TsDAMLM fond 646, op. 1, d. 21, ll. 4–6v. See also TsDAMLM, fond 646, op. 1, d. 33 for correspondence from membership campaigns of 1874–1879. On ethnicity in Kiev's public life, see Natan M. Meir, "Jews, Ukrainians, and Russians in Kiev: Intergroup Relations in Late Imperial Associational Life," *Slavic Review* 65, no. 3 (Fall 2006): 480–84, 486–89.

36. TsGIA SPb, fond 408, op. 1, d. 17, ll. 3–4, 5–6v, 7–8v, 9–10v, 11–12v, 13–14v.

37. TsDAMLM, fond 646, op. 1, d. 75a, l. 28v.

38. TsDAMLM, fond 646, op. 1, d. 107, ll. 9–9v.

39. TsDAMLM, fond 646, op. 1, d. 177a, l. 34–35.

40. TsGIA SPb, fond 408, op. 1, d. 378, ll. 10–11v.

41. TsGIA SPb, fond 408, op. 1, d. 373, l. 173v–174v.

42. TsGIA SPb, fond 408, op. 1, d. 511, ll. 18v–19.

43. Odesskoe otdelenie IRMO, *Otchet... za 1892–1893* (Odessa, 1893), 14–17.

44. E. K. Al'brekht, *Proshloe i nastoiashchee orkestra: ocherk sotsial'nogo polozheniia muzykantov* (St. Petersburg, 1886). See also, "S.-Peterburg, 5 oktiabr," *Teatr i iskusstvo*, no. 40 (1897): 605–606; and Manfred (pseud.), "Letopis provintsii: ego kar'era," *Muzyka*, no. 223 (1915): 338–41.

45. See the comments of the Kishinev, Orel', and other small branches of the RMO on this issue as late as 1907, TsGIA SPb, fond 408, op. 1, d. 538, ll. 58v–60v (Kishinev), ll. 5–6 (Orel).

46. TsGIA SPb, fond 408, op. 1, d. 378, ll. 7–8.

47. RIII, fond 66, op. 1, d. 2, "I. I. Slatin," ll. 1–2v. Although the archive dates this document to 1879, other evidence strongly suggests that this proposal dates from 1886. See Khar'kovskoe otdelenie IRMO, *Kratkii obzor deiatel'nosti Khar'kovskogo otdeleniia IRMO i sostoiashchogo pri nem muzykal'nogo uchilishcha za* 25 *let* (Kharkov, 1896), 16.

48. RIII, fond 66, op. 1, d. 2, ll. 3–4.

49. Figures compiled from Khar'kovskoe otdelenie IRMO, *Otchet... za 1888/89 g.* (Kharkov, 1890), 32–52.

50. Khar'kovskoe otdelenie IRMO, *Otchet... za 1890–91 g.* (Kharkov, 1892), 34–68. By comparison, in 1910 the Moscow Conservatory reported 144 orchestral players (99

strings, 55 winds) among its 749 students, less than 20 percent of the student body. TsGIA SPb, fond 408, op. 1, d. 559, ll. 114–114v.

51. See the views of K. K. Zike on the status of the Kharkov Music School *c.* 1889, TsGIA SPb, fond 361, op. 11, d. 221, ll. 5v, 38v–39, and 41v–49. On the curriculum of the Kharkov music school, see TsGIA SPb, fond 408, op. 1, d. 73, ll. 23–27.

52. TsGIA SPb, fond 408, op. 1, d. 378.

53. Scholarships funded 31/33 wind students, 10/12 cellists, and 14/37 violinists. "Otchet o sostoianii muzykal'nykh klassov," in Odesskoe otdelenie IRMO, *Otchet... za 1895–1896*, 46.

54. "Svedeniia ob okonchivshikh kurs muzykal'nogo uchilishcha i byvshikh ego ucheniki," in Odesskoe otdelenie IRMO, *Otchet... za 1907–1908* (Odessa, 1909), 3–16.

55. Odesskoe otdelenie IRMO, *Otchet... za 1907–1908* (Odessa, 1909), 17–18.

56. TsGIA SPb, fond 408, op. 1, d. 328, ll. 12–13.

57. TsGIA SPb, fond 408, op. 1, d. 318, ll. 49–51. The tuition fee was raised to 75 rubles in 1891.

58. Ibid., ll. 51v–52v.

59. RGIA, fond 1152, op. 11, 1894, d. 121, ll. 2v–3; TsGIA SPb, fond 408, op. 1, d. 318, ll. 51v–52v.

60. RGIA, fond 1152, op. 11, 1894, d. 121, ll. 2–8, esp. ll. 4 and 7–8.

61. Provincial branches emphasized the need to own the premises of their music schools and classes in the statements they supplied to the Main Directorate in support of the Society's petitions for state aid. TsGIA SPb, fond 408, op. 1, d. 538.

62. Saratovskoe otdelenie IRMO, *Al'bom fotograficheskikh spiskov dom Saratovskogo otdeleniia Imperatorskogo russkogo muzykal'nogo obshchestva* (Saratov, 1910).

63. On A. P. Engel'gardt, see Richard G. Robbins, *The Tsar's Viceroys: Russian Provincial Governors in the Last Years of the Empire* (Ithaca, N.Y., 1987), 67–71.

64. Saratovskoe otdelenie IRMO, *Torzhestvo otkrytiia i osviashcheniia novogo zdaniia Saratovskogo otdeleniia Imperatorskogo russkogo muzykal'nogo obshchestva, 28 oktiabria 1902 goda* (Saratov, 1903), 1–2.

65. Ibid., 2–22.

66. On the development of the Tiflis branch and its activities, see A. Mshvelidze, *Ocherki po istorii muzykal'nogo obrazovaniia v Gruzii* (Moscow, 1971).

67. In 1914, the Tiflis Music School enrolled 504 students, including 187 Armenians, 169 Russians, 65 Georgians, 37 Jews, and 25 Germans. TsGIA SPb, fond 408, op. 1, d. 783, l. 14v.

68. TsGIA SPb, fond 408, op. 1, d. 254, ll. 17–22.

69. M. M. Ivanov, "Muzykal'nye nabroski: proshloe i nastoiashchee izdatel'skoi firmy Rikordi; tifliskie muzykal'nye dela," *NV*, 16 November 1892; M. M. Ivanov, *NV*, 7 December 1892; Letter to the editor, *Kavkaz*, 12 December 1892. See also, TsGIA SPb, fond 408, op. 1, d. 314. ll. 60–61 and 68–75v.

70. TsGIA SPb, fond 408, op. 1, d. 254, ll. 31–32, V. D. K. "Vokrug teatra: 28; muzykal'noe uchilishche," *Kavkaz*, *c.* January–February 1896.

71. Ibid.

72. Tiflisskoe otdelenie IRMO, *Torzhestvo otkrytiia i osviashcheniia kontsertnogo zala v novom zdanii Tiflisskogo otdeleniia Imperatorskogo russkogo muzykal'nogo obshchestva* (Tiflis, 1905), 4–12, 13, 15, and 18.

73. Ibid., 27.

74. Ibid., 19–20.

75. TsGIA SPb, fond 361, op. 11, d. 221, ll. 1–1v.

76. See Anne Swartz, "Technological Muses: Piano Builders in Russia, 1810–1881," *Cahiers du monde russe* 43, no. 1 (January–March 2002), esp. 130–32. More generally, see Edwin M. Good and Cynthia Adams Hoover, "Designing, Making, and Selling Pianos," in James Parakilas, et al., *Piano Roles: Three Hundred Years of Life with the Piano* (New Haven, Conn., 2000), 31–75.

77. M. A. Etinger, *Muzykal'naia kul'tura Astrakhani* (Volgograd, 1987), 28.

78. TsGIA SPb, fond 361, op. 11, d. 221, ll. 1–1v.

79. Zike's final summary report is held at TsGIA SPb, fond 361, op. 11, d. 221, ll. 2–91. Additional correspondence, his notebook, and a draft of his report are held in the manuscript division of the Russian National Library, St. Petersburg, fond 816, op. 3, d. 2456–58.

80. TsGIA SPb, fond 361, op. 11, d. 221, l. 5v.

81. Ibid., ll. 6–6v.

82. Ibid., l. 9.

83. Ibid., ll. 14–15v.

84. Lomtev, *Nemetskie muzykanty v Rossii*, 110.

85. TsGIA SPb, fond 361, op. 11, d. 221, l. 17v.

86. Nikolai Findeizen, *Ocherk deiatel'nosti Poltavskogo otdeleniia Imperatorskogo russkogo muzykal'nogo obshchestva za 1899–1915 gg.* (Poltava, 1916). See also, TsGIA SPb, fond 408, op. 1, d. 465, ll. 41–42, 43–44v, and 113–14.

87. Findeizen, *Ocherk deiatel'nosti Poltavskogo otdeleniia IRMO*, 18.

88. RIII, fond 71, op. 1, d. 561/1.

89. RIII, fond 21, op. 3, d. 19, ll. 14–15, 34–35. See also D. Akhsharumov, "Volia preodolevaet," *NV*, 1909, nos. 11980 and 11987; "Putevye zametki o kontsertnoi poezdke po Rossii simfonicheskogo orkestra v marte i aprele 1910 g.," *NV*, 1910, no. 12458; "7500 verst po Rossii: desiataia kontsertnaia poezdka orkestra Poltavskogo otdeleniia Imperatorskogo russkogo muzykal'nogo obshchestva," *NV*, 1913, nos. 13357 and 13364.

90. Findeizen, *Ocherk deiatel'nosti Poltavskogo otdeleniia IRMO*, 25.

91. Ibid., 25 and 6–7.

92. Ibid., 33.

93. TsGIA, fond 408, op. 1, d. 567, l. 57–57v.

94. Ibid., l. 57v–60.

95. RGIA, fond 1152, op. 13, 1902, d. 312, ll. 9 and 10v.

96. TsGIA SPb, fond 408, op. 1, d. 803, ll. 15–15v.

97. "O stipendiatakh gubernskogo zemstva v muzykal'nom uchilishche," *Pedagogicheskii zhurnal dlia uchashchikh narodnykh shkol Poltavskoi gubernyi*, no. 1 (January 1916): 29–30.

98. DAMK, fond 297, op. 1, d. 158, ll. 1–2.

99. RMO, *Ustav muzykal'nykh uchilishch*, 1882. See also RGIA, fond 1149, op. 9, 1882, d. 19, ll. 1–15.

100. TsDAMLM, fond 646, op. 1, d. 88, 1883, l. 1.

101. RGIA, fond 1284, op. 223, 1899, group A, d. 75, "Ob utverzhdenii proekta ustava muzykal'nykh klassov IRMO, 1899–1900." TsGIA SPb, fond 408, op. 1, d. 420, "O vyrabotke obshchikh programm khudozhestvennykh predmetov, prepodavaemykh v muzykal'nykh klassakh IRMO, 1899–1900."

102. See TsDAMLM fond 646, op. 1, d. 12a, ll. 25–30, and d. 31, esp. ll. 9–11 and 41–42, as well as DAMK, fond 176, op 1, d. 28, l. 1, d. 66, ll. 4–5v, d. 123, ll. 51–52, and d. 239, l. 67. See also RGIA, fond 1149, op. 9, 1882, d. 19, l. 3, for ministerial debates regarding deferments for music school students. Because of their expense, the Kiev general education classes closed in 1883. See TsDAMLM, fond 646, op. 1, d. 89, ll. 1–5v, d. 236, ll. 1–4, and d. 91, ll. 9–10. In 1915, the Kiev Conservatory attempted to reinstate the classes in an effort to assist students seeking draft deferments. See TsDAMLM fond 646, op. 1, d. 177a, ll. 148–50, 151–54 and d. 221, ll. 1–1v, 7–7v and 13, 8–9v and 11–12.

103. TsGIA SPb, fond 408, op. 1, d. 356, "O vyrabotke obshchikh normal'nykh programm khudozhestvennykh predmetov, prepodavaemykh v muzykal'nykh uchilishchakh. 1894–1900, and d. 420, "O vyrabotke obshchikh programm khudozhestvennykh predmetov, prepodavaemykh v muzykal'nykh klassakh IRMO, 1899–1900." See also, DAMK, fond 176, op. 1, d. 156, "Kievskoe muzykal'noe uchilishche: protokol s'ezda direktorov muzykal'nykh uchilishch i konservatorii, 13–20 April 1898."

104. TsGIA SPb, fond 408, op. 1, d. 512, "Po pervomu obshchemu s'ezdu gg. direktorov muzykal'no-uchebnykh zavedenii IRMO v mae 1904 goda."

105. TsGIA SPb, fond 408, op. 1, d. 573, ll. 1–1v.

106. TsGIA SPb, fond 408, op. 1, d. 573, ll. 10, 11, 20–21.

107. Faculty had credentials from a variety of institutions, including the Warsaw (1), Prague (2), Moscow (2), and St. Petersburg (5) conservatories. Conservatory director S. K. Eksner held credentials from both the Leipzig and St. Petersburg conservatories. TsGIA SPb, fond 408, op. 1, d. 573, ll. 24–24v, 28–29, 47–48, 50, 54–55.

108. TsGIA SPb, fond 408, op. 1, d. 356, ll. 235v–38.

109. TsGIA SPb, fond 408, op. 1, d. 573, ll. 54–91v.

110. The student body also included 99 singers, 59 violinists, 25 cellists and 7 theorists. TsGIA SPb, fond 408, op. 1, d. 572, ll. 93–94.

111. TsGIA SPb, fond 408, op. 1 d. 710, ll. 89–89v.

112. Ibid., ll. 120–21v.

113. Ibid., ll. 20–22, 47–55.

114. TsGIA SPb, fond 408, op. 1, d. 260 and d. 440. See also the *otchety* of the Kazan RMO.

115. On the didactic role of the theater, see E. Anthony Swift, *Popular Theater and Society in Tsarist Russia*, Studies on the History of Society and Culture, vol. 44 (Berkeley and Los Angeles, 2002); and Gary Thurston, *The Popular Theatre Movement in Russia, 1862–1919*, Studies in Russian Literature and Theory (Evanston, Ill., 1998). On music in the schools as a form of social control, see Lynn Sargeant, "Singing the Nation into Being: Teaching Identity and Culture at the Turn of the Twentieth Century," *History of Education Quarterly* 49, no. 3 (August 2009).

116. TsGIA SPb, fond 408, op. 1, d. 556, ll. 60–63v. See also *otchety* of the Kazan RMO for 1907–1913. On the Russian temperance movement, see Patricia Herlihy, *The Alcoholic Empire: Vodka and Politics in Late Imperial Russia* (New York, 2002).

117. TsGIA SPb, fond 408, op. 1, d. 328, l. 66.

118. TsGIA SPb, fond 408, op. 1, d. 462, l. 15–16. Temperance choirs were particularly numerous in Perm province. See Permskoe Popechitel'stvo o Narodnoi Trezvosti, *Narodnopevcheskoe delo v Permskoi guberniia: otchet rukovoditelia po ustroistvu khorov Permskogo popechitel'stva o narodnoi trezvosti s 1896 po 1908 god* (Perm, 1909).

119. TsGIA SPb, fond 408, op. 1, d. 462, l. 15v.

120. N. A. Ern', "Neskol'ko slov po voprosu o deiatel'nosti komitetov popechit. o narod. trezvosti," *Teatr i iskusstvo*, 1909, no. 46: 805–6.

121. TsGIA SPb, fond 408, op. 1, d. 462, l. 16.

122. TsGIA SPb, fond 408, op. 1, d. 493, ll. 123, 124–24v, 125–26, 130–31v, 132, and 135.

123. TsGIA SPb, fond 408, op. 1, d. 219, ll. 53–54v; d. 315, ll. 40–44v; d. 577, ll. 10–13v; and d. 578, ll. 146–49 and 166–73. The city's determination to promote itself can be seen in the weighty volume detailing the city's institutional, economic, and cultural life that was distributed as a supplement to *Sibirskaia zhizn'* in 1912. See *Gorod Tomsk* (Tomsk, 1912), esp. 331–36 on musical life.

124. TsGIA SPb, fond 408, op. 1, d. 219, ll. 53–53v.

125. TsGIA SPb, fond 408, op. 1, d. 315, ll. 40–44v, esp. 41–41v.

126. TsGIA SPb, fond 408, op. 1, d. 382, l. 124.

127. TsGIA SPb, fond 408, op. 1, d. 538, ll. 203–6v.

128. TsGIA SPb, fond 408, op. 1, d. 362, ll. 45–46.

129. TsGIA SPb, fond 408, op. 1, d. 363, ll. 38–38v.

130. Compare, for example, the characterization of the People's House as "heaven on earth" in *Pered narodnym domom (razgovor), 2-go fevralia 1903 goda* (Khar'kov, 1903) and as a den of iniquity in *Tainy v S.-Peterburgskom narodnom dome* (St. Petersburg, 1905). See also *Desiatiletie narodnogo doma Khar'kovskogo obshchestva gramotnosti, 1903–1913* (Khar'kov, 1913), which indicates that in its first decade, this institution hosted 25 operas and 22 concerts, as well as 363 Russian and 282 Ukrainian plays (pp. 8 and 72).

131. TsGIA SPb, fond 408, op. 1, d. 328, ll. 84–84v.

132. TsGIA SPb, fond 408, op. 1, d. 538, ll. 1a–1av.

133. Ibid., ll. 5–6, 54–60v, 65–66v, 131–33.

134. Ibid., ll. 35–39.

135. Ibid., ll. 61–63v.

136. Ibid., ll. 65–66.

137. Ibid., ll. 96–97v.

138. Ibid., ll. 104–5.

139. Ibid., ll. 47v–48.

140. Ibid., ll. 115–16v.

141. Ibid., ll. 185–88.

142. Susan M. Vorderer, "Urbanization and Industrialization in Late Imperial Russia: Ivanovo-Voznesensk, 1880–1914," (Ph.D. diss., Boston College, 1990), 101–5.

143. TsGIA SPb, fond 408, op. 1, d. 803, ll. 12–13v.

144. TsGIA SPb, fond 408, op. 1, d. 512, ll. 7–7v and 31–34.

145. Ibid., ll. 36–37.

146. Ibid., ll. 40–42 and 120v–22.

147. For the British case, see Paula Gillett, *Musical Women in England, 1870–1914: "Encroaching on All Man's Privileges"* (New York, 2000), esp. 207–12.

Chapter 6

1. Leo Tolstoy, *What Is Art?* trans. Richard Pevear and Larissa Volokhonsky (New York, 1995 [1898]), 55.

2. Ibid., 55–57.

3. Ibid., 98 and 152.

4. V. G. Valter, *V zashchitu iskusstva: mysli muzykanta po povodu stat'i L. N. Tolstogo, "Chto takoe iskusstvo"* (St. Petersburg, 1899), 4.

5. Ibid., 14–17.

6. See for example, Beverly Whitney Kean, *All the Empty Palaces: The Merchant Patrons of Modern Art in Prerevolutionary Russia* (New York, 1983).

7. Cyril Ehrlich has identified at least four primary forms of musical patronage: personal, official, open market, and subvention. Ehrlich, *The Music Profession in Britain since the Eighteenth Century: A Social History* (Oxford, UK, 1985), 73.

8. William Weber, *Music and the Middle Class: The Social Structure of Concert Life in London, Paris, and Vienna* (New York, 1975).

9. Jaap van der Tas, "Dilettantism and Academies of Art: The Netherlands Example," in *Paying the Piper: Causes and Consequence of Art Patronage*, ed. Judith Huggins Balfe (Urbana, Ill., 1993), 30–39. In the same volume, see also Tia Denora, "The Social Basis of Beethoven's Style," 9–29; Judith Huggins Balfe and Thomas A. Cassilly, "'Friends of...': Individual Patronage through Arts Institutions," 119–33; and Vera Zolberg, "Remaking Nations: Public Culture and Postcolonial Discourse," 234–50.

10. van der Tas, "Dilettantism and Academies of Art," 38–39.

11. See *Materialy po voprosu o prieme evreev v sredniia i vysshiia uchebnyia zavedeniia* (St. Petersburg, [c. 1908]), 16–22, and TsGIA SPb, fond 361, op. 11, d. 577, ll. 10–16.

12. The subsidies awarded to the St. Petersburg and Moscow conservatories differed significantly from those awarded to the provincial schools. The avowed purpose of the subsidy to the Kiev Music School, for example, was to support its general education classes. RGIA, fond 1152, op. 8, 1876, d. 524, ll. 2–8 and 12, and TsDAMLM fond 646, op. 1, d. 48a, ll. 14–15v. Although general education courses justified state funding and reinforced the legitimacy of specialized music education, few of the Society's provincial branches proved able to sustain such courses financially and their effectiveness was open to question. The courses in the Kiev Music School opened in 1874 to much fanfare but closed a decade later without ever attracting a significant number of students. The idea that state subsidies should support general education classes persisted for decades, however. The very definition of a *muzykal'noe uchilishche* as opposed to either the Society's *muzykal'nye klassy* or a private *muzykal'naia shkola* presupposed the existence of general education classes. See RMO, *V Glavnuiu direktsiiu IRMO obrazovannoi po postanovleniiu glavnoi direktsii 13 dekabria 1915 g. komissy po raspredeleniiu posoby na 1915/1916 uchebnii god: doklad* (Petrograd, 1916), appendix.

13. RGIA, fond 1152, op. 9, 1882, d. 482, "O posobii iz kazny Kievskomu i Khar'kovskomu muzykal'nym uchilishcham"; op. 10, 1885, d. 629 "O posobii po 5,000 r. v god, Tiflisskomu muzykal'nomu uchilishchu IRMO"; op. 11, 1894, d. 121, "O proizvodstve ezhegodnogo posobiia Saratovskim muzykal'nym klassam"; op. 12, 1899, d. 306 "O proizvodstve s 1 ianvaria 1900 g. posobiia Odesskomu otdeleniiu IRMO po 5,000 r. v god, techenie 5-ti let." Subsidies included 5,000 rubles each to the Kiev, Khar'kov,

Odessa, Saratov, and Tiflis Music Schools, 2,000 rubles to the music classes of the Tomsk RMO, 15,000 rubles to the St. Petersburg Conservatory, and 20,000 rubles to the Moscow Conservatory. An additional subsidy awarded 3,000 rubles to the Main Directorate for administrative expenses.

14. RGIA, fond 1152, op. 13–1902, d. 312, esp. ll. 2–3v., 6–7, 16–18 and 19.

15. The five conservatories had total expenses of 571,765 rubles and a combined income of 618,364 rubles. The state subsidies for the five institutions amounted to only 53,578 rubles (9.37 percent of expenses or 8.66 percent of income). State subsidies covered 11.3 percent of aggregate annual expenses of 433,223 rubles for the Society's music schools. By this date, the total subsidy amount was set by the state but allocated to individual institutions by the Society. TsGIA SPb, fond 361, op. 11, d. 618.

16. M. M. Ivanov, "Nashi muzykal'nye dela." *NV*, 20 December 1910.

17. Editorial, *Muzykal'nyi truzhenik*, 15 November 1908.

18. Glavnaia direktsiia, IRMO, "Gospodinu Ministru vnutrennykh del, 23 iiunia 1908, no. 3763," 1–2, 5–6.

19. Ibid., 13–14.

20. Ibid., 14–15. The proposal included 65,000 rubles for the St. Petersburg Conservatory, 50,000 for the Moscow Conservatory, 14,000 for the Saratov Conservatory, 80,000 for the Society's sixteen existing music schools, 18,000 rubles for its music classes, and 8,000 rubles for the Main Directorate itself.

21. Glavnaia Direktsiia, IRMO, "Gospodinu Ministru vnutrennykh del 14 aprelia 1909, no. 4211," 1–4.

22. Ibid., 7–8. See also RGIA, fond 1158, op. 1–1910, d. 355, esp. l. 62.

23. RGIA, fond 1158, op. 1–1910, d. 355, ll. 83–84v.

24. TsGIA SPb, fond 408, op. 1, d. 451, ll. 139–42.

25. Katerina Clark, *Petersburg, Crucible of Cultural Revolution* (Cambridge, Mass., 1995), 64–65, and 304.

26. B. Ch., "Neobkhodimo li nam ministerstvo iziashchnykh iskusstv?" *Iskusstvo*, no. 41 (1883): 41–42.

27. Representative examples of the debate on this issue include editorials in *Teatr i iskusstvo* no. 18 (1909): 317 and no. 34 (1909): 573. See also "K voprosu o ministerstve iziashchnykh iskusstv," *Protiv techeniia*, 2 February 1913, 4–5. For a somewhat different formulation of this issue, see Anton Rubinstein's 1889 proposal for two state-supported conservatories, RGIA, fond 1284, op. 223, d. 115, 1889, ll. 1–6.

28. Starcheus, "Ob odnoi probleme," 52. See also I. F. Petrovskaia, *Istochnikovedenie istorii russkoi muzykal'noi kul'tury XVIII—nachala XX veka*. 2d ed. (Moscow, 1989), 167–72.

29. Harley Balzer, "The Problem of Professions in Imperial Russia," in *Between Tsar and People: Educated Society and the Quest for Public Identity in Late Imperial Russia*, ed. Samuel D. Kassow, James L. West, and Edith W. Clowes (Princeton, N.J., 1991), 184.

30. M. F. Gnesin, ed., *Mysli i vospominaniia o N. A. Rimskom-Korsakove* (Moscow, 1956), 212.

31. V. V. Yastrebtsev, *Reminiscences of Rimsky-Korsakov*, ed. and trans. Florence Jones (New York, 1985), 359, 525 n. 12. See also M. Iankovskii, *N. A. Rimsky-Korsakov i revoliutsiia* 1905 *goda* (Moscow, 1950), 30.

32. On the social composition of higher educational institutions, see Samuel D. Kassow, *Students, Professors, and the State in Tsarist Russia*, Studies on the History of Society

and Culture (Berkeley and Los Angeles, 1989), 407–11. On the tensions created by class and gender divisions within the *studenchestvo*, see Susan K. Morrissey, *Heralds of Revolution: Russian Students and the Mythologies of Radicalism* (New York, 1998), 80–88 and 160–68.

33. Yastrebtsev, *Reminiscences*, 352–53. The original "Zaiavlenie russkikh muzykantov" appeared in *Nashi dni*, 3 February 1905.

34. *RMG*, no. 7 (1905): 202 and no. 8 (1905): 238.

35. On the *Declaration of the* 342 and its educational and political resonance, see David Wartenweiler, *Civil Society and Academic Debate in Russia, 1905–1914*, Oxford Historical Monographs (New York, 1999), 47–48. The *Declaration of the 342* was eventually signed by over 1800 individuals.

36. During the 1904–1905 academic year, the St. Petersburg Conservatory enrolled 1137 students (720 women, 417 men). TsGIA SPb, fond 408, op. 1, d. 538, ll. 26v–28, 32v–33, and 251–56.

37. "Postanovlenie obshchego sobraniia uchashchikhsia konservatorii o prekrashchenii zaniatii do 1 sentiabria i o reformakh, v kotorykh nuzhdaetsia konservatoriia," *Novosti*, 14 February 1905, in A. L. Birkengof, et al., compilers, *Iz istorii Leningradskoi konservatorii: materialy i dokumenty, 1862–1917* (Leningrad, 1964), 227–29. See also "Obrashchenie skhodki uchashchikhsia konservatorii k professoram i prepodavateliam s prizyvom podderzhat' trebovanie uchashchikhsia o prekrashchenii zaniatii," February 1905, from TsGAOR, fond DP, op. 00, 1905, d. 3, ch. 150, ll. 8–8v, in the same volume, 233–34.

38. TsGAOR, f. DP, op. 00, 1905 g., d. 3, ch. 150, ll. 2–3, "Donesenie zhandarmskogo podpolkovnika Gerasimova direktoru departamenta politsii o skhodke uchashchikhsia konservatorii 10 fevralia," in Birkengof, et al., *Iz istorii Leningradskoi konservatorii*, 230–31.

39. Morrissey, *Heralds of Revolution*, 4–5.

40. TsGMMK im. Glinki, fond 80, op. 1, d. 3559, ll. 1–2.

41. TsGMMK im. Glinki, fond 80, op. 10, d. 2126, ll. 1–2.

42. Abraham Ascher, *The Revolution of* 1905*: Russia in Disarray* (Stanford, Calif., 1988), 194–96. See also Kassow, *Students, Professors, and the State*, 256–65.

43. Morrissey, *Heralds of Revolution*, 105–6.

44. "Anti-muzykal'nye pitomtsy i pitomitsy (k prekrashcheniiu zaniatii v konservatorii)," *Budil'nik*, 6 March 1905.

45. "Konservatorskiia zabastovki," *Budil'nik*, 6 March 1905.

46. Glavnaia direktsiia, IRMO, "O sobytiiakh v SPb konservatorii," *NV*, 28 March 1905.

47. N. A. Rimsky-Korsakov, "Otkrytoe pis'mo direktoru Peterburgskoi konservatorii (po telefonu)," *Russkie vedomosti*, 17 March 1905.

48. A. I. Puzyrevskii and L. A. Sakketti, *Ocherk piatidesiatiletiia deiatel'nosti S.-Peterburgskoi konservatorii* (St. Petersburg, 1912), 122–23.

49. TsGIA SPb, fond 361, op. 11, d. 491, ll. 7–9.

50. TsGIA SPb, fond 361, op. 11, d. 496a, "Ob uvol'nenii N. A. Rimskogo-Korsakova, A. K. Glazunova, i A. K. Liadova v sviazi s sobytiiami 1905 g. i ikh vozvrashchenie v konservatoriiu."

51. Savva Mamontov's private Moscow company premiered the opera in 1902.

52. Synopsis and libretto from N. A. Rimsky-Korsakov, *Kashchey the Immortal*, Kirov Chorus and Orchestra, Valery Gergiev, Philips compact disc 446704-2.

53. Gnesin, *Mysli i vospominaniia*, 216.

54. N. A. Rimsky-Korsakov, *My Musical Life*, ed. Carl van Vechten, trans. Judith A. Joffe (London, 1989 [1923]), 412–13.

55. See, for example, "Chestvovanie N. A. Rimskogo-Korsakova," *Russkie vedomosti*, 28 March 1905; and A. Ossovskii, "Teatr i muzyka: 'Kashchei bezsmertnyi,'" *Slovo*, 29 March 1905.

56. Yastrebstev, *Reminiscences*, 357–58.

57. Stasov's speech appears in "Chestvovanie N. A. Rimskogo-Korsakova," *Novosti i birzhevaia gazeta*, 28 March 1905. See also V. Stasov, "Russkoe muzykal'noe obshchestvo i Rimskii-Korsakov," *Novosti i birzhevaia gazeta*, 25 March 1905.

58. A. Ossovskii, "Prazdnik russkogo kompozitora," *Slovo*, 28 March 1905.

59. Gnesin, *Mysli i vospominaniia*, 220.

60. "Chestvovanie," *Novosti i birzhevaia gazeta*, 28 March 1905.

61. Gnesin, *Mysli i vospominaniia*, 220.

62. *Teatral'naia Rossiia*, 9 April 1905.

63. "K uvol'neniiu Rimskogo-Korsakova," *Rus'*, 7 April 1905.

64. Rimsky-Korsakov, *My Musical Life*, 413–14.

65. Guslar, "Listki iz al'boma svistunov: bezsmertnye Kashchei," *Peterburgskii listok*, 29 March 1905.

66. V. Burenin, "Stseny iz komedii 'Gore ot gluposti,'" *NV*, 29 April 1905.

67. There is no shortage of works by, on, or about Rimsky-Korsakov, either singly or in the context of the so-called *Moguchaia kuchka*. Help in sorting through this mass of material can be found in Gerald R. Seaman's *Nikolai Andreevich Rimsky-Korsakov: A Guide to Research* (New York, 1988).

68. Rimsky-Korsakov, *My Musical Life*, 3–40.

69. Ibid., 41–42.

70. Yastrebtsev, *Reminiscences*, 351.

71. Gnesin, *Mysli i vospominaniia*, 211.

72. "Khronika: novoe muzykal'noe uchilishche," *Rus'*, 27 April 1905.

73. Letter of V. Senilov and M. Chernov, in "Po povodu uvol'neniiu N. A. Rimskogo-Korsakova," *Russkie vedomosti*, 6 April 1905.

74. TsGIA SPb, fond 361, op. 11, d. 493, "Prosheniia ob uvol'nenii studentov konservatorii v sviazi s uvol'neniem professora N. A. Rimskogo-Korsakova." See also "K uvol'neniiu N. A. Rimskogo-Korsakova," *Russkie vedomosti*, 6 April 1905.

75. "K uvol'neniiu N. A. Rimskogo-Korsakova," *Russkie vedomosti*, 1 April 1905, and "Teatr i muzyka," *Slovo*, 28 March 1905.

76. Letter of Anna Esipova to *Novosti i birzhevaia gazeta*, 1 April 1905.

77. "Teatr i muzyka," *Slovo*, 27 March 1905.

78. "Po povodu uvol'neniia N. A. Rimskogo-Korsakova," *Novosti i birzhevaia gazeta*, 1 April 1905.

79. A. Oss[ov]skii, "Teatr i muzyka: k zlobe dnia," *Slovo*, 27 March 1905.

80. "Nashi muzykal'nye deiateli," *Peterburgskaia gazeta*, 30 March 1905.

81. Spectator, "Ob intsidente s N. A. Rimskim-Korsakovym," *Peterburgskaia gazeta*, 26 March 1905.

82. A. Ziloti, "Otkrytoe pis'mo k A. M. Klimchenko," *Rus'*, 31 March 1905. Klimchenko's letter precedes Ziloti's response.

83. A. Livin, "Zametki: XXI; nazrevshie voprosy," *RMG*, no. 11 (1905): 297. Italics in original.

84. Editorial, *Teatr i iskusstvo*, no. 14 (1905): 216.

85. "Otgoloski pechati," *Zaria*, 29 March 1905 and 30 March 1905.

86. "Russkaia pechat'," *Novosti i birzhevaia gazeta*, 27 March 1905.

87. M. Ivanov, "Uvol'nenie N. A. Rimskogo-Korsakova," *NV*, 28 March 1905.

88. "Kak my pooshchriaem talanty," *Novosti i birzhevaia gazeta*, 27 March 1905.

89. Pero, "K uvol'neniiu N. A. Rimskogo-Korsakova," *Slovo*, 26 March 1905.

90. "V konservatorii," *Peterburgskii listok*, 27 March 1905.

91. "Oni uvolili," *Peterburgskii listok*, 29 March 1905.

92. "Konservatoriia v blizhaishem budushchem," *Teatr i iskusstvo*, no. 16 (1905): 261.

93. "O chem govoriat," *Novosti i birzhevaia gazeta*, 3 April 1905.

94. TsGIA SPb, fond 361, op. 11, d. 496a, ll. 10–16.

95. Ibid., esp. ll. 13v, 15–15v.

96. Yastrebtsev, *Reminiscences*, 361.

97. Kassow, *Students, Professors, and the State*, 238.

98. Wartenweiler, *Civil Society and Academic Debate*, 44–50.

99. See, for example, in *Novosti i birzhevaia gazeta*, "V Peterburgskoi konservatorii," 23 September 1905, "V uchebnom mire: skhodka v konservatorii," 2 October 1905, "V uchebnom mire: v SPb konservatorii," 7 October 1905, and "V uchebnom mire: v konservatorii," 10 October 1905.

100. TsGMMK im. Glinki, fond 80, d. 3557.

101. TsGIA SPB, fond 361, op. 11, d. 492, l. 13.

102. TsGIA SPb, fond 408, op. 1 d. 710, ll. 133–134v, 144–45.

103. See IRMO, "Proekt ustava konservatorii, vyrabotannyi kommissiei, izbrannoi khudozhestvennym sovetom 5 dekabria 1905 g," ([1906]).

104. TsGIA SPb, fond 361, op. 11, d. 518, ll. 1–14.

105. Ibid., ll. 28–39.

106. Ibid., l. 40.

107. Ibid., l. 51.

108. Ibid., ll. 64–77.

109. Pecheneg, "Otkliki dnia," *Sel'skii vestnik*, 20 December 1912.

110. "50-letnyi iubilei konservatorii," *Kommercheskaia gazeta*, 17 December 1912.

111. IRMO, 50-*letie Imperatorskogo russkogo muzykal'nogo obshchestva i S.-Peterburgskogo otdeleniia* (St. Petersburg, 1909); and S.-Peterburgskoe otdelenie IRMO, 50-*letie S.-Peterburgskoi konservatorii: protokol torzhestvennogo akta* (St. Petersburg, 1912). See also RIII, fond 4, op. 2, d. 17.

112. "Eskizy i kroki," *Peterburgskaia gazeta*, 23 December 1909.

113. "50-letnii iubilei Peterburgskoi konservatorii," *Kievskaia mysl'*, 19 December 1912.

114. Chernomor, "Teatr i muzyka", *Za 7 dnei*, December 1912.

115. [V. G.] Karatygin, "Iubilei Peterburgskoi konservatorii," *Sovremennoe slovo*, 16 December 1912. See also N. Negorov, "K iubileiu Peterburgskoi konservatorii (1862–1912)," *Teatr i iskusstvo*, no. 50 (9 December 1912): 990–92.

116. Negorev, "K iubileiu."

117. Ibid. See also, "K 50-letnomu iubileiu konservatorii," *Obozrenie teatrov*, 16 December 1912, 17–18.

118. Grigorii Timofeev, "Piatidesiatiletie Imperatorskogo russkogo muzykal'nogo obshchestva," *Rech'*, 21 December 1909.

119. "Vtoroi den' iubileia konservatorii," *Peterburgskaia gazeta*, 18 December 1912. See also N. Bernshtein, "Teatr i muzyka: konservatorskii iubilei," *SPV*, 19 December 1912.

120. A. G., "50-letnyi iubilei Peterburgskoi konservatorii," *Golos iuga*, 22 December 1912.

121. Nik. Bernshtein, "Teatr i muzyka: piatidesiatiletie Russkogo muzykal'nogo obshchestva," *Vechernyi peterburg*, 18 December 1909.

122. *Muzyka i zhizn'*, 10 December 1909, 1.

123. Puzyrevskii and Sakketti, *Ocherk piatidesiatiletiia deiatel'nosti S.-Peterburgskoi konservatorii*; Puzyrevskii, *IRMO v pervye 50 let*; and Findeizen, *Ocherk deiatel'nosti S.-Peterburgskogo otdeleniia IRMO (1859–1909)*.

Conclusion

1. X., "Konservatoriia v 1905 g.," *Russkaia molva*, 18 December 1912. Veisberg was both a pupil of Rimsky-Korsakov and, ultimately, his daughter-in-law, albeit only after his death. On Veisberg's career in the early Soviet period, see Simo Mikkonen, "State Composers and the Red Courtiers: Music, Ideology, and Politics in the Soviet 1930s (Ph.D. diss., University of Jyväskylä, 2007).

2. M. F. Gnesin, ed., *Mysli i vospominanie o N. A. Rimskom-Korsakove* (Moscow, 1956), 214.

3. X., "Konservatoriia v 1905 g."

4. See Dana Ohren, "All the Tsar's Men: Minorities and Military Conscription in Russia, 1874–1905 (Ph.D. diss., Indiana University, Bloomington, 2006), 146–48, as well as Joshua A. Sanborn, *Drafting the Russian Nation: Military Conscription, Total War, and Mass Politics, 1905–1925* (DeKalb, Ill., 2003), 21–25.

5. TsDAMLM, fond 646, op. 1, d. 65, ll. 2–2v; DAMK, fond 176, op. 1, d. 540, ll. 16–27, esp. l. 26. TsDAMLM fond 646, op. 1, d. 36, ll. 35–35v; RGIA, fond 1149, op. 9, 1882, d. 19, ll. 3, 9–10.

6. "V vidu obshchei voinskoi povinnosti, u mnogikh mirnykh grazhdan vdrug poiavilis' muzykal'nye sposobnosti," *Maliar*, 14 September 1875, 2.

7. See the exchange between the critic of *NV* and the St. Petersburg Conservatory: *NV*, "Nashi konservatorii," 7 July 1889; A. G. Rubinstein, "Eshche o konservatoriiakh (pis'mo v redaktsiiu)," *NV*, 11 July 1889; and *NV*, "O konservatoriiakh," 12 July 1889.

8. "Letopis provintsii: Samara," *Muzyka*, 251 (1916): 206.

9. See, for example, DAMK, fond 297, op. 1, d. 74, l. 9. For a discussion of the complex relationship between the real and perceived rate of Jewish draft evasion, see Ohren, "All the Tsar's Men," 178–91, 194–98, and 207–21, as well as Yohanan Petrovsky-Shtern, "Jews in the Russian Army: Through the Military towards Modernity (1827–1914)" (Ph.D. diss., Brandeis University, 2001), 125–26, and 134–44.

10. TsDAMLM, fond 646, op. 1, d. 185, l. 3 and d. 227, l. 7–7v.

11. It reached 9.4 percent in October 1916. TsGIA SPb, fond 408, op. 1, d. 559, ll. 97–98, 114–14v, 143–44, 223–24, 282–83, 304–5v, 345–46, and 410–12; d. 773, ll. 1–2v, 25–26, 72–74, 167–69; d. 774, ll. 17–18, 61–61v, 161–63.

12. TsGIA SPb, fond 408, op. 1, d. 649, ll. 79–79v, 90–90v, 92–93.

13. TsGIA SPb, fond 408, op. 1, d. 328, ll. 186–86v (22 April 1915).

14. TsGIA SPb, fond 408, op. 1, d. 817. ll. 6–7.

15. TsDAMLM, fond 646, op. 1, d. 200, ll. 26–26v, and TsGIA SPb, fond 408, op. 1, d. 817, esp. ll. 11–12, 15–15v, and 53–59v.

16. See, for example, TsGIA SPb, fond 408, op. 1, d. 777, which details how attempts by the Poltava Music School to fight the requisitioning of its new building led to an investigation into draft evasion.

17. TsGIA SPb, fond 361, op. 11, d. 618, ll. 73–74.

18. The conservatory suffered a loss of more than 50,000 rubles in student fees alone. In evacuation, the conservatory enrolled only 255 students in the fall of 1915. After returning to Kiev for the spring 1916 semester, enrollment rebounded to approximately 800 students. TsDAMLM, fond 646, d. 177a, ll. 184–86.

19. TsGIA SPb, fond 361, op. 11, d. 618, ll. 1–8, 27–29, 30, 45, 54–57, 71.

20. TsGIA SPb, fond 408, op. 1, d. 824, ll. 3–3v.

21. Ibid., ll. 6–6v.

22. DAMK, fond 297, op. 1, d. 128, ll. 6–7v (pp. 11–14) and ll. 16–16v (pp. 31–32), Appendix 5.

23. TsGIA SPb, fond 361, op. 11, d. 518, l. 81. See also TsDAMLM, fond 646, op. 1, d. 227, l. 15–15v.

24. TsGIA SPb, fond 361, op. 1, d. 518, ll. 82–89. See also DAMK, fond 297, op. 1, d. 127, ll. 1–8, pp. 1–16 and RGALI, fond 2099, op. 1. d. 325, ll. 89v–90.

25. "Protokoly zasedanii komissii, izbrannoi Glavnoi direktsii Russkogo muzykal'nogo obshchestva 27 marta 1917 goda, dlia peresmotra ustava RMO," 1–3.

26. Ibid., 3–4.

27. TsGIA SPb, fond 408, op. 1, d. 580, ll. 231–32.

28. Three-quarters of the twenty-four faculty members had conservatory credentials. Ten held diplomas from the St. Petersburg or Moscow conservatories; one possessed equivalent credentials from the Musical-Dramatic School of the Moscow Philharmonic Society. Four low-ranked piano instructors and the trombone teacher lacked conservatory diplomas, but had graduated from the Kharkov Music School. Another voice teacher lacked credentials but boasted a successful stage career. Even the orchestral faculty possessed sterling credentials, with diplomas from a range of European conservatories, including not only Moscow and St. Petersburg, but also Prague, Budapest, Vienna, Amsterdam, and several German conservatories. TsGIA SPb, fond 408, op. 1, d. 580, ll. 241, 246, 247–49.

29. TsGIA SPb, fond 408, op. 1, d. 783, ll. 4–7, 23–26, 29–30v, 35, 37–37v, 38, 39–39v, 41–42, 43–44v, 45–48, 49–49v.

30. RGALI, fond 661, op. 1, d. 140, ll. 17–18v, 19–19v.

31. "Dekret o Moskovskoi i Petrogradskoi konservatoriiakh," 12 July 1918, "Postanovlenie Muzykal'nogo otdela Narodnogo komissariata po prosveshcheniiu," 5 October 1918, and "Dekret o perekhode gubernskikh i gorodskikh otdelenii Russkogo muzykal'nogo obshchestva i sostoiashchikh pri nikh konservatorii i drugikh uchrezhdenii v vedenie Narodnogo komissariata po prosveshcheniiu i o natsionalizatsii vsego imushchestva etikh otdelenii i sostoiashchikh pri nikh uchrezhdenii," 22 October 1918, in *Sbornik dekretov, postanovlenii i rasporiazhenii po muzykal'nomu otdelu Narodnogo komissariata po prosveshcheniiu*, vol. 1 (Petrograd, 1919), 3–5.

32. Sheila Fitzpatrick, *The Commissariat of Enlightenment: Soviet Organization of Education and the Arts under Lunacharsky, October 1917–1921* (New York, 1970), esp. 11–25, 236–42.

33. See Timothy Edward O'Connor, *The Politics of Soviet Culture: Anatolii Lunacharskii*, Studies in the Fine Arts: The Avant-Garde, no. 42 (Ann Arbor, Mich., 1983), 67–85; and Fitzpatrick, *Commissariat of Enlightenment*, esp. chap. 6.

34. See, for example, TsDAMLM, fond 646, op. 1, d. 234, ll. 1–2. See also RGALI, fond 2099, op. 1, d. 325, ll. 113–24v, esp. 113–14.

35. Amy Nelson, *Music for the Revolution: Musicians and Power in Early Soviet Russia* (University Park, Pa., 2004), 162–64, 179–81; on the groupings of the musical left in general, see 67–93. See also Neil Edmunds, *The Soviet Proletarian Music Movement* (New York, 2000), 90–96 on conservatory politics in the 1920s.

36. M. N. Buianovskii, "V klassakh dukhovykh instrumentov," in *Leningradskaia konservatoriia v vospominaniiakh*, 2d ed., vol. 1., eds. G. G. Tigranov, et al. (Leningrad, 1987), 160.

37. S. L. Ginzburg, "V poroga muzykal'nogo nauki," in *Leningradskaia konservatoriia v vospominaniiakh*, 178–79.

38. F. A. Rubtsov, "Iz vospominaniia," in *Leningradskaia konservatoriia v vospominaniiakh*, 2d ed., 27.

39. On early Soviet cultural policy, see Lynn Mally, *Culture of the Future: The Proletkult Movement in Revolutionary Russia*, Studies on the History of Society and Culture (Berkeley and Los Angeles, 1990); O'Connor, *The Politics of Soviet Culture*; Fitzpatrick, *Commissariat of Enlightenment*, esp. chaps. 4 and 6; and Sheila Fitzpatrick, *Education and Social Mobility in the Soviet Union, 1921–1934*, Soviet and East European Studies (New York, 1979).

40. Fitzpatrick, *Commissariat of Enlightenment*, 68–88.

41. James C. McClelland, "Proletarianizing the Student Body: The Soviet Experience during the New Economic Policy," *Past and Present*, no. 80 (August 1978): 130.

42. "Otnoshenie Narkompros o poriadke priema v konservatorii," 23 sentiabria 1918 g., in *Iz istorii sovetskogo muzykal'nogo obrazovaniia: sbornik materialov i dokumentov, 1917–1927* (Leningrad, 1969), 31.

43. On the student purge, see Fitzpatrick, *Education and Social Mobility*, 97–102.

44. See for example, "Metodicheskie pis'ma Glavprofobra: o tselevoi ustanovke ispolnitel'skogo fakul'teta konservatorii," *Muzykal'noe obrazovanie*, no. 3 (1926): 47–51. For an introduction to Soviet-era musical periodicals, see Gerald R. Seaman, "Soviet Musical Life in the 1920s as Seen in Contemporary Music Periodicals," *Fontes Artes Musicae* 53, no. 3 (2006): 233–38.

45. See, for example, Edmunds, *The Soviet Proletarian Music Movement*, 85.

46. The 1924 purge of the Moscow Conservatory student body initially expelled 372 of 963 students (some were later readmitted), almost half of whom (180/372) were pianists. Whereas in 1910 pianists had comprised 44.4 percent of the Moscow Conservatory's student body, and before the 1924 purge 33.2 percent of the student body, after the purge pianists constituted only 23.7 percent of the remaining students. "Po muzykal'nym shkolam: v Moskovskoi konservatorii," *Muzykal'naia nov'* no. 8 (1924): 35–36. See also, in the same issue, "Priemochnaia kompaniia," 36, which details how the 100 newly admitted students were to be apportioned by specialty.

47. L. Lebedinskii, "Po muzykal'nym shkolam: priemochnaia kompaniia," *Muzykal'naia nov'*, no. 8 (1924): 36.

48. The 278 applicants for the Moscow Conservatory included 159 men (57 percent) and 119 women (43 percent). The one hundred admitted students included 61 men and 39 women. 82 applicants were either workers or children of workers (29.5 percent), and 36 were peasants or children of peasants (13 percent). Members of the categories "employees" [*sluzhashchie*] and "persons from the laboring intelligentsia" [*litsa intel. truda*] together comprise 88.1 percent of the applicant pool. Peasants in any case comprised only 1.1 percent of the applicants and 3 percent of the admittees. "Tablitsa so svedeniiami o rezul'tatakh priema studentov v Moskovskuiu gosudarstven. konservatoriiu na 1924–25 akademich. god.," *Muzykal'naia nov'*, no. 9 (1924): 31. On the difficulty of determining the social and political status of students during the 1924 student purge, see Fitzpatrick, *Education and Social Mobility*, 101–2.

49. *Muzykal'naia nov'*, no. 9 (1924): 31. On the gendered impact of the purge and new patterns of student recruitment, see Fitzpatrick, *Education and Social Mobility*, 100, 108–109.

50. On Briusova's ideas and career, see N. N. Minor, *N. Ia. Briusova i ee shkola muzykal'nogo obrazovaniia* (Saratov, 1994). See also N. Briusova, *Voprosy professional'nogo muzykal'nogo obrazovaniia* (Moscow, 1929). On the People's Conservatories, see RGALI, fond 2009, Briusova, N. Ia., esp. op. 1, d. 145, Avtobiografii Briusovoi Nadezhdy Iakovlevny s prilozheniem spiskov ee nauchnykh rabot.

51. On the status hierarchies of music, see the work of sociologist Brian A. Roberts. In addition to *A Place to Play: The Social World of University Schools of Music* (St. John's, NF, 1991), see his *I, Musician: Towards a Model of Identity Construction and Maintenance by Music Education Students as Musicians* (St. John's, NF, 1993), and *Musician: A Process of Labeling* (St. John's, NF, 1991), as well as the ethnomusicological studies of conservatories by Bruno Nettl, *Heartland Excursions: Ethnomusicological Reflections on Schools of Music* (Urbana, Ill., 1995); and Henry Kingsbury, *Music, Talent, and Performance: A Conservatory Cultural System* (Philadelphia, 1988), esp. 35–46, on artistic lineages.

52. The constructed memory of the "conservatory revolution" achieved its most complete formulation in Iankovskii's *N. A. Rimsky-Korsakov i revoliutsiia* 1905 *goda*. On the Soviet and post-Soviet interpretations of the "conservatory revolution," compare L. S. Ginzburg, et al., eds., *Moskovskaia gosudarstvennaia konservatoriia, 1866–1966* (Moscow, 1966) and N. A. Mironova, *Moskovskaia konservatoriia: istoki (vospominaniia i dokumenty, fakty i kommentarii* (Moscow, 1995).

53. Iuliia Veisberg, "Konservatoriia v 1905 g: vospominaniia," part 1, *Krasnaia gazeta*, 20 December 1925, evening edition.

54. Anatolii Drozdov, "1905 god v Leningradskoi konservatorii (vospominaniia uchastnika sobytii)," *Muzyka i revoliutsiia*, no. 2 (1926): 6–17. Reprinted in Gnesin, *Mysli i vospominanie*, 313.

55. Ibid., 311, 330. Drozdov suffered for his active participation in the conservatory student movement and his vocal criticism of the Russian Musical Society. In 1908, he was arrested and exiled to the provinces, along with other conservatory student leaders. Nevertheless, Drozdov continued his association with the RMO. By 1912, he was director of the Ekaterinodar branch's music classes. TsGIA SPb, fond 408, op. 1, d. 660, ll. 58–60.

56. "O prieme v konservatorii," *Muzykal'noe obrazovanie*, no. 3–4 (1926): 112. On the Rabfak system in general, see Frederika M. Tandler, "The Workers' Faculty (Rabfak) System in the USSR" (Ph.D. diss., Columbia University, 1955); and Fitzpatrick, *Education*

and Social Mobility, 48–51, 91–92. Edmunds overestimates the success of the musical Rabfak in *The Soviet Proletarian Music Movement*, 99–102, while Nelson argues for its failure as a means of proletarianizing the conservatory in *Music for the Revolution*, 175–78.

57. "Otkrytie Rabfaka pri Moskovskoi konservatoriia," *Muzykal'naia nov'*, no. 2 (1923): 25. Until 1929, the musical Rabfak was a subsection within the general artistic Rabfak.

58. E. Vilkovir, "Obshchestvennyi otdel: ob uchrezhdenii rabfakov pri konservatoriiakh," *Muzykal'naia nov'*, no. 1 (1923): 19–22.

59. Tandler, "The Workers' Faculty (Rabfak) System," 295–96. In 1924–1925, only 40 of 8,201 Rabfak graduates went on to study at fine arts institutions. In 1926–1927, only 197 of 25,000 former Rabfak students were in the fine arts. Rabfak graduates made up only 6 percent of the total enrollment of fine arts institutions in 1926–1927.

60. B. Khvatskii, "Zhizn' v shkoly: v Leningradskoi konservatorii," *Muzyka i revoliutsiia*, no. 9 (1928): 33. The Leningrad Conservatory did not receive a Rabfak of its own until 1930. See Brigada myzykal'nogo rabfaka pri LGK - Kinn, Gorshechnikov, Ivanov, Loginov, "Otkrytoe pis'mo," *Proletarskii muzykant*, no. 9–10 (1930): 72.

61. A. Koposov, "Voskresnaia rabochaia konservatoriia," *Muzyka i revoliutsiia*, no. 12 (1927): 27–28. See also Milashevich, "Moskovskaia gosudarstvennaia konservatoriia: Voskresnaia rabochaia konservatoriia i kul'turnyi front," *Muzykal'noe obrazovanie*, no. 2 (1928): 49–53.

62. Ibid., 51. On the Sunday Workers' Conservatory, see also V. B., "Itogi dvukhletnei raboty Voskresnoi rabochei konservatorii pri M. G. K.," *Muzyka i revoliutsiia*, no. 5 (1929): 25–26.

63. See V. F. Shevliagina, "Moskovskaia narodnaia konservatoriia i ee rol' v muzykal'nom prosveshchenii narodnykh mass Rossii (1906–1916 gody)" (Kand. diss., Moskovskii gos. institut kul'tury, 1975). See also I. A. Sats, "B. L. Iavorskii v Moskovskoi narodnoi konservatorii" in *B. Iavorskii: stat'ia, vospominaniia, perepiska* (Moscow, 1972).

64. On the cultural revolution in higher education and the arts, see Fitzpatrick, *Education and Social Mobility*, 180–98, 209–12, and 234–36, as well as "Cultural Revolution as Class War," in *Cultural Revolution in Russia, 1928–1931*, ed. Sheila Fitzpatrick (Bloomington, Ind., 1978), 8–40.

65. For a thorough discussion of the cultural revolution in the Moscow Conservatory, see Nelson, *Music for the Revolution*, 207–40.

66. B. Pshibyshevskii, "Puti reorganizatsii Moskovskoi konservatorii," *Muzykal'noe obrazovanie*, no. 3 (1929): 11–12.

67. "Ofitsial'nyi otdel: rezoliutsiia Glavprofobr po Moskovskoi i Leningradskoi konservatorii," *Muzykal'noe obrazovanie*, no. 1 (1930): 44–47, esp. 44–45.

68. Juri Jelagin, *Taming of the Arts*, trans. Nicholas Wreden (New York, 1951), 189–90.

69. Nelson, *Music for the Revolution*, 237–40, 242.

70. On the organizational and institutional development of Soviet musical life under Joseph Stalin, see Kiril Tomoff's thorough study *Creative Union: The Professional Organization of Soviet Composers, 1939–1953* (Ithaca, N.Y., 2006).

BIBLIOGRAPHY

Archival Collections

Rossiiskii gosudarstvennyi istoricheskii arkhiv (RGIA)
Fond 733, op. 194 (1880–1895), Departament narodnogo prosveshcheniia, Ministerstvo narodnogo prosveshcheniia, razriad obshchikh del
Fond 1149, Departament zakonov gosudarstvennogo soveta
Fond 1152, Departament ekonomii gosudarstvennogo soveta
Fond 1158, Finansovaia komissiia gosudarstvennogo soveta
Fond 1284, Departament obshchikh del, Ministerstva vnutrennykh del
Tsentral'nyi gosudarstvennyi istoricheskii arkhiv Sankt-Peterburga (TsGIA SPb)
Fond 361, Petrogradskaia konservatoriia
Fond 408, Russkoe Muzykal'noe Obshchestvo
Manuscript Division, Russian National Library (OR RNB), St. Petersburg, Russia.
Fond 816, Nikolai Findeizen
Rossiiskii institut istorii iskusstv (RIII)
Fond 1, Sobranie rukopisei i pisem deiatelei muzyki i teatra
Fond 4, Sobranie materialov k istorii muzykal'nykh organizatsii
Fond 7, N. A. Rimsky-Korsakov
Fond 17, A. I. Ziloti
Fond 21, E. F. Napravnik
Fond 24, A. G. Rubinstein
Fond 53, D. P. Gubarev
Fond 66, I. I. Slatin
Fond 67, V. P. Tolstov
Fond 71, Sobranie spravochnykh materialov
Fond 96, M. A. Bikhter
Fond 119, N. S. Mikkel'
Tsentral'nyi derzhavnyi arkhiv-muzei literatury i mistestva (TsDAMLM)
Fond 646, Kievskoe otdelenie IRMO

Derzhavnyi arkhiv mista Kyiva (DAMK)
Fond 176, Kievskoe muzykal'noe uchilishche
Fond 297, Kievskaia konservatoriia
Tsentral'nyi gosudarstvennyi muzei muzykal'noi kul'tury im. M. I. Glinki (TsGMMK)
Fond 80, Moskovskaia konservatoriia.
Rossiiskii gosudarstvennyi arkhiv literatury i iskusstva (RGALI)
Fond 2009, N. Ia. Briusova
Fond 2099, Moskovskaia konservatoriia

Principal Periodical Sources

Iskusstvo 1883–1884
Muzyka 1910–1916
Muzyka i zhizn' 1908–1912
Muzykal'nyi listok 1872–1877
Muzykal'noe obozrenie 1885–1888
Muzykal'nyi i teatral'nyi vestnik 1883
Muzykal'nyi sezon 1869–1871
Muzykal'nyi svet 1852–1878
Muzykal'nyi truzhenik 1906–1910
Muzykal'nyi vestnik 1870–1871
Novoe vremia 1868–1917
Orkestr 1910–1912
Russkaia muzykal'naia gazeta 1894–1918
Russkii muzykal'nyi vestnik 1885–1888
Sankt-Peterburgskie vedomosti
Teatr i iskusstvo 1897–1918

*Annual Reports (*otchety*) of Branches of the Russian Musical Society*

Astrakhan 1891–1896
Baku 1908–1916
Chernigov 1907–1913
Ekaterinburg 1914–1915
Ekaterinodar 1909–1910; 1912–1913; 1915–1916
Ekaterinoslav 1907–1908; 1914–1915
El'nia 1912–1913
Ialta 1910–1911
Irkutsk 1902–1908
Kazan 1904–1915
Kharkov 1878–1879; 1886–1895; 1896–1904; 1905–1906; 1907–1913; 1914–1915
Kherson 1910–1914
Kiev 1874–1902; 1905–1915
Kronshtadt 1874–1876
Kursk 1893–1895
Moscow 1864–1878; 1879–1886; 1887–1895; 1897–1906
Nikolaev 1898–1899; 1911–1912

Nizhnii Novgorod 1906–1915
Novocherkassk 1911–1912
Odessa 1888–1908; 1909–1911; 1912–1914; 1915–1916
Orel 1907–1908; 1915–1916
Penza 1902–1904
St. Petersburg 1859–1865; 1870–1871; 1872–1877; 1878–1885; 1886–1887; 1888–1898; 1899–1904; 1905–1909; 1910–1913
Poltava 1909–1910; 1911–1914
Pskov 1911–1912
Rostov-on-Don 1914–1915
Russkoe Muzykal'noe Obshchestvo/Glavnaia direktsiia 1860–1861; 1897–1898; 1905–1907; 1907–1908
Sarapul 1909–1910
Saratov 1909–1912
Tambov 1910–1916
Tiflis 1884–1891; 1894–1895; 1900–1902; 1904–1908
Tobolsk 1878–1879; 1894–1895; 1897–1898; 1902–1903; 1904–1905
Tomsk 1908–1915
Tsaritsyn 1911–1913
Tula 1908–1915
Ufa 1915–1916
Uman 1915–1916
Vilnius 1903–1904; 1906–1908
Vladimir 1914–1915
Vladivostok 1914–1915
Voronezh 1908–1915

Documents and Pamphlets relating to the Imperial Russian Musical Society and its Branches from the Russian National Library, St. Petersburg

Arkhangel'skoe otdelenie IRMO. *Programma kursa khudozhestvennykh predmetov muzykal'nykh klassov*. Arkhangel'sk, 1914.
Ekaterinodarskoe otdelenie IRMO. *Programmy prepodavaniia khudozhestvennykh predmetov muzykal'nogo uchilishcha Ekaterinodarskogo otdeleniia IRMO*. Ekaterinodar, 1911.
Gerke, A. A. *Zaiavlenie deistvitel'nogo chlena S.-Peterburgskogo otdeleniia Imperatorskogo russkogo muzykal'nogo obshchestva*. St. Petersburg, 1884.
Imperatorskoe russkoe muzykal'noe obshchestvo. *50-letie Imperatorskogo russkogo muzykal'nogo obshchestva i S. Peterburgskogo otdeleniia: telegrammy*..., 1909.
Instruktsiia muzykal'nym uchilishcham, 1904.
K gospodinu Ministru vnutrennikh del, 23 June 1908.
K gospodinu Ministru vnutrennikh del, 14 April 1909.
Kazanskoe otdelenie IRMO. *Muzykal'noe uchilishche Kazanskogo otdeleniia IRMO: pamiatnaia i poverochnaia knizhka* (exemplar).
Khar'kovskoe otdelenie IRMO. *Usloviia priema v muzykal'noe uchilishche Khar'kovskogo otdeleniia IRMO*. Khar'kov, 1894.

———. *Usloviia priema v muzykal'noe uchilishche... i programma prepodavaniia nauchnykh predmetov*. Khar'kov, 1899.

———. *Usloviia priema v muzykal'noe uchilishche Khar'kovskogo otdeleniia IRMO*. Khar'kov, 1904.

———. *Kratkii obzor deiatel'nosti Khar'kovskogo otdeleniia IRMO i sostoiashchego pri nem muzykal'nogo uchilishcha za 25 let 1871–1896*. Khar'kov, 1896.

Kievskoe otdelenie IRMO. *Pamiatnaia i poverochnaia knizhka na... 188... goda*. (exemplar).

———. *Usloviia priema v Kievskuiu konservatoriiu IRMO s prilozheniem programm na 1913–14 uch. god*. Kiev, 1913.

Ministerstvo vnutrennykh del. "O ezhegodnom posobii IRMO na poderzhanie muzykal'nykh uchilishch." 1902.

Moskovskoe otdelenie RMO. *Zapiska direktorov Russkogo muzykal'nogo obshchestva v Moskve o neobkhodimosti obezpechit' prochnost' sushchestvovaniia sostoiashchei pri obshchestve konservatorii*. Moscow, 1870.

———. *Ocherk po postroike i torzhestvennomu otkrytiiu zdanii konservatorii*. Moscow, 1905.

———. *Usloviia dlia priema i pravila dlia postupleniia v Moskovskuiu konservatoriiu*. Moscow, 1886.

Odesskoe otdelenie IRMO. *Otchet po postroike zdaniia Odesskogo muzykal'nogo uchilishcha RMO*. Odessa, 1906.

Peterburgskaia konservatoriia. *Polozheniia po Sanktpeterburgskoi konservatorii RMO*. St. Petersburg, 1887.

Peterburgskoe otdelenie IRMO. *Zhurnaly direktsii Petrogradskogo otdeleniia IRMO po smete konservatorii na 1914–1915*. Petrograd, 1914.

Petrogradskaia konservatoriia. *Instruktsiia po Petrogradskoi konservatorii*. Petrograd, 1914.

Polozheniia po Sanktpeterburgskoi konservatorii RMO, 1887.

Pravila dlia sostavlenie muzykal'nogo obshchestva, *c*. 1861.

Proekt izmenenii ustava IRMO, 1911.

Proekt ustava gosudarstvennoi konservatorii, 1917.

Proekt ustava konservatorii, vyrabotannyi kommissiei, izbrannoi khudozhestvennym sovetom 5 Dekabria 1905.

Proekt ustava konservatorii, 1910.

Proekt ustava muzykal'nykh uchilishch RMO, 1917.

Proekt ustava Russkogo muzykal'nogo obshchestva, 1869.

Proekt ustava Russkogo muzykal'nogo obshchestva, 1873.

Protokoly pervogo obshchego s'ezda gg. direktorov muzykal'no-uchebnykh zavedenii. Moscow, 1904.

Protokoly zasedanii komissii, izbrannoi glavnoi direktsiei RMO 27 marta 1917 goda, dlia peresmotra ustava RMO, 1917.

S.-Peterburgskoe otdelenie IRMO. *50-letie S.-Peterburgskoi konservatorii: protokol torzhestvennogo akta....* St. Petersburg, 1912.

———. *Instruktsii po Petrogradskoi konservatorii*. St. Petersburg, *c*. 1916.

———. *Usloviia priema v S.-Peterburgskuiu konservatoriiu IRMO i izvlecheniie iz pravil konservatorii*. St. Petersburg, 1908.

———. *Zhurnaly direktsii Petrogradskogo otdeleniia IRMO po smete konservatorii na 1914–1915*. Petrograd, [1914].

Saratovskoe otdelenie IRMO. *Torzhestvo otkrytiia Saratovskoi konservatorii*. Saratov, 1912.

———. *Torzhestvoe otkrytie i osviashcheniia novogo zdaniia Saratovskogo otdeleniia IRMO 28 oktiabria 1902 goda*. Saratov, 1903.

———. *Usloviia priema v Saratovskuiu konservatoriiu IRMO i izvlecheniie iz pravil konservatorii*. Saratov, 1912.

S'ezd v Petrograde deiatelei Russkogo muzykal'nogo obshchestva, 1917.

Tambovskoe otdelenie IRMO. *Pravila dlia chlenov i gostei obshchestva i dlia sushchestvuiushchikh pri otdlenii muzykal'nykh klassov*. Tambov, 1886.

Tiflisskoe otdelenie IRMO. *Torzhestvo otkrytiia i osviashcheniia kontsertnogo zala v novom zdanii Tiflisskogo otdeleniia IRMO*. Tiflis, 1905.

Ustav konservatorii, 1911.

Ustav muzykal'nykh uchilishch, 1910.

Ustav muzykal'nykh uchilishch, 1882.

Ustav muzykal'nogo uchilishcha pri Russkom muzykal'nom obshchestve, 1861.

Ustav Russkogo muzykal'nogo obshchestva, 1873.

Ustav Russkogo muzykal'nogo obshchestva, 1885.

Vglavnuiu direktsiiu IRMO obrazovannoi po postanovleniiu glavnoi direktsii ot 2 ianvaria 1910 goda komissii. 1910.

Vglavnuiu direktsiiu IRMO obrazovannoi po postanovleniiu glavnoi direktsii ot 31 ianvaria 1910 goda komissii.

Vglavnuiu direktsiiu IRMO obrazovannoi po postanovleniiu glavnoi direktsii ot 29 Oktiabria 1910 g. komissii po raspredeleniiu posobii na 1911 g.

Vglavnuiu direktsiiu IRMO obrazovannoi po postanovleniiu glavnoi direktsii ot 6 Noiabria g. komissii po raspredeleniiu posobii na 1911/12 uchebnyi god.

Vglavnuiu direktsiiu IRMO obrazovannoi po postanovleniiu glavnoi direktsii...komissii po raspredeleniiu posobii na 1914–1915.

Vglavnuiu direktsiiu IRMO obrazovannoi po postanovleniiu glavnoi direktsii ot 13 Dekabria 1915 g. komissii po raspredeleniiu posobii na 1915/1916 uchebnyi god.

Vglavnuiu direktsiiu IRMO obrazovannoi po postanovleniiu glavnoi direktsii...komissii po raspredeleniiu posobii na 1915.

Voronezhskoe otdelenie IRMO. *Programmy khudozhestvennykh predmetov muzykal'nogo uchilishcha*. Voronezh, 1913.

———. *Programmy khudozhestvennykh predmetov muzykal'nogo uchilishcha Voronezhskogo otdeleniia IRMO*. Voronezh, 1915.

———. *Usloviia priema v muzykal'noe uchilishche....* Voronezh, 1913.

Published Primary Sources and Document Collections

100-letnyi iubilei S.-Peterburgskogo filarmonicheskogo obshchestva, 1802–1902. St. Petersburg, 1902.

Abaza, A. M. "O muzykal'nom obrazovanii v tochnom smysle: rech', proiznesennaia direktorom muzyk. klassov Kurskogo otd. RMO na akte 5 febralia 1889 g." *Baian*, no. 10 (1889).

Afanas'ev, N. "Vospominaniia N. Ia. Afanas'eva." Parts 1 and 2. *Istoricheskii vestnik*, 1890 (July): 23–48; 1890 (August): 255–76.

Al'brekht, E. K. "Programmy kontsertov St.-Peterburgskogo filarmonicheskogo obshchestva sosnovaniia ego v 1802 g. do 1883 g. *vkliuchitel'no*." In *Obshchii obzor deiatel'nosti vysoch. utv. S.-Peterburgskogo filarmonicheskogo obshchestva*. St. Petersburg, 1884.

———. *Proshloe i nastoiashchee orkestra (ocherk sotsial'nogo polozheniia muzykantov)*. St. Petersburg, 1886.

———. *S.-Peterburgskaia konservatoriia*. St. Petersburg, 1891.

Alekseev, M. P., et al. *Muzykal'noe nasledstvo: sborniki po istorii muzykal'noi kul'tury SSSR*. Vol. 1. Moscow, 1962. Vols. 2–3. Moscow, 1968–1970.

Alekseeva, E. N., and G. A. Pribegina, comps. *Vospominaniia o Moskovskoi konservatorii*. Moscow, 1966.

Amori [Ippolit Rapgof]. *Pianofily i pianofoby: o fortepiannoi igre i otvet doktoru Gorinevskomu*. St. Petersburg, 1894.

———. *Kak sleduet obuchat' detei muzyke*. St. Petersburg, 1910.

Argamakov, Konstantin. *Pedagogicheskiia stat'i o ser'eznoi muzykal'noi podgotovke uchitelei muzyki i o kursakh pianistov-metodologov*. Vol. 1. Kiev, 1909.

Asaf'ev, B. V. *Izbrannye stat'i o muzykal'nom prosveshchenii i obrazovanii*. Leningrad, 1973.

Auer, Leopold. *My Long Life in Music*. New York, 1923.

Bakhtiiarova, Ch. N., ed. *Muzykal'naia kul'tura narodov Povolzh'ia: sbornik nauchnykh trudov*. Moscow, 1978.

Barenboim, L. A., S. M. Vil'sker, and P. A. Vul'fius, eds. *Iz istorii sovetskogo muzykal'nogo obrazovaniia: sbornik materialov i dokumentov, 1917–1927*. Leningrad, 1969.

Bekhter, A. N. *Neskol'ko slov o muzykal'nom obrazovanii*. St. Petersburg, 1882.

Beliaev, M. P. and I. Ia. Bilibin. *Russkie simfonicheskie kontserty i Russkie kvartetnye vechera, osnovanye M. P. Beliaevym*. St. Petersburg, 1906.

Bezekirskii, V. V. *From the Notebook of a Russian Violinist, 1850–1910*. Translated by Samuel Wolf. Linthicum Heights, Md., 1984 [1910].

Birkengof, A. L. et al., comps. *Iz istorii Leningradskoi konservatorii: materialy i dokumenty, 1862–1917*. Leningrad, 1964.

Boborykin, P. D. *Vospominaniia*. Vols. 1–2. Moscow, 1965.

Bogatyrev, P. I. "Moskovskaia starina." In *Ushedshaia Moskva*, edited by L. Kuznetsova, 76–153. Moscow, 1964.

Bogdanov, N. A. *Ocherk deiatel'nosti Kievskogo otdeleniia IRMO i uchrezhdennogo pri nem muzykal'nogo uchilishcha so vremeni ikh osnovaniia*. Kiev, 1888.

Briusova, N. *Voprosy professional'nogo muzykal'nogo obrazovaniia*. Voprosy massovoi muzykal'noi kul'tury. [Moscow], 1929.

Bukhovtsev, A. *Zapiski po elementarnoi fortepiannoi pedagogii: rukovodstvo dlia molodykh prepodavatelei*. 2d ed. Moscow, 1890.

Bulgakov, S. *Znachenie muzyki i peniia v dele vospitaniia i v zhizni cheloveka: prilozhenie k tsirkuliaru po Kievskomu uchebnomu okruga za 1901 god*. Kiev, 1901.

Campbell, Stuart, ed. and trans. *Russians on Russian Music, 1830–1880: An Anthology*. New York, 1994.

Chechott, V. A. *Dvadtsatipiatiletie Kievskoi russkoi opery: 1867–1892 gg*. Kiev, 1893.

Cherepnin, N. N. *Vospominaniia muzykanta*. Leningrad, 1976.

Chizhov, A. P. *Obzor pervogo desiatiletiia sushchestvovaniia Russkogo khorovogo obshchestva v Moskve (1878–1888)*. Moscow, 1890.

Chto takoe muzykal'nyi rabfak i kak na nego postupit'. Moscow, 1930.

Clyman, Toby W. and Judith Vowles, eds. *Russia through Women's Eyes: Autobiographies from Tsarist Russia*. New Haven, Conn., 1996.
Cui, Cesar. *Muzykal'no-kriticheskiie stat'i*. Petrograd, 1918.
Demianskii, V. V. *O pervonachal'nom prepodavanii igry na fortepiano v sem'e*. St. Petersburg, 1896.
Dolotov, A. *Nashi muzykal'nye dela*. St. Petersburg, 1900.
Dulova-Zograf, A. Iu. "Moi vospominaniia." Parts 1–6. *Muzyka*, 1912, no 68: 267–72; no. 69: 283–89; no. 70: 299–304; no. 71: 315–19; no. 72: 338–40; no. 73: 356–61.
———. "Moi vopsominaniia o N. G. Rubinshteine." Parts 1–7. *Muzyka*, 1912, no. 84: 582–84; no. 86: 614–16; no. 87: 630–34; no. 88: 646–47; no. 89: 662–65; no. 96: 800–2; no. 106: 1029–32.
Elanskii, Petr. *Otkrytie v g. Nikolaeve otdeleniia Imperatorskogo russkogo muzykal'nogo obshchestva. Rech' Petra Elanskogo o vospitatel'noi znachenii muzyki v razlichnyia istorichie epokhi {sic}*. Nikolaev, 1893.
Elson, Arthur. *Woman's Work in Music: Being an Account of Her Influence....* Boston, 1904.
Engel', I. "Programmy istoricheskikh simfonicheskikh kontsertov RMO [v] Moskve v 1907–1909 gg." In *Ocherki po istorii muzyki: lektsii, chitannye v istoricheskikh simfonicheskikh kontsertakh IRMO* [v] *Moskve v 1907–1908 i 1908–1909 gg*. Moscow, 1911, 213–18.
Engel', I. D. *Narodnaia konservatoriia: ocherk*. Moscow, 1908.
Findeizen, Nikolai. *Ocherk deiatel'nosti S.-Peterburgskogo otdeleniia Imperatorskogo russkogo muzykal'nogo obshchestva (1859–1909)*. St. Petersburg, 1909.
———. *Ocherk razvitiia russkoi muzyki (svetskoi) v 19-m veke*. St. Petersburg, 1909.
———. *Vasilii Vasil'evich Bessel': ocherk ego muzykal'no-obshchestvennoi deiatel'nosti*. St. Petersburg, 1909.
———. *Ocherk deiatel'nosti Poltavskogo otdeleniia Imperatorskogo russkogo muzykal'nogo obshchestva za 1899–1915 gg*. Poltava, 1916.
Gabrilovich, A. *Muzykal'nyi kalendar: spravochnaia i zapisnaia knizhka*. St. Petersburg, 1895–1904, 1907–1915.
Glazunov, A. K. *Avtobiograficheskaia spravka*. St. Petersburg, 1907.
———. *Pis'ma, stat'i, vospominaniia: izbrannoe*. Moscow, 1958.
Glebov, Igor [B. V. Asaf'ev] and P. P. Suvchinskii, eds. *Melos: knigi o muzyke*. St. Petersburg, 1917.
Glier, R. M. *Reingol'd Moritsevich Glier: stat'i, vospominaniia, materialy*. Leningrad, 1965.
Gnesin, M. F., ed. *Mysli i vospominaniia o N. A. Rimskom-Korsakove*. Moscow, 1956.
———. "Avtobiografiia." In *M. F. Gnesin: stat'i, vospominaniia, materialy*. Moscow, 1961.
Iastrebtsev, V. V. *Nikolai Andreevich Rimsky-Korsakov: vospominaniia V. V. Iastrebtseva*. Leningrad, 1960.
Illiustrirovannyi slovar sovremennykh russkikh muzykal'nykh deiatelei. Parts 1 and 2. Odessa, 1907–1908.
Ippolitov-Ivanov, M. M. 50 *let russkoi muzyki v moikh vospominaniiakh*. Moscow, 1934.
Ivanov, M. M. *Istoricheskii ocherk 50-letnei deiatel'nosti muzykal'nogo zhurnala "Nuvellist"*. St. Petersburg, 1889.

Ivanov-Boretskii, M. V., ed. *Muzykal'noe nasledstvo: sbornik materialov po istorii muzykal'nogo kul'tury*. Moscow, 1935.
Jelagin, Juri. *Taming the Arts*. Translated by Nicholas Wreden. New York, 1951.
K desiatiletiiu Oktiabria, 1917–1927: sbornik statei. Moscow, 1927.
Kak postupit' na muzykal'nyi rabfak. Moscow, 1934.
Kalendar dlia uchitelei i uchashchikhsia muzyke. Annual. Moscow, 1901–1915.
Kapustin, S. Ia. *K voprosu o russkoi narodnoi muzyke*. [St. Petersburg, 1882].
Karasev, A. *Besplatnye vechernie shkoly khorovogo peniia*. Viatka, 1903.
Kashkin, N. D. *Pervoe dvadtsatipiatiletie Moskovskoi konservatorii: istoricheskii ocherk*. Moscow, 1891.
———. "Iz vospominanii o N. G. Rubinshteina i Moskovskoi konservatorii." *Russkii arkhiv*, 1897, kn. 3, no. 11: 441–72.
———. *Russkiia konservatorii i sovremennyia trebovanii iskusstva*. Moscow, 1906.
———. *Ocherk istorii russkoi muzyki*. Moscow, 1908.
———. "Russkoe muzykal'noe obshchestvo (po lichnym vospominanii)," parts 1–9. *Moskovskii ezhenedel'nik*, 1908, nos. 16, 18, 20, 21, 22, 24, 26, 27, 29.
———. *Moskovskoe otdelenie IRMO: ocherk deiatel'nosti za 50-letie 1860–1910 g*. Moscow, 1910.
———. *Stat'i o russkoi muzyke i muzykantakh*. Russkaia klassicheskaia muzykal'naia kritika. Moscow, 1956.
Kazak, Svetlana. "Samyi bol'shoi muzykant v nizhnem: avtobiografiia V. Iu. Villuana." *Istoricheskii arkhiv*, no. 6 (1999): 209–13.
———. "Ot vsei dushi blagodariu vas: pochta V. Iu. Villuana." *Istoricheskii arkhiv*, no. 2 (2001): 153–67.
Khar'kovskoe obshchestvo gramotnosti. *Desiatiletie Narodnogo doma Khar'kovskogo obshchestva gramotnosti, 1903–1913*. Khar'kov, 1913.
Khar'kovskoe obshchestvo liubitelei khorovogo peniia. *Adres podnesennyi Khar'kovskim obshchestvom liubitelei khorovogo peniia direktsii Khar'kovskogo otdeleniia IRMO*. Khar'kov, 1896.
Kochetov, N. R. *Muzykant: na rasput'e; sbornik statei o vybore professii*. Moscow, 1917.
Komitet po delam iskusstv pri SNK SSSR, Glavnoe Upravlenie Uchebnykh Zavedenii. *Uchebnye programmy dlia fakul'tetov strunnykh i dukhovykh instrumentov konservatorii*. Moscow, 1941.
Kontserty A. Ziloti: programmy kontsertov za desiat' sezonov (1903/1904–1912/1913). St. Petersburg, 1913.
Koptiaev, A. P. *Evterpe: vtoroi sbornik muzykal'no-kriticheskikh statei*. St. Petersburg, 1908.
Korev, S., ed. *Na putiakh k proletarskoi muzyke: rezoliutsii vserossiiskoi muzykal'noi konferentsii, iiun' 1929 g*. Moscow, 1929.
Korganov, V. D. *Muzykal'noe obrazovanie v Rossii (proekt reform)*. St. Petersburg, 1899.
———. *Kavkazskaia muzyka: sbornik statei*. 2d ed. Tiflis, 1908.
Kuznetsov, K. A., ed. *Istoriia russkoi muzyki v issledovaniia i materialakh*. Moscow, 1924.
Lad, 1-i sbornik. Petrograd, 1919.
Larosh, G. A. "Vospominaniia Antona Grigor'evicha Rubenshteina, 1829–1889." *Russkaia starina* 64, no. 11 (1889): 516–600.
———. *V zashchitu muzykantov*. St. Petersburg, 1895.
Lebedev, V. Vl. *Penie i muzyka kak sredstva esteticheskogo razvitiia naroda*. Tambov, [n.d.].

Leningradskaia gosudarstvennaia konservatoriia. *Trebovaniia dlia postupleniia v konservatoriiu i na muzykal'nyi rabfak pri nei na 1933–34 uch god*. Leningrad, 1933.

———. *Trebovaniia dlia postupleniia v konservatoriiu i na muzykal'nyi rabfak pri nei na 1934–1935 uch god*. Leningrad, 1934.

———. *Otkrytaia sessiia uchenogo soveta posviashchennaia 80-letiiu konservatorii, 1862/63–1942/43*. Tashkent, 1943.

———. *Tezisy reorganizatsii Leningradskoi gosudarstvennoi konservatorii*. Leningrad, [n.d.].

Lineva, E. E. "Mysli V. V. Stasova o narodnosti v muzyke." In *Nezabvennomu Vladimiru Vasil'evichu Stasovu: sbornik vospominanii*, edited by S. A. Vengarov. St. Petersburg, 1910.

Lipaev, I. V. *Ocherk byta orkestrovykh muzykantov*. Moscow, 1891.

———. *Orkestrovye muzykanty: istoricheskie i bytovye ocherki*. St Petersburg, 1904.

Lisovskii, N. M. *Muzykal'nyi almanakh i spravochnaia knizhka na 1891 g*. St. Petersburg, 1890.

———. *Obozrenie literatury po teatru i muzyke za 1889–1891 gg.: bibliograficheskii ocherk*. St. Petersburg, 1893.

Malinovskii, I. A. *Gorod Tomsk*. Tomsk, 1912.

Malishevskii, V. *Kratkii istoricheskii ocherk deiatel'nosti Odesskogo otdeleniia IRMO i sostoiashchego pri nem muzykal'nogo uchilishcha za 25 let (1886–1911)*. Odessa, 1911.

Manykin-Nevstruev, N. A. *Imp. russkoe muzykal'noe obshchestvo, Moskovskoe otdelenie: simfonicheskie sobraniia 1–500; statisticheskii ukazatel'*. Moscow, 1899.

———. *Kratkii istoricheskii ocherk Moskovskogo otdeleniia IRMO 1860–1900*. Moscow, 1900.

[Markovich, A. N.] *Imperatorskoe russkoe muzykal'noe obshchestvo*. Offprint from *Pravitelstvennyi vestnik* 1883, no. 76.

Maslov, A. L. *Narodnaia konservatoriia: muzykal'no-teoreticheskii i obshcheobrazovatelnyi kurs; stat'i i lektsii*. Moscow, 1909.

Materialy po voprosy o prieme evreev v sredniia i vysshiia uchebnyia zavedeniia. St. Petersburg, [*c*. 1908]. [Harvard Pre-Soviet law preservation microfilm project; 03975.]

Matsnevoi, A. I. *Ustav i programma muzykal'nykh klassov uchitel'nitsy muzyki Ol'gi Ivanovny Matsnevoi*. Tambov, 1913.

Mikhnevich, V. O. *Ocherki istorii muzyki v Rossii v kulturno-obshchestvennom otnoshenii*. St. Petersburg, 1879.

Miklashevskii, Ios. *Ocherk dieiatelnosti Kievskogo otdieleniia Imperatorskago russkogo muzykalnago obshchestva, 1863–1913*. Kiev, 1913.

Miropol'skii, S. *O muzykal'nom obrazovanii naroda v Rossii i v Zapadnoi Evrope*. 3d ed. St. Petersburg, 1910.

Mollengauer, N. *O muzykal'nom obrazovanii*. Moscow, 1909.

Mordvinov, I. P. *Narodnyi khor i pevcheskiia obshchestva*. Novgorod, 1916.

Moskovskaia gosudarstvennaia konservatoriia. *Pravila priema v konservatoriiu*. Moscow, 1933.

Moskovskaia gosudarstvennaia konservatoriia, popechitel'stvo ob uchenitsakh. *Ustav Popechitel'stva Eleny Grigor'evny Torletskoi o nedostatochnykh uchenitsakh, sostoiashchei pri Moskovskom otdelenii RMO konservatorii*. Moscow, 1874.

Muzykal'noe obrazovanie: sbornik po pedagogicheskim, nauchnym i obshchestsvennym voprosam muzykal'noi zhizni. Moscow, 1925.

Muzykal'nyi kalendar'-al'manakh (s illiustratsiiami) na 1895 god. St. Petersburg, 1895.
Muzykal'nyi kalendar'-al'manakh (s illiustratsiiami) na 1896 god. St. Petersburg, 1896.
Narodnyi komissariat po prosveshcheniiu. *O tom, chto sdelano*. Petrograd, 1919.
———. *Sbornik dekretov, postanovlenii i rasporiazhenii po muzykal'nomu otdelu Narodnogo komissariata po prosveshcheniiu*. Petrograd, 1919.
———. *Kalendar'-spravochnik muzykal'nogo otdela Narodnogo komissariata po prosveshsheniiu na 1919 g*. Petrograd—Moscow, 1919.
———. *Muzykal'no-instruktivnoe pis'mo, No. 6: o sostoianii muzykal'nogo obrazovaniia v RSFSR*. [Moscow], 1931.
Narodnaia konservatoriia. *Materialy dlia otcheta za pervyi uchebnyi god, 1906–1907*. Moscow, 1907.
Nevedomskaia-Dinar. "Ocherki moikh vospominaniia." *Russkaia starina* 128, no. 12 (1906): 652–84.
Nikolaevskii, M. *Neobkhodimye sovety i ssvedeniia vsem uchashchimsia na fortepiano v konservatoriiakh, muzykal'nykh shkolakh i u chastnykh prepodavatelei*. Moscow, 1915.
Nikitenko, A. V. *Moia povest' o samom sebe*. Vol. 1. St. Petersburg, 1904.
Obiazatel'nyia pravila dlia orkestrovykh muzykantov, sluzhashikh v teatre Shelaputina. Moscow, 1897.
Obolenskii, A. D., Prince. *Rech' proiznesennaia na akte 18 dekabria 1909 goda vitse-predsedatelem Imperatorskogo russkogo muzykal'nogo obshchestva kniazem A. D. Obolenskim po sluchaiu 50-ti letiia sushchestvovaniia obshchestva*. St. Petersburg, [1909].
Obolenskii, Dm. A., Prince. *Moi vospominaniia o velikoi kniagine Elene Pavlovne*. St. Petersburg, 1909.
Obshchestvo liubitelei muzykal'nogo i dramaticheskogo iskusstv. *Ustav obshchestva liubitelei muzykal'nogo i dramaticheskogo iskusstv*. Moscow, 1881.
Obshchestvo iziashchnykh iskusstv. *Kratkii obzor sostoianiia shkol Obshchestva iziashchnykh iskusstv, prochitannyi g. vitse-prezidentom na publichnom akta muzykal'noi i risoval'noi shkol, byvshem 21-go dekabria 1873 goda*. Odessa, 1874.
———. *Doklad komissii, izbrannoi obshchim sobraniem Obshchestva iziashchnykh iskusstv 18 maia 1886 goda, po delu o muzykal'noi shkole obshchestva*. Odessa, [1886].
Odesskaia konservatoriia: kharakteristika prepodavatelei. Odessa, 1914.
Odesskaia konservatoriia. Odessa, 1916.
Odoevskii, V. F. *Muzykal'no-literaturnoe nasledie*. Moscow, 1956.
Ostrogorskii, V. *Pis'ma ob esteticheskom vospitanii*. 3d ed. 1908.
Otzyvy bol'shogo simfonicheskogo orkestra (70 chelovek) pod upravleniem dirizhera i kompozitora G. Ia. Fistulari, v S.-Peterburge, na Mezhdunarodnoi khudozhestvenno-promyshlennoi vystavke v Mikhailovskom manezhe s 31-go avgusta po 19-e oktiabria 1908 goda. St. Petersburg, 1908.
"Perechen' kontsertov v Peterburge v sezon 1885/86 g." In *Muzykal'naia pamiatnaia i zapisnaia knizhka na 1887 god*, edited by M. M. Ivanov and P. D. Perepelitsyn. St. Petersburg, 1886.
Pered narodnym domom (razgovor), 2-go fevralia 1903 goda. Khar'kov, 1903.
Perepelitsyn, P. D. *Istoriia muzyki v Rossii s drevnieishikh vremen i do nashikh dnei*. St. Petersburg, 1888.
Permskoe popechitel'stvo o narodnoi trezvosti. *Narodnopevcheskie khory Permskogo popechitel'stva o narodnoi trezvosti v 1902 godu*. Perm, 1903.

———. *Narodnopevcheskoe delo permskoi gubernii: otchet rukovoditelia po ustroistvu khorov Permskogo popechitel'stva o narodnoi trezvosti za 1906 god*. Perm, 1908.

———. *Narodnopevcheskoe delo permskoi gubernii: otchet rukovoditelia po ustroistvu khorov Permskogo popechitel'stva o narodnoi trezvosti c 1896 po 1908 god*. Perm, 1909.

———. *Narodnopevcheskoe delo permskoi gubernii: otchet rukovoditelia narodnykh khorov Permskogo popechitel'stva o narodnoi trezvosti za 1913 god*. Perm, 1915.

Peterburgskie gorodskie muzykal'nye klassy im. M. I. Glinki. *K desiatiletiiu gorodskikh muzykal'nykh klassov imeni M. I. Glinki, 1906–1916 g*. Petrograd, 1916.

Peterburgskoe obshchestvo narodnykh universitetov, Muzykal'naia sektsiia. *Instruktsiia sektsii muzyki pri S.-Peterburgskom obshchestve narodnykh universitetov: polozhenie o SPb. narodnoi konservatorii*. St. Petersburg, 1908.

Porten, A. *Zaveshchanie muzykanta (Testament d'un musician)*. St. Petersburg, 1891.

Programmy muzykal'nykh predmetov i istorii iskusstv Moskovskogo sinodal'nogo uchilishcha tserkovnogo peniia: v ob'eme kursa vysshego muzykal'no-uchebnogo zavedeniia. Moscow, 1911.

Prokin, N. G. *Kak izuchat' muzyku?* Kishinev, 1900.

Puzyrevskii, A. I. *Penie v semeinom vospitanii (s notam)*. St. Petersburg, 1901.

———. *Muzykal'noe obrazovanie: osnovy muzykal'no-teoreticheskikh znanii*. St. Petersburg, 1903.

———. *Imperatorskoe russkoe muzykal'noe obshchestvo v pervye 50-let ego deiatel'nosti (1859–1909 g.)*. St. Petersburg, 1909.

Puzyrevskii, A. I., and L. A. Sakketti. *Ocherk piatidesiatiletiia deiatelnosti S.-Peterburgskoi konservatorii*, St. Petersburg, 1912.

Rimskii-Korsakov, N. A. *Letopis moei muzykal'noi zhizni*. 8th ed. Moscow, 1980.

———. *Polnoe sobranie sochinenii*. 8 vols. Moscow, 1955–1982.

Rimsky-Korsakov, N. A. *My Musical Life*. Edited by Carl van Vechten. Translated by Judith A. Joffe. Boston, 1989 [1923].

———. *Kashchey the Immortal*. Kirov Chorus and Orchestra. Valery Gergiev. Philips compact disc 446704-2.

Ritter, Fanny Raymond. *Woman as a Musician: An Art-Historical Study*. London, 1877.

Rodkin, B. S. *Al'manakh-spravochnik: vsia teatral'no-muzykal'naia Rossiia, 1914–1915 god*. Petrograd, 1914.

Rubets, A. I. "Vospominaniia o pervykh godakh Peterburgskoi konservatorii." *Novoe vremia*, (1912), nos. 12985, 12998, 13012, 13019, 13003, 130075, 13096, 13103, 13110, 13124, 13180, 13187.

Rubinshtein, M. *Esteticheskoe vospitanie detei*. Moscow, 1915.

Rubinstein, Anton. "Vospominaniia A. G. Rubinshteina." *Russkaia starina*, 1889 (November): 516–88.

———. *Autobiography of Anton Rubinstein, 1829–1889*. Translated by Aline Delano. Boston, 1890.

———. *Literaturnoe nasledie*. Edited by L. A. Barenboim. Vols 1–3. Moscow, 1983–1986.

Sabaneev, L. L. *Muzyka posle oktiabria*. Moscow, 1926.

Safonov, V. I. *Proekt ustava konservatorii Russkogo muzykal'nogo obshchestva, sostavlennii direktorom Moskovskoi konservatorii V.I. Safonovym*. Moscow, 1901.

Sakketti, L. A. "Muzykal'noe obrazovanie v shkole i zhizni." *Vestnik evropy*, 1879 (April). Partially reprinted as *O muzykal'nom obrazovanii*. Sapozhok, 1919.

Saratovskoe otdelenie IRMO. *Al'bom fotograficheskikh spiskov dom Saratovskogo otdeleniia Imperatorskogo russkogo muzykal'nogo obshchestva*. Saratov, 1910.

S.-Peterburgskii muzykal'no-dramaticheskii kruzhok liubitelei. *Pamiatnaia knizhka S.-Peterburgskogo muzykal'no-dramaticheskogo kruzhka liubitelei: sezon 1880/1881*. St. Petersburg, 1880.

———. *Prilozhenie k pamiatnoi knizhke S.-Peterburgskogo muzykal'no-dramaticheskogo kruzhka liubitelei, sezon 1880–1881*. St. Petersburg, 1881.

Saratovskii khudozhestvennyi kruzhok liubitelei muzyki i stseny. *Ustav*. Saratov, 1912.

Serov, A. N. *Stat'i o muzyke*. Vols. 1–6. Moscow, 1984–1988.

Serova, V. S. *Muzyka v derevne*. Moscow, 1897.

Shchurovskii, P. *Kak nado uchit' nashikh detei muzyke*. Moscow, 1898.

Shebuev, N. G., ed. *Vse teatry: sezon 1910/11*. Moscow, 1910.

Shemianin, M. M. "Konservatoriia glazami ochevidiia." In *Iz proshlogo i nastoiashchego otechestvennoi muzykal'noi kul'tury*, edited by E. B. Dolinskaia. Nauchnye trudy MGK. Vol. 2. Moscow, 1993.

Sherman, N. S. *Kak postupit' na muzykal'nyi rabfak*. Moscow, 1932.

Shevig, V. S. *O prepodavanii muzyki*. St. Petersburg, 1879.

Siloti, V. P. *V dome Tret'iakova*. Moscow, 1992.

Simpson, Eugene E. *Travels in Russia, 1910 and 1912*. Self-published, 1916.

Spasskaia, A. L. *Sovety po muzykal'noi pedagogiki*. Warsaw, 1896.

Stasov, V. V. *Sobranie sochinenii V. V. Stasova, 1847–1886: s prilozheniem ego portreta i snimka s podnesennago emu adresa*. Vols 1–4. St. Petersburg, 1894.

———. "Programmy russkikh simfonicheskikh kontsertov za vremia 1884–1885 g.: programmy russkikh kvartetnykh vecherov (1891–1894 gg)." In *Mitrofan Petrovich Beliaev: biograficheskii ocherk*, edited by A. S. Ogolevtsa, 33–57. Moscow, 1954.

Tainy v S.-Peterburgskom narodnom dome. St. Petersburg, 1905.

Taneev, S. I. *3-e zaiavlenie v khudozhestvennyi sovet Moskovskoi konservatorii*. Moscow, 1898.

———. *V khudozhestvennyi sovet Moskovskoi konservatorii*. Moscow, 1898.

Tigranov, G. G., et al. *Leningradskaia konservatoriia v vospominaniiakh, 1862–1962*. Leningrad, 1962.

———. *Leningradskaia konservatoriia v vospominaniiakh*. 2d ed., suppl. Vols. 1–2. Leningrad, 1987–1988.

Tolstoi, L. N. *Chto takoe iskusstvo?* Letchworth, UK, 1963 [1897].

Tolstoy, Leo. *What Is Art?* Translated by Richard Pevear and Larissa Volokhonsky. New York, 1995.

Towers, John. *Woman in Music*. Winchester, Va., 1918.

Trebovaniia dlia postuplenniia na muzykal'nyi rabfak pri Moskovskoi gos. konservatorii. Moscow, 1930.

Tsybul'skii, S. O. *Muzyka i penie v gimnaziiakh*. St. Petersburg, 1891.

Upton, George P. *Woman in Music*. 4th ed. Chicago, 1892 (1886).

Uslovie [musicians' contract]. Kazan, 1886.

Valter, V. G. *V zashchitu iskusstva: mysli muzykanta po povodu stat'i L.N. Tolstogo, "Chto takoe iskusstvo."* St. Petersburg, 1899.

———. *Eduard Frantsevich Napravnik: k 50-letiiu ego artisticheskoi deiatel'nosti*. St. Petersburg, 1914.

Veber [Weber], Karl Ed., comp. *Kratkii ocherk sovremennogo sostoianiia muzykal'nogo obrazovaniia v Rossii, 1884–1885*. Moscow, 1885.

———. *Putevoditel' pri obuchenii igre na fortepiano: ped-prakticheskoe rukovodstvo s planom obucheniem ot 1-go nachala do vyshchego usovershenstvovaniia*. 4th ed. Moscow, 1909.

Vigdorchik, Ia. *Khudozhestvennomu sovetu SPb konservatorii: neobkhodimye reformy otdela peniia SPb konservatorii*. St. Petersburg, 1907.

Voinskaia povinnost' i konservatoriia. Odessa, 1915.

Wallace, Robert K. *A Century of Music Making: The Lives of Josef and Rosina Lhevinne*. Bloomington, Ind., 1976.

Yastrebtsev, V. V. *Reminiscences of Rimsky-Korsakov*. Edited and translated by Florence Jones. New York, 1985.

Zagoskin, N. P. *50-letie opery "Zhizn' za tsaria": rech', proiznesennaia v kazanskom teatre 27 noiabria 1886*. Kazan, 1887.

Zeifert, I. I. *Vospominaniia professora Petrogradskoi konservatorii*. Petrograd, 1914.

Selected Secondary and Reference Sources

Abdullin, R. K. *Kazanskaia gosudarstvennaia konservatoriia: 1945–1995*. Kazan, 1998.

Adishchev, V. I. *Muzykal'noe vospitanie v kadetskikh korpusakh Rossii (konets XIX – nachalo XX veka)*. Perm, 2000.

———. *Muzyka v zhenskikh institutakh Rossii kontsa XIX–nachala XX veka: teoriia i praktika obrazovaniia*. Perm, 2001.

Alekseenko, M. I. *Kul'tura na Dal'nem vostoke, XIX–XX veka*. Khabarovsk, 1993.

Alekseev, A. D. *Muzykal'noe obrazovanie v kontekste kul'tury: voprosy teorii, istorii, metodologii; nauchno-prakticheskaia konferentsiia, 25–29 oktiabria 1994 goda; sektsiia obrazovaniia ispolnitelei*. Moscow, 1996.

Alekseev, B. *Muzykalnaia zhizn' Riazani*. Riazan, 1961.

Anfimov, A. M. and A. P. Korelin, eds. *Rossiia 1913 goda: statistiko-dokumental'nyi spravochnik*. St. Petersburg, 1995.

Apraksina, O. A., ed. *Iz istorii muzykal'nogo vospitaniia: khrestomatiia*. Moscow, 1990.

Asaf'ev, B. V. *Anton Grigorevich Rubinshtein v ego muzykal'noi deiatel'nosti v otzyvakh sovremennnikov (1829–1929)*. Moscow, 1929.

———. *Izbrannye stat'i o muzykal'nom prosveshchenii i obrazovanii*. Moscow, 1965.

Baker, Jennifer. "Glinka's *A Life for the Tsar* and 'Official Nationality.'" *Renaissance and Modern Studies* 24 (1980): 92–114.

Balfe, Judith Huggins. *Paying the Piper: Causes and Consequences of Art Patronage*. Urbana, Ill., 1993.

Barantsev, A. P. "Obuchenie igre na dukhovykh instrumentakh v Rossii kontsa XVIII–nachala XX vekov." Avtoref. Ph.D. diss., Leningradskaia gosudarstvennaia konservatoriia, 1974.

Barenboim, Lev. *Nikolai Grigor'evich Rubenshtein: istoriia zhizni i deiatel'nosti*. Moscow, 1982.

Barkin, Elaine, and Lydia Hamessley. *Audible Traces: Gender, Music, and Identity*. Zurich, 1998.

Barutcheva, E. S., et al., compilers. *Sankt-Peterburgskaia konservatoriia: dokumenty i materialy na fondov biblioteki i muzeia*. St. Petersburg, 2002.

Baryshnikov, M. N. *Delovoi mir Rossii: istoriko-biograficheskii spravochnik*. St. Petersburg, 1998.

Beliaev, S. E. *Istoriia muzykal'noi kul'tury Urala: XVIII–nachalo XX v.; kurs lektsii.* Ekaterinburg, 1996.

———. *Muzykanty starogo Urala: biobibliograficheskii spravochnik*. Ekaterinburg, 1997.

———. *Deiateli muzykal'noi kul'tury Urala XVI–nachala XX vv.: biobibliograficheskii slovar'-spravochnik*. Ekaterinburg, 1999.

———. *Iz muzykal'nogo proshlogo Urala XVII –nachalo XX veka: muzykal'noe obrazovanie v starom Ekaterinburge*. Ekaterinburg, 1999.

Beliakaeva-Kazanskaia, L. *Siluety muzykal'nogo Peterburga: putevoditel' po muzykal'nym teatram, muzeiam, kontsertnym zalam proshlogo i nastoiashchego*. St. Petersburg, 2001.

Beliakov, B. N., V. G. Blinova, and N. D. Bordiug. *Opernaia i kontsertnaia deiatelnost v Nizhnem Novgorode – gorode Gorkom*. Gorky, 1988.

Belousov, A. F. and T. V. Tsiv'ian, comps. *Russkaia provintsiia: mif – tekst – real'nost'*. Moscow, 2000.

Belov, S. V. *Muzykal'noe izdatel'stvo P. I. Iurgenson*. St. Petersburg, 2001.

Berezin, V. V., ed. and comp. *Ispolnitel'skie i pedagogicheskie traditsii Moskovskoi konservatorii: sbornik statei*. Moscow, 1993.

Berezovskii, B. L. *Filarmonicheskoe obshchestvo Sankt-Peterburga: 1802–1915, 1992–1997*. St. Petersburg, 1997.

———. *Filarmonicheskoe obshchestvo Sank-Peterburga: istoriia i sovremennost'*. St. Petersburg, 2002.

Bernandt, G. B., I. M. Iampol'skii, and T. E. Kiseleva. *Kto pisal o muzyke: bio-bibliograficheskii slovar' muzykal'nykh kritikov i lits, pisavshikh o muzyke v dorevoliutsionnoi Rossii i SSSR*. Moscow, 1971–1979.

Bobylev, L. B. "Istoriia i printsipy kompozitorskogo obrazovaniia v pervykh russkikh konservatoriiakh (1862–1917)." Avtoref. Ph.D. diss., Moskovskaia gosudarstvennaia konservatoriia, 1992.

Bochkareva, N. R. *Iz istorii muzykal'noi kul'tury*. St. Petersburg, 1999.

Bogdanov-Berezovskii, V. M. and I. Gusin, eds. *V pervye gody sovetskogo muzykal'nogo stroitel'stva: stat'i, vospominaniia, materialy*. Leningrad, 1959.

———. *Muzykalnaia zhizn' Leningrada: sbornik statei*. Leningrad, 1961.

Bolotin, S. *Biograficheskii slovar' muzykantov-ispolnitelei na dukhovykh instrumentakh*. Leningrad, 1969.

Borisov, G. P. "Muzykal'naia kult'tura Ekaterinodara s nachala XIX veka po 1920 god." Avtoref. Ph.D. diss., Moscow, 1992.

Brezhneva, I. V. and G. M. Malinina. *Russkie muzykal'nye arkhivy za rubezhom: zarubezhnye muzykal'nye arkhivy v Rossii; materialy mezhdunarodnoi konferentsii*. Moscow, 2000.

Bronfin, E. *Muzykal'naia kul'tura Petrograda pervogo poslerevoliutsionnogo piatiletiia, 1917–1922*. Leningrad, 1984.

Broyles, Michael. *"Music of the Highest Class": Elitism and Populism in Antebellum Boston*. New Haven, Conn., 1992.

Bruk, Mirra. "Iz proshlogo sovetskoi muzyki: Pedfak Moskovskoi konservatorii 1920-kh godov." In *Iz proshlogo i nastoiashchego otechesvennoi muzyki*. Moscow, 1991, 7–24.

Buckler, Julie. *The Literary Lorgnette: Attending Opera in Imperial Russia*. Stanford, Calif., 2000.

Campbell, Stuart. *V. F. Odoyevsky and the Formation of Russian Musical Taste in the Nineteenth Century*. Outstanding Dissertations in Music from British Universities. New York, 1989.

Chernykh, M. P. "Muzykal'naia zhizn' Rostova-na-donu ot serediny XVIII do 20-kh godov XX stoletiia: puti razvitiia, osobennosti muzykal'nogo uklada." Avtoref. Ph.D. diss, Rossiiskii institut iskusstvoznaniia, 1991.

———. "Obrazovanie i kul'tura v Rostove na Donu (40-90-e gody XIX veka)." In *Kul'tura Donskogo kraia: stranitsy istorii; sbornik nauchnykh trudov*. Rostov on Don, 1993.

Chow, Maria M. "Representing China Musically: A Chinese Conservatory and China's Musical Modernity, 1900–1937." Ph.D. diss., University of Chicago, 2005.

Cornwell, Neil. *V. F. Odoyevsky: His Life, Times, and Milieu*. Athens, Ohio, 1986.

Dagilaiskaia, E. R. "Muzykal'naia zhizn' Odessy XIX–nachala XX v.: kontsertnaia i pedagogicheskaia deiatel'nost' pianistov. Avtoref. Ph.D. diss., Moscow, 1975.

Dan'ko, L. G. and T. V. Broslavskaia. *Peterburgskie stranitsy russkoi muzykal'noi kul'tury: sbornik statei i materialov*. St. Petersburg, 2001.

Drinker Bowen, Catherine. *"Free Artist": The Story of Anton and Nicholas Rubinstein*. New York, 1939.

Dukov, E. V. *Kontsert v istorii zapadnoevropeiskoi kul'tury*. Moscow, 1999.

Dunlop, Carolyn C. *The Russian Court Chapel Choir, 1767–1917*. Amsterdam, 2000.

Edmunds, Neil. *The Soviet Proletarian Music Movement*. New York, 2000.

———. *Soviet Music and Society under Lenin and Stalin: The Baton and the Sickle*. New York, 2004.

Ehrlich, Cyril. *The Music Profession in Britain since the Eighteenth Century: A Social History*. Oxford, UK, 1985.

———. *The Piano: A History*. New York, 1990.

Emelianova, N. N. *Muzykal'nye vechera: khronika muzykal'noi zhizni Tambovskogo kraia za 100 let*. Voronezh, 1977.

Ershova, E. D. et al., eds. *Iz istorii Saratovskoi konservatorii*. Saratov, 2004.

Etinger, M. A. *Muzykal'naia kul'tura Astrakhani*. Volgograd, 1987.

Fend, Michael and Michel Noiray, eds. *Musical Education in Europe (1790–1914): Compositional, Institutional, and Political Challenges*. 2 vols. Musical life in Europe 1600–1900: Circulation, Institutions, Representation. Berlin, 2005.

Filenko, Taras. "Ethnic Identity, Music, and Politics in Nineteenth-Century Ukraine: The World of Mykola Lysenko." Ph.D. diss., University of Pittsburgh, 1998.

Findeizen, N. F. *Pavlovskii muzykal'nyi vokzal: istoricheskii ocherk, 1838–1912*. Reprint. St. Petersburg, 2005 [1912].

Fomin, V. P., ed. *Muzyka, mif, bytie: sbornik statei*. Moscow, 1995.

Fooks, Jacquetta Beth. "The Serf Theatre of Imperial Russia." Ph.D. diss., University of Kansas, 1970.

Foulkes, Julia L. "Review Essay: Social History and the Arts." *Journal of Social History* 39, no. 4 (Summer 2006): 1177–85.

Fradkina, Eleonora. *Zal dvorianskogo sobraniia: zametki o kontsertnoi zhizni Sankt-Peterburga*. St. Petersburg, 1994.

———. "Zal dvorianskogo sobraniia: zametki o kontsertnoi zhizni Sankt-Peterburga, 1839–1914 gg." *Muzykal'naia akademiia*, no. 2 (1994): 212–22.

Frame, Murray. *The St. Petersburg Imperial Theaters: Stage and State in Revolutionary Russia, 1900–1920*. Jefferson, N.C., 2000.

———. *School for Citizens: Theatre and Civil Society in Imperial Russia*. New Haven, Conn., 2006.

Frolova-Walker, Marina. "On 'Ruslan' and Russianness." *Cambridge Opera Journal* 9, no. 1 (March 1999): 21–45.

———. "The Disowning of Anton Rubinstein." In *"Samuel" Goldenberg und "Schmuyle": Jewish and Anti-Semitic Elements of Russian Musical Culture*, edited by Ernst Kuhn, Jascha Nemtsov, and Andreas Wehrmeyer. Berlin, 2003, 19–60.

———. *Russian Music and Nationalism: From Glinka to Stalin*. New Haven, Conn., 2007.

Fulcher, Jane F. *French Cultural Politics and Music: From the Dreyfus Affair to the First World War*. New York, 1999.

Gaidamovich, T. A., et al. *Iz istorii muzykal'noi zhizni Rossii: XVIII–XIX vv*. Moscow, 1990.

———. *Iz istorii muzykal'noi zhizni Rossii, XIX–XX vv*. Moscow, 1992.

Gasparov, Boris. *Five Operas and a Symphony: Word and Music in Russian Culture*. New Haven, Conn., 2005.

Gessele, Cynthia M. "The Conservatoire de Musique and National Music Education in France, 1795–1801." In *Music and the French Revolution*, edited by Malcolm Boyd. New York, 1992.

Gillett, Paula. *Musical Women in England, 1870–1914: "Encroaching on All Man's Privileges."* New York, 2000.

Ginzburg, L. S., et al., eds. *Moskovskaia konservatoriia 1866–1966*. Moscow, 1966.

Ginzburg, S. L. *K. Iu. Davydov: glava iz istorii russkoi muzykal'noi kul'tury i metodicheskoi mysli*. Leningrad, 1936.

———. ed. *N. A. Rimskii-Korsakov i muzykal'noe obrazovanie: stat'i i materialy*, Leningrad, 1959.

Glukhov, L. V. *Moskovskoe sinodal'noe uchilishche: dirizhersko-khorovoe obrazovanie Rossii i pedagogicheskaia deiatel'nost V. S. Orlova, konets XIX– nachalo XX stoletii: istoriko-pedagogicheskii ocherk*. Perm, 2001.

Golubovskaia, N. Ios., and L. A. Barenboim, eds. *V fortepiannykh klassakh Leningradskoi konservatorii*. Leningrad, 1968.

Gor'kovskii gosudarstvennyi muz-teatral'nyi tekhnikum. *60 letnii iubilei Gor'kovskogo gosudarstvennogo muz-teatral'nogo tekhnikuma*. Gorky, 1934.

Gozenpud, A. A. *Dom Engel'gardta: iz istorii kontsertnoi zhizni Peterburga pervoi poloviny XIX veka*. St. Petersburg, 1992.

Graboedova, N. V., and F. E. Purtov. *Voprosy muzykal'nogo istochnikovedeniia i bibliografii: sbornik nauchnykh statei*. St. Petersburg, 2001.

Gramit, David. *Cultivating Music: The Aspirations, Interests, and Limits of German Musical Culture, 1770–1848*. Berkeley, Calif., 2002.

Green, J. Paul. *Music Education in Canada: A Historical Account*. Toronto, 1991.

Green, Lucy. *Music, Gender, Education*. New York, 1997.

Guenther, Roy J. "Evenings in Old St. Petersburg: The Balakirev Circle and Its Origins." *Canadian-American Slavic Studies/Revue canadienne-américaine d'etudes slaves* 34, no. 1 (Spring 2000): 5–31.

Hays, Tim. "Development of the Music Conservatory in Europe and the United States." *Journal of the Midwest History of Education Society* 23 (1996): 4–10.

Heller, George N. *Historical Research in Music Education: A Bibliography*. Lawrence, Kans., 1995.

Hildebrandt, Dieter. *Pianoforte: A Social History of the Piano*. New York, 1988.

Hondré, Emmanuel. "L'etablissement des succursales du Conservatoire de musique de Paris, de la Restauration à la Monarchie de Juillet: un exemple de decentralization artistique." Ph.D. diss., Université de Tours, 2001.

Hoops, Richard. "Vladimir Vasil'evich Stasov: The Social and Ethical Foundations of His Relation to Russian Music." *Canadian-American Slavic Studies/Revue canadienne-américaine d'etudes slaves* 34, no. 1 (Spring 2000): 63–97.

Hughes, Carol Bailey. "*Muzykal'naia starina* (1903–1911)." *Periodica musica: Newsletter of the Répertoire international de la presse musicale du XIX siècle* 5 (1987): 1–8.

Hyde, Derek. *New Found Voices: Women in Nineteenth-Century English Music*. Brookfield, Vt., 1998.

Iablonskii, A. "List v Rossii." *Sovetskaia muzyka* 50, no. 12 (1986): 97–103.

Iakovlev, V. *Izbrannye trudy o muzyke*. Vol. 3. Moscow, 1983.

———. *Muzykal'naia kul'tura Moskvy*. Moscow, 1983.

Iankovskii, M. *N. A. Rimskii-Korsakov i revoliutsiia 1905 goda*. Moscow, 1950.

Il'in, V. *Iskusstvo millionov: iz istorii muzykal'noi samodeiatel'nosti Petrograda-Leningrada*. Leningrad, 1967.

Iubileinyi komitet po chestvovaniu sester Gnesenykh, osnovatel'nits gosudarstvennogo muzykal'nogo tekhnikuma imeni Gnesenykh. *Za tridtsat' let, 1895–1925*. Moscow, [1925].

Ivanov-Boretskii, M. V., ed. *Muzykal'noe nasledstvo: sbornik materialov po istorii muzykal'nogo kul'tury*. Moscow, 1935.

"Iz dokumentov po istorii Moskovskoi konservatorii." In *Esteticheskie ocherki*. Vol. 1. Edited by S. Rapoportas, et al. Moscow, 1963.

Johnson, James H. *Listening in Paris: A Cultural History*. Berkeley, Calif., 1995.

Kabalevskii, D. V., et al. *Rimskii-Korsakov: issledovaniia, materialy, pis'ma*. 2 vols. Moscow, 1953–1955.

Kantor, G. M., L. V. Brazhnik, and V. I. Iakovlev. *Iz istorii muzykal'noi kul'tury i obrazovaniia v Kazani*. Kazan, 1993.

Kartsovnik, V. G. and Iu. Kudriashov. *Iz istorii instrumental'noi muzykal'noi kul'tury: sbornik nauchnykh trudov*. Leningrad, 1988.

Kazak, S., and S. M. Leberskaia. *Gor'kovskomu muzykal'nomu uchilishchu 100 let: 1873–1973; ocherk*. Gorky, 1972.

Kean, Beverly Whitney. *All the Empty Palaces: The Merchant Patrons of Modern Art in Pre-Revolutionary Russia*. New York, 1983.

Keldysh, Iu. V. *Sto let Moskovskoi konservatorii: kratkii istoricheskii ocherk*. Moscow, 1966.

Kharkeevich, I. Iu. *Muzykalnaia kul'tura Irkutska*. Irkutsk, 1987.

Kingsbury, Henry. *Music, Talent, and Performance: A Conservatory Cultural System*. Philadelphia, Pa., 1988.

Kogan, Judith. *Nothing but the Best: The Struggle for Perfection at the Julliard School*. New York, [1987].

Kollar, V. A. *Muzykalnaia zhizn Nizhnego Novgoroda – goroda Gorkogo*. Gorky, 1976.

Kolominov, V. "Puteshestvie gardemarina Rimskogo-Korsakogo." *Morskoi sbornik*, no. 1 (1989): 93–95.

Koltypina, G. B., ed. *Spravochnaia literatura po muzyke: slovari, sborniki biografii, kalendari, khroniki, pamiatnye knizhki, putevoditeli, sborniki libretto, sborniki tsitat; ukazatel' izdanii na russkom iazyke, 1773–1962*. Moscow, 1964.

Kopytova, G. V. "Evraiskaia muzyka v Peterburge – Petrograde." *Muzykal'naia akademiia*, no. 3 (1993): 156–59.

Korabel'nikova, L. "Muzyka." In *Russkaia khudozhestvennaia kul'tura vtoroi poloviny XIX veka*. Moscow, 1988, 98–138.

———. "Muzykal'noe obrazovanie." In *Istoriia russkoi muzyki v 10-ti tomakh*, edited by Iu. V. Keldysh, O. E. Levasheva, and A. I. Kandinskii. Vol. 6. Moscow, 1989.

Korabel'nikova, L. Z. *S. I. Taneev v Moskovskoi konservatorii: iz istorii russkogo muzykal'nogo obrazovaniia*. Moscow, 1974.

Koraleva, V. "Muzykal'noe obrazovanie na Dal'nem vostoke: 1900–1929." In *Istoriia kul'tury Dal'nego vostoka Rossii XVII–nachala XX veka*. Vladivostok, 1996, 221–41.

Koreniuk, O. J. "Iz istorii muzykal'nogo obrazovaniia v Kieve (XIX-nachalo XX v.)." Kievskaia gosudarstvennaia konservatoriia, 1972.

Korev, Iu. *Russkaia professional'naia muzyka do 1917 goda*. Moscow, 1958.

Kosmovskaia, M. L. *Voprosy muzykal'nogo prosvetitel'stva i kritiki, obrazovaniia i vospitaniia v kontse XIX –nachale XX veka*. Kursk, 1990.

———. *Nasledie N.F. Findeizen*. Kursk, 1997.

Kovaleva, L. P. "Fortepiannoe isponitel'stvo i pedagogika v Rostove (1890–1917)." In *Kul'tura Donskogo kraia: stranitsy istorii; sbornik nauchnykh trudov*. Rostov on Don, 1993.

Kravchenko, S. P., ed. *Iz istorii muzykal'noi kul'tury Rossii: konets XIX–nachalo XX vv.: kraevedcheskie ocherki; uchebnoe posobie po kursu "Istoriia russkoi muzyki."* Moscow, 1993.

Kremlev, Iu. *Leningradskaia gosudarstvennaia konservatoriia 1862–1937*. Moscow, 1938.

———. *Russkaia mysl' o muzyke: ocherki istorii russkoi muzykal'noi kritiki i estetiki v XIX veke*. Vol. 1, 1825–1860. Leningrad, 1954.

———. *Russkaia mysl' o muzyke: ocherki istorii russkoi muzykal'noi kritiki i estetiki v XIX veke*. Vol. 2, 1861–1880. Leningrad, 1958.

———. *Russkaia mysl' o muzyke: ocherki istorii russkoi muzykal'noi kritiki i estetiki v XIX veke*. Vol. 3, 1881–1894. Leningrad, 1960.

"Krepostnye orkestry v Rossii XVIII–XIX vv (tablitsy)." In *Russkoe skripichnoe iskusstvo: ocherki i materialy*, vol. 1, edited by I. M. Iampol'skii, 368–98. Moscow–Leningrad, 1951.

Legkii, D. M. "Dmitrii Vasil'evich Stasov." *Voprosy istorii*, no. 7 (2003): 54–73.

Leningradskaia gosudarstvennaia konservatoriia. *100 let Leningradskoi konservatorii, 1862–1962*. Leningrad, 1962.

Leppert, Richard. *Music and Image: Domesticity, Ideology, and Socio-Cultural Formation in Eighteenth-Century England*. New York, 1988.

———. *The Sight of Sound: Music, Representation, and the History of the Body*. Berkeley and Los Angeles, 1993.

Leung-Wolf, Elaine. "Women, Music, and the Salon Tradition: Its Cultural and Historical Significance in Parisian Musical Society." DMA diss., University of Cincinnati, 1996.

Litvinov, M. *Voronezhskoe muzykal'noe uchilishche: 1904–XXXV–1939*. Voronezh, 1939.

Liubomudrova, N. "Fortepiannye klassy Moskovskoi konservatorii v 60–70-kh godov proshlogo stoletiia." *Voprosy muzykal'no-ispolnitel'skogo iskusstva*, 1962, no. 3: 263–97.

———. "Fortepiannye klassy Moskovskoi konservatorii v 80–90-kh godov proshlogo stoletiia." *Voprosy muzykal'no-ispolnitel'skogo iskusstva*, 1967, no. 4: 337–71.

Liuter, A. *Iz istorii muzykal'no-prosvetitel'noi raboty progressivnykh legal'nykh obshchestv v gody novogo revoliutsionnogo pod'ema (1910–1914)*. Moscow, 1960.

Livanova, T. N. *Ocherki i materialy po istorii russkoi muzykal'noi kul'tury*. Moscow, 1938.

———. *Pedagogicheskaia deiatel'nost' russkikh kompozitorov-klassikov*. Moscow, 1951.

———., comp. *Muzykal'naia bibliografiia russkoi periodicheskoi pechati XIX veka*. Vols. 1–6. Moscow, 1960–1968.

Locke, Ralph P., and Cyrilla Barr. *Cultivating Music in America: Women Patrons and Activists since 1860*. Berkeley and Los Angeles, 1997.

Logan, George M. *The Indiana University School of Music: A History*. Bloomington, Ind., 2000.

Loeffler, James. "'The Most Musical Nation': Jews, Culture, and Nationalism in the Late Russian Empire." Ph.D. diss. Columbia University, 2006.

Loesser, Arthur. *Men, Women and Pianos: A Social History*. New York, 1951.

Lokshin, D. L. *Khorovoe penie v russkoi dorevoliutsionnoi i sovetskoi shkole*. Moscow, 1957.

Lomtev, Denis. *Nemetskie muzykanty v Rossii: k istorii stanovleniia russkikh konservatorii*. Moscow, 1999.

———. *U istokov nemetskie muzykanty v Rossii: k istorii stanovleniia rossiiskikh konservatorii*. Moscow, 1999.

Maes, Francis. "Modern Historiography of Russian Music: When Will Two Schools of Thought Meet?" *International Journal of Musicology* 6 (1997): 377–94.

———. *A History of Russian Music from Kamarinskaya to Babi Yar*. Berkeley and Los Angeles, 2002.

Malozemova, A. I., and Popova, N. V. *Kievskaia gosudarstvennaia ordena lenina konservatoriia im. P. I. Chaikovskogo*. Kiev, 1988.

Marchenko, Iu. G. *Istoriia muzykal'noi kul'tury Sibiri (na rubezhe XIX–XX vv.): sbornik statei*. Sbornik trudov – Gosudarstvennyi muzykal'nyi pedagogicheskii institut im. Gnesinykh, Vol. 37. Moscow, 1978.

Matveichuk, V., and Vl. Fedotov. "Izuchenie muzykal'noi kul'tury Vladivostoka (dorevoliutsionnyi period) v uchilishche i VUZe." In *Puti razvitiia metodiki prepodavaniia v muzykal'nom VUZe*. Vladivostok, 1989.

McCarthy, Marie F. "Music Education and the Quest for Cultural Identity in Ireland, 1831–1989." Ph.D. diss., University of Michigan, 1990.

McQuere, Gordon D. "The Moscow Conservatory 1866–1889: Nikolai Rubinstein and Sergei Taneev." *Canadian-American Slavic Studies/Revue canadienne-américaine d'etudes slaves* 34, no. 1 (Spring 2000): 33–61.

Medushevskii, V. V., et al., eds. *Muzykal'noe obrazovanie: uroki istorii; sbornik nauchnykh trudei*. Moscow, 1991.

Menninger, Margaret Eleanor. "Art and Civic Patronage in Leipzig, 1848–1914." Ph.D. diss., Harvard University, 1998.

Metzelaar, Helen H. *From Private to Public Spheres: Exploring Women's Role in Dutch Musical Life from c. 1700 to c. 1800 and Three Case Studies*. Utrecht, 1999.

Minor, N. N. *N. Ia. Briusova i ee shkola muzykal'nogo obrazovaniia*. Saratov, 1994.

———. "Problemy massovogo muzykal'nogo vospitaniia v pedagogicheskom nasledii N. Ia. Briusova." Kand. diss., Moskovskii pedagogicheskii institut, 1998.

———. *N. Ia. Briusova – muzykant, pedagog, uchenyi*. Saratov, 2000.

Mironova, N. A. "Reforma muzykal'nogo obrazovaniia kak problema muzovedcheskogo issledovaniia." Avtoref. Ph.D. diss., Moskovskaia gosudarstvennaia konservatoriia, 1991.

———. *Moskovskaia konservatoriia: istoki (vospominaniia i dokumenty, fakty i kommentarii)*. Moscow, 1995.

———. ed. *Moskovskaia konservatoriia: ot istokov do nashikh dnei; istoriko-biograficheskii spravochnik*. Moscow, 2005.

Miroshnichenko, S. V., et al., eds. *Odesskoe muzykal'noe uchilishche: 100 let*. Odessa, 1997.

Miroshnichenko, S. I. *Stanovlenie khorovogo ispolnitel'stva na iuzhnom urale*. Magnitogorsk, 1999.

Mitchinson, Paul Gregory. "Music and Politics in Early Soviet Russia: 1917–1929." Ph.D. diss., Harvard University, 1997.

Mizrahi, Joan Berman. "The American Image of Women as Musicians and Pianists, 1850–1900." DMA diss., University of Maryland, 1989.

Mshvelidze, A. *Ocherk po istorii muzykal'nogo obrazovaniia v Gruzii*. Moscow, 1971.

Mussulman, Joseph A. *Music in the Cultured Generation: A Social History of Music in America, 1870–1900*. Evanston, Ill., 1971.

Muzykal'naia zhizn' Moskvy v pervye gody posle Oktiabria: oktiabr 1917–1920; khronika, dokumenty, materialy. Moscow, 1972.

Myers, Margaret. "Blowing Her Own Trumpet: European Ladies' Orchestras and Other Women Musicians 1870–1950 in Sweden." Ph.D. diss., Göteborg University, 1993.

Natanson, V. A. *Iz muzykal'nogo proshlogo Moskovskogo universiteta*. Moscow, 1955.

———. ed. *Voprosy fortepiannoi pedagogiki*. Vol. 1. Moscow, 1963.

Neiman, V. "Iz istorii russkogo muzykal'nogo obrazovaniia." *Voprosy fortepiannoi pedagogiki* 3 (1971): 317–32.

Nelson, Amy. *Music for the Revolution: Musicians and Power in Early Soviet Russia*. University Park, Pa., 2004.

Nettl, Bruno. *Heartland Excursions: Ethnomusicological Reflections on Schools of Music*. Urbana, Ill., 1995.

Nikol'skaia-Beregovskaia, K. F. *Russkaia vokal'no-khorovaia shkola IX–XX vekov: metodicheskoe posobie*. Moscow, 1998.

Ohrenych, M. L. *Odesskaia konservatoriia: zabytye imena, novye stranitsy*. Odessa, 1994.

Oldani, Robert W. "Sing Me Some Glinka or Dargomyzhsky." *History of European Ideas* 16, no. 4–6 (1993): 713–19.

Olkhovsky, Yuri. *Vladimir Stasov and Russian National Culture*. Ann Arbor, Mich., 1983.

Olle, M. I., ed. *Sbornik statei po muzykal'nomu obrazovaniiu*. Vol. 4. Sverdlovsk, 1961.

Olmstead, Andrea. *Julliard: A History*. Urbana, Ill., 1999.

Orfeev, S. *Istoriia Odesskoi konservatorii: istoricheskii ocherk*. Odessa, 1963.

Parakilas, James, et al. *Piano Roles: Three Hundred Years of Life with the Piano*. New Haven, Conn., 2000.

Pekacz, Jolanta T. *Music in the Culture of Polish Galicia, 1772–1914*. Rochester, N.Y., 2002.

Pendle, Karin, ed. *Women and Music: A History*. Bloomington, Ind., 1991.

Petrovskaia, Ira, ed. "K istorii muzykal'nogo obrazovaniia v Rossii." In *Pamiatniki kul'tury: novye otkrytiia*. Leningrad, 1979.

Petrovskaia, I. F. *Istochnikovedenie istorii russkoi muzykal'noi kul'tury XVIII – nachala XX veka*. 2d ed. Moscow, 1989.

———. *Muzykal'noe obrazovanie i muzykal'nye obshchestvennye organizatsii v Peterburge, 1801–1917: Entsiklopediia*. St. Petersburg, 1999.

———. *Kontsertnaia zhizn' Peterburga: muzyka v obshchestvennom i domashnem bytu 1801–1859 gody; materialy dlia entsiklopedii "Muzykal'nyi Peterburg."* St. Petersburg, 2000.

Phillips, Leonard M. "The Leipzig Conservatory: 1843–1881." Ph.D. diss., Indiana University, 1979.

Plante, Anne Marie. "The Iconography of the Piano in Nineteenth-Century Art." Vols. 1 and 2. D.Mus. document, Indiana University, 1984.

Podbolotov, P. A. *Russkaia khorovaia kul'tura: istoriia, traditsii, sovremennye problemy*. St. Petersburg, 1995.

Podzemskaia, L. *M. M. Ippolitov-Ivanov i gruzinskaia muzykal'naia kul'tura*. Tbilisi, 1963.

Pribegina, G. A., ed. and comp. *Moskovskaia konservatoriia: 1866–1991*. Moscow, 1991.

Ramazanova, N. V. *Iz istorii muzykal'noi kul'tury*. St. Petersburg, 1999.

Rapatsksaia, L. A. *Istoriia russkoi muzyki ot drevnei Rusi do "Serebrianskogo veka."* Moscow, 2001.

Reich, Nancy B. "Women as Musicians: A Question of Class." In *Musicology and Difference: Gender and Sexuality in Music Scholarship*, edited by Ruth A. Solie. Berkeley and Los Angeles, 1993.

———. "Women and the Music Conservatory." In *Aflame with Music: 100 Years of Music at the University of Melbourne*, edited by Brenton Broadstock, et al. Parkville, VIC, 1996.

Ridenour, Robert C. *Nationalism, Modernism, and Personal Rivalry in Nineteenth-Century Russian Music*. Russian Music Studies. Ann Arbor, Mich., 1981.

Rideout, Roger, ed. *On the Sociology of Music Education*. Norman, Okla., 1997.

Rimsky-Korsakov, A. N. *N. A. Rimskii-Korsakov: zhizn' i tvorchestvo*. Moscow, 1933.

Roberts, Brian A. *A Place to Play: The Social World of University Schools of Music*. St. John's, NF, 1991.

———. *Musician: A Process of Labeling*. St. John's, NF, 1991.

———. *I, Musician: Towards a Model of Identity Construction and Maintenance by Music Education Students as Musicians*. St. John's, NF, 1993.

Roell, Craig A. *The Piano in America, 1890–1940*. Chapel Hill, N.C., 1989.

Rohr, Deborah Adams. "A Profession of Artisans: The Careers and Social Status of British Musicians, 1750–1850." Ph.D. diss., University of Pennsylvania, 1983.

Rosselli, John. *Music and Musicians in Nineteenth-Century Italy*. London, 1991.

Rozanov, A. S. *Muzykal'nyi Pavlovsk*. Leningrad, 1978.

Sargeant, Lynn. "Singing the Nation into Being: Teaching Identity and Culture at the Turn of the Twentieth Century." *History of Education Quarterly* 49, no. 3 (August 2009).

Sats, I. A. "B. L. Iavorskii v Moskovskoi narodnoi konservatorii." In *B. Iavorskii: stat'ia, vospominaniia, perepiska*. Moscow, 1972.

Savel'eva, Iu. Vl. "Muzyka v prazdnichno-razvlekatel'noi kul'ture Peterburga pervoi treti XIX veka." Kand. diss., Rossiiskii gosudarstvennyi universitet im. A.I. Gertsen, 2003.

Seaman, Gerald. "Amateur Music-Making in Russia." *Music and Letters* 47, no. 3 (July 1966): 249–59.

———. "Nineteenth-Century Russian Music Periodicals: An Annotated Checklist." Part 1. *Periodica musica: Newsletter of the Répertoire international de la presse musicale du XIX siècle* 2 (Spring 1984): 14–16.

———. "Nineteenth-Century Russian Music Periodicals: An Annotated Checklist." Parts 2–3. *Periodica musica: Newsletter of the Répertoire international de la presse musicale du XIX siècle* 4 (Spring 1986): 6–11.

———. *Nikolai Andreevich Rimsky-Korsakov: A Guide to Research*. New York, 1988.

———. "Nineteenth-Century Italian Opera as Seen in the Contemporary Russian Press." *Periodica musica: Newsletter of the Répertoire international de la presse musicale du XIX siècle* 6 (1988): 21–24.

———. "Contemporary Music as Revealed in Nineteenth-Century Russian Periodicals." *Revista de Musicologia* 16, no. 3 (1993): 54–62.

———. "The *Russkaya Muzykal'naya Gazeta* (Russian Musical Gazette)." *Fontes Artis Musicae* 49, no. 1–2 (2002): 55–66.

———. "Soviet Musical Life in the 1920s as Seen in Contemporary Music Periodicals." *Fontes Artis Musicae* 53, no. 3 (2006): 233–38.

Scott, Derek B., *Music, Culture, and Society: A Reader*. New York, 2000.

Shamaeva, K. I. *Muzykal'noe obrazovanie na Ukraine v pervoi polovine XIX veka*. Kiev, 1992.

Shcherbakova, T. *Mikhail i Matvei Viel'gorskie: ispolniteli, prosvetiteli, metsenaty*. Moscow, 1990.

Shchurov, G. S. *Arkhangel'sk - gorod muzykal'nyi: khronika sobytii muzykal'noi zhizni g. Arkhangelska 1820–1917 gg*. Vol. 1. Arkhangel'sk, 1995.

Shepelev, L. E. *Chinovnyi mir Rossii XVIII – nachalo XX v*. St. Petersburg, 1999.

Shestopalov, A. P. "Velikaia kniaginia Elena Pavlovna." *Voprosy istorii*, no. 5 (2001): 73–94.

Shevliagina, V. F. "Moskovskaia Narodnaia Konservatoriia i ee rol' v muzykal'nom prosveshchenii narodnykh mass Rossii (1906–1916 gody)." Kand. diss., Moskovskii gos. insitut kul'tury, 1975.

Shindin, B. A. *Muzykal'naia kul'tura Sibiri*. Novosibirsk, 1997.

Shostakovich, D. ed. *B. L. Iavorskii: vospominaniia, stat'i, i pis'ma*. Vol. 1. Moscow, 1964.

Shteinpress, B. S., ed. *Iz muzykal'nogo proshlogo: sbornik ocherkov*. Vols. 1 and 2. Moscow, 1960–1965.

Shvarts, A. (Anna Schwarz). "Pokrovitel'stvo sem'i romanovykh muzykal'noi kul'ture Rossii v kontse XVIII – seredine XIX veka." *Novaia i noveishaia istoriia*, no. 6 (2001): 190–92.

Skinner, Frederick W. "A Shakespeare of the Masses: Beethoven and the Russian Intelligentsia, 1830–1914." *Canadian-American Slavic Studies/Revue canadienne-américaine d'etudes slaves* 38, no. 4 (Winter 2004): 409–29.

Small, Christopher. *Music, Society, Education*. Hanover, N.H., 1996.

Soboleva, N. A. "Sozdanie gosudarstvennykh gimnov Rossiiskoi imperii i Sovetskogo soiuza." *Voprosy istorii* no. 2 (2005): 25–41.

Soboleva, N. A. "Iz istorii otechestvennykh gosudarstvennykh gimnov." *Otechestvennaia istoriia* no. 1 (2005): 3–21.

Sokolova, A. M. "Kontsertnaia zhizn'." In *Istoriia russkoi muzyki v 10-ti tomakh*, edited by Iu. V. Keldysh, O. E. Levasheva, and A. I. Kandinskii. Vol. 4. Moscow, 1989, 276–80.

Sorokina, E. G., et al., eds. *Moskovskaia konservatoriia: materialy i dokumenty iz fondov MGK imeni P. I. Chaikovskogo i GTsMMK imeni M. I. Glinki*. Moscow, 2006.

Starcheus, M. S. *Moskovskaia konservatoriia: traditsii muzykal'nogo obrazovaniia, iskusstva i nauki, 1886–2006*. Moscow, 2006.

Stites, Richard. "The Domestic Music: Music at Home in the Twilight of Serfdom." In *Intersections and Transpositions: Russian Music, Literature, and Society*, edited by Andrew Baruch Wachtel. Evanston, Ill., 1998.

———. *Serfdom, Society, and the Arts in Imperial Russia: The Pleasure and the Power*. New Haven, Conn., 2005.

Stolpianskii, P. *Muzyka i muzitsirovanie v starom Peterburge*. 2d ed. Leningrad, 1989.

Strub-Ronanye, Elgin. "Liszt and the Founding of the Weimar Conservatory." *The Hungarian Quarterly* 34, no. 130 (1993): 148–54.

Stupel', A. *Russkaia mysl' o muzyke, 1895–1917: ocherk istorii russkoi muzykal'noi kritiki*. Leningrad, 1980.

Swartz, Anne. "Technological Muses: Piano Builders in Russia, 1810–1881." *Cahiers du monde russe* 43, no. 1 (2002): 119–37.

Tambovskii muzykal'nyi tekhnikum. *Piatidesiatiletie so dnia osnovaniia Tambovskogo muzykal'nogo tekhnikuma, 1882–1932*. Tambov, 1932.

Tarasova, L. A. *Muzykal'naia kul'tura Tverskogo kraia: uchebnoe posobie*. Tver, 1997.

Taruskin, Richard. "How the Acorn Took Root: A Tale of Russia." *Nineteenth-Century Music* 6, no. 3 (Spring 1983): 189–212.

———. "Some Thoughts on the History and Historiography of Russian Music." *The Journal of Musicology* 3, no. 4 (Autumn 1984): 321–39.

———. *Defining Russia Musically: Historical and Hermeneutical Essays*. Princeton, N.J., 1997.

Taylor, Philip S. *Anton Rubinstein: A Life in Music*. Bloomington, Ind., 2007.

Terent'eva, N. A. *Istoriia i teoriia muzykal'noi pedagogiki i obrazovaniia: uchebnoe posobie v 2 ch*. Vol. 1. St. Petersburg, 1994.

Thorpe, Richard Gordon. "The Management of Culture in Revolutionary Russia: The Imperial Theaters and the State, 1897–1928." Ph.D. diss., Princeton University, 1990.

Tick, Judith, "Passed Away Is the Piano Girl: Changes in American Musical Life, 1870–1900." In *Women Making Music: The Western Art Tradition, 1150–1950*. Edited by Jane M. Bowers and Judith Tick. Urbana, Ill., 1986, 325–48.

Tigranov, G. G. *Muzyka v bor'be za gumanizm i progress*. Leningrad, 1984.

Tomoff, Kiril. *Creative Union: The Professional Organization of Soviet Composers, 1939–1953*. Ithaca, N.Y., 2006.

Usov, Iu. A. *Istoriia otechestvennogo ispolnitel'stva na dukhovykh instrumentakh*. Moscow, 1986.

Veselovskaia, L., et al. *Bol'shoi put' (iz istorii partiinoi organizatsii Moskovskoi konservatorii)*. Moscow, 1969.

Viner, E. N., V. Kal'fa, and B. L. Kandel', eds. *Vladimir Vasil'evich Stasov: materialy k bibliografii, opisanie rukopisei*. Moscow, 1956.

Voik, P. "Dinamika kul'turnoi politiki Rossii v 1917–1991 g. i ee vliianie na razvitie sistemy muzykal'nogo obrazovaniia." In *Sosiokul'turnaia dinamika: teoretiko-metodologicheskie i istoricheskie aspekty*. Kemerovo, 2001, 182–202.

Vorontsov, Iu. V. *Muzykal'naia zhizn dorevoliutsionnogo Voronezha: istoricheskie ocherki*. Voronezh, 1994.

Weber, William. *Music and the Middle Class: The Social Structure of Concert Life in London, Paris, and Vienna*. New York, 1975.

———. "Artisans in Concert Life of Mid-Nineteenth-Century London and Paris." *Journal of Contemporary History* 13, no. 2, Special Issue: Worker's Culture (April 1978): 253–67.

———. "Toward a Dialogue between Historians and Musicologists." *Musica e storia* 1, no. 1 (1993): 7–21.

———. "Beyond Zeitgeist: Recent Work in Music History." *Journal of Modern History* 66 (June 1994): 321–45.

Weickhardt, George G. "Music and Society in Russia, 1860s–1890s." *Canadian-American Slavic Studies/Revue canadienne-américaine d'etudes slaves* 30, no. 1 (Spring 1996): 45–68.

Wolff, Janet and John Seed, eds. *The Culture of Capital: Art, Power, and the Nineteenth-Century Middle Class*. Manchester, UK, 1988.

Wright, David. "The South Kensington Music Schools and the Development of the British Conservatoire in the Late Nineteenth Century." *Journal of the Royal Musical Association* 130, no. 2 (2005): 236–82.

Zagurskii, B. I. *Kratkii ocherk istorii Leningradskoi konservatorii*. Leningrad, 1933.

Zenkin, Konstantin. "The Liszt Tradition at the Moscow Conservatoire." *Studia Musicologica Academiae Scientiarum Hungaricae* 42, no. 1–2 (2001): 93–108.

Zlotnikova, T. S., and Iu. Iu. Ierusalimskii. *Rol' tvorcheskoi lichnosti v razvitii kul'tury provintsial'nogo goroda: materialy regional'noi nauchnoi konferentsii, posviashchennoi 100-letiiu Iaroslavskogo khorovogo obshchestva i 125-letiiu Iaroslavskogo obshchestva liubitelei muzykal'nogo i dramaticheskogo iskusstv*. Iaroslavl', 2000.

Zvereva, O. M., and Pavlova, G. *Spravochnaia literatura po muzyke: annotirovannyi ukazatel'izdanii na russkom iazyke: 1979–1995*. Moscow, 2000.

Zvereva, Svetlana. *Alexander Kastalsky: His Life and Music*. Translated by Stuart Campbell. Burlington, Vt., 2003.

INDEX